I0094452

"In the current contentious and divisive climate that surrounds the treatment of homosexuality, the well-being of thousands of patients is at stake. Therefore, it is imperative that militant attempts at censorship and ideologies that would limit open inquiry be set aside in the interest of clinical integrity. The right of the patient to choose his or her therapeutic goals is paramount, and attempts to stifle the patient's freedom of choice are not only egregious but also contrary to the basic commitment of all health care itself.

For this reason, even though I disagree with some cause-and-effect relationships proffered in this book, Dr. Nicolosi's point of view must be part of the equation in an honest, open deliberation until we arrive at ultimate scientific and clinical fact. In my over 60 years of practice as a psychologist I have seen many conditions, both medical and psychological, that were once regarded as incurable but are now readily treatable. In this early stage of the heated debate on the treatment of homosexuality and same-sex attraction, to prematurely remand all homosexuals to an unchangeable life style would be a disservice of the worst order."

Nicholas A. Cummings, Ph.D., Sc.D., Distinguished Professor, University of Nevada, Reno; president, Cummings Foundation for Behavioral Health; board chair, The Nicholas & Dorothy Cummings Foundation; executive board chair, CareIntegra; and former president, American Psychological Association

"Nicolosi brings extensive professional clinical perspective and deep immersion in the historical literature in this area to his reflections on work with individuals experiencing unwanted same-sex attraction. This volume offers fruitful clinical hypotheses for exploration. Nicolosi shows balance in acknowledging possible biological and psychological contributors to causation, in exploring what full informed consent for consultation entails, in respecting appropriate clinical boundaries in professional consultation, and in acknowledging the experiences of those who find such work unproductive as well as those reporting success."

Stanton L. Jones, Ph.D., provost and Professor of Psychology, Wheaton College, and author of *Homosexuality: The Use of Scientific Research in the Church's Moral Debate* and *Ex-Gay? A Longitudinal Study of Religiously Mediated Change of Sexual Orientation*

"For the therapy of unwanted same-sex attraction, very few people have had the depth of experience and wide-ranging success of Joe Nicolosi. A master in the field has here distilled that experience equally for the professional and the interested layperson.

Every genuinely open-minded therapist should be familiar with the important insights that Dr. Nicolosi provides. This book can and should likewise provide the foundation for courses that train interested professionals in the art and science of helping to reverse homosexuality and restore heterosexual desire and functioning to those who seek such changes."

Jeffrey Burke Satinover, M.D., diplomate, American Board of Psychiatry; diplomate, American Board of Neurology; diplomate, C.G. Jung Institute of Zurich, Switzerland; and author of *Homosexuality and the Politics of Truth*

"In this richly detailed book, Dr. Nicolosi shares his experiences of many years working with same-sex attracted men who want to diminish their unwanted attractions and develop their heterosexual potential.

Nicolosi is convinced that the world's great religious traditions are right: humanity was designed for gender-complementary coupling. The mental-health associations must respect this viewpoint; to do otherwise would be a gross violation of worldview diversity as well as the client's right to freedom and self-determination.

This new book is a rich source of information – written by an astute clinician whose work with same-sex attracted clients has been groundbreaking, beginning with his 1991 book, *Reparative Therapy*.

A. Dean Byrd, Ph.D., M.B.A., M.P.H., Clinical Professor of Psychiatry, University of Utah; president, National Association of Research and Therapy of Homosexuality (NARTH)

"As readers have come to expect from Dr. Nicolosi, *Shame and Attachment Loss: The Practical Work of Reparative Therapy* again is an enormous contribution to making the complexities of homosexuality and its treatment more coherent for parents, therapists and anyone concerned about cultural issues. Dr Nicolosi continues his pathway of contributing clinically and philosophically in the traditions of a scholar."

Benjamin Kaufman, M.D., Clinical Professor of Psychiatry, University of California at Davis; psychoanalyst

"As an internationally recognized clinical expert on reparative therapy for unwanted homosexual attractions, Dr. Joseph Nicolosi has written a theoretically sound, clinically insightful, intellectually brilliant and highly compassionate practical book that will no doubt become a standard professional reference for psychologists, psychiatrists and other mental health clinicians treating individuals troubled by their homosexual impulses. This book is not only psychologically sound and theoretically insightful, but it is consistent with the Judeo-Christian theological understanding of the creation of humans as male and female, and the normality of close emotional, nonsexual, relationships among men."

George A. Rekers, Ph.D., Th.D., FAACP, Distinguished Professor of Neuropsychiatry and Behavioral Science Emeritus, University of South Carolina School of Medicine

"I have just finished reading this book, and I only wish there had been such research and words of hope earlier in my ministry in counseling homosexuals. Nicolosi's book offers a refreshing, cool cup of reason and hope on one of the most heated topics today. This is a must-read not only for the homosexual who is struggling over his sexuality but for every parish pastor, counselor and therapist. As a university professor of graduate studies in family ministry, it will be on my list of required textbooks."

Roger Sonnenberg, M.Div., M.A. (pastoral psychotherapy), Professor of Graduate Studies in Family Ministry, Concordia University, and author of *Human Sexuality: A Christian Perspective*

"A legend in the world of gender affirmation, Joe Nicolosi has devoted much of his professional career to educating the Western world that a change of sexual orientation is possible. Having written three other books on the subject, this latest book, *Shame and Attachment Loss: The Practical Work of Reparative Therapy*, represents his most recent insights and personal growth in understanding and treating those with unwanted same-sex attractions. Initially conceptualizing homosexual attraction as a striving 'to repair gender deficits,' he now sees it more broadly as a striving 'to repair deep self-deficits' and as a 'defense against trauma to the core self.' From this profoundly insightful premise, the text principally addresses mental health professionals and faith-based ministry leaders to explain the psychodynamics of homosexuality, its treatment modalities, and the role and resolution of grief in reparative therapy. Not only are brilliant new insights found throughout this volume, but it shows how the Judeo-Christian worldview is aligned with practical psychological techniques for healing. I recommend this must-read book to anyone who cares to learn about either the causes or the treatment of homosexuality. The library of every mental health professional, ministry leader and individual concerned about the sexual confusion that runs rampant in today's world should include this book."

Arthur Goldberg, codirector, JONAH, and author of *Light in the Closet: Torah, Homosexuality, and the Power to Change.*

"Dr. Nicolosi's latest book is, as ever, a continuation of insightful writing based firmly on his clinical experience. Although the basic therapeutic approach has stood the test of time, it has been refined in the light of experience. Many myths about reparative therapy are refuted by this book, and no one reading it could believe any longer that such therapists are primarily motivated by anti-gay feelings. Considerable care of clients is clearly evident in the many transcripts included. The approach is refreshingly non-doctrinaire. Although the book is intended for therapists, there is also much here that would deepen the understanding of nontherapists. Even critics who abhor this type of therapy might find their opinions modified if they read this book."

Neil Whitehead, Ph.D., scientific research consultant, and author of *My Genes Made Me Do It: A Scientific Look at Homosexual Orientation* and over 120 published scientific papers

"Joseph Nicolosi has achieved in this book what could only be the culmination of decades of clinical observation and scholarly integration of what is known today about the origins and treatment of homosexuality when it is not ego-syntonic. The popular press fosters an idea that the reason for rejecting homosexual impulses must be traditional social disapproval. Objective scientific study says otherwise. Nicolosi uncovers complex shame- and attachment-based motivations behind homosexual behavior, and provides clinical examples to show how reparative work can be freeing to those with the courage to explore sources of pain so long hidden from consciousness. For those in the field who want to hold on to prevailing notions about homosexuality, *Shame and Attachment Loss* is a book to avoid. But anyone who does read it will be rewarded with a cogent understanding of personality development and family dynamics and our need to take the psychotherapeutic journey with each individual as a fresh adventure."

Johanna Tabin, Ph.D., member, American Psychological Association; member, Division 38 Psychoanalysis; and author of *On the Way to Self: Ego and Early Oedipal Development*

"In this groundbreaking book, Nicolosi, a pioneer in the field of reparative therapy, introduces clinicians to the influence of shame and attachment loss within a same-sex drive. By integrating multiple theoretical bases, Nicolosi has developed, and effectively presents, a fresh and comprehensive framework for understanding and treating male SSA. The techniques and strategies discussed within this cutting-edge work not only guide therapists in their work with homosexual strugglers but also will provide insight into many other clinical cases. This is a must-read and an essential resource for any counselor's library. It will have a lasting impact on how the scientific and professional mental health communities view and comprehend homosexuality."

Janelle Hallman, M.A., L.P.C., author of *The Heart of Female Same-Sex Attraction*

"For those who have freely made up their mind to find a different way forward in dealing with the challenges of homosexuality, this book is a godsend. Joseph Nicolosi has provided a first-rate manual that tackles the issues head-on, that works from the best evidence available, and that is rooted in years of therapeutic practice. We have long needed a book like this: respectful of human choices, realistic in its central claims, clear about its theoretical foundations, aware of relevant objections and robust in its proposed clinical solutions. Every pastor and therapist, whatever their personal theological or moral commitments, should have this book in their library. They owe this to all those who are reaching for an alternative to the sexual ideology of our culture; they also owe it to the demands of common honesty and of intellectual virtue."

William J. Abraham, Ph.D., Albert Cook Outler Professor of Wesley Studies, Altshuler Distinguished Teaching Professor, Perkins School of Theology, Southern Methodist University

SHAME
AND
ATTACHMENT
LOSS

The Practical Work of
Reparative Therapy

Joseph J. Nicolosi, Ph.D.

Forewords by H. Newton Maloney, Ph.D.,
and Robert Perloff, Ph.D.

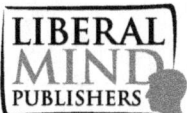

LIBERAL
MIND
PUBLISHERS

Liberal Mind Publishers
Publisher@liberalmindpublishers.com

© *2016 by Joseph Nicolosi*

All rights reserved. No part of this book may be reproduced in any form
without written permission from Liberal Mind Publishers.

All Scripture quotations, unless otherwise indicated, are taken from the Holy Bible, New International Version®. NIV®.
Copyright © *1973, 1978, 1984 by International Bible Society. Used by permission of Zondervan Publishing House.*
All rights reserved.

Design: Janelle Rebel, Shanie Cooper
Images: plainpicture/fStop
Typesetting: Raphaël Freeman, Renana Typesetting
ISBN *978-0-9976373-0-4*

Printed in the United States of America

The Library of Congress has cataloged the original IVP Academic edition as follows:

Nicolosi, Joseph,
 Shame and attachment loss: the practical work of reparative therapy
 / Joseph Nicolosi.
  p. cm.
 Includes bibliographical references and index.
 ISBN *978-0-8308-2899-9 (pbk.)*
 1. Gay men – Mental health. 2. Male homosexuality. 3. Sexual
 reorientation programs. 4. Psychotherapy. I. Title.
 RC558.3.N533 2009
 616.85'83 – dc22

2008054480

*To dearest Linda, a loving wife and tireless working partner.
Her commitment to our work transformed
my ideas into readable language.
She has made all my writings possible.*

Contents

List of Figures and Tables

TABLES

Foreword

I would like to take this opportunity to recommend to you the publication of this important volume by Dr. Joseph Nicolosi. Having served in the education and training of therapists for many years, I commend his work for the following reasons. First, although reparative therapy has been maligned by some in Division 12 (Clinical) of the American Psychological Association, it has not been rejected as a therapeutic modality for those seeking to change their sexual orientation, especially Christians or other religious or morally motivated persons.

Second, while there is a currently a strong emphasis on empirically validated treatment modalities, all approaches initially began as theories which were clinically applied long before they were subjected to controlled clinical studies. Reparative therapy as described in Nicolosi's volume is one such modality. Empirical validation will be the next step in its development, but it should not be discounted merely for being at this stage in its development.

Third, reparative therapy, as detailed by Nicolosi, is not presented as a therapeutic cure-all nor is it presented as a model that explains each and every incidence of homosexuality. Reparative therapy is offered as a hopeful remedy grounded in one environmentally significant determinant – namely family interaction. It is also offered as an option for religiously motivated persons who are seeking some alternative to the view that they cannot change.

In summary, Nicolosi is making room for the "social/environmental" hypothesis. His theories are a significant upgrading of the classic psychoanalytic model, one that accords well with classical Judeo-Christian teachings. Although in our current atmosphere there may be some risk in the publication of this book, I welcome Nicolosi's bold and valuable contribution to psychotherapy in the hope that it would influence the field to become more balanced in its approach.

H. NEWTON MALONY, PH.D.
Senior Professor, Graduate School of Psychology, Fuller Theological Seminary

Foreword

An advocate for gay men and women who are serious about striving to overcome their same-sex orientation and achieving sexual fulfillment heterosexually, Nicolosi – like a voice in the wilderness – audaciously defies conventional psychologists who cling to the belief that changing from homosexuality to heterosexuality is neither possible nor advisable.

Disseminating his point of view is desirable and necessary for society, as well as for gay men and lesbians. Now this is not to definitively assert that for many homosexuals, heterosexuality is preferable to homosexuality; only that this quest should be freely accessible to the homosexual person, if indeed that is his or her wish.

Nicolosi's treatise on reparative therapy is a groundbreaking and courageous navigation of the tricky shoals, perilous undertows, and precipitous twists and turns required to bypass the psychological community's declaration that homosexuality is appropriate for all homosexual men and women. Though still controversial, his treatise is punctuated and made more believable through his reliance on the client's perceptions, feelings and family dynamics.

In a word, Nicolosi's thrust in promoting his point of view on behalf of this contentious hot-button issue is broad and deep, abstract and experiential, and theoretically and practically depicted.

The policies and resolutions of organizations such as the American Psychological Association, and probably the American Psychiatric Association as well, would be better framed and more truthfully based were these organizations cognizant of, and open to, the sentiments promoting reparative therapy.

Nicolosi's book deserves widespread readership, by friend and foe alike, whether or not, truth to tell, it is still a work in progress; even if in the long run, he is shown to be right, wrong, or somewhere betwixt and between. The paths to ultimate truth can only be forged when consummated fully and unconditionally, and certainly not with impeding and competing ideological polestars misdirecting their voyages.

The author has contributed enormously to the sexual literature by offering his not unreasonable views for consideration by gays and lesbians, by scholars in the field, by the man in the street, and by practicing psychotherapists. His challenging and forceful commentary is must-reading from top to bottom, from stem to stern.

ROBERT PERLOFF, PH.D.
Former President, American Psychological Association
Distinguished Service Professor Emeritus, University of Pittsburgh

Acknowledgments

I would especially like to thank Howard and Roberta Ahmanson for their generosity in the service of our shared, passionate belief – that men and women were designed for heterosexuality.

I would also like to express my deep gratitude for the assistance of Alan Schore, Ph.D., Johanna Tabin, Ph.D., and Donald Nathanson, M.D.

My thanks to Don Schmierer and Lela Gilbert for their assistance, and to my colleagues Tim Long, Cynthia Winn, David Pickup, Scott Sutherland and Robert Vazzo for their very helpful suggestions. I also wish to thank my very able assistants, Sara Trevino and Linda Overbeck.

Last, my deepest appreciation to all the men who have revealed their shame to me – teaching me so much about true masculinity.

Introduction

My first act of free will, shall be to believe in free will.

— WILLIAM JAMES

This book is for psychotherapists who seek techniques to assist a systematically ignored group, the non-gay homosexual – a population thought by most of my colleagues not to exist.

Non-gay homosexuals are same-sex attracted men whose deeply held values and sense of self prevent them from embracing a gay identity. In the past twenty years I have worked with thousands of such clients, all of whom seek to diminish their unwanted homosexuality and develop their heterosexual potential. These men now compose about 95 percent of the caseload at our clinic.

As a result of "politically correct" graduate school training and of relentless promotion by the media, the vast majority of my colleagues now erroneously believe that their clients' sexual destiny is biologically sealed. Approximately 50 percent of the clients we have seen were previously told by another psychotherapist that they could not change – that they were "born gay." They were advised that their sole choice was to "resolve your internalized homophobia," and to "embrace these feelings – because whether you like it or not, this is who you really are."

Describing his previous therapy, one teenager said: "My first shrink told me that I had gay DNA, and to basically have a coming-out party!"

But we do not accept the fatalism of the "born that way" concept. Instead, we propose an alternative model – addressing and resolving the underlying conflicts that have, in our view, laid the foundation for the symptom of same-sex attraction.

In a detailed informed-consent form at our clinic, we explain to our clients that our theoretical position differs from that of the American Psychological Association. We clarify that we do not offer gay-affirmative therapy, yet we respect our clients' viewpoints, which sometimes change radically during the course of therapy. Some clients decide to make a complete about-face and self-identify as gay, leaving reparative therapy. Others may go back and forth for months – into and out of a gay lifestyle during the course of our sessions together. Respecting these changes of heart and mind, I always tell my clients, "Don't accept anything I say unless it rings true for you."

Born That Way?

Our profession has been swept away by the media blitz promoting the "born that way" theory. However, there is no evidence to support the idea that homosexuality is simply and solely inborn. On the other hand, biological factors indeed probably *influence* some people toward homosexuality – either genetic (inherited) factors that cause gender nonconformity, or prenatal-hormonal influences, especially in men, that may result in a low-masculinized brain.

In all likelihood, any factor – biological or social-environmental – that leads a male to feel less secure in his maleness has the potential to affect his gender identity and thus his sexual orientation.

But none of these factors mean that homosexuality is normal and a part of human design. Further, none of them prove that homosexuality is inevitable in any particular person – or that it is unchangeable.

This work is dedicated to those men who seek to live out the sexual orientation that corresponds to their biological design. Our theories pose a radical challenge to the gay-identified man's narrative that at his deepest level of self, homosexuality is "who he really is."

Our Bodies Tell Us Who We Are

Philosophically, I am an essentialist – not a social constructionist: I believe that gender identity and sexual orientation are grounded in biological reality. The body tells us who we are, and we cannot "construct" – assemble or disassemble – a different reality in which gender and sexual identity are out of synchrony with biology.

The belief that humanity is designed for heterosexuality has been shaped by age-old religious and cultural forces, which must be respected as a welcome aspect of intellectual diversity. This viewpoint is not a phobia or pathological fear.

Natural-law philosophy says this view derives from humankind's *collective, intuitive* knowledge – a sort of natural, instinctive conscience. This would explain why so many people, even the nonreligious, sense that a gay identity is a false construct.

The very man who was instrumental in removing homosexuality from the list of mental disorders – psychiatrist Robert Spitzer, a self-proclaimed atheist – said that in homosexuality, "something's not working." He sensed, on an intuitive level, that homosexuality was sub-optimal.

Putting this same intuitive knowledge into blunt terminology, one of my clients asked, "How could I have been designed by the Creator for anal sex?" He scoffed at the American Psychological Association's idea that homosexuality is equivalent to heterosexuality. "Anal sex is damaging to the body," he said. "It's demeaning to a man's dignity; it's unhealthy. I couldn't have been created for a same-sex relationship whose *very design* makes biological parenthood impossible."

He laughed ironically. "So I was designed this way? Then I have been created by an absurd god."

Many other men have told us, "I tried homosexuality, but I found out that it didn't work."

The fact is, the vast majority of clients who come to us have found same-sex attraction to be maladaptive in their lives. Their impetus for change comes from their deep conviction that underneath it all they really are heterosexual men, and they seek a therapist who sees their inner potential. But, as George Orwell said, "In a time of universal deceit, telling the truth is a revolutionary act."

Not an Easy Road

Like all authentic commitments to self-improvement, efforts to change will make for a very challenging task. Change cannot be motivated primarily by social or religious guilt. Rather, the man must find his strength from a profound and abiding commitment from within. Success in treatment can only come from an *intrinsic* motivation, expressed in terms of a strong personal aspiration or a deep commitment to a worldview or a particular faith tradition. This is distinct from an extrinsic motivation, such as pressure by outside influences – "My wife wants me to come to therapy," "My church said I need help," "My parents said I should change," and so forth.

For these men the journey begins with the internal conviction that homosexuality is not merely wrong but that – on yet a broader dimension – homosexuality simply isn't "true." Most men cannot explain it any better than that, but in their own ways they express the conviction that gay sex doesn't "work" – it never satisfies their inner longings, and it doesn't reflect who they are as gendered beings.

Calling gay life "a bait-and-switch game," one client described his disillusionment. "It is not the sex that I want, but it always ends up that way – as just sex. What I'm really looking for is to be close to someone, to hold and to be held, to love and to feel loved, to whisper and to be heard, to reveal myself to another person. But in the end gay sex always feels empty. It doesn't feel honest. It doesn't feel true."

Another man said, "In gay sex the parts don't fit. Most psychologists think homosexuality is normal, but I *know* it's not normal."

Honoring Client Self-Determination

The only remaining debate within psychology, at the time of this writing, is this: "Should treatment for unwanted homosexuality be considered *permissible?*"[1] In response to this question, various authors have argued persuasively that it must *not* be banned.

The push within my profession to *outlaw* treatment for unwanted same-sex attractions (SSA) is in striking violation of contemporary liberalism's own professed commitment to diversity. Only a few members of our profession have had the courage to speak up for a true diversity of worldviews. The men I am about to quote represent those striking exceptions. Both are champions of gay rights, self-professed liberals and former presidents of the American Psychological Association – and both were keynote speakers at annual conferences of the National Association of Research and Therapy of Homosexuality (NARTH), of which I am the former president.

At the 2004 NARTH Conference Robert Perloff, Ph.D., past-president of the American Psychological Association, said:

> The individual has the right to choose whether he or she will accept a gay identity. It is his or her choice, not that of an ideologically driven interest group. To discourage a psychotherapist from undertaking a client wishing to convert is anti-research, anti-scholarship, and antithetical to the quest for truth.

Nicholas Cummings, Ph.D., past-president of the American Psychological Association, who has personally helped homosexual clients reorient to heterosexuality, observed at the 2005 NARTH Conference:

> I remain fiercely dedicated to freedom of choice for all people, and especially in their right to choose the goals for their own individual psychotherapy.
>
> Patients should have the right to explore their heterosexual potential.

Robert Spitzer, M.D., who led the team that deleted homosexuality from the diagnostic manual, said in 2001:

> Contrary to conventional wisdom, some highly motivated individuals, using a variety of change efforts, can make substantial change in multiple indicators of sexual orientation, and achieve good heterosexual functioning.

And Sigmund Freud, M.D., wrote in 1918:

> We refuse most emphatically to turn a patient...into our private property, to decide his fate for him, to force our own ideals upon him...in the service of a particular philosophy. In my opinion, this is...to use violence [upon the patient].

The Mainstream Mental Health Groups

At the 2006 Annual Conference of the American Psychological Association there were fifty picketers greeting conference attendees. All were ex-gay men and women carrying signs that said, "APA, Please Help Us!" "Keep My Choice Ethical!" and "Diversity Includes Us!" Most of the psychologists who spoke to the picketers expressed surprise that their profession would wish to restrict reparative or reorientation therapies. If a person isn't satisfied being gay, why shouldn't he have help to reduce his unwanted homosexuality and develop his heterosexual potential?

Why not, indeed? Asked this very question during an open meeting at the same conference, APA's then-president, Gerald Koocher, agreed. Highlighting the importance of client autonomy and self-determination, Dr. Koocher stated to the audience, "APA has no conflict with psychologists who help those distressed by unwanted homosexual attraction." As long as there was no coercion, and proper informed consent was obtained, he said, reorientation therapy could indeed be ethical.

As he left the meeting, however, Koocher was surrounded by angry gay-activist psychologists, and he quickly issued written clarifications, including the insistence that homosexuality must not be presented to the client as a mental illness.

In an e-mail to psychologist David Blakeslee on August 15, 2006, Koocher offered this reasoning: "In fact the data show that gay and lesbian people do not differ from heterosexuals in their psychological health. By that I mean that they have no greater instance of mental disorders than do heterosexuals."

Remarkable Misinformation

Regarding this crucial subject President Koocher was actually remarkably uninformed. In recent years all the available data has converged on the incontrovertible conclusion that gays and lesbians have a markedly higher level of mental health problems than do heterosexuals.

The *Archives of General Psychiatry*, an established and well-respected peer-reviewed journal, offered three such papers (Fergusson et al., 1999; Herrell et al., 1999; Sandfort et al., 2001; and a commentary by Bailey, 1999). J. Michael Bailey concluded with a commentary on the article, which had summarized all the available research on the subject. (Bailey, it should be noted, conducted the much publicized gay-twin studies, which were used by gay advocates as support for the "born that way" theory.) Bailey said,

> These studies contain arguably the best published data on the association between homosexuality and psychopathology, and both converge on the same unhappy conclusion: *homosexual people are at substantially higher risk for some forms of emotional problems,* including suicidality, major depression, and anxiety disorder, [and] conduct disorder.... The strength of the new studies is their degree of control. (Emphasis added)

Yet here we were seven years later, and the APA president – who has evidently "turned the henhouse over to the foxes" when it comes to gay issues – continues to believe that homosexually oriented people *do not differ from heterosexuals in their psychological health.*

But What If the Client Doesn't Change?

Of course, reorientation therapy is a long and difficult process, with no guarantee of success. We do know that change is possible.[2] But, what if the man doesn't change? Will he have gained anything of value?

There is far more to reparative therapy than change of sexual behavior. In fact, people are often surprised to hear that there is very little discussion about sex. Good therapy addresses the whole person and aims to change him on many levels.

Reparative theory holds that the origin of SSA is in unmet emotional and identification needs with the same sex. I typically tell clients in the very first session, "Rule number one is: Never accept anything I say unless it resonates as true for you." His experience, whatever that may be, must always trump any preconceived theory. If that theory doesn't feel true to him, he will usually decide to leave therapy after one or two sessions. He may then decide to see a gay-affirmative therapist, who will affirm his homosexuality as an intrinsic part of his identity.

But if he continues, the therapeutic setting will provide an opportunity in which he can explore, reexperience and assimilate past trauma. Here, he begins to liberate himself from old patterns of shame and self-sabotage.

He grows beyond the emotional isolation and chronic loneliness that have so long limited him, and develops a renewed emotional investment in authentic relatedness.

Most especially, through a relationship with an attuned therapist, the client discovers how it feels to emotionally disclose to another man and to reveal those long-buried feelings of gender shame. He receives a deep acceptance of wherever he is in his life at that point in time, whether he changes or not. Such an experience is always therapeutic.

Besides an enhanced ability to develop genuine male friendships, the client will discover healthier relationships with females – where he learns to prohibit the boundary violations with women that may have been causing him to compromise his separate, masculine selfhood.

He will also learn how to examine himself with appropriate criticism. As one client put it, "In the past I simply assumed the worst about myself. But now there is a clarity of wants and needs – strength in my voice – and a deeper way of communicating."

Rather than focusing on sexual-orientation change, the primary work of therapy is to teach the client to relate from a place of authenticity, openness and honesty. This is what we call the "assertive stance," where the person matches up his inner feelings with his outer dealings – to paraphrase psychologist Diana Fosha, who defines the healthy individual as the person who is actively "feeling and dealing."

We believe that "feeling and dealing" is the essential ingredient to the healing of SSA: teaching the person to live and love from his authentic self. When he truly does so, we believe, his unwanted SSA will greatly diminish, thus releasing him to develop his heterosexual potential.

As one struggler expressed it, "My homosexuality is like a snake, always trying to wrap itself around my identity." Treatment is carried out not by focusing on the "snake" but on the whole person around whom it has wrapped itself.

And another young man told me, "The sinister nature of homosexuality is that it gets me to focus on *it* rather than on *me*." Therapeutic success requires not a mere elimination of the same-sex symptom but the growth and maturation of the whole man.

But what about the client who fails to change; will he be left in a sort of "intimacy limbo" – not heterosexual, yet unable to be intimate with men? The truth is, our client was never intimate with men. That is why he came to therapy. He also came to us because he believes that true sexual intimacy with a person of the same gender is, in fact, not possible: same-sex eroticism simply fails to match his biological and emotional design and does not reflect who he is as a man.

Some clients, of course, alter their worldview. Jason left reparative therapy to live in a gay relationship. He had come to believe that homosexuality was indeed (contrary to his earlier beliefs) truly compatible with his religion. His worldview had changed so much that he and I were no longer in fundamental agreement about the meaning of homosexuality, and we agreed to end our working relationship. He told me, "I didn't change sexual orientation, but I can truly say that I no longer fear straight men – and I've learned to be my own person."

A few men enter reparative therapy as gay-identified from the start, and not desirous of change. With those clients we agree on a precondition to our working together – that is, we will not address the issue of sexual-identity change, but we will work on all of their other problems in living. And so we work on issues like capacity for intimacy, problems with self-esteem, internalized shame, childhood trauma and the search for identity.

The good therapist always conveys his complete acceptance of the client, even if that client eventually decides to gay-identify. Like Jason, some of our clients decide to change course and embrace homosexuality as "who they are." Others remain ambivalent about change, while going in and out of gay life over a period of months. We accept their choices even if we don't agree with them, because we accept the person.

The overall focus of this book is on isolating "what works." I have attempted to minimize the theoretical discussion and instead concentrate on practical techniques for the reparative therapist.

And yet this book is not an explicit "how to," but a suggestive "how might." At first glance some of the specific techniques will appear reductionistic, rigid and neglectful of the complexity, nuance and individuality of each client. Since each client presents a unique history and personality, we can only offer here guiding principles, not absolute formulas and dictums.

In particular, the diagrams throughout this book can be criticized as crude, simplistic, even naive. And in a sense they are. Still, having conceded that, I offer the practitioner these diagrams as a rudimentary tool to describe the clinical art of reparative therapy.

Of course, there is still something artificial in the attempt to reduce what is essentially a creative process into a schematized set of clinical interventions. But if psychotherapy is more art than science, then – like all art – it must be guided by certain procedures and rules within which the artist executes his creative work. These interventions should be applied without compromising the primacy of the client's experience. The danger is to squeeze the client into a predetermined framework. The good psychotherapist is challenged to honor each person's unique narrative, while loosely applying methodologies and techniques that are dictated by his careful empathic attunement.

The fact remains that people do not change through the application of techniques. *People change through relationships* – relationships with caring people who apply those effective techniques.

Staying Politically "Safe" in Dangerous Territory

A Christian psychologist contacted me to discuss reorientation therapy for same-sex attracted (SSA) men. Hoping to find a political compromise with the APA, he was anxious to avoid value judgments, preserve his standing in his profession and remain safely noncommittal about the homosexual condition. The solution, he thought, would be to develop a simple behavior-modification program that helped clients change their unwanted behavior but did not value heterosexuality as preferable to homosexuality.

Speaking from my twenty-five years of experience in this field, I told him I found his approach naive and ultimately unworkable. Our men do not come to us to change their unwanted behavior. They come to us to change their sense of self – to *be* more heterosexual, not just to "act" heterosexual; to feel comfortable in relationships with straight men, to learn to hold on to their masculine autonomy with women – in short, to fulfill their heterosexual potential. A behavior-modification program might be politically safe, but because of its shallowness it would inevitably fail.

"Why should I refuse to reveal my philosophical position," I told him, "when gay-affirmative therapists are working very hard as boosters of their own philosophy? They tell clients that same-sex feelings are 'sacred.' They push them to revolutionize society's and the church's attitudes. Any client's conviction that heterosexuality is the norm will be redefined by the therapist as a 'psychological illness – homophobia.'"

"The fact is, neutrality fails for clinicians on both sides of this issue," I told this psychologist. "Clinicians like you and me, who believe that humanity was designed for heterosexuality, must speak up to defend our worldview. These men with unwanted SSA want boosters, allies, advocates, as they claim their masculine identity – someone who believes in them and stands strongly at their side."

A Clinical Picture Is Essential

Furthermore, what will happen when the uncommitted ("neutral") therapist hears his client revealing self-destructive behaviors that are statistically proven to be associated with SSA? How will he interpret these behaviors? Staying out of philosophical territory with the client would require a "Rogerian neutrality" that even Carl Rogers himself couldn't live up to. And once seen, how can these factors – including their meaning and likely origins – be ignored?

The men that stay with us in therapy do in fact believe that "something happened to them." We offer them an understanding of the traumas they tell us about – and one that deeply resonates with them. We also offer a way out, albeit a difficult one, that has been proven to work with other men.

Client and Therapist Together

Indeed, the most powerful dimension of the working alliance can only come into play when therapist and client together view SSA the same way. When the therapist takes a neutral position ("I see gay and straight as equally OK outcomes"), this dilutes the power of the transference and leaves the client feeling incompletely understood and incompletely supported.

What sustains the client during difficult periods of therapy is the therapist's unwavering conviction that he does possess a latent heterosexual nature. For these men, to know that a salient man sees this potential, however hidden – even when they themselves are undergoing doubts – is a powerful inspiration.

Reconnecting the Man to His Gendered Self

In discussing their family backgrounds, over and over our clients tell us that they never felt known and loved for *who they really are*. This is not to say their families didn't love them – most of their parents loved and wanted the best for the children. But with this particular son, there was a disconnect... a malattunement. The majority of my clients say they never felt truly "seen" by their parents. And so it is the work of therapy to undo the shame, repair the attachment loss and reconnect the man back to the gendered being he was designed to be.

*   *   *

Postscript: In the clients' stories and transcripts I have used in this book, all identifying names and details have been changed to protect confidentiality. The client stories and quotes are composites; therefore any resemblance to a person known to the reader is coincidental.

PART ONE

Psychodynamics of Homosexuality

CHAPTER 1

Overview

Advances in Reparative Therapy

Homosexuality may not be a problem for the American
Psychological Association, but it is a problem for me.

— A NINETEEN-YEAR-OLD STUDENT

⁓

I hitched my wagon to the wrong star.

— A FIFTY-YEAR-OLD MAN

In recent years, significant advances have been made in our understanding of the etiology and treatment of male same-sex attraction (SSA). This book brings together the new understandings gained since my earlier works, *Reparative Therapy of Male Homosexuality; A New Clinical Approach* (1991), *Healing Homosexuality: Case Stories of Reparative Therapy* (1993) and *A Parent's Guide to Preventing Homosexuality* (2002).

No Model of Healthy Homosexual Development

At this writing it has been over thirty years since the 1973 American Psychiatric Association depathologized homosexuality. Since that time, no theorist has yet presented a credible model of *nontraumatic* early development that would result in homosexuality. The best attempt to offer a nonpathological model of homosexual outcome is made by psychologist Daryl Bem (1996).[1] I have critiqued his model elsewhere.

Bem, a psychologist who is himself a gay activist, explains in his "Exotic Becomes Erotic" model that what is *exotic* – that is, mysterious – to a boy in childhood is what will become *erotic* to him in adulthood. I agree with that concept; a person eroticizes what he or she does not identify with. Yet remarkably the fact that masculinity should be exotic to a boy is not seen by Bem as problematic. He clearly does not believe, as we do, that normality is *that which functions according to its design.*

When a man finds masculinity mysterious and exotic, and seeks it outside himself, we believe he is living in a false self, and, as prominent psychiatrist Robert Spitzer recently observed, "something's not working."

Social-Parental Factors Remain the Focus

While recognizing the predisposing role of gender-atypical temperament for at least some homosexuals, we continue to focus on the influence of social-environmental factors in the development of SSA. Our emphasis is on the triadic-narcissistic family: the features of narcissism and gender-identity deficit that are associated with SSA, and the etiological role of early parental malattunement. The father's influence is particularly critical in the case of a boy born with a sensitive temperament.[2]

In terms of our treatment principles, we continue to emphasize the powerful healing experience of the relationship with an accurately attuned, same-sex therapist and the ongoing (indeed, lifelong) necessity of close male friendships.

The essential principle of reparative therapy remains the same – simply stated by one client as "When a real man sees me as a real man, then I become a real man."

Recognizing Gender Deficits and Self-Deficits

Recently, reparative theory has expanded to conceptualize homosexual attraction as more than a striving to repair gender deficits. We now see it more broadly, as a striving to repair deep *self*-deficits.

My longtime clinical observation suggests one repeated trend in early childhood: *specifically, an accumulation of early, core emotional hurts that have led to an attachment injury.* I believe that homosexuality is not only a defense against gender inferiority *but a defense against a trauma to the core self.*

Beyond the previously recognized needs of same-sex identification and affirmation, we now better understand the condition as an attempt to heal an abandonment-annihilation trauma. We see homosexuality as typically an attempt to "repair" a shame-afflicted longing for gender-based individuation. As such, homosexuality can be seen as a pathologic form of grieving. Adopting concepts from bereavement and grief literature, we thus turn new attention to the contributions of attachment theory and the role of shame.

An Interactional Model

Within our etiological parameters there are many plausible combinations of causes for homosexuality. For each person these factors come together in a unique way. Our model focuses on biological influences (a sensitive temperament), but more importantly on the parents' failure to support the boy's emerging identity. Negative childhood same-sex peer experiences play a role as well.

All of those factors lead to the sense of estrangement from males that gay-activist psychologist Bem has also identified – where the boy with SSA considers other males to be mysterious, different from him, in a word, *exotic*.

Over the years in working with thousands of men struggling with unwanted SSA, I have repeatedly heard the same childhood themes of painful relational deception, betrayal and, ultimately, inconsolable disappointment. Clients repeatedly complain of feeling weak, inadequate and out of control, and demonstrate a guarded stance toward life and relationships.[3] It is in addressing those profound hurts that therapist and client encounter one another on the deepest level. At this level of human encounter, the healing begins.

The Big Picture

> Thank you, homosexuality! Through the misery you've caused me, you forced me to look at myself – face all those things that I've pushed under, avoided. I'm more alive because I faced my homosexuality.

A major step forward in therapy occurs when the client's focus of concern shifts from his perceived original problem at the start of treatment, namely, his unwanted SSA, to the deeper and more consequential issues that prompt his susceptibility to homosexual enactment. Understanding this distinction, one client explained what so many others have also told me: "My problem is this low-grade emptiness in my life that sets me up for male attractions."

Another client, grasping the larger context of his homosexual problem, announced after six months of therapy, "The good news is that my problem is not my homosexuality. The bad news is that it's about everything else!" By "everything else" this man meant his compromised style of engaging others – his pervasive difficulty relating in mutuality with other men, and his need to present a false self to the world.

Another man described the same conviction that he was facing a much more fundamental problem than unwanted homosexuality: "It's like what my singing teacher used to say to me: 'The problem with your singing is in the way you breathe.'"

This idea that *emotional inauthenticity* is what leads a man into homosexual enactment is most clearly evidenced in an analysis of what we call "The Scenario Preceding Homosexual Enactment." This is our model of ordinary day-to-day events that tells us when the client is most likely to be tempted into unwanted sexual activity. Closely following the details of our clients' lives and their shifting self-states, we see that it is the assertion-versus-shame conflict that most consistently propels the man into the depressive state that we call the "gray zone." And it is from within the gray zone that homosexual desire is most compelling.

This understanding that homosexuality is a symptom of a larger issue of self-identity is supported by the almost universal complaint of clients that they feel "insecure," "inadequate," "a little boy in an adult world," "out of control" and lacking relational authority. For years I have heard clients express this interpersonal powerlessness: "She *upsets* me, they *annoy* me, he *doesn't take me seriously.*"

Shame as Integral to SSA

The struggle with shame is reported by almost all therapists in describing the SSA men they work with. In fact, virtually all gay-*affirmative* therapists – those who actively encourage clients to embrace a gay identity – identify shame as a primary therapeutic issue. However, they see this shame as "internalized homophobia" – a socially induced conflict that is said to prevent the man from accepting his normal and healthy homoeroticism. While it is apparent that society's reaction to the homosexual condition produces shame, I believe the origins of the homosexual condition *began* with shame – specifically, in the person's unsuccessful struggle for secure attachment and masculine identity.

Based on this premise the therapeutic approach we take at our clinic draws the client's attention beyond his presenting complaint to address the larger question of the role or "stance" he assumes in his relational world. We have come to believe that a felt compromise of personal integrity prompts shame, which in turn prompts the need for self-esteem regulation (reparation), which in its turn, motivates the man to seek a same-sex erotic attachment. Thus a particular focus of reparative therapy is on helping the client reject shame to live life in the assertive stance.

Unlike gay-affirmative therapists, who see shame as a consequence of socially disapproved homosexuality (homophobia), we see homosexuality as a narcissistic solution to a shame problem. Referring to his day-to-day struggle with homosexuality – which he calls "It" – one man composed the diary entry below:

The False Comfort of "It"

It is my shame

That gives "**It**" power over me.

"**It**" always goes back to my shame.

There are moments when the **It** is not there,

Not present in my life, and I think,

"Wow this is beautiful, peaceful." But then my shame

Comes – and with that, once again, the **It**.

When shame takes over my life, then **It** looks like

THE BIG PROMISE OF COMFORT!

My challenge is to live my life without shame.

Then I won't need the false comfort of **It**.

Therapeutic Body Work

In a new approach to reparative treatment, we have adopted a set of inter-ventions from the therapeutic school known as Affect-Focused Therapy

(AFT). The most influential writers within this movement are Davanloo (1980); Neborsky (2004); Alpert (2001); Coughlin Della Selva (1996) and Fosha (2000).

AFT's intensive technique centers around reducing core intrapsychic conflicts and trauma. Particular core conflicts occur with almost predictable regularity in the life of the SSA man, for which the principles and techniques of AFT are especially useful.

We call our own model of AFT "body work." (No touching is ever involved.) We have modified this treatment approach, which in other applications can be very confrontational, into a "kinder, gentler" version for our men. Our client population has a history of feeling victimized by manipulation and control; therefore our modality emphasizes not so much confrontation but a collaborative and supportive working alliance.

Body work necessitates the client's responding with his authentic feelings in the present, rather than reacting to present situations as if they were events in the past. It focuses on the expression and resolution of emotional conflict, and is reminiscent of Fritz Perls's Gestalt Therapy. By addressing the client's defensive structure of affect inhibition, while using an "overdrive" or accelerated method, body work offers quick access to effective emotional breakthrough and consequent self-insight. These techniques work well to unblock defenses and gain immediate access to feelings. They are especially applicable to the SSA client, whose presenting symptomatology is very often a consequence of affect inhibition – the consequence of traumatic shame.

The goal for the client in reparative therapy is to no longer act out his past hurts in the present but to experience those authentic feelings about his past while in the presence of the therapist. When the therapist supports and encourages the client to open up, the client reexperiences those feelings and their associations while in the presence of an attuned other. He is then able to "take in" the new insights. His identified conflict is thereby redefined and transformed, imbuing it with a new, coherent meaning.

Body work thus helps the client understand his same-sex attractions not just cognitively but "from the inside." Through this process clients almost invariably uncover an awareness of profound feelings of unworthiness.

Tracing Back to Attachment

Attachment is the foundation of our self-identity. It is through the mother-child attachment that we develop our sense of self and discover who we are. Shame felt during this process of attachment and individuation subverts development of both self-identity and gender identity.

Since our clients report a core experience of not having felt "seen" by their parents for who they are, they inevitably also felt that they were not loved – at least in the deepest and most genuine sense. There is a deep perception that the parents, even though they may have been truly well-meaning, have failed to fully see, know and accept them. This trauma is at the foundation of their attempt to individuate. Feeling abandoned because they were not truly known, they developed the maladaptive response of the false self. While the false self is adaptive to protect the ego in childhood, it becomes maladaptive in adulthood. Because it is a defense against the authentic exchange of feelings, it cuts off all future opportunities for authentic attachment. The client must drop his defense of the false self in order to receive the male affirmation necessary for the resolution of his SSA.

We invariably see lingering effects of this childhood shame trauma of not having felt truly seen. Thus we encourage the SSA man to reexperience the trauma – particularly its associated anger and sadness – and thus be "seen and known" by the therapist in the process of grief work (see part 3). In grief work the therapist also points out to the client the negative consequences of holding on to the illusions and distortions that have protected him from acknowledging and reexperiencing those core attachment losses.

The Parenting Challenge of the Gender-Nonconforming Son

Among SSA men we often see a temperament that is sensitive, emotional, relational and more aesthetically oriented than the gender-typical male. Most homosexual men, in fact, report having felt "different from other boys." This contributes to the boy's often-reported feeling of discomfort around other males (including their fathers).

Fathers find themselves facing a particular challenge with a temperamentally sensitive son. These sons will encounter special difficulty in negotiating the gender-identification phase of childhood. Fathers often recall that this one boy, unlike their other sons, seemed to reject *them*. It will be vital for the father to "go out and get" this boy and actively pull him into the masculine sphere, for unlike his more masculine brothers, this boy will find it all too easy to retreat into the comfort of the feminine.

Recognizing Biological Factors

Efforts within my profession to present homosexuality as solely and simply "biologically *predetermined*" have failed, even, in fact, by the admission of the researchers themselves (many of whom are gay). All behavior, of course, has some biological basis; and some children may indeed have a biological predisposition to homosexuality. But "predisposition" is not the same as "predetermination." *Susceptibility is not the same as inevitability.* No research has proven that some children are inevitably destined to be homosexual.

Is an incompletely masculinized male brain – if research later confirms this intriguing theory to be a factor in SSA – "normal"? It is often mistakenly assumed that if something is inborn, it is normal. Yet many of us come into life with inborn conditions like short tempers, inclinations toward obesity and alcoholism, nearsightedness, and attention-deficit disorder. Individuals with these conditions were, so to speak, "born that way," but they were not *designed* that way; these are anomalies and problems to be overcome. It is easy to confuse the concept of "born that way" with "designed that way." To the extent that an incompletely masculinized brain is biological, we must say that it would be (like attention-deficit disorder, for example) a *biological developmental error.*

A Benign Variant?

Further, when we take an honest look at the homosexual condition, we see that it is not a benign expression of human diversity. Even without considering its many negative consequences for society, we see that it is also about a pervasive sense of despair and a characteristic emotional disengagement.

Our own clients, not surprisingly, reveal a despairing attitude toward life and a distrust of relationships. There is an anticipation that all good things will, in the end, betray. This is not surprising; homosexuality must be, after all, inevitably about a struggle for belonging in a gendered world.

Furthermore, we cannot fail to recognize the narcissistic self–preoccupation so often exhibited in SSA men, which continually weakens the normal human drive toward emotional connectedness. One thirty-five-year-old client described his private (but very typical) battle with narcissistic self-absorption this way: "For me, it's a mindful effort to reach out, to connect. It's always an exercise, an act of the will to push myself out of isolation, to let others in." This characteristic fear of emotional engagement leads to frustration, loneliness, general cynicism about life and ultimate resignation to a lifestyle of relational superficiality.

Another man spoke of his lifelong depression, saying that was why the gay social scene had long attracted him: "I ask myself, 'What about gay life was most compelling for me?' and I think, *The frivolity – it's, Oh, let's talk about fun things*. But those 'fun things' have led me downward to despair."

In the end, then, clients discover that the hard work of therapy is not so much about removing all homosexual temptation as it is all about learning to develop personal and interpersonal authenticity. And it is about retracing the roads taken in childhood that brought them onto this unfortunate path.

Asked what he would tell other men in reparative therapy, one client told me:

> I would say, "Don't believe the gay agenda. Go with what your heart and mind are really telling you. This life can never be authentic. If you're on the path to change, don't stop – don't give up. This is so much more joyful than anything I ever did in my crazy, acting out days."

CHAPTER 2

Family Dynamics

My mother abandoned half of me – the man – and
clung to the other half, the good little boy.

࿈

Every time I see a father and his little son, I want to be
that little boy. It's the same stab – a deep yearning.

The family model that produces a homosexual son has, in our view, typically failed to validate the boy's masculine individuation during the formative phase of gender identification. Masculinity is an achievement, not a "given," and one that is vulnerable to developmental injury.

There is a particular family pattern that we often find in the histories of SSA men. This pattern unifies two models that disrupt gender individuation: the *classic triadic family*, and *the narcissistic family*. Together, they form what I term the triadic-narcissistic family (Nicolosi, 2001).

By unifying these two models we better understand some commonly observed aspects of the homosexual condition – particularly, the narcissism-shame dimension. Our model better incorporates our profession's growing knowledge of infant attunement-malattunement. It also helps explains the conflicting findings about mothers of SSA men, who are most often observed to be overinvolved but can also be the opposite –

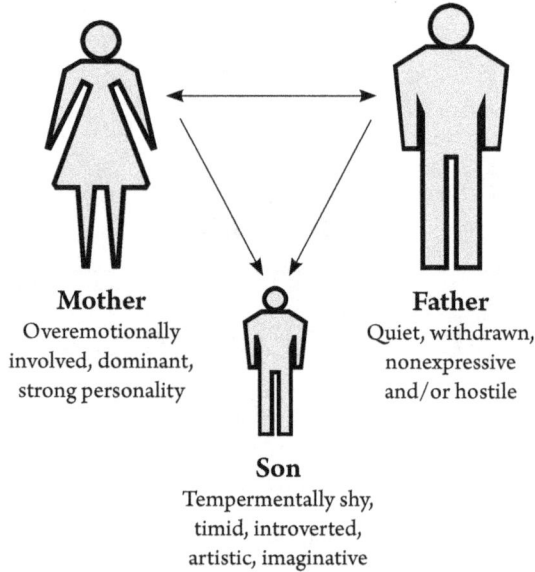

Mother
Overemotionally
involved, dominant,
strong personality

Father
Quiet, withdrawn,
nonexpressive
and/or hostile

Son
Tempermentally shy,
timid, introverted,
artistic, imaginative

Figure 2.1 Classic triadic relationship

underinvolved/inadequate in parenting style. In both cases the result is insecure attachment.

The Classic Triadic Family System

The triadic family system, described in the foundational psychoanalytic literature on homosexuality by Bieber, Socarides, Kronemeyer and others, is the system that identifies the overinvolved mother and critical/detached father. Later writers found this same family pattern (Moberly, 1983; Fitzgibbons, 2005; van den Aardweg, 1997). This model lays the foundation for gender-identity deficit, particularly in the boy who is temperamentally sensitive.

This classic triadic pattern (see fig. 2.1) is described in the literature as follows:

- *Father.* The boy experiences his father as hostile, emotionally detached or both. Although he may be highly competent in the business world, he is seen by the boy as nonsalient in family life – failing to be both "good enough" and "strong enough." (He may be seen as "good" but weak, or he may be seen as "strong" but critical/nonbenevolent.) In either case, the result is the same: the boy experiences the father as an unsafe/unworthy object of identification.

- *Mother.* The mother's attentions are typically described by the son as overinvolved, intrusive, possessive and controlling. The relationship between them is particularly close and excludes the father. Their bond has been described by many homosexual men as "special and intimate," with the two being "soul mates and confidantes." She confides her own emotional needs to the son, as well as her chronic dissatisfaction with the father. Both mother and son experience the father as emotionally limited or inaccessible. They share their mutual grievances about the limitations of the father/husband. The criticism expressed by the mother lays the groundwork for the son to develop a negative view of men and, by extension, of masculinity in general. Masculinity comes to seem mysterious, "other-than-me," dangerous and unapproachable, or, as gay-activist psychologist Daryl Bem observes, *exotic.*

- *Son.* The boy is temperamentally sensitive, timid, passive, introverted, artistic and imaginative. Mothers describe these sons as more intuitive, verbal, gentle and perfectionistic than their other sons. While temperament is usually a biological given, some of these traits (especially

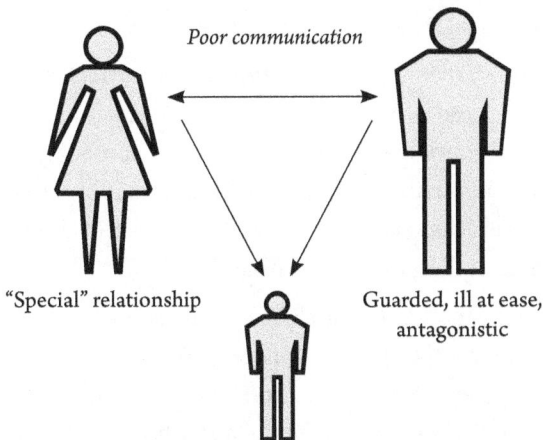

Figure 2.2 Closer look at the classic triadic relationship

timidity and passivity) may also be acquired and can be a symptom of insecure attachment. This sensitive and intuitive temperament causes the mother to gravitate to this particular son, which diverts him from the normal developmental path toward masculine individuation.

When we look more closely at the classic triadic relationship, we see the following relational patterns:

- *Husband-wife relationship.* Due to his psychological limitations the father maintains a distance from the mother, whom he avoids because he finds her emotionally draining. The marriage is characterized by a lack of emotional compatibility, with minimal intimacy. He does not want to engage her because he risks "upsetting" her and thus stimulating burdensome new emotional demands. He maintains his equilibrium by offering her the sensitive and relational son, who serves as a spousal surrogate.

  The mother invests herself in this particular son (whom she can control and mold – fortunately, he has none of the objectionable aspects of her husband), but in her possessive love, she engulfs him. When the couple argues, the son sides with his mother and identifies with her hurt and anger.

  In less common cases the mother is cold and detached. This is most common with the post-gender-identity phase type of homosexual, but the result is the same – an insecure attachment.

- *Mother-son relationship.* There is typically a particularly close relationship between mother and son; many clients will describe their relationship with their mother as "best friends" or "soul mates." Mother will often share her marital problems with the son, sometimes using him as a husband surrogate to compensate for a lack of emotional support and understanding from her husband.

- *Father-son relationship.* Our clients commonly say: "I never knew my father." "He was there, but not there." "He was a 'shadow figure.'" "He was as unapproachable as the Lincoln Monument."

  Minimal or nonexistent, their relationship is characterized by poor communication and a lack of openness and trust. The father is seen by the boy as distant or critical. Father and son almost never speak about meaningful issues, and personal disclosure is avoided. Whenever there is any communication between them, the mother is the go-between.

- *Older brother.* Freud said that if the homosexual has an older brother, the brother is likely to be feared, and the relationship will be hostile. We have found this pattern to be common. This older brother may have behavioral adjustment problems and be experienced by the pre-homosexual son as an intimidating bully; he may be the family "bad boy," while the prehomosexual son is the "good boy." Or he may be the high achiever for whom "everything comes easy," especially in sports. But in either scenario the client feels intimidated by the older brother and finds little support and encouragement from him.

  In only one case that I have seen, there was an adequate relationship with the older brother, but he, like the father, was unable to protect the client from a very disturbed mother. (In this regard, the client fit the post-gender-identity phase type of homosexual to be discussed later.)

- *Father-older brother relationship.* The father and this older brother typically get along better, share common interests and are more alike. Sometimes, this companion-to-father role is taken by a younger (more masculine) brother.

  An alternative scenario involves a great deal of hostility – even violence – between the father and older brother. But in both situations, the older (heterosexual) brother identifies with the father and his power enough, significantly, to be able to confront and engage him directly. This is in contrast to the prehomosexual son; his rebellion is indirect and he maintains emotional disengagement. The SSA son remembers of his family, "My brother was always my father's son; I was my mother's son."

The father inevitably resents this special mother-son relationship. Recognizing that this boy gets along so well with the mother causes the father to withdraw even further. The son, feeling further rejected, exacts his revenge on the abdicating father by using the privileged role he enjoys as Mom's confidante and best friend to usurp Dad's spousal role.

The Liability of "Specialness"

The "special place" so often held by the prehomosexual son with his mother was won without having to resolve any conflict with the father, and without the boy's achieving the masculinity the father represents. This becomes the basis for the gay man's often-stated contempt – rooted in envy – for the "boring, ordinary" straight man.

"I got the message from Mom that my charms, sociability, verbal and social skills, and emotional sensitivity made me better than the ordinary male," one client said. This specialness conferred on him meant that he did not have to achieve masculinity to win his place in the world. The scenario of "it's Mom and me together against those powerful, aggressive and hurtful males" subverts the boy's separation-individuation, preventing him from internalizing his masculine power.

Gradually, inevitably, the boy begins to develop a fascination for that essential part of his own identity that he has failed to claim. He will begin to seek it "out there" in the form of another male, feeling intense romantic longings. In puberty these longings for his own masculine power will become eroticized.

The Narcissistic Family

> To my father, I was a nothing.
> To my mother, I was a conditional something.
>
> I know that on some level my mom loves me.
> But she stops me from being myself.

In the previous section I described the basic features of the classic triadic family. Here we detail the essential features of the narcissistic family.

In the narcissistic family the son's separation-individuation (not just his gender individuation) poses a threat to the parental team's investment in this son as the "good little boy." This family – also known as the "parent-centered model" – places the child in the position of having to gratify (and assume upon himself, as if they were his own) his parents' emotional needs, particularly to help maintain the status quo between the detached father and overinvolved mother. The father and mother, who may on one level be nurturing, attentive, loving and consciously well-meaning, nevertheless see the child not so much in terms of who he is as a separate individual but how he makes them feel. Ultimately, the needs of the narcissistic parental system take precedence over the needs of the child (Donaldson-Pressman & Pressman, 1994).

This model is frequently reported by our homosexually oriented clients. One of our clients described an incident that illustrates this dynamic:

> When I was six years old, I got pulled into some kind of sex play with an older boy in our house. On some level I knew that doing this was wrong, and so I told my mom. The first thing she said was, "No! In our house?" Even at that age, I felt there was something wrong about her reaction.
>
> Today, in hindsight, I realize it's because she made the incident about her, not about me. Instead of responding to my need as a child, she was thinking mainly about her own embarrassment.

Narcissistic parents live overdramatized lives; what is happening to them at the moment is all-important. They transition from one drama to another, while their children are left as passive spectators or manipulated participants. The man who grew up in such a family often expresses an excessively pained sympathy for his parents, even an intense sadness and anguish for them. He was conditioned, early on, to be emotionally entangled in the never-ending drama of their lives, while neglecting his own. When he upsets them by presenting his own problems, they respond to him with disapproval. Thus the family structure creates a reversal of affect; the child feels sympathy not for himself but for his mother and father.

Narcissistic Features in Homosexual Men

The triadic-narcissistic family model helps explains a source of the narcissistic features so often found in the homosexually oriented male (Freud, 1914; Fenichel, 1945; van den Aardweg, 1985, 1986; Hatterer, 1970). Children of narcissistic parents are not seen for who they really are but are recognized for a false-positive self that is gratifying to the parent (or parents). Therefore they tend to develop narcissistic character structures, or at least narcissistic features, themselves. Narcissism causes a person to blur the boundaries between self and other, and to confuse his own needs with those of other people. Such persons are likely to have low self-esteem, difficulty in committing to long-term goals and problems with delayed gratification. They may start a new project with intensity, only to be unable to maintain commitment to it over time. Since they lacked an attuned parent to help them identify and express their true emotional needs and realistically assess their strengths and weaknesses, they do not know themselves.

Other narcissistic features we have often seen in homosexually oriented men include self-preoccupation, emotional distancing, excessive concern with external appearances, restricted self-insight, a tendency to choose image over substance, and a tendency to be easily hurt and offended by others. There is an excessive need for reassurance and a persistent need to be made to feel "special." They frequently hold unrealistic expectations of other people – setting others up to have to reflect back this specialness to them. There is a sense of entitlement and self-absorption, yet the grandiosity they feel alternates with deflated self-abasement.

Underinvolved or Overinvolved?

In the narcissistic family the parents' positive regard, in the form of warmth, affection and love, is generally dispensed for the purpose of shaping the child's behavior. At the same time, love may be given or taken away according to the moods, whims, impulses or sentiments of the parent. Rather than providing an understanding, accepting and supportive emotional environment for their son's developing individual self, such parents routinely and systematically "fail to see" the boy as a separate person with rights and needs of his own. What they do see is selectively determined by how the child affects them.

In the narcissistic, parent-centered family there are two "camps" that separate the children and the parents. One client put it this way: "It was always two families. My mother and father were one family, and we kids were the other – the haves and have-nots. When I was 11, they went on vacation and left me with my younger brother and sister. They wanted me to be the head of the house while they were gone. I was abandoned with that responsibility. They didn't teach us anything." As another client explained, "Our parents just 'watched us' raise ourselves."

The boy who later becomes homosexual is often the family member whose unspoken role was to "hold the family together" and to "keep Mom happy." He is tasked with consoling, comforting and taking responsibility for her feelings. Mom's feelings are especially unpredictable when she has a tumultuous marital relationship, and because she feels a chronic restlessness, emptiness and dissatisfaction with herself and with life itself.

Violation of Boundaries

Violations of boundaries are common to the narcissistic family. Thus we see unfair infringements on the child's privacy, time, emotionality, physicality and property. All of these are made available for the parent's use. The child is taught that his behavior determines his mother's happiness, although it is not so much his behavior as his mother's idiosyncratic feelings in the moment that determine her response to him. Consequently, rewards are given on a hit-or-miss basis.

Not surprisingly, the boy's inability to consistently gratify his mother through the right behavior (i.e., being "good," "nice," "considerate," "sweet," etc.) causes him to feel chronically dissatisfied with himself. His accomplishments are not consistently rewarded and never seem to be enough. It is here that the seeds of interpersonal inadequacy are planted. He represses his hurt feelings – especially his anger. He cannot internalize a sense of competence. He remains intensely confused about his real needs and real identity.

And so he develops a false self characterized by outward compliance and passivity. He becomes the "good little boy" on the outside, but begins to feel a need for some distraction – eventually undertaking a manic search for "something" because of this nagging, seemingly irresolvable inner discontentment and helplessness.

For the child of the narcissistic family, this is learned helplessness – a consequence of the repeated childhood experience that "nothing I ever do or say will make a difference."

The Importance of Image

A primary need of the narcissistic family is always to maintain an appropriate image. Acceptable appearance is very important, since it conveys desirability. This family may appear to have "no problems" and is often religious and socially conservative, attending church services regularly. The boy may remember it as all having been "very typical, middle class and apple pie." But in reality the family is actually "the shiny red apple with a worm inside: It looks great, until you bite into it and discover the worm. The rest of the apple may be fine, but you've lost your appetite" (Donaldson-Pressman & Pressman, 1994, p. 18).

In the narcissistic family we see that the boy's individuation is undermined. In the triadic family it is the boy's emerging masculine individuation that is discouraged. When we combine the two family systems – narcissistic and triadic – the boy's expression of his *individual* and *gendered* self is undermined by this family dynamic.

Children of these families later say that they were never allowed to acknowledge the reality of their family's brokenness; instead, their parents presented an idealized image of family life which the family was not only expected to project to the outside world but to believe. This "pretend family" environment implicitly approves the use of fantasy as a way of dealing with any unpleasant realities. This fantasy-option way of dealing with reality lays the foundation not only for his good-little-boy identity but for what will be his own later denial of male-female design ("I can be both male and female." "It is normal for men like me to feel uncomfortable around other guys." "I have a male body, but feel like a girl inside – this is me, this is 'who I am'").

Feeling thus emotionally abandoned, he becomes an object to himself – an object to be continually perfected. He fears that any spontaneous behavior would meet with shaming, so his personal identity is continually revised. Any hope of real personhood is abandoned for image.

As one client said, "How other people relate to me is how I define myself." Another explained:

Everything about myself is the promotion of an image: my apartment, my clothes, everything about me. I have this hyper self-awareness: *What are they thinking of me? What should I say? How am I appearing? How am I standing?* All the time, I am aware of watching myself through this kind of "third eye."

The Life of Montgomery Clift

In the biography of actor Montgomery Clift we see a striking example of many features of the narcissistic family – the classic maternal and paternal parenting style; the "good little boy" who does not rebel and becomes the perfectionistic high-achiever, but does not seem to ever know or trust his own feelings; the siblings who harbor a "family secret" that something was very wrong behind the family image, although they are not sure what it is; and the SSA son whose restless drivenness gradually leads to self-destruction.[1]

The Family Secret

A common feature of the triadic narcissistic family system is the existence of some unspoken secret that was kept from outsiders, and even from themselves. Beneath the normal, even "ideal," family image, there is something wrong, something too weird to discuss even among siblings. Perhaps it is the secret that his parents actually didn't love each other, or else (as Montgomery Clift's siblings suspected, see endnotes), perhaps their parents weren't the happy people they presented themselves to be.

Adults who enter treatment often speak to their siblings to confirm their own perception of some kind of distortion: "Was it true," they ask their brothers and sisters, "that it really happened that way?" When they do share their tentative impressions, they are often surprised to discover they shared the same "strange" impressions. The family's conflicting messages were too confusing to sort out, making it easier to retreat to the belief that "everything is OK."

As Montgomery Clift's brother, Brooks, said:

> Psychologically we couldn't take the memories...so we forgot. But at the same time we were obsessed with our childhood. We'd refer to it among ourselves, but only among ourselves. Part of each of us desperately wanted to remember our past, and when we couldn't, it was frustrating. It caused us to weep, when we were drunk enough. (Bosworth, 1978, p. 49)

The client from the narcissistic family rarely recognizes the pathology in his upbringing. At the start of therapy he may report a very normal family life – despite his inability to feel and express anger, his low self-esteem, feelings of inadequacy in relationships, depression, cynical and pessimistic moods, and difficulty in making decisions. There is often no obvious parental neglect; the malattunement was subtle – not easily detected. Things in the family "looked normal," as one client said, "yet somehow, felt strange":

> My parents were not verbally or physically abusive. I always had plenty
> of food and education and clothes and vacations, and always felt well-
> cared for. Because they have always been "nice" to me, it is really hard
> to hold them accountable for the emotional support they didn't give.

The Allure of Theater and Acting

The child of the triadic-narcissistic family must develop a coping mechanism to survive. He does so by creating a false self, which we see in his role of the "good little boy." This allows him to bury his "bad" self and adapt to the demands of his environment. But in doing so, he must necessarily sever his connection with his own emotional life.

In compensation he often develops a fascination with fantasy, theater and acting, taking on the emotional life of someone else. If he was born with the temperamental traits of creativity and sensitivity, he will find it especially easy to retreat to fantasy.

As Montgomery Clift's brother said, when Monty played someone else, he was at last freed from his old role as the good son, and he no longer had to live up to the image his mother imagined for him. Without guilt, he could wrest himself free of the "good boy" and claim the persona of someone else.

Another place where we often find gay men seeking meaning and spiritual solace is in the reality-denying and gender-blurring archetypes of New Age philosophy.

Failure to Emotionally Connect Leads to a Sense of Existential Meaninglessness

The child of the narcissistic family simply does not know himself because his parents confused their own needs with his needs. He can never fully satisfy his parents' perceived needs, so he feels like a failure. He feels inadequate, immature, unprepared for adult responsibility and unready to assume control over his life. He continues to look to the expectations of others. He has grown up without knowing "who owns the 'should,'" because he never received accurate mirroring.

Because he cannot maintain genuine emotional connectedness with himself or others, he suffers from a pervasive sense that life is meaninglessness. One man explained it this way: "Life is just so … [searching for a word]."

Another client explained the same sense of disconnection and unhappiness:

> I hide pieces of myself from other people. Different friends will see different pieces of me. But no one will see all of me. I don't even know all of me. I only know different pieces of me at different times, depending on who I'm with. When I'm alone, I get uncomfortable because I don't know who I'm with.

"Mother's Favorite Child" Evokes Her Love, Guilt and Resentment

In the following autobiography, written by a gay man, we see more of the features of the triadic-narcissistic family. We hear the son's confusion about who he is; his pain and estrangement from his father, who was a negative, shadowy figure; and his inability to separate his own feelings from those of his mother. Finally (in this all-too-typical scenario), the lonely and vulnerable young man was offered sexual attention by another male:

> It was no secret in my family that I did not have a father. … I was the son of a man with whom my mother, then married, had had an affair, to the lasting shame of her Mexican-Catholic family. … All I knew about my natural father was his name, and I saw him only once, when I was five years old and he turned up, drunk, at our house. My stepfather drove him out of the yard, screaming invectives. After that, I never asked about him and was ashamed when my mother mentioned him to me.
>
> This one incident aside, my stepfather showed little paternal interest in me. More often, he used my mother's infidelity to her first husband against her when they fought. Once, during a drunken argument, I

heard him call her a whore, and the humiliation I felt was as much for myself as for her.

Practically speaking, I was my mother's child, her favorite, she told me occasionally, and both she and her own mother indulged me. But even then, at five and six, I was aware that my mother's solicitude was due as much to pity as love, not to mention her own complicated shame.

What I felt toward my mother in return was a confusion of love, guilt and resentment. At that early age, in my innermost self, I was no one's child, and as I grew older, my sense of estrangement from my family deepened. When, at eleven, I was sexually molested by an adult family member, I felt cast off completely.

They, [my mother and grandmother] had no idea what to do with me, a moody boy, precocious at one moment and withdrawn the next, who sometimes accepted their solicitude and at other times angrily rejected it. And it was beyond my power – because it was beyond my understanding – to tell them how I hurt. (Michael Nava, quoted in Preston, 1992, pp. 15–18)

Impairment of the Child's Gender Maturation

The boy who grows up within the triadic-narcissistic family will develop trust issues that center around the gendered self – that is, he will fear that men will "diminish" and "degrade" him, while women will manipulate and control him, and drain him of his masculine power.

One man explained: "My mother abandoned half of me – the man – and clung to the other half, the good little boy. But she booted out the masculine."

Many of our clients report recurrent nightmares and fears replayed over and over regarding threats to their masculinity and their assertive self. This client describes this fear about his masculine self-worth, along with the shame he felt that his father did not rescue him:

My mother was a doctor, and I felt very loved by her whenever I was sick; she would take care of me in a very kind and attentive way. However, when angry, she would say the most insensitive, hurtful and shaming things to me. When I did something wrong, she would call me "Idiot Tom." When I got upset about something, she would ask me if the reason I was irritated was because I was "having my period." For sure, she devalued my masculinity.

Even though basically my father was an easygoing guy, he emotionally abandoned me. When my mother abused me, he never intervened, as if I weren't worth rescuing. I never remember him initiating any activities with me. If I had been content to spend all of my time alone in my room, he would not have budged an inch to seek me out.

The Parents' Role in Eliciting Masculinity

In his classic study of effeminate boys, titled the *Sissy Boy Syndrome*, psychiatrist Richard Green says that parents of gender-disturbed boys did not necessarily encourage their sons' girlish behavior – but in their failure to discourage it, they were implicitly condoning it.

The healthy boy knows and delights in the fact that "not only am I 'me,'" but "I am a 'boy-me.'"[2] In some cases, the parents actively punished male behavior because they found it threatening or inconvenient. In other cases, where the boy was born temperamentally sensitive, the parents did not elicit the masculine identification for which that particular boy needed special, validating support. "Masculinity," as Stoller points out, "is an achievement," not a given – and one that is vulnerable to developmental injury.

The "Delight-Deprived" Boy

In my search for the particular quality of father-son bonding that is fundamental to the development of the boy's masculine identity, I have been led to what I call "a shared delight." I am convinced that the healthy development of masculine identification depends on this phenomenon. This special emotional exchange should be between the boy and his father, although a father figure or grandfather may serve the purpose where no father is available. It is not a single event or one-time occurrence, but should characterize the relationship.

This particular style of emotional attunement is especially important during the critical time of gender identification. Homosexual men rarely if ever recall father-son interaction that includes activities they both enjoy together. In this vital experience father and son share in the enjoyment ("delight") in the boy's success.

Psychotherapist Robert Rupp observes that the homosexual man is "delight-deprived" by his father, which is to say he cannot recall his father generally taking pleasure in his son's activities, accomplishments or success. On the other hand, most nonhomosexual men do, in fact, recall sharing an activity with their fathers that involved the possibility of failure, injury, fear and danger.

Homosexual men have great difficulty recalling childhood father-son activities that were fun, exciting and enjoyable, and included success for the son. They rarely have positive memories of their father's teaching, coaching or encouraging them to gain a new accomplishment that involves bodily activity or strength. Indeed, many clients specifically lament this deprivation.

An example of "a shared delight" is found in writer and social commentator Malcolm Muggeridge's autobiography. Malcolm's father was his hero, and as a teenager Malcolm would travel to his father's office in London. When the young man arrived, he noticed an embodied shift in his father:

> When he saw me, his face always lit up, as it had a way of doing, quite suddenly, thereby completely altering his appearance; transforming him from a rather cavernous, shrunken man into someone boyish and ardent. He would leap agilely off his stool, wave gaily to his colleague . . . and we would make off together. There was always about these excursions an element of being on an illicit spree, which greatly added to their pleasure. They were the most enjoyable episodes in all my childhood. (Wolfe, 2003, p. 26)

In contrast to the shared delight which lies at the core of the true father-son bonding experience, there is instead a shame experience remembered by many homosexually oriented men. As one of my clients explained:

> When I recall my father, I feel this big, black, heavy-weighted force that washes over me in a powerful, oppressive wave. My dad looked at me not as a person, a child, his son but as a "thing." His look at me said

"I made a mistake" – literally, I made a mistake, I made *that* mistake – "and I don't want to interact with that." That's the oppressive wave that washes over me.

A twenty-two-year-old client lamented missing the shared delight experiences: "I wish he could have gotten excited by my activities, my accomplishments. I want him to be proud of me. I want him to make me feel proud of myself. I wish he had worked with me, pushed me, challenged and encouraged me."

Another client recalled:

I don't think my father was happy with me. Somehow he seemed unhappy, and I couldn't help think it was about me. When my father came home and sat at the table, he had a look of unhappiness. I'm sitting there and he's unhappy. Somehow I felt, 'I'm failing to make him happy.' It's confusing; I couldn't be sure if Dad felt bad about himself or bad about me.

The shared delight typically occurs within the context of physical activity involving success or failure. There is the quality of risk, danger and adventure in which the boy is first terrified – then with encouragement and coaching from Dad, achieves success and feels good about himself. The excitement is no doubt intensified by the risk of failure. Father and son both share in the delight of son's achievement.

This interaction is an example of how mothers and fathers care for their sons differently. While mothers will attend to the child – protecting him from harm – fathers engage their sons in play. Often this play includes reckless, even seemingly dangerous, activities.

We have all observed a young father tossing his infant son in the air and catching him. Anyone observing this universal ritual will see that the dad is laughing, while the son looks full of fear. Soon the boy begins to laugh because Dad is laughing. The boy has just learned an important lesson that older males teach younger males: "Danger can be fun." More importantly, the boy learns another lesson; he can trust his father – "Dad will catch me." And from that early relationship, he begins to learn to trust other men.

Let's contrast this bonding ritual with a quite different early memory related by a temperamentally sensitive man who experienced his father's well-meaning but rough play in an entirely different manner:

> I was probably three or four years old and Dad was throwing me up into the air and catching me. I think I liked it for a while, but soon his hand and thumbs began to chafe and poke into my armpits. I either cried or complained. I do not remember if my father said anything, but he did stop throwing me. I felt ashamed, as if I had spoiled his fun. I felt separated from him and that made me feel sad. I was afraid that I had disappointed Dad and that he wouldn't play with me anymore.

In this case the boy sensed his father's disappointment in him. Over the years an emotional gulf slowly grew wider between this father and son – one which the father never attempted to understand or to break down.

Positive physical interaction between father and son appears essential in making the father feel familiar, nonmysterious, approachable and "just like me" in the boy's eyes.

So much of what lies behind adult same-sex attraction is a deep, lingering, unsatisfied desire for physical closeness with a male. When there has been a healthy, childhood internalization of the father's masculinity, there will be no need to sexualize another man.

Being "Pulled In, Then Dropped" by Parents

In a healthy family, children know that their feelings matter and their needs are important. The children of the narcissistic family, having been used as extensions of their parents, are not so sure. Healthy families recognize and support their children as discrete individuals with their own needs. In the narcissistic family, parents may be overattentive and solicitous – but then, when the child makes demands on the parental system that clash with their needs, they abruptly withdraw. His own emotional needs are seen as self-centered, disruptive or upsetting. Sensing himself to be emotionally manipulated, he feels powerless and helpless. He has the disturbing sense of being intermittently pulled in, seduced, but then dropped.

Children of narcissistic families lack a reasonable sense of entitlement. They are not given the right to own their own feelings, their property, their time and even – in the scenario of early sexual abuse – their own bodies. In adulthood they find it very hard to establish clear personal boundaries.

As the child of this family becomes more independent, he increasingly finds himself labeled "selfish and disrespectful." Placed in the hopeless position of having to make Mom happy, and finding himself unsuccessful in gaining his father's love and attention, he grows up with a sense of helplessness and pessimism about life and relationships. As an adult he won't trust his feelings or his internal judgment, because he was never taught to attune to his interior promptings.

Black or White
Children of these families are inclined to "split," which is to say, to perceive other persons as "all good" or "all bad." Significant relationships are seen in terms of absolutes – the other person is "great" or "terrible," and either "They love me" or "They hate me." The child of this family, who is himself likely to have narcissistic features, cannot see the realistic ambiguities inherent in all relationships, the nuances and gray areas. This splitting is done to avoid intense, often overwhelming, anxiety, for there is a sense of control to be gained by interpreting things as all positive or negative.

Yet even this black-or-white perception changes: the other person may suddenly go from good to bad, depending on how they make the child of the narcissistic family feel about himself. This is because his parents related to him as if he were "all good" (i.e., they were loving, attentive) when his behavior made them feel good about themselves, but they treated him as "all bad" (by being cold, rejecting) when his behavior made them feel bad about themselves.

The family thus deprives this child of the experience of object constancy, and the understanding that all relationships will inevitably contain both deep satisfactions and deep disappointments.

Family Reconciliation
When the client recognizes his family dysfunction, this need not destroy the family relationship and end in bitterness. It may, in fact, eventually lead to forgiveness. As one man explained:

Initially, I felt anger, resentment and confusion about why my parents chose to do the things that they did. Today, though, I have come to understand more of how they too were wounded emotionally, and that they couldn't give what they didn't have. Recognizing that has led to a much more authentic relationship with them.

Now I have been able to feel more compassion toward them, and to move on to a place of forgiveness and understanding.

CHAPTER 3

Homosexuality as a Shame-Based Symptom

An ocean of oblivion sweeps over a child when it is shamed.

— ROBERT BLY

The developmental theme I described in the previous chapter fits the backgrounds described to us by most of the SSA men who come to our clinic seeking change.

This model is what we call the pre-gender-identity phase type of client. It does not apply to the approximately 20 percent of our cases that we identify as the "post-gender-identity phase" type of homosexuality.

The triadic-narcissistic family model, described in chapter two, is activated in two successive phases. First, the boy suffers an insecure attachment with the mother due to her narcissistic parenting style, which confuses the child's needs and identity with her own needs. Then, when confronted with the second developmental challenge of bonding with a hostile/critical or distant/uninvolved father, the boy lacks the secure maternal attachment that he needs to successfully negotiate the phase of gender individuation. Thus we posit that for some – perhaps many – homosexual men, there was not only a failure to identify with the father but an earlier foundational attachment insecurity with the mother.

Seeing and Being Seen

Over and over, we encounter our clients' expression of a profound sense of emotional abandonment. Hearing these same stories we suspect that there was also an early maternal attachment deprivation that preceded their problems with masculine gender identification.

The gender-identification/separation-individuation phase of identity development occurs at a time of heightened self-awareness, which is also a time of heightened narcissistic sensitivity. At around two years old, the child first discovers that he can be "seen." This striking discovery – the awareness of self – is born through the realization that others, in fact, see him. How others mirror *who he is* will shape his developing perception of self.

In the first phase of our model the mother-son insecure attachment prompts a shame response when the boy reveals his autonomous strivings. This results in a heightened sensitivity to shame, leaving the boy ill-prepared for the second phase: achieving the secure father-son attachment.

Biology May Set the Stage

Today, we have evidence that there may be a biological predisposition to gender deficit and subsequent homosexuality in some people, especially boys. But biology is only one of several influences that shape gender identity and sexual orientation.

On a parallel plane we see new empirical support for the power of parental influences, particularly, in the case of male homosexuals, new evidence for a family background of absent fathers and broken homes. (This finding is detailed at <www.narth.com/docs/influencing.html>.) In addition, recent advances in attachment theory and in our neurobiological understanding of gender development cause us to direct additional attention to attachment problems that occur in the early infant-mother bond.

An Interactional Model: Biology and Social Environment

A helpful way to understand the interaction of biology and social environment is as follows. First are the "givens": genes and prenatal hormonal influences. These biological factors work together to create a temperamental predisposition, either to gender conformity and the likelihood of normal heterosexuality or to gender *non*conformity and the possibility of homosexual development. Layered on top of those biological givens is the social environment of parents, peers and life experiences; and last, there is the influence of free will and choice.

The biological and social factors work together to shape gender identity and eventual sexual orientation. The element of choice operates in terms of the values we choose to identify with, the social group we select and the behavioral avenues we pursue – all of which serve to reinforce or modify our early shaping experiences.

Most boys who become homosexual have a sensitive nature, which makes them especially vulnerable to emotional injury. This same sensitivity is a great gift in some ways: it often includes keen aesthetic abilities. But when such a child is driven into isolation by an insecure attachment with the parents, these same gifts provide an easy escape from reality.

Driven into isolationism, the boy who has been wounded is tempted to escape into a secret world of pretense and make-believe. One client describes this common scenario: his boyhood was spent "wrapped up in those wonderful stories that weren't mine, those consoling dreams, the other-worldliness." That style of coping contrasts with the play and interest of the pre-*heterosexual* boy, who more often strives for mastery of the environment rather than a withdrawal from it.

Sadly, the prehomosexual boy often learns, early on, to be a detached spectator. From a safe vantage point, he watches the actions of others. His is a vicarious way of living rather than a direct engagement. His contact with the world is mediated through the imagination – envisioning interactions and scenarios that never happened, and people who never existed where he can observe, report and create, but without the risk of real emotional engagement. Typically neglected (by his father) and emotionally manipulated (by his mother), the only time when he can safely *be with himself* is in the artistic-imaginative world he has come to know so well. There, his relationships can be built with people in fantasy situations over which he does have control.

Boyhood gender nonconformity has been shown to be a high predictor of adult homosexuality. Saghir and Robins (1973) report, "About two-thirds of male homosexuals [67 percent in their sample] describe themselves as having been girl-like during childhood" (p. 18). Green's

(1985) study of boys who were diagnosed with Gender Identity Disorder (GID) showed that approximately two-thirds later identified themselves as either bisexual or homosexual. Zucker and Green (1992) also found that 66 percent to 75 percent of GID boys would later become homosexual.

Imitative Feminine Attachment: An Explanation for GID

Boys with GID overidentify with their mothers. They are far more likely to wish to be like their mother and less likely to be like their father than boys who show typical gender-role behavior.

GID in boys can be an attempt by the child to hold onto a mother who is only intermittently available. The overwhelming stress of maternal insecure attachment causes the boy to adopt a feminine role in order to compensate for the attachment loss. He thus restores the lost love object through the enactment of "fantasy fusion," employing the feminine introject as a defense against the terror of maternal abandonment. Researcher Susan Coates (Coates & Wolfe, 1995) says that when the attachment bond has been derailed,

> massive separation anxiety in the child is then defended against by a recitative self-fusion fantasy with the mother. In essence, the child substitutes an identification for a relationship, and comes to confuse *being* mommy with *being with* mommy – this during a period when he lacks stable internal representation of self and other, and when his cognitive understanding of the permanent gender classification is still immature. (p. 9)

The boy thus develops a "fantasized fusion" of himself with his mother: "By thus identifying with women, the boy disassociates himself from his own rage and protects the internal tie" (p. 650).

But the boy's effeminacy is not truly feminine. It is actually a caricature. As some mothers report, their GID sons are actually more effeminate than their sisters. In fact the GID boy "does not truly behave like girls his age; rather he acts like his highly stereotyped idea of what being a girl is like" (Coates & Wolfe, 1995, p. 10).

Coates (Coates & Zucker, 1988) analyzed the Rorschach responses of GID boys and – supporting the view that GID is symptomatic of self-object confusion – found evidence of impairment in self- and object-representations, and a disturbance of boundaries between fantasy and reality.

Similarly, Susan Bradley (2003) states:

> I conceptualize the symptom of GID as a child's solution to intolerable affects. This is confirmed in the fact that GID typically has its onset at a time in a child's life when the family has been particularly stressed and the parents are either more angry, or less available, or both. The GID symptoms, particularly the assumption of the role and behaviors of the opposite sex, act to quench the child's anxiety and to make him or her feel more valued, stronger, or safer. (p. 202)

Gender-Confused Boys and Acting

The idea that GID is an imitative defense is further supported by the evidence that gender-confused boys have a particular interest in theater and acting. Coates (Coates & Wolfe, 1995) mentions the "notable acting ability and talent for mimicry that has been described by many observers of GID boys" (p. 31). Fenichel (1945) has noted that homosexuals seem to be disproportionately represented in the acting profession. Green and Money (1966) also found a relationship between early boyhood effeminacy, role-taking and stage acting. The boy's ability to adopt an effeminate role is, they believe, due to the development of a "chameleon-like" talent that might be related "to the fundamental personality mechanism of dissociation" (p. 536).

GID and General Psychopathology

Is Gender Identity Disorder a biologically based behavioral trait and "normal" for that child (as advocated by gay apologists), or is it suggestive of a pervasive maladaptation within the personality? That the condition is not just an isolated disorder but indicative of more pervasive underlying psychopathology has been suggested by the following writers: Bates, Bentler and Thompson (1973, 1979); Bates, Skilbeck, Smith and Bentler (1974); Tuber and Coates (1989); Coates and Person (1985); Bates et al. (1973, 1974, 1979); and Bradley (1980).

Within the general body of research on psychopathology, data suggests that GID can be symptomatic of separation anxiety (Bradley et al., 1980; Coates & Person, 1985; Lowry & Zucker, 1991).

This is supported by the high rate of separation-anxiety disorder found in studies of GID children (55–60 percent) as well as the high rate of depressive symptoms.

The Contributions of Alan Schore: Maternal Attachment

With the integration of attachment theory and neurobiology into the reparative-therapy model, we see how the sensitive boy's shame response to parental malattunement would negatively affect areas of the developing brain that are associated with gender-identity formation.

Looking to the earliest developmental period with the mother, we thus have an intriguing possible explanation for why the SSA male has had such difficulty in securely identifying with the father and the father's masculinity.

In this section I will summarize the literature, particularly the seminal contributions of Schore (1994, 2003) toward developing a unified model of neurophysiology, interactional theory and self-psychology in the development of homosexuality. This multidimensional developmental model demonstrates how interpersonal events trigger neurophysiological changes in the brain, which in turn can result in the perception of gender inferiority.

This model of insecure attachment to the mother also explains some of the commonly encountered defenses of our SSA clients, such as tendencies toward dissociation, projective identification and addiction, especially sexual addiction.

Gender Is Best Actualized in a Securely Individuating Self

During the boy's earliest years of life, he is confronted with two important developmental challenges: the separation-individuation phase, in which his autonomous self is developed, and the gender-identity phase of masculine identification.

As has been well established (Greenson, 1968; Horner, 1991; Coates, 1990; Fast, 1984; Tabin, 1985), these two phases occur at about the same time, at about a year-and-a-half to three years old.

The child's sense of gender awareness is a crucial aspect of his identity formation. It is through gender that he grows to understand who he is in relation to other people. By understanding his place within the natural dichotomy of *male-female*, he is able to create an organized view of himself in the world (Tabin, 1985; Tabin & Tabin, 1988).

Structurally, we might say that for the boy, *masculinity* is to the autonomous self what a *steel beam* is to an edifice. More than a mere "cultural or social construct," gender is biologically based and is most readily actualized in a securely individuating self. Gender identity supports personal identity; in turn, personal identity is the basis on which gender is constructed. Because each developmental task supports the other, failure in one area threatens success in the other.

Especially for the boy, an awakened maleness acts in the service of his newly developing autonomous self. The drive toward masculine identification supports his ongoing and vital task of separation from the mother. Irene Fast (1984) summarizes the process: "For boys, separation-individuation and gender differentiation issues interpenetrate in a particular way: regressive temptations to merge with the mother threaten gender identity" (p. 106).

Mother as Affect Regulator

During the first year of life the infant shows a separation-anxiety response only in regard to the absence of the mother. She is the major interactive regulator, especially when he is in a distressed state. If, during the first year of the child's life, the mother is extremely depressed, the child will not learn through her how to regulate his affect, so he may subsequently turn to the father. But in most cases the development is sequential, with the mother being the first object of attachment and affect-regulation, and later the father.

The father's role is distinctly different; his interactive style is to play and hyper-arouse, while the mother's role is the regulation of negative states, such as hunger and physical distress.

In the child's second year this second attachment system (toward the father) becomes well established, so that by the middle of the second year we see the father's absence prompting a genuine separation-anxiety response in the toddler.

The Influence of Maternal Attachment on Gender Identity

> We understand failure at gender acquisition to be rooted in the attach-
> ment dynamic between the mother and baby. (Allan Schore, personal
> communication, September 30, 2005)

It is through the primary relationship with the mother that the child
develops the ability to trust other human beings. When we see difficulties
in the child regarding trust and emotional connection, we recognize these
as affect-regulation problems which originated in that primary, maternal
relationship. The mother acts as a social reference for all other human
beings – in particular, as a social reference to the infant when he experiences the father. The boy's first experience of the father is through the
mother's eyes, and a number of studies suggest that poor relations between
mother and father are an influencing factor during this phase of the boy's
development. The mother can convey that the father is safe or that he is
dangerous. Or she may devalue the father, block the son's access to the
father, and transmit disapproving messages not only about her husband
but also about the boy himself as a male.

Early mother-child malattunement can be a result of either the mother's excessive engagement or her lack of engagement. Excessive engagement results in intense hyper-arousal, while neglect results in the child's
hypo-arousal. Sometimes we will find shifts back and forth between the
two polarities of overstimulation and understimulation, depending on the
idiosyncratic needs of the mother from moment to moment. A mother
with manic-depression, for example, generates high levels of arousal in the
child and then leaves him in a depressive state through her abandonment.
The result of either mothering style is overwhelmingly stressful, forcing
the boy to adapt by resorting to the defenses of dissociation and projective identification.

The Hyper-Intrusive Type of Mother

The narcissistically interactive mother often acts as an intrusive, overstimulating caregiver to her child. Here, the mother is using the child for her
own affective self-regulation. When she persists in this interactive style

of hyper-intrusiveness and hyper-stimulation, the child finally must shut down. Clinical observation of children as young as four months old show the infant in a hyper-aroused state trying to defend himself by giving back cues to the mother such as gaze-averting; the mother ignoring the gaze averts; and the child arching its back to get away from her while she keeps looming in and attempting to engage him face-to-face.

In this situation all of the child's active coping strategies are overridden by the mother's persistence. Her intrusiveness drives the infant into either hyper-arousal or protest. If pushed further into extremely high arousal, he will shut down (dissociation).

If the mother engages the husband through the same overstimulating relational style, he (especially if he is the passive-avoidant type) will distance himself from his wife, placing himself on the periphery of family life.

Attachment Loss with the Nonresponsive Mother

In an opposite but equally problematic scenario, the mother is nonresponsive to the boy's animation and displays of pride, which causes the boy to shut down. This type of mother is extremely disengaged, which in turn causes massive emotional disengagement in the child, triggering his affective collapse and eventual dissociation.

With both maternal styles, the end result is the boy's adaptation of dissociation: he has become habituated to this infantile defense by the time he approaches the second developmental phase (engaging with the father).

Moving From Mother to Father

The boy now moves into the second developmental phase: where he must develop an attachment to the father. But when the boy has previously acquired the defense of emotional disengagement (dissociation) in the primary relationship with the mother, and now experiences a father who is emotionally unavailable, there is likely to be a secondary failure in the father-son attachment bond.

With this general overview of the two-phase model, I now return to a more detailed description of each parent's role in this model.

The Practicing Subphase: Separation from Mother

The mother-son attachment phase first begins with the practicing phase and is then followed by the rapprochement (return to mother) phase.

At the start of the practicing phase the boy begins to demonstrate spontaneous gestures toward the actualization of his individuated self. During this time he discovers his power and autonomy. He revels in his newly discovered "embodied self," which is to say, a self that is capable of physicality and separateness from his mother. This new identification with his body establishes the groundwork for his later masculine identity.

In her classic study of childhood, *The Magic Years*, Selma Fraiberg (1959) beautifully captures the boy's first euphoric discovery of his body:

> To stand unsupported, to take that first step is a brave and lonely thing to do; so, independent standing and walking represent, truly, a cutting of the moorings to the mother's body. In such moments there is a heightened awareness of self, a feeling of being absolutely alone in an empty world, that is exalting and terrifying.... [T]his moment must bring the first sharp sense of the uniqueness and separateness of his body and his person, the discovery of the solitary self....
>
> [A]nd he is quite 'in love with himself' for being so clever. From dawn to dusk he marches around in an ecstatic, drunken dance, which ends only when he collapses with fatigue. He can no longer be contained within the four walls of his house, and the fenced-in-yard is like a prison to him. Given practically unlimited space, he staggers joyfully with open arms toward the end of the horizon. (pp. 60–61)

During the practicing phase the mother must match and support the boy's hyper-aroused state. She should not be threatened (i.e., upset) by his vitality, nor convey fear of his physical injury. Rather, through bodily and facial expression, she needs to be "happy" for him, showing enthusiasm for his individuation from her.

This phase – one of emotional imbalance and unregulated overexcitation – leaves the child especially sensitive to any maternal empathetic break. It is a phase of self-exhibition, elation and overstimulation when the boy feels a heightened shame-sensitivity that makes him uniquely vulnerable to his mother's response. His increased self-rapture and narcissistic investment in his growing separateness require a mother who provides a particularly attuned demonstration of support and approval.

During this phase the mother should neither exaggerate the child's hypo-depressive state, nor hyper-arouse him; instead, he requires supportive attunement. If he is overwhelmed by the over-stimulating mother or depressed by the under-responsive mother, he may dissociate and develop a reactive "shutdown" response.

This mother-son affective communication system is critical to the infant's integration of his own affect and his discovery of how to maintain (or regain) emotional contact with others as well as with himself.

Particularly for the temperamentally sensitive boy, when the maternal response fails to match and reflect back his own level of arousal, we see the very first experience of "shaming."

"Central moments" requiring attunement. Upon return from these exploratory forays, Schore (2003) notes, the boy's earlier symbiotic relationship with the mother is challenged now that he has had a taste of the world. Coming back to her after interacting in these new social and physical realms, whenever he "encounters a facially expressed affective misattunement" with his mother, this prompts a "sudden shock-induced deflation of positive affect," which propels the infant into a shamed/depressive state (pp. 159–60).

Such "central moments" of reunion, as Schore calls them, last only thirty seconds to three minutes, yet they can be critical ones. Learning to regulate affect is essential for successful completion of the separation-individuation phase. Successful completion establishes the foundation for the next bonding challenge, the one with the father, and the process through which the boy's masculine identification is attained.

Schore describes the damage that can be done through the "prototypical shame transaction," which involves "an expectation of seeing the gleam in the mother's eye in a reunion, but suddenly, he encounters frustration, and experiences instead a bodily-based autonomic stress response" (p. 163).

During this time the child's "hyperstimulated, elated, grandiose, narcissistically charged state of heightened arousal" (p. 155) means that the return to the mother will involve high expectations. It is at this critical point of return that the boy is most vulnerable to shame. Coming back from his euphoric explorations, when he unexpectedly encounters the mother's facial expression denoting a negative emotional state, through her muted response and "strange face" (Basch, 1976, p. 765) we see an abrupt disregulation of the infant's arousal state. A "shame moment" ensues, with a break in the attachment bond accompanied by an actual internal, physiological change, that is, an abrupt biological shift from the sympathetic to the parasympathetic mode. He now enters a state of unfocused attention and diminished affect. He becomes deflated and passive, with less interest in his surroundings (Schore, 2003, pp. 154–55).

This research on the neurophysiology of mother-infant interaction offers a possible biological explanation for our own clients' frequently observed ready inclination to shift from the assertion state into shame. Schore describes this shift as "the rapid-state transition" from hyper-arousal to hypo-arousal, and it is the same shift we observe over and over in our adult SSA clients.

Schore (1994) points out that the critical times for gender-role imprinting and shame-socialization regulation both occur during the same period of orbito-frontal development. "These shame transactions," he explains, "critically influence gender identification processes that emerge in the middle of the second year" (p. 268).

Learning the skill of attunement reparation. The attuned mother will rescue the infant from his affective collapse so that he is able to recoup his lost energetic state through her response. Her accurate attunement has the effect of modulating the infant's shame state through emotional reengagement. This helps the boy develop his own ability to regulate mood shifts. Thus the mother teaches him "self-affect regulation" and helps him develop the capacity to maintain his internal equilibrium during periods of high stress.

Miscoordination and repair, even with attuned mothers, is a typical feature of mother-infant interaction. In fact, studies in infant-mother face-to-face exchanges show that it occurs every few seconds in the form of a cyclical interactive pattern of coordination, miscoordination and then the return to mutual understanding. This is how the infant learns interpersonal competence and the ability to stay in the assertive self-state. Toleration of malattunement during times of miscoordination serves to facilitate the child's developing sense of personal autonomy (Winnicott, 1965).

Whenever maternal detachment is followed by reattachment (successful reengagement), the infant's stress-coping ability is increased. By rescuing the child from his shame posture, the attuned mother supports his self-identity and self-continuity. Through his participation in this attunement reparation, the child develops his own internal resources for later self-regulation so that he need not remain deflated (i.e., stay stuck in the "gray zone").

This cyclical process of detachment and reattachment also helps the child learn the difference between his own behaviors and needs and his mother's behaviors and needs.

Learning this skill of "miscoordination and repair" teaches the child interpersonal competence. He discovers that he has the ability to affect others – specifically, that he has the power to reengage another person after a relational breach. Without this power to emotionally reengage others within a relationship, the child will be more inclined, later in life, to learn an unhealthy, impersonal form of affect-regulation through addictive behaviors, especially sexual and substance addiction.

But when the child's efforts to repair the miscoordination fail to be reciprocated by the mother, a sense of powerlessness results. This lays the foundation for interpersonal compliance and passivity, helplessness and hopelessness, and the tendency to develop hostile-dependent relationships as a result.

We may speculate that many of the mothers of these homosexual men were limited in their ability to appropriately reengage and reattach with their sons, and to support their sons' separation and individuation from them.

Alienation from masculine gender vitality. The prehomosexual boy grows up "disembodied" – that is, alienated from his own body, especially his genitals, which disconnects him from his biologically based gender vitality. Not surprisingly, he then begins to envy the masculine bodies of other boys, in a compensatory (reparative) attempt to acquire other male bodies by erotically joining with them.

Part of this alienation could be rooted in a childhood shame-based scenario that involves the boy's exploration of his male body. "Parental affective response to the toddler's exhibitionistic sexual displays, if shame-producing," Schore (2003) states, "can critically influence gender-identity formation during this period of time" (p. 994).

The male genitals are the embodied symbol of the boy's essential difference from his mother. A negative parental reaction when the child is engaged in genital exploration or play may (especially in the very sensitive child) prompt the boy's shame-filled disavowal of his masculinity.

Many of our adult clients feel deeply alienated from – and ashamed of – their bodies; other men, in compensation, are caught up in a narcissistic fascination with their body and genitals as if they were not their own. In gay men we see an almost universal fascination, indeed obsession, with the penis.

Treatment, especially through the modality of body work, will later aim to reconnect the client with his body.

The Second Phase of Homosexual Development: Father-Son Insecure Attachment

The second phase of our two-phase model involves the boy's attachment to the father, which occurs during the "practicing" phase. In his desire to fulfill his natural masculine strivings, the boy reaches out to the father, seeking his attention, affection and approval. It is through the fulfillment of these affective needs that the boy's masculine identity is acquired.

During this paternal attachment phase the boy is challenged to leave the safety of the mother and attach to his father in order to secure his masculine gender identity. We have suggested that the boy is unprepared for this challenge because of a prior insecure attachment with the mother, resulting in his readiness to dissociate.

Mother and father together. Mother and father can work in tandem, providing alternative and compensatory attunement, with the child attuning to one parent or the other at different periods during his development. Attunement problems developing with the mother, for example, will be mitigated if during that particular time the boy feels understood and supported by the father.

But where there is a family system that itself is narcissistic, the enmeshment of each parent within the parental team prevents any compensatory attachments. Preoccupation with their own dysfunctional system prevents either parent from "breaking rank" and offering the child an alternative attachment. Consequently, neither parent rescues the child when the relationship with the other parent becomes faulty.

Said one client, "My father would join my mother in her attacks on me, or say nothing to help me. He supported her against me, even when he actually knew she was wrong. He needed to stay in Mom's good graces."

The father's personality: A characteristic "failure to engage." My clinical experience has, with strong consistency, shown the fathers of homosexual men to be unable or unwilling to reconnect with their sons after their sons emotionally detach from them. As a group these fathers seem to lack the traits of salience that are necessary to reengage an avoidant son who is inclined to dissociate from them. Fathers will typically report, "My son rejects *me*," yet they do not initiate the sustained, long-term emotional connection necessary for surmounting their son's emotional detachment. Consideration of the fathers' personality limitations are discussed elsewhere (Nicolosi & Nicolosi, 2002). In spite of their failure with this particular son, however, these fathers may have been "good enough" with another, less shame-prone son.

The prehomosexual boy thus approaches this second phase with two handicaps: the inclination to dissociate, and a nonsalient father incapable of breaking through his dissociation. When challenged to bond with an uninvolved father, who has a detached or critical style and fails to "go out and get" his son, the boy with a malattuned mother will maintain his dissociative defense: he withdraws and affectively collapses into the shamed self-state.

Shaming by the father can be either active or passive, in the form of explicit physical or emotional abuse, name-calling and shows of contempt, or passively in the form of disregard and neglect that implies that the boy is unimportant. In this latter case the father's interaction does harm through a "not doing"; that is, he displays an indifference and nonresponse to the boy's need for paternal affirmation. The father's incomplete, unpredictable or less than enthusiastic response to the boy has failed to match the boy's narcissistic investment in masculine attachment.

Mother		Father	
(Narcissistic)		(Nonsalient)	
Practicing subphase	Rapprochement subphase	Pre-oedipal supportive subphase	Pre-oedipal challenging subphase
Nonresponsive hypo-stimulation	Intrusive hyper-stimulation		

Disregulation

| Defenses of dissociation and projection | Gender-identity deficit |

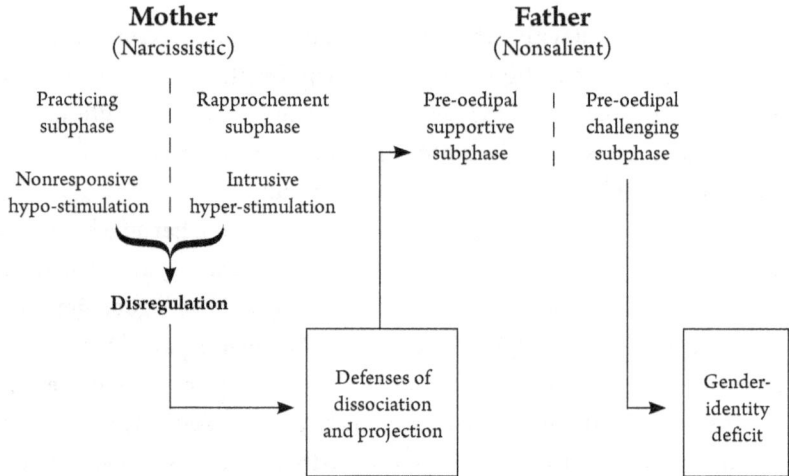

Figure 3.1 Failure of paternal bonding

Facing either the passive or active mode of paternal negativity, the boy experiences an internal "sinking" or "dropping" associated with his desire for affirmation. His embodied (parasympathetic) shame response for this desire for masculine attachment is eventually imprinted as a lifelong lesson.

Describing the hurt and shame he felt from having been "on the outs" with his father and brothers, a client described the profound, soul-destroying effect of this "delight deprivation" from his father as follows: "All the time this is happening to me, I'm losing my soul – losing my innocence."

We may see a favorable scenario, however, where the father takes notice of the boy's reaction and rescues him from his deflation. But if the father repeatedly fails to notice his son's bonding needs, the boy abandons the desire for paternal attachment, internalizes the message of unworthiness and returns to an imitative attachment with the mother.

By thus "being" feminine, the boy not only symbolically attaches to the mother but manifests a hostile rejection of the father. The father's repeated failure to respond to his defensive detachment sets in motion a lifelong antagonism between father and son, which we see time and again as characteristic of the homosexual condition.

In summary then, the boy's insecure attachment to the mother, followed by the father's abuse or indifference, creates in the boy a deep sense of emotional deprivation and loss. Where neither parent reengages the boy out of his dissociative defense, the foundation is laid for a lifelong, shame-based relational style and a pervasive feeling of not belonging and of not feeling truly loved.[1]

The shamed self is internalized. Thus the child's first narcissistic injury lays the foundation for all future shame experiences. He will forever hear that internalized parental voice: *My parents are right, there is some-thing _____ [bad, weak, unworthy, etc.] about me being a boy. Something inside of me that wants to be like Daddy is _____ [bad, weak, unworthy, etc.].*

Children of the narcissistic family often have a poor memory of their childhood, recounting only vague themes of hurt and alienation, betrayal and painful misunderstanding. They feel a deep yet unarticulated sense of injustice. There is an overwhelming feeling that somehow "this is not fair," but no one else seems to notice the unfairness. It seems as if their parents secretly conspire to keep them powerless for some unknown purpose.

One might expect the reaction of the boy to be anger toward those who have shamed him, with a sadness for himself. But for the child in such a family those feelings are reversed, and he himself takes the responsibility for the shamer's actions. He is angry at himself for "upsetting" his parents, for whom he "feels sad." This reversal of sadness and anger "preserves the loved one" (Freud, 1917) in his seemingly "rightful" position of honor and power, but at the same time, it derails the child's ability to perceive and grieve parental failure.

Our adult clients are particularly susceptible to shame during attempts at self-assertion, and this inhibitory response is self-induced. There is an old, body-held association of ego-deflation contained within memories of being in the assertive self-state. Thus the man has learned to associate assertion with this thought: *Get ready – you're about to be disappointed.*

In the course of therapy, clients offer particular words represent-ing their "personal unworthiness" to be assertive. Over and over, they describe themselves as "weak," "flawed," "defective," "damaged," "bad" and "unlovable." These critical labels represent the internalization of a negative parental message. And from these negative self-assumptions, there evolves an inevitable legacy of self-defeating, self-destructive and maladaptive behaviors in adulthood.

One man explained the broad effect of this shame in his life:

> When I'm shamed, I lose a sense of my masculinity. When I lose that, others will pick up on it and see that I'm vulnerable. At work, they'll want to assign me more projects because I'm not able to defend myself. When I'm at the gym, men will see that about me, and some might want to act out sexually. Even my mother notices this shame state, and when she sees it, she'll capitalize on it to get something she wants. She'll say, "Why don't you spend more time at home with me?"

The child of the narcissistically involved family has been faced with an overwhelming threat of abandonment annihilation. The only solution – or more accurately, the adaptation he must make for his emotional survival – is to accept and internalize the message that *I am weak, and I am unmasculine.* By disavowing his gendered and autonomous self, he is rewarded with a semblance of parental love and approval. Distressing as it may be to consider himself inferior, this message is preferable to feeling the trauma of parental attachment loss. Indeed, for a child to abandon a biologically based core part of his personality, that is, his gender identity, requires trauma of powerful, negative impact, which on some level seems actually to threaten his very existence.

Among our clients, time and again we hear this sense of being weak, unmasculine and unlovable, and of having never, in their whole lives, felt genuinely "seen." Trying to make sense of their parents' ambivalent acceptance of them, many clients report: "Yes, I do think on some level I was loved, but I know I was not understood." One man explained, "I know that my parents love me, but I've never really experienced them 'being there' for me. They say they love me, but it doesn't actually feel like they love me."

Ambivalent relationship with the mother in adulthood. Homosexual men often maintain overattached yet highly ambivalent relationships to their mothers throughout their entire lives. These relationships are characterized by a hostile dependency.

We often hear reports of mothers who were on one level overinvolved, but on a deeper level unsupportive. For example, while paradoxically praising their mother for her loyal support and encouragement, many clients express a fear that their mother's love is actually conditional. Of his rejecting-smothering mother, one man said: "She's the best mom in the world, she gave so much of herself. I got a lot of material things and a lot of attention, but she didn't ever fill the hole in my heart."

Said another client of his narcissistically involved mother: "My mother is very interested in my life; she's loving, but when I make a mistake, she just explodes. It's like all of a sudden I become the bad guy. I just become completely worthless." Another nineteen-year-old praised his mom for always supporting him, but "I remember her criticism all the time. She could suddenly turn on me, and it would be vicious." Describing the uninvolved type of mother, a sixteen-year-old said, "My mom is like a stuffed animal – she doesn't give back."

Temperamental disposition or insecure attachment? Many men in reparative therapy report having always been timid, shy and introverted, and preferring artistic pursuits such as art, theater and music. There was an almost universal avoidance of rough-and-tumble play. They felt overly concerned about physical injury and avoided dangerous activities.

But what has generally been attributed to inborn temperament might also, in some cases, be the consequence of insecure attachment. Bowlby (1977) believed that a secure sense of self requires consistent contact with a parent perceived as "stronger and/or wiser" (p. 203). Psychologist Diana Fosha summarizes this correlation: "The freedom to explore the world is the behavioral consequence of being and feeling safe" (2000, p. 35). Insecure attachment, however, causes the child to feel anxious and vulnerable, and deprives him of the emotional reserve necessary for developing confidence, curiosity and boldness in order to explore the world beyond the mother's sphere. Bowlby (1988) points out that the child who is truly secure in his parental attachment is less likely to be inhibited in exploring the world. In fact, he says, "Exploring the environment, including play and varied activities with peers is ... *antithetical to attachment [insecurity]*" (p. 121, emphasis added). Similar to Bowlby, Jerome Kagan (1994) found that parents' treatment of their children could influence their degree of shyness.

Many homosexual men recall their mothers as having been weak, unstable and inconsistent in their emotional responsiveness. Emotionally

insecure mothers interact with their children through their own idiosyncratic needs, leaving them anxious and uncertain. Consequently, the sons
feel responsible for their mother's emotional stability.

The homosexually oriented client typically reports feeling a pervasive
vulnerability. Insecure attachment often manifests as irrational fears (see
Nicolosi, 1991, p. 100). One client explained, "As a kid I just felt alone and
scared even though everyone else was around. I was scared of the dark; I
always thought someone was in my closet or under my bed." Said another
man, "My parents never made me feel secure within myself. My mother
didn't believe in me, didn't encourage me. My dad may have tried, but he
was such a poor example."

Supportive statements from the parents were often absent, inconsistent
or (as in the following client's statement) lacking in credibility.

> Even as a little kid, as far back as I can remember, I avoided sports,
> competition. I didn't go out there and do things. I stayed at home. I was
> a loner, isolated and shy. My brothers were doing things, they joined
> right in and participated, but I shied away and just did not put myself
> out there. I was a sad, stay-at-home introvert.
>
> Mom always told me I was great, that I could do anything I wanted.
> But I never believed her. I don't think she believed it, either.

When fathers are also perceived as weak or hostile, we see how the
parental team would have failed to offer the consistent emotional support
necessary for the child's bold, aggressive and outgoing attitude toward
life. A minimally involved, emotionally detached father combined with a
narcissistically involved mother do not offer the boy a secure emotional
base. This compromises the boy's bold exploration of the world, as well
as his strength, independence and self-sufficiency.

When he is securely attached to his parents, the child can tolerate
loss or rejection by his peers, including those who tease him for poor
performance in sports or for not being typically masculine. The security
that comes from such an attachment provides a lifelong safety net, even
when others in his life fail him.

Thus I propose that the timidity generally attributed to biological causes may be, for some homosexual men, actually the result of insecure attachment.

Defenses Against the Negative Introject: Narcissism and the False Self

Thus I have proposed that for many – probably most – homosexually oriented men, a childhood injury has occurred to the gendered self. That injury, I believe, is rooted in shame. The experience feels like what Walt Whitman described in "A Hand Mirror" as

> Outside, fair costume;
> Within, ashes and filth.

Unable to tolerate the sense of worthlessness that this shamed self engenders, the boy develops two particular defenses: the false self and narcissism. Working together, these defenses compensate for the felt deficit caused by the shamed self. The false self and the narcissistic self serve not only as a survival tactic for managing present interactions but also as a defense against any future attachment losses. These defenses are mutually supportive, so much so that some writers consider them synonymous (Johnson, 1987).

While the argument can be made that narcissism and the false self are actually two aspects of the same phenomenon, for the purposes of diagnosis and more effective treatment, as well as the client's own self-understanding, we treat them as separate and distinct phenomena.

The False Self in Comparison to the Narcissistic Self

To maintain his sense of acceptance and belonging within a family that does not see him as a separate individual with needs of his own, the child develops a compromise identity. As one client explained, "I'd rather be a 'false somebody' than a nobody." To avoid the annihilation of being a nobody, he complies with the family system, giving his parents the false self that seems necessary for recognition. The price paid, of course, is a restriction of genuine self-expression and relational attachment.

The quintessential false self of prehomosexuality is the "good little boy," the survival adaptation of the "nice," inoffensive, genderless child. But this persona comes at high cost: it blocks the boy from expressing his natural masculine strivings and from satisfying his same-sex attachment needs. This persona causes a deep affective void and eventually leaves the person with a chronic, unsatisfied longing for deep human connectedness.

In adulthood the residual symptom of the good little boy is manifested as "the nice guy." Such a man is often described as "compliant," "passive" and "obsequious." He displays a one-dimensional, codependent pleaser personality, habitually seeking the approval of others.

The nice guy is displayed in a restricted body posture that conveys introjected shame. It is a shield (how can anyone not like a "nice guy"?) protecting against the core-self injury of the shame-damaged self. The nice guy generally avoids conflict and is inclined to be tentative, confined, defensive and overcontrolled, with a rigid, restrictive one-dimensionality. The man is bound in an emotional straitjacket in which he is unable to fully know and experience his own emotions or openly receive those of others. He is hesitant and inhibited and particularly fearful of being hurt.

The Insatiable Need to Be "Seen"
Another common defense of homosexually oriented men is narcissism. In contrast to the false self of the nice guy, the narcissistic style is grandiose, with a sense of entitlement. The man seems active and vital, in comparison to the nice guy's static, confined and wooden manner. Both types are constructions against anticipatory shame, but the narcissistic style can be seen as active/offensive, while the nice guy is passive/defensive.

The narcissistic style is more multidimensional, complex and interesting than the nice guy, but is typically much more abrasive and difficult. Ever motivated to create an effect, the narcissist manipulates other people for special attention rather than engaging them authentically. He is concerned above all with the promotion of an idealized image, and his efforts to gain special attention must necessarily involve manipulation. Beneath this is a grandiose illusion that he can reshape the world, including, for the gay-identified man, refashioning nature's inevitable gender realities into a new reality that better suits his desires.

Truth, too, is subject to his manipulation: driven by the powerful need for his life to be better than it is, he devotes years to the pursuit of various illusions. He idealizes people who fulfill the image of what he wishes he himself could be. Idealization, in fact, is the foundation of his homoerotic attraction. It acts in the service of his narcissism to compensate for his hidden gender shame and the emotional starvation that results from his isolationism.

With this inordinate need to *be seen*, the narcissist never gets enough validation. People in his life are continually alienated by his unrelenting sense of entitlement. He is ever ready to counter against any feeling of being slighted, hurt, unappreciated or ignored. Mired in self-preoccupation, he will be limited in his ability to offer real empathy. Quick to feel victimized, he is often left feeling resentful and retaliatory. The narcissist has been described as the person "for whom it is never enough." The price for "having it his own way" is that he will be ultimately find himself alone.

The Gray Zone and the Desire for Same-Sex Eroticism

Trapped in emotional isolationism and inhibited in his ability to relate to others authentically, the man with SSA will often feel defeated, hurt and let down, which subsequently propels him into the self-state we call the gray zone.

The gray zone is experienced as discouragement, powerlessness, disappointment, loneliness and weakness. These feelings are especially likely to occur when a significant person in this person's world fails to gratify his expectations, which, because of his constricted view of people and relationships, are inclined to be driven by unrealistic, narcissistically based needs. When these expectations of others are frustrated, he feels disappointed, humiliated, even worthless. It is at such times that his homosexual attractions are most likely to surface.

Same-sex eroticism offers the promising illusion of masculine infusion and in fact actually delivers an immediate affective shift, with great excitement and a sense of rebellious liberation, in marked contrast to the flat, depressive affects of the gray zone's deflated narcissism. A symbolic contact with the idealized masculine image (i.e., the projected idealized self) through same-sex enactment has temporarily restored his depleted self-esteem. The idealized image serves as a self-object, and homoerotic contact will temporarily "reassure" the depleted narcissistic self.

The defense of dissociation. Among our clients we have noted the frequent utilization of the defense of dissociation. This may be what Elizabeth Moberly (1983) originally identified as "defensive detachment."

People who use the defense of dissociation are likely to have experienced early attachment trauma with the mother (Schore, 2003). In adulthood they respond to certain triggers associated with the original trauma by disconnecting from the outer world and shifting into a vitality-depleted state.

The attachment-traumatized person becomes highly sensitive to implicit cues of disapproval and rejection, such as a certain vocal tone, facial expression or subtle gesture, particularly when these cues come from significant others or representatives of past significant others.

The cues are often perceived below the level of awareness, prompting the dissociative response. This infantile defense is maladaptive in adulthood and leads to a variety of secondary symptoms. For our clinical population the most pronounced maladaptive response is the inability to emotionally bond with other men, thus perpetuating homoerotic fantasy and desire.

In the therapeutic setting we see dissociation occurr when the client is confronted with highly stressful material. The therapist observes the client's gaze suddenly becoming flat and unfocused, and his face grows blank. He has just entered into a subjective field and is, for a time, unreachable. At such moments the therapist observes that the client has become disengaged, unfocused, and with greatly diminished affect. The client may be parroting back in a flat voice exactly the interpretation he was just given, but he is emotionally closed off.

How does the therapist help the client out of that state? He may disclose to him that he is noticing his detachment and, in an unthreatening manner, point out his facial expression as evidence, while inviting the client to "return to the session." The therapeutic objective is to make the client conscious of the ways in which certain cues, including nonverbal communication, inhibit his affective states – particularly how these cues propel him out of the healthy state of assertion and into the constricted state of shame.

The client learns that he can take comfort in the client-therapist conjoined state, working in collaboration to co-regulate not only positive affects such as joy and love but also his negative affective states such as shame, terror and rage.

Projection. In addition to dissociation the second defense against overwhelming stress that we see in our clients is projection. This was visible earlier in the boy's projecting onto the father the same experience of affect disregulation that he had with the mother.

Projection is an infantile defense mechanism developed as early as the first year of life, in which the child creates an internal representation of a particular traumatic event and projects those representations onto others. These nonverbal, presymbolic representations serve to anticipate and therefore protect the child from any such future trauma. The internal constructs he creates will then become the basis for the phenomenon of the repetition compulsion. As a survival and coping mechanism the repetition compulsion is reactivated in response to particular social cues.

In the therapeutic situation, subliminal cues triggering memories of others who have shamed the client will bring about this negative projection. In a worst-case scenario a counter-transferential reaction is activated that prompts the therapist to react to the expectation of the client's projection, shattering the working alliance. Negative projection onto the therapist is often at the root of the critical therapeutic impasse called the "double bind," which we resolve through the therapeutic "double loop" procedure (see part two).

Addiction. The two previous defenses – dissociation and projection – are learned in early infancy and for this reason are called primitive defenses. There is another common defense – addiction – that manifests itself later.

Early malattunement in many of our men's backgrounds, experienced as betrayal, has created a difficulty with affect regulation. When affect regulation cannot be managed interpersonally, many SSA men use drugs, alcohol or compulsive sexual encounters. Incapable of modulating internal distress, they chooses mood-altering options as a pleasurable, quick alternative to the task of internal self-management.

For many men, there is the unconscious hope that same-sex erotic contact will replicate the symbiotic bliss of secure parental attachment.

One nineteen-year-old man succinctly explained his "ultimate fantasy": "I want to sit in the lap of a big man, and never wake up."

Drugs, alcohol and sex provide immediate relief from internal, shame-based distress. Substance abuse and sexual promiscuity offer temporary relief from emotional emptiness, personal inadequacy and chronic depression. All these serve to distract the person from his fundamental inability to establish authentic emotional attachments.

This tendency to use sex as a distraction from the pain of deep alienation is echoed by a former lover of the great ballet dancer Rudolf Nureyev. Speaking of Nureyev, the former lover said, "It was as if there was some inner loneliness, some sense of rejection that could never be overcome, and he provoked this frenzied eroticism to hide from it a little while" (Segal, 2007).

Substance abuse and sexual addiction, especially with anonymous partners, also satisfy the drive for grandiosity and omnipotence, and are acts of infantile defiance against the constraints of reality. They reinforce the illusions (false-positive perceptions) that buttress the fragile sense of self.

Addictive behavior, sexual or otherwise, is typically prompted in the moment by a disappointment over some unmet expectation, particularly a perceived slight to the client's dignity by another man or the experience of disappointing a mother figure. Faced with sudden deflation that triggers rage against the inadequate self, the man seeks some sort of auto-regulatory, ritualistic enactment.

But as with all other narcissistic enactments, addictions are a fantasy option. Sex, food, compulsive hyperactivity and the drive for "distraction" and "entertainment" will not override the distress of emotional disequilibrium for long. After enactment the disequilibrium returns.

In our client population we especially see the use of sexual arousal as a way of prompting oneself out of a depressive state. The homosexually oriented client uses dissociated sexuality (anonymous sexual encounters) to regulate his chronic depression. But sexual behavior does not address the depressive core.

An essential therapeutic goal is to diminish the client's drive to utilize anonymous sex as an auto-regulator and to substitute genuine, relationally oriented forms of affect regulation.

	Phase 1 Insecure attachment	Phase 2 Gender Identity	Phase 3 Erotic	Phase 4 Social role
Significant other	Mother	Father	Peers/Siblings	Social/Cultural
Age	First year	1½–3 years	5–11 years	Mid-teens
Result	Defense of dissociation Projective identification	Gender-identity deficit	Homosexuality	Gay self label

Figure 3.2 The four phases of gay identity

The Four Phases of Gay Identity

Chapter two detailed the two phases resulting in gender-identity deficit. We may extend those two phases to the additional phases of the eroticization of masculinity and, then, the social role of a gay identity.

In the first phase, insecure attachment, the "significant other" is the mother, resulting in the defenses of dissociation and projection. In the second phase, gender identity (which occurs at approximately a year-and-a-half to three years), a failure to bond with the father results in a gender-identity deficit. In the third (erotic) phase (occurring at approximately five to eleven years), the significant others are peers and siblings, who are often traumatically hostile and rejecting. The result is the defense of eroticization, which is expressed in homosexuality. The fourth stage, the social phase, is when significant social and cultural forces introduce the concept of a gay identity, typically in the person's early to mid teens. The result is a self-labeling of "gay" in an attempt to "narratively explain" past experiences.

A Different Model: Post-Gender Homosexuality

Up to this point our model of homosexuality has explained the condition as a failure to negotiate the gender-identity phase of one-and-a-half to three years old, which, if successful, involves the boy's disidentification from the mother and secure identification with the father. That model resonates as true with the majority of the homosexual clients we have seen in our clinic during the past twenty years.

However, approximately 20 percent of the men we have seen in treatment present a distinctly different clinical picture.

The distinction we make between a "pre-gender type" and "post-gender type" of SSA is somewhat parallel to the psychoanalytic distinction between the pre-oedipal and post-oedipal models. In the post-oedipal/post-gender model, we theorize that the developmental trauma occurred later and involved a wider spectrum of influences – especially damage to the ego during the latency period (five to twelve years old).

We postulate that the post-gender type client successfully completed the gender identity phase but later experienced another form of trauma for which homoerotic desire became conditioned as an affect regulator. (As such, this "post-gender" scenario does not necessarily involve gender identity.) Possessing masculine attributes and lacking effeminate behavior, these clients appear "straight" yet feel within themselves a disturbing need for masculine affection. This client often has distinct sexual attractions to women but little or no interest in female friendship. He is only interested in "being around the guys," and in this regard behaves like a boy does during the latency period. He demonstrates the ability to establish reasonably good relationships with straight men, but does not feel he can openly share his struggle with them about his homosexual attractions.

Post-gender trauma typically seems to have occurred from an older brother, the father, cruel and teasing peers at school, from sexual abuse or from a very disorganizing, "crazy-making" mother who invoked intense fear and anger, which the client now generalizes toward all women and which keeps him out of deeper relationships with them. These men appear to be "regular guys," but have a distinct insecurity about their masculinity. It is not a desire for the other's masculine qualities that drives this client's same-sex attractions; instead, he seeks the anxiety-reducing reassurance of male support and comfort against his inner insecurity.

With this post-gender type there is no real deep grievance against the father – yet the client typically sees the father as weak or ineffectual for lacking the salience to defend him against an abusive older brother; cruel, teasing peers at school; or a disorganizing, destabilizing mother. The father was "good enough" for attachment but failed to rescue the son during the latency phase from repeated trauma.

Sometimes these past abusive relationships will "repeat" in his homosexual fantasies and in the type of relationship he seeks with a partner. But he is less likely to develop an addiction to gay pornography, as the male image alone has less powerful sexual appeal. Rather, he looks for masculine affirmation, sometimes from a youthful, gentle, boyish, passive (and more effeminate) type of man. Here, the image sought in a partner is not the idealized masculine type (which is the type most desired by the "pre-gender identity phase" client), but a man who represents his own lost, innocent, younger self.

Table 3.1 outlines the basic distinction between these two types of male homosexuals.

Table 3.1 Basic Distinctions Between Pre-Gender and Post-Gender Male Homosexuals

PRE-GENDER TYPE	POST-GENDER TYPE
Approximately 80% of client population*	Approximately 20% of client population*

*(we assume this percentage to be representative of the general homosexual population)

General Impression

Effeminacy or non-masculine fragility.	Masculine, ordinary male; generally comfortable with his body. In group psychotherapy, other members are especially attracted to him. He holds higher group status.
Rigid, fastidious, self-conscious.	Rugged, relaxed, casual about his body.

Attitude Toward Treatment Plan

Reactive, emotional, moody, volatile.	Uses rational, intellectual defenses; prefers cognitive approach. Appreciates goals, objectives and progress reports. Resilient; can move into his fears and approach new challenges.

Narcissism

Easily emotionally injured, offended, crushed, slighted, insulted.	Greater resilience, less easily hurt, can hear criticism.

Unmet Needs

Masculine identification and affectional needs.	Masculine affectional needs.

Greatest Source of Developmental Trauma

Father (most often weak, non-salient; less often hostile/tyrannical).	Hostile, tyrannical father or older brother, or highly disorganizing ("crazy-making") mother.

Relationship with Father

Traumatic father-hurt. Narcissistic injury; son feels deep resentment, grievance, contempt.	Father was (minimally) adequate for identification/attachment, but failed to defend son against sources of trauma.

Relationship with Father (continued)

Repair of relationship with father occurs very rarely.

Can more readily repair relationship with father.

Relationship with Mother

More enmeshment with mother; intense ambivalent relationship, easily upset by her.

Less enmeshment with mother, less emotional dependency; usually less easily upset by her.

Relationship with Women

Little or no sexual attraction toward women.

Definite (if weak) attraction to women, but deep fear of sexual inadequacy.

Easy to establish and maintain female friendships.

Does not share the same affinities and interests to sustain friendships with females.

Relationship with Other Men

More male authority problems; suspicious, anticipates injustice; lack of close male friendships.

Fewer male authority problems; has history of fairly good male friendships, but they could take on a sexual dimension.

True Self–False Self

Pervasive false self; difficulty finding and staying in the true self.

No false self; is more readily able to relate to men from the true self.

Prognosis

More difficult therapy, slower change; more trust issues; will stay much longer on "ex-gay plateau."

Faster treatment, better prognosis.

CHAPTER 4

Homosexuality as a Repetition Compulsion

*Looking for another guy always seemed an answer
to my pain, but it never worked.*

⁓

*Homosexuality has robbed me of life and leaves me empty.
The very thing that I use to soothe and distract and
relieve the pain, actually keeps me in the pain.*

Psychoanalytic theory defines repetition compulsion as the continual re-creating of a past, traumatic incident. Through a symbolic reenactment of the traumatic situation the person unconsciously seeks to gain final victory and to resolve his core injury. And so he recreates "in the here-and-now, the original traumatic failure situation, in the hope that perhaps this time, the outcome will be better" (Stark, 1994a, p. 23).

Repetition compulsion contains three elements:

1. Attempt at self-mastery
2. A form of self-punishment
3. Avoidance of the underlying conflict

We will look at these three elements of repetition compulsion and see how they are evidenced in homosexual enactment.

A Symbolic Attempt at Self-Mastery

What the psychoanalytic literature refers to as an attempt at self-mastery, we term "the reparative drive." This reparative attempt at mastery is made through the effort to conquer and gain the love of a feared object, the unavailable man (usually the father), and thus to repair a felt deficit of masculine affirmation through an input of virility, power and confidence.

The repetition compulsion is evidenced in the client's relentless attempts to achieve mastery of the unavailable male, even though his efforts always prove self-defeating. As with all forms of repetition compulsion, this is a fantasy option – a futile, repetitive grasping at emotional resolution.

For such men the pursuit of fulfillment and emotional intimacy through same-sex behavior is spurred by the fearful anticipation that their own masculine self-assertion will inevitably fail and result in humiliation. Rather than face the pain in their past, they opt for a ritualized reenactment with the hope that, unlike all other past occasions, *This time, I will finally get what I want; with this man I will find masculine power for myself,* and *This time, the nagging sense of internal emptiness will finally disappear.*

On one level the repetition compulsion represents a healthy, reparative drive to be proactive – an attempt to gain victory over a previous humiliating experience. But to the extent that it is a function of narcissistically based illusions, the repetition compulsion is doomed to defeat, because any attempt at resolving early attachment loss through erotic enactment will not work.

One client explains the frustration of his attachment loss as follows:

> I can never get close enough to the male body. However close I am, it is never enough. I fantasize elaborate impossible things in which I can get closer to a man than is possible in reality. I want to be the sock on his foot; I want to be the shirt on his back… still not close enough. I want to be the tattoo on his skin, I want to be *in* the other man's penis, I want to *be* the other man's penis. Still not close enough! That does not work. I try to get from another man what I feel that I lack in myself.
>
> I compensate for my pain by getting sexual release, but ultimately the realization is this: I can *never* get close enough! Even in fantasy; even

augmented by masturbation. I can never get close enough to assuage my pain of being separate from – *other* than – *less than* other men.

Why can't I get close enough? Shame. Shame for wanting to be that close. That intense longing is what separates me from other men. Shame is the enemy. My enemy is not homosexuality; my enemy is the shame.

A Form of Self-Punishment

Beneath the drive for same-sex contact is gender-based shame, carrying with it a feeling of unworthiness and unlovableness. Inevitably, there will be anger toward the shamer, which is turned against the self, as well as a despairing suspicion that life will never get better. One client said it this way:

> When I have sex with a guy, I don't care what happens; I know I'll hate myself afterward, but I don't care. I'm in a self-destructive mode; I'm saying, "F—k you" to everybody, including myself.

The self-defeating, self-punishing aspect of the repetition compulsion is a result of shame-based distortions: the false-negative belief that somehow, he must really deserve this shame.

In many cases the repetition compulsion becomes an insidious game that gradually consumes the client's emotional resources. He stays stuck in this compulsion because he has not overcome the hurt from those who failed him; in fact, he "keeps the shamer alive" by subjecting himself to the abuse of still another shamer. Of course, he does so under the illusion that *this* time he will actually be loved and empowered and thus achieve vindication. Yet by making another man his narcissistic object to achieve vindication, he has given one more person the power to reject him, shame him and make him feel worthless. But he truly believes it is "only about" this one new man in the present.

When the shame-producing scenario is played out over and over again, this only reinforces his conviction that he really is a hopeless victim and ultimately unworthy of love.

That his homosexual enactment really is a repetition compulsion, not a freely given form of love, is revealed by the "adrenaline zap," which contains (and is heightened by) an element of raw fear. Gay men very often report that they are attracted to men of whom they are afraid, thus revisiting the relationship with the unavailable father. In fact, there is an entire gay subculture of public sex that revels in the thrill of acting out in places like parks, public bathrooms and truck stops, and is erotically driven by the fear of discovery and humiliating exposure.

The act of sodomy itself is intrinsically masochistic. Anal intercourse, as a violation of our bodily design, is unhealthy and anatomically destructive, damaging the rectum and spreading disease because the rectal tissues are fragile and porous. Furthermore, the act humiliates and demeans a man's dignity and masculinity.

Avoidance of an Underlying Conflict: The Defense Against Grief

Two opposing aspects of the repetition compulsion – reenactment of the distortion that he deserves shame, and reenactment of the illusion that this time he will master the shame – serve to defend the client against the grief of parental emotional abandonment.

For the child whose parents were profoundly malattuned to his deepest needs, some defense is required against his actually acknowledging and truly feeling "the horrid reality of just how bad things were" (Stark, 1994a, p. 136).

This compelling reenactment of the internal drama prevents the client from mourning the loss of what was earlier denied. Essentially, therefore, the repetition compulsion is a refusal to grieve.

Bloch (1984) acknowledges the depth of this abandonment-annihilation trauma – the dread of being "a nothing," and describes the homosexual man's "fantasy that he is 'simply fulfilling his true nature' or that he was 'born that way'" as being "in the service of...his conviction that his life depends on preserving his assumed identity" (p. 53).

Compulsive sexual acting out, with its high drama and its promise of infantile-like gratification, is well suited as a defense against memories of childhood abandonment. *If only I can get this man to make me feel better about myself* deflects attention from the real tragedy of a childhood characterized by nagging emptiness.

The therapeutic task is to reveal the repetition compulsion to the client. He must recognize the inherent, underlying illusions and distortions.

When the illusions and distortions are faced and understood, the client can confront parental limitations and early attachment losses.

Based on our clinical experience, the client is most receptive to abandoning the repetition compulsion and facing his grief during a time when he is experiencing the loss of a narcissistic love object. When his self-defeating behaviors lead him to a confrontation with uncompromising reality, he is most ready to face the losses of his past. At such a time, what he often finds buried within is a profound sense of emptiness and sadness. This discovery will mark the beginning of productive grief work.

Grief work often involves memories of the father:

> Why do I grieve? I grieve the lack of connection with men. What causes such a division between me and other men? I think of Dad. Dad is a great man, but he is not good at connecting emotionally. He does not talk feelings. I would have liked to be able to express my heart to him and have him hear me and acknowledge that he has heard and understood. Dad shuts down; he falls asleep when the topic goes there.
>
> My sister recognizes that as well; she thinks that's because he is not interested in her. She's incorrect; it's a limitation of Dad. And we all grieve that limitation. I, especially, grieve that limitation – that lack.
>
> But when I try to avoid the grief, it comes out wrongly in all that I do. When I refuse to feel it, when I fall into shame, when I fantasize and masturbate, I am only setting myself up for greater shame. Shame leads to depression, and depression leads to sexual acting out, which leads to a greater sense of separation from other men.
>
> And so the cycle goes on and on and on.

Avoidance of the Conflict Through Narcissistic Entitlement

A forty-five-year-old surgeon, Dr. M., came from a background in which he had never been acknowledged by his father and felt, on a deep level, unmasculine and unlovable. He befriended a twenty-five-year-old medical student, Connor, and provided him with undeserved career opportunities at his teaching hospital, for which the younger man was not prepared, as well as many expensive "gratuities," even at the risk of losing his own job.

Consciously, Dr. M. only expected in return "some gratitude and appreciation." In truth, he wanted – using Eli Siegel's (1971) term – to be "adored."

CLIENT   (*irritated and annoyed*) Connor hasn't been giving me any attention lately. Nothing. He shows no interest or concern for me. I keep returning to him, reaching out to him – even humiliating myself to him – but I get nothing back.

THERAPIST   What's the feeling as you say this?

CLIENT   A lack of gratitude and betrayal.

THERAPIST   Yeah, but what's the feeling inside you?

CLIENT   It's hurtful.

THERAPIST   Sure. Stay with it.

CLIENT   (*deep sigh, long pause*) Profound sadness.

Dr. M.'s "profound sadness" ultimately proved to be not so much about Connor's inability to show gratitude, but about Connor's failure to live up to Dr. M.'s narcissistic expectation to make him feel good about himself. Dr. M.'s profound sadness was a consequence of the depletion of his defenses against feeling a much deeper loss, the one which lay behind his reenacted drama.

At this point in the session the therapist could gently begin to interpret the narcissistic nature of the relationship. For example, Dr. M. might be asked if Connor reminds him of someone from his past. To this line of inquiry Dr. M. might feel threatened and renew his defenses against the interpretation, perhaps feeling betrayed by the therapist. But in a more favorable scenario, he might abandon his illusions about Connor's ability to make him feel better about himself and begin to work toward resolution.

Indeed, homosexual enactment is very compelling: it offers a radical shift of the depleted affective state, lifting the man out of depression and into a peak moment of intense, visceral arousal. With its power to manage internal disequilibrium, it distracts from more important underlying issues – particularly the healthy developmental challenge of learning to assert the true gendered self.

Resolution of the Repetition Compulsion

As clients proceed in therapy, they often come to see their ritualistic reenactment of emotional conflicts as motivated by a powerful need to keep things as they are, even if "things as they are" are, in fact, self-defeating.

There is a healthier alternative to their unsatisfying enactments; rather than re-creating the traumatic failure, they can develop healing relationships that offer the chance to do now in adulthood what they could not do as children, namely, to acknowledge and truly grieve their loss.

When a client confronts the fact that his unwanted behaviors are indeed a repetition compulsion, he faces the reality that happiness and fulfillment can never be "imported" from any other human being. The acknowledgment of this fact often opens the client up to doing the necessary grief work.

Accepting the traumatic reality that his parents never "saw" him, one eighteen-year-old client trapped in a repetitive cycle of sexual acting out admitted (concerning the painful emotional work of therapy) that it was, in fact, better than staying stuck in an endless cycle of fantasy about other guys. "I'd rather cry," he said, "than keep on masturbating."

Many clients, through therapeutic body work, come to see that they have been attempting to gain male connectedness in a self-defeating way that protects them against feeling deep grief. Through same-sex erotic contact they are seeking resolution of the powerful and very normal human need to be known and loved by another man. Beneath their homosexual behavior is a *healthy drive* to gain authentic attachment.

For them the challenge is to give up the dream of finding another man who will provide the masculinity they themselves lack. Instead, they must accept male affirmation in a realistic way – through mutuality, not idealization.

CHAPTER 5

Homosexuality as a Reparative Drive

I devalue a man who doesn't turn me on.

֍

When I turn a man into an object of narcissism, I "consume"
him. Doing this destroys people, and it has destroyed me.

During over twenty years of clinical work with ego-dystonic homosexu-ally oriented men, I have come to see homosexual enactment as a form of reparation. The general concept of reparative drive has been well established within the literature. It is an unconscious attempt to compensate for a defi-cit. We could say it's a symbolic "settling of the score." In our application, the man with same-sex attraction is attempting to repair unmet same-sex affective needs (attention, affection and approval) and gender-identification deficits through homoerotic behavior (Nicolosi, 1991, p. 93).

Homosexual enactment temporarily relieves the stressful self-states that we repeatedly observe in our clients, most particularly the shame self-state, often followed by the depressive mood of the "gray zone." Homo-sexual acting out, for these men, is an attempt at restoring psychic equi-librium in order to maintain the integrity of the self-structure. Through sex with another man, they unconsciously seek to attain a self-state of authenticity, assertion, autonomy and gender-relatedness, but they have found that it brings them none of those things, only a nagging feeling of inauthenticity and a still deeper sense of unfulfillment.

In the following section we will consider homosexual behavior as a reparation for three self-states: inhibited assertion, shame, and the gray zone. In addition we will also consider the ways in which homosexual enactment serves as reparation for the false self of the "nice guy."

Homosexual Enactment as Reparation of Inhibited Assertion

As our clients begin to live more authentically, they discover a growing ability to be assertive. Living in an authentic self-state brings a person freedom, self-possession and healthy social relatedness. At first, clients may confuse assertion with childish acting out. Acting out is troublesome behavior, an old, maladaptive way of being in the world. But healthy assertion is quite different: it forms the foundation of authentic relationships and direct communication. It is a positive adaptive medium for learning new ways of relating, and involves intentionality and responsibility. Assertive behaviors help fulfill male identification needs and propel the client toward mastery of interpersonal conflicts, especially those that repeatedly arise in his interactions with other men.

Growth in assertion means that the client will begin to experiment with new behaviors – sometimes even homosexual behavior. Some men leave therapy at this pivotal point, making the decision to embrace a gay identity as "who they are" in the deepest and most essential sense of being.[1]

But for those men who are deeply convicted that SSA does not represent who they are, the choice to assert will eventually take the opposite form, meaning a deliberate self-denial, with the willful determination to refrain from acting out with other men.

Assertion versus acting out. The exhilaration of the transgressive, the false vitality clients typically feel when engaging in sex with other men, is, they feel intuitively, a maladaptation in their lives. Their acting out is compulsive, stereotypic and repetitive; it represents an unproductive attempt to resolve an intrapsychic conflict – most often the conflict between love and fear, having to do with memories of the father figure. Their same-sex drive is an attempt to connect with their own free, expressive, spontaneous, gendered selves.

The intent of this impulse is "reparative" in that its goal is gender affirmation; the man strives to be "seen" by other men as an attractive male. But the behavior never resolves the original conflict and creates even more distress.

Both assertion and homosexual enactment contain an energy, a vitality, an "aliveness." Assertion's vitality is deeply resonant, relationally connected, long-lasting and emotionally transformative. Homosexual enactment's energy is similarly intense, but it is shallow and short-lived.

Homosexual enactment: A reaction against the false self ("role reparation"). No man can live perpetually in the false self of the "nice guy" role because it is a repressed, inauthentic and inhibited presentation of self to the world. In an effort at relief from this role, men often carry on a second life as the rebellious, shocking, "naughty," offensive "sexual outlaw." There is a repressed longing for liberation and rebellion, a chance to be transgressive, outrageous, "free."

When there is the perception of danger, this adds to the excitement. This sometimes means that the man allows (or even actively seeks) exposure to the AIDS virus. This may explain the gay subculture devoted to "barebacking" with HIV-positive partners. Or the man may seek sex in a semi-public place, such as a bathroom or park, where there is a risk of being seen or possibly arrested. One client, a conservative-appearing corporate lawyer, described the thrill as

> the possibility of getting caught, doing something "naughty," risky and illicit. In that moment I get an adrenalin rush. "F—k you, world!" It gives me energy, purpose. I feel alive.
>
> It's empowering, it's powerful. "The hell with you, I'm in charge of my life." Yeah, it's actually a temper tantrum.

A twenty-one-year-old student who reported feeling intimidated by the straight guys at college explained his anonymous sexual contacts:

> My sexual exploits are like, "You know what? I can be bad like you guys. I can have battle scars. I've been there, I can tell you stories." It's like showing off to my friends, "I've done this, and this, and this. I've got something to talk about," like, "Here I am!"

A mild-mannered businessman, returning from a vacation in Amsterdam, had explored the gay scene in Europe and involved himself in some homosexual activity. He explained his motivations as follows:

> I wanted to feel I could go out and do whatever I wanted. I wanted to feel independent. I can make my own decisions, and be open to anything. I could check things out and decide for myself...go explore, and feel my own power.
>
> After all, my power to say no has to be based on my freedom to say yes.

To what extent was this client's homosexual acting out a true effort to "explore his own power" through self-assertion? Or in this case, was it just a rationalization to take a step backwards in the therapeutic process? Here we see a possible avenue of therapeutic exploration.

Homosexual enactment as esteem reparation (*a reaction against shame*). Shame is a double-edged sword; it cuts the person off from both self and others. The shamed self believes it is defective, insignificant and worthless. As a form of narcissistic reparation, gay sex seems to offer relief from negative self-evaluations through masculine attention, admiration and reassurance. It offers the promise of

- a reparation of depleted masculinity
- intimate contact to reassure himself against the alienation that characterizes the shame experience
- special attention – a narcissistic reflection of his identity that mitigates his secret feelings of defectiveness and insignificance
- reassurance that he truly does possess a worthy male body

But these promises inevitably fail to deliver. A twenty-one-year-old client described his obsession with men's bodies through gay pornography:

> I've always asked myself why all these other distractions don't satisfy. The whole power of the fantasy is that I'm not good enough. All that I seek, everything I do, is to keep me away from the feeling of inadequacy; that I'm nothing.
>
> The empty pleasure of porn is like every other anesthesia; it dulls

life. Its roots are in darkness. It's a pleasure that closes off life [with] a turning-away from relationships.

What makes me want to do it is an emptiness inside, an emptiness that comes from a condemnation about me. The pleasure of porn temporarily defeats that condemnation.

Homosexual enactment as a reaction against the gray zone. Feeling alive, excited, connected, aroused: homosexual activity promises a visceral charge, that "zap" of primitive arousal that rescues the man out of the impotent, "shut down" depressive mood he feels in the gray zone.

> I'm so used to covering up my sadness with sexual arousal that when I feel sad, I know arousal is right around the corner. I used masturbation ever since I was a kid. I'd [do it] three times a day, so as not to feel like a loser and not to feel weak, sad.

The gray zone appears to be a "dead" state emotionally, but underneath it is profound despair, and in this sense the gray zone is a pseudo-grief state. Anticipation of deeply felt despair prompts manic defenses, including the homosexual enactment that our clients most want to resist.

As one man explained, "If I grab hold of my sadness and pull it close to my chest, I believe it will absorb me, consume me." And so he relieves his sadness with sexual acting out.

Shame and the Abdication of Gender

The shame moment. The shame moment is a moment of conflict between two opposing impulses – gendered-self assertion and shame for failing in such assertion. It is the collision of a vital affect hitting up against an inhibitory affect. The feeling is, *I can't explain myself, and no one will understand me. I can never win.* The man feels frozen, paralyzed and unable to defend himself against an overwhelming, unarticulated injustice. Thus his assertion shuts down.

One client describes it as "that palpable fear that stops me from connecting with others. I'm completely still and numb, my mind goes blank, and I'm just taking the abuse."

The double bind and the creation of shame. Shame is not an "emotion," since emotion means "to move" or "to emote"; rather, it is a counteremotion and an affect inhibitor. For SSA men, it is the wedge that splits gender identity off from the totality of the person. The result is an incompletely masculine-identified and ultimately false self.

Children who grew up in the triadic-narcissistic family were often caught in the communications structure of the double bind: the "no-win predicament." If the boy assumes responsibility for the fact that he does not feel loved *for who he really is*, he is rewarded with a semblance of parental love and attention. That is the nature of shame – assuming responsibility for not having felt loved – that is, accepting the idea that *I must therefore be unlovable*. But if the child maintains his assertive stance, holding onto the integrity of his own perception and his own internal state, he is punished with parental inattention and withdrawal.

To comprehend the profound gravity of this choice, we need to understand what we mean by a parent's often well-intentioned yet malattuned love. When one is a very small child, parental malattunement feels like expulsion: a shunning that is experienced as nothing less than hopeless abandonment. The price of choosing to maintain his own perception means, to the small child, having to confront the primal fear of abandonment-annihilation.

Abandonment-annihilation. Essentially, shame is about not being seen, becoming nonexistent, invisible. As one man said, "At that moment I could disappear, hide under a rock." The southern-Italian dialect word for shame, *scomparire*, means literally "to disappear." Indeed, shame is an "affective death" of the self.

One twenty-eight-year-old man admitted, "As a kid I felt like I didn't belong to my family. I have flashbacks of smirks, contemptuous glances, disparaging looks. I tried to understand it. I thought, *What did I do? My behavior? My looks?*"

Field observations of wolves reveal the social function of this shame posture. The wolf's acceptance by the pack is essential to its individual survival, because expulsion from the group almost inevitably results in death. The outcast wolf displays a slinking, cowering posture in an effort to be readmitted to the pack, and that behavior is strikingly reminiscent of our clients' own embodied experience of the shame moment. Their shoulders cave in, with a bodily collapse.

Self-blame. Many clients say they received the message that "you do not belong to us because you are flawed/defective/weak/damaged" and the like. Reinstatement into the family may mean the requirement to accept the message "You do not qualify to be masculine." This perception results in long-term emotional devastation, with the shamed person taking upon himself the responsibility for having been worthy of the shame. Sadness and anger will thus be made to switch places, with the child taking responsibility for the parent's emotional abandonment of him. Thus he becomes angry at himself, and sad for his parents.

In a paradoxical way, taking responsibility for feeling unloved offers a sense of power and control, because the shamed person now assumes culpability for his threatened expulsion. As "the shamed one," the boy holds a particular place of his own. Rather than accepting the alternative, which is a feeling of annihilation, he assumes his "rightful role" as the genderless "good little boy." As long as he represses his grief and assumes responsibility for his unlovability, he avoids the psychic death of abandonment-annihilation trauma.

Shame thus preserves the boy's relationship with the parent by deflecting his rage at them and his sadness for himself. His implicitly recognized "shamed self" remains preserved within the pathological family system.

Shame has another important function: it preserves the relationship with a parent and keeps alive the false hope that if he keeps trying, someday that parent will see him, attune to him and love him for who he really is. It preserves the hope that if he gratifies the family's narcissistic expectations of him by remaining in his proper place as "the shamed one," they will someday give him what he actually needs.

The shame is a defense against abandonment grief, felt as a hollow emptiness. As one client explained, "There's a hollowness inside that I used to fill with shame." The often-heard phrase *"filled" with shame* suggests its actual function. It fills up the emptiness that results from abandonment. But only when he begins to abandon the defense of shame is the client able to fully feel the impact of the loss, the interior "hollowness."

Parental nonresponse to gender strivings. Clients often cannot, in fact, recall an explicit negative parental message in response to their gender strivings. But many can recall an implicit nonresponse that subtly conveyed a message of discouragement about their masculine individuation.

Most people have difficulty understanding how a person can feel shame when other people have done nothing to them – all they have offered is a nonresponse. To this I answer, Have you ever told a joke and no one laughed?

Faced with the choice between his biologically based drive to be an authentic, separate, gendered individual and the shame-inducing experience of parental nonresponse to that biological drive, the boy who became homosexual has chosen the latter. The perceived threat of expulsion from the pack has induced him to accept the message that he is defective.

Some parents' nonresponse takes the form of consistently failing to defend their temperamentally sensitive son from a bullying older brother or teasing peers, which is experienced by the boy as emotional abandonment.

Example of anticipatory shame for masculine ambition. In planning a home visit, a twenty-three-year-old client expressed the desire to spend time with his older brother. In preparation for his visit, I encouraged him to make a plan to achieve his goal. He was hopeful, imagining how they might enjoy time together as they took bikes and went out for a day's ride in the mountains. Continuing his fantasy, he imagined how his mother, who considered him her "special" son, would disapprove when they returned home:

> She'll say [imitating a patronizing voice], "Oh, did you boys have a nice time?" She'll be smiling, but I know she disapproved, like I did something wrong. *I violated something between us....*
>
> That's when I want to go into my gay-defiant, "I can-stand-on-my-own" self.

Shame's domination comes from the unexamined assumption that "I am shame-able." The person assumes responsibility for this situation, thus essentially blaming himself for being unworthy of affiliation. As one forty-five-year-old man confessed, "I am rejected because I am rejectable.

I am unloved because I am unlovable." It is an affective shutting down of the desire to authentically assert oneself.

Many clients feel deeply embarrassed about their desire, as an adult, to receive male attention, affection and approval, admitting to the therapist that they actually feel weak, flawed, silly, stupid or simply bad for wanting it. As one man said, "I recognize my need to be affirmed by a man. But to *pursue it* seems so weak."

Anticipatory shame is generated from within, but for the client, it seems to come from "out there." Here the therapist points out that this punishing distortion is representative of the internalized, critical parent that he has created through projective identification. In this way, the man is simply doing to himself what he felt his parents and peers did to him. There is the ever-present fear of devastating rebuke. Always underneath, we see the little boy ready to be punished.

The shame posture: Bracing for the next shame moment. The shame posture is a stance toward the world in which the person is always braced for the next assertion-shame collision. He is in a state of continual vigilance against suddenly and unexpectedly becoming an "object of contempt" while in the act of some sort of innocent, spontaneous self-expression. Thus he assumes the shame posture in anticipation of "getting slammed" by another humiliation.

One man described this stance:

> I don't feel I relate to people as people, but as negative judges of me, harboring mean thoughts about me. I think, *Yeah, they're right about me; I am a failure, loser…weak, fake, stupid, defective, weird, "sissy," "queer," not male.* I live with the fear of someone discovering I am fake. I'm always anticipating rejection, but when the moment comes, I never seem prepared for it.

Another man described his anticipatory shame as

> this interior sense that I am unlovable. On some level I convey this sort of unspoken plea: "Please don't do anything to remind me that I'm unlovable. In fact, if you want to be my friend, you'll work hard at distracting me from that truth."

The anticipatory stance against shame is literally a "posture," in that it is carried in the body and observable. Many clients display a meek, cautious, diminished body posture. Some gay-identified men adopt an exaggerated, campy, flamboyant posture that is a reaction against the same sense of shame.

A lifestyle of hiding. This ever-present vigilance creates a lifestyle of hiding, avoidance, withdrawal and passivity. In clinical settings we have seen that anticipatory shame can become so intense as to approximate paranoia, with the client harboring the frightening conviction that another person has the power to turn everybody against him. The assumption is that he is helpless against slander.

The omnipotence he projects on the other person obliterates any belief that he can have a direct impact on others; the "offended other" has all the power. He is still a child in the world of adults, powerless to directly influence others' opinions of him. Past associations to this frightening anticipation often go back to early adolescence, when a bully turned the other boys against him, and perhaps even earlier yet, to the "omnipotent" mother who could control the opinions of other family members and either turn them against him or prevent them from defending him.

While children experience shame for a wide repertoire of behaviors, the prehomosexual boy somehow felt shamed for desiring attachment to his father, and shamed for exposing his masculine ambitions. If he was a particularly sensitive child, he felt shame for desiring the emotional needs associated with male bonding; he felt unworthy of the three A's of attention, affection and approval. Often, his masculine assertion violated the "special" mother-son relational stability. Whatever its source, the result of this shame was the boy's ultimate abandonment of his true gendered self.

No boy can simply "take" masculinity from his father. It can only be offered, bestowed. As Leanne Payne says, the father "blesses" his son with his masculinity.

But to feel that he has somehow been denied masculinity is not all that the boy suffers. Many clients have been made to feel like a "nothing" by the world for exposing their ambition to enter the world of men. The tragic result is that the boy joins with the rest of the world in turning against the part of himself that wanted to be male.

The prehomosexual boy thus develops into an intrapsychic system that turns against itself. The original *vitality* affect expressed as the desire for masculine relatedness triggers a shame *inhibitory* affect. The result is a devastating shutdown, a chronic inhibition against subsequent opportunities for male attachment.

This developmental understanding helps explain the clinical features associated with homosexuality – namely, unusual shame sensitivity and personality traits suggestive of narcissism. Shame and narcissism are two sides of the same coin – where there is narcissism, there is shame, and where there is shame, there is narcissism. For our clients, homosexual acting out defends against the shame they feel for the sense of masculine inferiority.

In fact, we can view shame as the "knife" that severs the self, separating off the disavowed aspects that have to do with gender. Homosexual enactment is an attempt to repair the wound of this cut-off part of the self through fusion with another man. The central challenge during the transition out of homosexuality is confronting the illusion that gender-based shame can, in fact, be relieved by same-sex behavior.

Narcissism: Pride and self-contempt. One client said, "My mom always made me feel that I was somehow 'special.' But I don't know why, and I don't know 'special about what.'" The narcissistic function of same-sex attraction was illustrated in a recent gay TV program where two characters were discussing a third attractive man. One gay man said to the other: "I was so attracted to him, I either had to *be* him, or *have* him."

The gender-identity phase, as with all other phases of a child's development, contains a surge of ambition to achieve competence. Along with this biologically driven ambition comes a narcissistic investment in gender achievement and a converse vulnerability to humiliation if he should fail. Ego-identification with gender mastery makes the boy sensitive to shame.

Narcissistic behavior involves manipulating external variables in order to reassure oneself against shame. Shame is the "underside of narcissism" (Morrison, 1989), with its alternating feelings of pride and self-contempt. "Pride and self-hate belong inseparably together; they are two expressions of one process" (Horney, 1945).

Narcissistic personality disorder, Shore (1991) says, is characterized by an insufficient capacity to regulate shame. H.B. Lewis (1980) also sees the narcissistic personality as suffering from shame, and Adler (1969) describes the narcissistic superiority complex as a compensation for an inferiority complex. As one client explained:

> I remember looking at those other boys and thinking, *Oh, I'm so much better-looking than them. And they're dumb, too.*
>
> Whenever I saw a guy better-looking than me, I got angry. I had to get his attention any way I could. It's not about them, it's about me. It's always about me. I'm so vain! My whole life is predicated on my looks and being the "pretty one" in the room. My narcissism permeates every aspect of my life; it fills every corner and crevice.... It controls me.
>
> I'm angry at my preoccupation with myself. It's been the great distraction and ruin of my life.

Developing male friendships: A challenge to shame and narcissism. "When I'm with other guys, they seem so at ease, but I feel locked out. I'm acting like I'm 'with' them, but I'm just acting," one client told me.

In relating to other men, the primary challenge for the SSA struggler is to shift out of his narcissistically driven anticipatory shame posture. He must relinquish the false self of the nice guy, and stay in the true self. In this assertive self-state, attachment and gender identification will become possible.

The therapist must closely attend to the client's tendency to shift between the two pendulum extremes of self-debasement and grandiosity, and help him develop a realistic perception of self in relation to the other. Simply stated, *the task is to see the other man as a real person while seeing himself as a real person at the same time.*

Many clients begin male relationships with exaggerated expectations grounded in overidealization and infatuation. They are not ready to acknowledge these distortions until they experience a painful disappointment. Then the illusions are shattered, and they are forced to look more honestly at the structure of the friendship.

As C.S. Lewis points out in *The Four Loves*, "Those who cannot conceive Friendship as a substantive love, but only as a disguise or elaboration of Eros, betray the fact that they have never had a Friend" (1960, p. 61).

The following transcript reveals one twenty-eight-year-old man confronting some painful realities about his relationship with "Jack," with whom he had hoped to have a friendship.

CLIENT   Jack has been avoiding me. He says I'm overly sensitive, I'm too intense. It's painful to realize that my desperation pushed him away. I create these relationships which I fantasize will fill my emptiness. It's hopeless; I'm going to feel like this for the rest of my life. I'm a piece of s——t. I ain't gonna find it anywhere.

THERAPIST   How do you feel now as you are saying this?

CLIENT   Alone. Scared, hurt and (*deep breath*) missing Jack.

THERAPIST   This is a grieving process, and the surrender of your illusion that Jack will meet all your needs. This is seeing and accepting Jack as an individual, as who he really is.

CLIENT   Yeah, not trying to make him over, mold him into something that gratifies me. I manufacture these relationships. I engineer the interactions. And then they never turn out the way I hope.

THERAPIST   (*returning to his feeling*) How are you feeling right now about Jack?

CLIENT   It's a fantasy relationship. It can't be what I want it to be. Even when it's good, it's never good *enough*. What I want is his undying devotion, but he doesn't have a clue of what I really want, and I have to suffer that.

THERAPIST   Yes.... It's about your own suffering.

CLIENT   Yeah, I know. And no one is ever gonna fill that void. I've always lived with the hope that someone will come along and make me happy. I would fanatically work to plan my contacts with certain guys, running from one chosen guy to the next, trying to fill that void. But there was always a background sense of, *This ain't gonna do it for me*. I need to learn to build friendships that are not aimed at "fixing" me.

THERAPIST   What's the feeling right now as you say this?

[Client knows exactly what is happening but is not actually feeling the implication of his words.]

CLIENT	A fear and a dread about the future. Then I move into anger that I have to carry all this around.
THERAPIST	Who are you angry at?
CLIENT	Dad (*pondering*)... and God. (*long pause, then suddenly*) Here is a memory that I've wanted to mention but I keep forgetting to tell you. There is some titillation about it. I have a memory from the third grade, when I was about seven or eight, of lying on the grass and looking at my father as he mowed the lawn. He was bare-chested. I hoped he would see me and come to me. Of course, he never did. There is some sexual arousal about that memory.
THERAPIST	How are you feeling as you are telling me this?
CLIENT	Embarrassed.
THERAPIST	Which is probably why you kept forgetting to tell me.
CLIENT	(*slight laugh*) Yeah. I just wanted to connect with my dad, and I've been scheming about ways to connect with men like that for thirty years. I haven't had a healthy relationship my entire life. I've spent so much of my life looking forward to the next titillation: *Oh, in five days I'm going to be with...* fill in the guy's name.
THERAPIST	What's the feeling?
CLIENT	Scared. (*pause*) There's a panic. Who can I find to make me feel good?
THERAPIST	Those are ideas. What's the feeling? Where do you feel it?
CLIENT	(*deep breath, pause*) Around my eyes. They're heavy. There's a tension in my face. When I'm clear-minded I see the price is too high, but when I'm weak, I think I don't care. I'll pay whatever price.
THERAPIST	Let's stay with "heavy around the eyes."
CLIENT	A sadness. (*pause*) Yeah, a sadness.
THERAPIST	Where?
CLIENT	Besides the tension in my face? (*pause*) My chest.
THERAPIST	(*waits*)
CLIENT	(*seems lost and vague*) All over, I guess.

[Therapist suspects the client is moving away from his body.]

THERAPIST   Let's go back to your chest. How does sadness feel in your chest?

CLIENT   Like a hard ball at my solar plexus.

THERAPIST   Yeah, stay with that.

CLIENT   (*long pause; seems stuck*)

THERAPIST   A big ball or a little one?

CLIENT   Small...and hard...and dark. Black. (*pointing to center of chest*)

THERAPIST   Yeah. Let's stay with this.

CLIENT   It's like a hollow, empty, black place there.

THERAPIST   (*waits*)

CLIENT   (*seriously considering*) Yeah. Really bleak. Big, empty, dropping, heavy.

[Client becomes very still.]

THERAPIST   When have you ever had this same dropping, sinking feeling?

CLIENT   (*softly*) All my life. When the boy next door would invite me over, we'd fool around in his room. When I'd come home, I'd feel dirty, stuck with that same old feeling of "empty and alone."

This client's task of establishing mutual friendships is complicated by powerful, frustrated longings for intense closeness that are in conflict with his even greater dread of rejection. He sees his options as being two extremes: either abandonment or enmeshment. Many of our clients, having known this dichotomy before in the maternal relationship, tend to think in these same absolutes of either-or.

Psycho-education is called for at this time to clarify that "instant intimacy" is not how friendships are formed with other men; it is not realistic. Rather, I explain to the client that friendships must develop in phases, over time. I offer him a model of two concentric circles. In the center of the circle we see the client with one to three intimate friends, while in the outer circle are six to eight casual friends. From the pool of casual friends, I explain, he can expect a few intimate friendships to gradually develop. But they don't happen instantly, and they can't be forced. This generalized working model reduces the client's anxiety and allows him to focus on a realistic game plan to develop healthier, less enmeshed relationships with men.

Eros versus philia: From shame to assertion. Reparative therapy distinguishes between two distinct modes of relating to other men: *eros*, the sexual or erotic mode, and *philia*, the brotherly or fraternal mode. This distinction is more fully understood within the larger context of living within the narcissistically driven shame posture versus living in a state of healthy assertion.

Once the idea is suggested to him, the client easily recognizes that when he feels better about himself, his homosexual attractions diminish. He may have suspected this inverse relationship before entering therapy yet never have given it such serious consideration. In one rare case, a fifteen-year-old knew the difference. When I suggested he develop a friendship with the boy at school that he sexualized, he quickly retorted, "No! Then I won't be attracted to him any more!"

A significant advance is achieved when the client realizes that his homosexual attractions are generated primarily *not by the attractiveness of the other man,* but by the way *he is feeling about himself.* He discovers that his same-sex attractions result from his tendency to relate to other men not as equals but from the shame posture. Conversely, his homoerotic interests are absent or insignificant when he relates to other men from the assertive self-state.

Making the connection between strengthened feelings of masculinity and diminished same-sex attractions, one client reported: "I notice that when I'm secure in my masculinity I'm not operating from my 'Perma-Scan': you know, that constant cruise mode, visually checking out guys. When I feel good, I'm not even thinking about thinking about it."

Another client described this experience in more detail:

CLIENT   On Saturday night I was invited to a party. There were three guys, rather good looking. I felt some attraction. They spoke to me a little bit, but I felt uncomfortable. I did not know what to say. I left the party early and didn't even finish my drink.

THERAPIST (*nods*)

CLIENT Then the next day I hiked with five guys who were at the party. We went for hours, which included crossing a river to an abandoned mining shack, and we went swimming in a lake. Then we all hiked back. I felt totally like one of the guys.

THERAPIST Tell me, of the two experiences – the Saturday night party and the Sunday hike with your friends – when did you feel more intense homosexual feelings?

CLIENT All day on the hike, I felt none at all. But (*embarrassed laugh*) after leaving the party on Saturday night, I went online to some gay porn sites.

In another example of this shift from eros to philia, a twenty-one-year-old college student who had felt a strong sexual attraction to another student cautiously cultivated a friendship with him. As the friendship developed and deepened, the client began to feel less anxious. He could recognize his friend as indeed good looking, but felt no sexual arousal. He reported, "We were sitting on the lawn and I was looking down his shirt and I noticed his hairy chest, which always gets me turned on. But I couldn't get turned on because I was talking to him." In that conversation in which mutuality and assertion were in evidence, the client was relating from a healthy position and saw himself as an accepted equal; this removed the sexual dimension.

A twenty-eight-year-old described his internal shift between eros and philia, moving from shame to assertion while showering at a gym with two friends.

CLIENT I've become friends with these two good-looking guys that live in my apartment complex. They're straight, real friendly guys. Anyway, we have this exercise facility we all belong to, and we go there during our lunch hour. They're really good looking, but when I'm with them in the shower I feel no arousal. Like the three of us are talking, and there's no turn-on, no nothing.

THERAPIST   And why is that, do you think?

CLIENT   I don't know... because we're talking.

THERAPIST   What does talking have to do with it?

CLIENT   I just feel we're relating differently, and it just doesn't become an issue. (*pause*) But then sometimes I'll "take a snapshot."

THERAPIST   A what?

CLIENT   You know, like a snapshot; I'll snatch a glimpse, an image that I can recall later.

THERAPIST   A sexual image that you can use later. For masturbation?

CLIENT   Well, yeah.

THERAPIST   OK, let's think about this. While taking your "snapshot" were you relating? Connected to these guys?

CLIENT   No. I clearly had to disconnect.

THERAPIST   You had to essentially drop out of the conversation – even for a second – in order to take your snapshot.

CLIENT   Yeah, then shift back into the true self and reconnect emotionally with them. Now, they've become just "guys" again. But good-looking guys.

THERAPIST   Sure. But are you sexually attracted to them?

CLIENT   No, but I could be.

THERAPIST   Sure. That's what the snapshot is about. But to see them in a sexual mode, you had to shift your way of being with them, and in so doing, they shifted from friends to sexual objects. For that moment, you consciously chose to disconnect from them, making them objects for your use, in order to evoke a desired sexual excitement.

CLIENT   Yes, I remember that, in fact, I felt a little devious doing it, like I was using them.

Narcissistic attention as distinct from authentic affirmation. Treatment attempts to sensitize the client to the felt difference between two states: the exciting (even thrilling) but shallow gratification of narcissistic attention, and the less exciting (but richer) gratification of a full, mutually affirmative connection.

There is an often seen "frantic" side to narcissism, as if the man is in rebellion against the passive false self of the nice guy. Confusing his narcissistic needs for authentic connection, one client said, "I need to feel special before I can feel connected with someone. Specialness allows me to feel connected." Through narcissistic manipulation, he would cajole flattery from the other man in order to maneuver him into a relationship that would reinforce his vulnerable inner self. Consequently, he created a self-defeating paradox: other people's positive attention had no power to improve his fragile self-esteem, since the men that he could successfully manipulate into admiring him would soon become objects of his contempt for their gullibility.

Another client confessed, "When I'm around people, I'm not really with them. I can't really get interested in them. Instead, I'm focused on getting them to pay attention to me, getting them to like me. The fact is, I don't really care about other people."

To clarify the difference between getting narcissistic attention and receiving authentic affirmation, we distinguish between the two qualitatively distinct forms of "being seen":

1. *Getting narcissistic attention: Feeling admired, adored.* This form of being seen is based on external appearance and feels gratifying and exciting. Because it is intense but shallow, it results in no internal transformation. Narcissistic attention is not affirmation that has been freely given but involves a "taking" from the other man.

2. *Authentic affirmation: Feeling respected, esteemed.* This form of being "seen" affirms interior character qualities and feels calming, strengthening and deeply transforming. It involves not a manipulative taking but receipt of a benevolent bestowal from the other man.

The SSA man attempts to "repair" his shame by establishing narcissistic relationships with particular men who are selected for their physical or character traits reminiscent of a past shamer. Thus he uses them as self-objects. In this way these people are used as extensions of the narcissistic self. Through fantasy projection, the man sees these men as offering the opportunity to master the past trauma. Reenactment of the shame-narcissism duality with these select men represents a repetition compulsion.

However, no narcissistically based relationship can ever offer emotional growth but rather only feeds the insatiable need for special attention. And when the other person fails to gratify his need, the man resorts to the familiar narcissistic maneuvers of flattery, moodiness, guilt trips or temper tantrums.

Working through the narcissistic illusion in order to achieve *true mutuality* with the other person is achieved through the therapeutic working alliance. The client must risk the dread of anticipated shame and hold on to the healing stance of *being seen by a man as a man,* along with all his fears and weaknesses. The challenge also includes seeing the other man (the therapist) as an autonomous person with his own needs, flaws and foibles. In short, growth in gender esteem occurs for the client when both men engage each other without illusions and distortions.

Narcissistic relationships: "My special [girl]friend." The drive for narcissistic attention, as distinct from authentic affirmation, is most often the therapeutic focus in the situation of male friendships. However, clients sometimes also speak of their special girlfriend (which is to say, a friend who is female). We hear, "We do everything together; shopping, movies, talking intimately for hours." The cohesive element in the friendship is each party's unspoken obligation to make the other feel special. These nonsexual, mutually narcissistic relationships are typically a replication of the client's relationship with his mother or older sister. We occasionally hear of Hollywood movie stars known to be grandiose personalities who seek out gay men as best friends and admirers.

These "special girlfriend" relationships continue until a dramatic crisis ensues when someone fails to live up to the unspoken agreement to narcissistically gratify the other. The result is a profound disappointment and a final, bitter cutoff.

Narcissistic relationships: Idealized men. The narcissistic dimension of same-sex attraction is apparent in this admission, often made by homosexual clients: "I devalue a man who doesn't turn me on." The illusion is that he can attain the masculinity of this sexually attractive other man by making him into a narcissistic self-object. This idea springs from the shame-based, "gender-empty" perspective from which he views other men.

As treatment proceeds the client begins to see that the apparent intensity of the other man's attractiveness depends not on that man's appearance as much as his own negative self-perception at the time. The "fun" of homosexual sex is diminished as he grows in awareness of the narcissism-shame polarity that drives his attraction.

In the following transcript, we see the client's struggle with shame-based unworthiness:

CLIENT	There have been good men like Arthur all my life who I've turned away, I've turned down. So I haven't been filling the empty hole; I've actually been building a fence around that hole: I don't let them in. When I think about Arthur, I think that I don't deserve his friendship. Why does he waste his time with me?
THERAPIST	You generate reasons to disqualify your friendship. Why?
CLIENT	Fear of his rejection, his not caring about me. I put up a barrier... then I want to get him to pity me so I can get more attention from him. I over-dramatize to get him to pay attention to me. I know I'm probably burning him out on the relationship, but I never really got this attention at home. I would cry to get my parents' attention, but it never really touched my need. It felt good on one level... but it didn't satisfy. So I have to dramatize my need – I always have to make a scene, I can't just relax.
THERAPIST	The lesson in childhood is that "who you were" was not good enough to get love and attention. Being ordinary meant being alone.
CLIENT	Right.... When I was in junior high, I felt left out with the cool kids. I remember Billy, when I was in the second grade. I wanted to invite him to my birthday party, but he didn't want to come. I felt awful. Now, I want Arthur's attention. When I get his attention I feel relaxed, I feel secure.
THERAPIST	Yeah, he reassures you that you're OK.

CLIENT   Yeah, it's pathetic, I'm so dependent on this guy. In fact, I'm completely ruining my life running after him. I feel powerless, very angry in ways that I can't express. I'm sexually attracted to him. I worry that if I ever express any anger, I'll lose out. When I'm with him I become "hyper," obsessed, and I want to act out.

THERAPIST   So for you, being ignored makes you angry.

CLIENT   (*nods*) Yes.

[Therapist revisits the no-win relationship with parents.]

THERAPIST   So you become afraid your anger will push him away from you, and as a result, you just suppress it.

CLIENT   And then I become self-critical. It's awful, it's really stupid. People must look at me like I'm an idiot.

THERAPIST   But why do you do this to yourself?

CLIENT   I'm not worth his attention. Why would he want to be my friend? I'm pathetic. I can't just relax, I'm always looking somewhere for a script. I even don't anticipate return calls from my friends. The reality is, I deserve to be ignored until I become "perfect."

The only recourse that the child possesses to compensate for the disavowed gendered part of himself is the narcissistic idealization of another male, where traits and features "owned" by the other are, through fantasy, incorporated into the self.

But the problem with the narcissistic solution is that it does not work. The reality principle will inevitably intervene in each relationship to shatter the illusion, consequently evoking even greater shame.

Whenever such collisions occur between narcissism and reality, they should be exposed for the client to recognize them.

Illusions and Distortions

Guiding the client toward his true gendered self, the therapist attempts to show the client how he vacillates between the two unrealistic extremes of shame and narcissism. Their cognitive distortions are, respectively, distortions and illusions.

Shame	True-Gendered Self	Narcissism
Distortion	*Reality*	*Illusion*

- Distortions are shame-based thoughts, beliefs and perceptions that have been introjected through a negative parental message.

- Illusions are narcissistically based thoughts, beliefs and perceptions that are unrealistically positive and serve to defend against the negative messages.

- Reality is the necessary reference point from which we assess the illusions and distortions.

Illusions and distortions find their origin in early childhood trauma. They form as a survival tactic for staying in relationship with "the parent who promises something good but fails to deliver" (Stark, 1994a).

Illusions include the man's belief that someone (a significant other, such as the therapist) will compensate for those original parental losses, finally providing the attuned love and attention that the man did not receive as a child. Today, as an adult, he still harbors this wish for others to be the "good parent," but always holds onto the fearful anticipation that they will actually prove to be the "bad parent."

The client's continuing need to work through his traumatic past causes him to repeatedly develop illusions and distortions about people in his present life. His illusions about finding a "special" connection to others, including the therapist, shield him against facing and grieving the reality of his core relational loss.

One constructive aid to help enable the client to recognize his illusions and distortions is the journaling format (see chap. 15).

Illusions and distortions: A defense against grief work. For the client who has experienced a profound attachment loss, illusions and distortions represent his "refusal to face the reality of how bad it really was" (Stark, 1994a, p. 136). By holding on to these misperceptions, he aborts the grief process, deflecting or minimizing the reality that he did not feel truly seen and loved. Further, they insulate him from the challenge of taking responsibility to make things better.

Successful grief work means not only facing the reality of past losses but also the painful truth that no one in his present life will ever be able to make up for those losses (for further discussion, see chap. 21).

The child who has been misunderstood, abused or neglected often preserves the illusion of the parent's goodness by taking responsibility for the parent's badness. Repeatedly traumatized by an alternately loving but then rejecting mother or father, the child of the narcissistic family system gains emotional security by "rescuing" the parent, assuming the parent's flaws. He has not learned the lesson of object constancy, for instance, "My mother (or father) is sometimes good and sometimes bad, but I can still see her (or him) as the same, whole person." Without having learned this lesson, he develops the pattern of switching radically between two extreme perceptions of others: unrealistic idealization and dehumanizing devaluation.

Masochism versus sadism. Shame is masochistic (self-punishing) in that it assumes the burden of the parents' failure. The child chooses to carry the shame and to believe in empty promises of future gratification in a new relationship rather than to fully experience his disappointment and rage at their failures. In contrast, sadism (punishment of others) is the way the masochist reacts to disappointment about the loss of an illusion.

Humility. Shame and narcissistic grandiosity alternate within a mutually reinforcing dichotomy. The only antidote to the shame-narcissism pendulum is accepting reality, and that requires embracing a deep humility. Humility means realistically accepting one's own limitations and surrendering the need to overvalue or undervalue either the self or others. Humility releases the person from self-preoccupation and permits him to focus on his own and others' authentic needs.

As treatment progresses, the client's narcissistic manipulations and shame-based self-defeating behaviors slowly give way to a greater toleration for the painful ordeal of facing life's circumstances. This adjustment to reality is achieved not only through his relationship with the therapist (through insight and working through the transference) but as a result of his growing perception of others as real people with their own separate needs.

Authentic human contact and taking responsibility for how his behavior affects others will begin to shift the person's perspective from self-protection into empathy. The healing of shame and narcissism is gained through a growing compassion for self and others, and through consistently being real with other people, that is, relating in an authentic way.

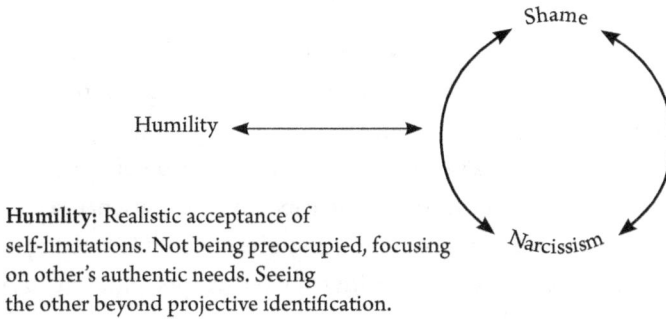

Humility: Realistic acceptance of
self-limitations. Not being preoccupied, focusing
on other's authentic needs. Seeing
the other beyond projective identification.

Figure 5.1 Humility

Seeing other individuals as autonomous and self-governing persons also helps to diminish the client's self-focused expectations. This is the transformative process that "humanizes" the person with narcissistic personality features (Johnson, 1987).

Reality testing, not idealizing. From the very beginning of his work, Freud (1895) distinguished two regulatory principles of psychic functions – the "reality principle" and the "pleasure principle." In infantile development, the child, faced with repeated disappointment, yields to the pleasure principle and consoles himself with pleasing but inaccurate representations of the external world. Later, he must accept the reality principle. This is a "momentous step" (p. 219), during which he abandons the pleasure principle and can accept what is no longer agreeable yet is nevertheless real.

The reality principle as applied to reparative therapy is the resolution of the duality of shame and narcissism.

These two polarities (contempt and idealization) dominate the thinking of the narcissistic personality, and for the homosexual these polarities are primarily fixated on symbols of masculinity. The other man is judged as either ideal or contemptible according to the quality of his maleness. The alternative to the idealized-versus-contemptible perception, of course, is to accept the other as a flawed, real person.

Mental health as acceptance of reality. There are different and sometimes conflicting ways to define mental health, but a primary component (especially by today's criteria) is self-acceptance. Unfortunately, many mental health organizations have come to define the healthy person *primarily* as someone who accepts him- or herself. The profession is less concerned with how he has adapted to the real (gendered) world or whether he is living in conformity with his biological design.

I see validity in Stark's (more traditional) definition of a primary defining quality of mental health: it is the capacity to experience reality as it is, and to accept others in this life as they are, uncontaminated by a need for them to be otherwise. The healthy person accepts others in his life for whatever they can or cannot give.

In our model, the reality principle – addressed with greatest impact during the analysis of the transference – is the opposing force that overcomes shame (with its self-punishing distortions) and narcissism (with its self-inflating illusions).

Illusions and distortions in transference. The phenomenon of transference, arguably Freud's greatest discovery, is the client's act of placing on the therapist the negative or positive features of the good or bad parent. Through careful analysis of the transference, the client has the opportunity to work through unresolved parental trauma. Transference reflects the client's need to make the therapist other than the person he actually is. A negative transference is the distortion of making the therapist like his bad parent (or anticipating that he will become like the bad parent).

Positive transference is the illusion that the therapist will be the idealized good parent he never had. In the positive transference, the client projects onto the therapist the good (idealized) parent, who "has all the answers that will make everything better."

Stark (1994a) summarizes the transference in terms of illusions and distortions by stating, "the patient both fears that his therapist will be bad and, on some level, needs his therapist to be bad" (p. 7). Most clients have the capacity to perceive the therapist as a real and therefore imperfect person. But on some level they choose to "forget" due to an unconscious need to work through past parental trauma. Through this narcissistic investment, he makes the therapist into a self-object. Consequently, there is always a tension within the client between his realistic vision of the therapist and his need for an unrealistically positive or negative perception of him. Misrepresentations of reality are worked through, via the person of the therapist, toward an authentic human encounter. The therapeutic goal is for the client to see the therapist (and consequently all other people) as they really are, with the good they offer and all their human imperfections as well.

For the SSA client, transferential distortions and illusions onto the male therapist are often representations of the loved but unavailable father. A female therapist may also be the recipient of the male client's "mother issues," with his expectation of encountering another woman who will manipulate him and diminish his personal power.

Sensitizing the client to his narcissistic illusions. The client typically reacts with shame when the therapist exposes his narcissistic motivations and the infantile needs behind them.

One man explained his growing understanding of his narcissism:

> Now I'm seeing the narcissism for what it is. They must "exist for me." When I turn a man into an object of narcissism, I consume him. It destroys people, including me.
>
> I called up Tom, and while I was talking to him I could hear in the background that he was watching a baseball game. I could sense he was distracted and only partially listening to me, and I could feel myself getting offended.
>
> I made it high drama: what he was doing was rubbing salt in a narcissistic wound. Of course, I can't really expect people to be totally receptive to me whenever I want. That is a sickness, and I can see that now.

In this quote, we hear shame-based self-contempt at the awareness of his narcissistic needs. But this only further intensifies the client's narcissistic defenses. Instead, the therapist tries to substitute the client's self-criticism for self-compassion by framing the narcissism within his personal history. In so doing, the therapist models compassionate understanding for the client's original need to develop narcissistic maneuvers in order to receive the love and attention that he needed.

One client explained:

> I pick the usual target. I watch myself doing it. I always choose young guys who have problems of their own, and I run in and rescue them, becoming their mentor. Most of these guys are cute blockheads –

teenage boys in men's bodies. I hypermanage and mentor them, receiving nothing back, and then I resent them. I don't know if I am doing these good things for their benefit or for me to feel needed, wanted and appreciated. It's hard for me to tell.

This therapy session reveals another client's struggle with reality:

CLIENT   When I look back on my life I see how I've kept replacing these special guys with other special guys. When they don't respond to me, I feel like a zero, a nothing. Like I'd be better off dead.

THERAPIST   Yes, that's a shame moment.

CLIENT   Yeah, they shame me.

THERAPIST   No, they don't shame you. They fail to help you cover the shame that's already there by not joining in the narcissistic game.

CLIENT   Oh...?

THERAPIST   You are learning how to walk a tightrope of reality between two extremes – special guys who make you feel great about yourself versus guys who ignore you and make you feel, as you say, "like a nothing." But the reality about these guys is somewhere in between.

CLIENT   Yes. It's always been one or the other, but I don't know how it can be any other way.

THERAPIST   Your task is to see the other guy as a real person, while staying real yourself.

When the therapist exposes the illusion, very often the client will turn against him in a narcissistic rage. In that moment the therapist has suddenly become "the bad, shaming parent."

Alternatively, the therapist may encounter a form of resistance in which the client's acknowledgment of his narcissistic behavior is followed by a self-directed shame response. Recognition of his narcissistic manipulation leads to despair: "You're right. I can see that I'll never be normal!" In short, being made aware of his narcissism evokes yet more self-induced shame. This shame reaction is evoked by the observing self's recognition of the source of the narcissistic manipulation: it is based on the childhood memory that attempts at masculine individuation evoked shame.

As the personification of the reality principle, the therapist attempts to expose the client's illusions while avoiding shaming him. This is achieved by showing the historical necessity for his illusory creation. Highlighting his childhood need for his narcissistic defense diminishes the client's shame reaction to such exposure.

With most clients, I have found it more beneficial to avoid direct "head-on" confrontation of defenses, and rather to gently highlight and name defenses as they present themselves while allowing the client freedom to accept or reject what he will about my comments.

Speaking to the client who grew up in the triadic-narcissistic family, the therapist might put it this way: "As a child you could not directly express your authentic needs, so you learned to do so by manipulation. Since you felt neglected and unacknowledged, you believe [this other person] is ignoring you, when he really isn't." With compassion and tolerance the therapist reveals how the illusion was a necessary childhood adaptation: "In view of how ignored you felt as a boy, it is understandable that you would manipulate your friend for special attention. Since your father showed you little attention, I can see how you'd hope that [this other person] would totally love and totally accept you, to fill that unmet need."

One thirty-five-year-old client who had developed a narcissistically driven relationship with a much younger man had been fostering a healthy, observing ego in order to identify how he manipulates others for special attention.

> I was with Tom this weekend, and there were times when I would catch myself grasping for any sort of compliment from him, and then a small voice inside me would say, *Oh, good job catching what you just did!* but then a bigger voice would say, *There! So you were fishing for compliments from someone again; you are such a little boy!* That always brings with it a heavy, sinking feeling.

Here the therapist intervenes to model the self-compassion that must replace self-criticism. The client must accept, for the present time, the existence of his narcissistic behaviors as he works toward developing true authenticity with other men. The therapist shows attuned compassion for the client as he works toward developing mutual, realistic, more mature friendships.

In the course of therapy, this twenty-eight-year-old man began to distinguish the difference between narcissism and altruism:

> When I would get these special guys' attention, it would only satisfy for a short time because I knew that I had pressured and manipulated them for it.
>
> But when I release them – allowing them to show interest in me on their own terms, in their own way, on their own time – then it feels awesome, truly affirming.

When the client is in his self-punishing shame mode, he not only deprives himself but also denies and punishes loved ones. Trapped in self-loathing, he cannot give anything good to those people for whom he cares. These include not only the therapist but his friends and (if he is married) his wife and children. But as he grows in the ability to see other people realistically, he also grows in acceptance of himself, along with all his human imperfections.

True Self Versus False Self

The earliest and most common form of false self is the "good little boy" persona. It is an attempt to present a socially acceptable self while maintaining emotional hiding. As a social role or public image, it functions to pacify and ingratiate potential shamers. The false self accommodates the need for social belonging and acceptance, while simultaneously offering self-protection against possible future shame moments.

Origins of the false self: The good little boy and the necessity for pretense. "As a kid, I remember making the conscious decision to be false or be eaten alive."

The false self is a defensive split resulting from a hurtful family system. We frequently see it emerge as a boyhood defense against a distant, rejecting, critical father and a manipulating, intrusive mother. Such family dynamics cause the boy to be shamed for the authentic and spontaneous expressions of his true gendered self, so he retreats into a compliant, genderless caricature. The good little boy is a one-dimensional persona of conformity and obedience who defends against the profound grief about feeling not fully known and fully loved.

Most clients trace the origins of their false self to their relationship with the mother. In some more rare cases, it appears to have grown out of the relationship with a seductive father who had a narcissistic need to foster a genderless identity in the son, whom the father feared as a potential competitor.

The prehomosexual boy is likely a temperamentally sensitive, creative, lonely child, and he has discovered that it is so easy, so "natural," to pretend. Having to develop a false self to survive has led him very easily into the rich, escapist world of fantasy and acting. Blocked from full and satisfying participation in family and, later, social life, he quickly discovers the ways in which fantasy reduces the painful loss.

While both parents may contribute to the boy's failure to develop his true gendered self, mother and father each contribute differently. The detached and critical father does so by neglecting to elicit the sensitive boy's emerging masculine identity and failing to provide a positive model to facilitate the development of his gendered self. The manipulative and intrusive mother does so by subtly but consistently discouraging the boy's formation of the true self; her love and attention are conditional, based on whether the boy gratifies her needs. Her emotional needs are particularly great when (as is often the case) her marriage is unsatisfying.

Within this scenario the abdicating father did not provide the boy with a secure masculine perspective from which he could accurately "see" his mother. Thus the father fails to give the boy the opportunity to observe how another male can have a relationship with a woman who he feels close to and is nurtured by while at the same time, not lose himself and surrender his masculine autonomy and power.

Different styles of the false self. The psychological concepts of the true self and false self first originated in religious and philosophical literature. They were adapted in the 1960s into the psychological literature by Winnicott. They have since been integrated into object relations theory and self psychologies, and are of central importance in our understanding of homosexuality.

The false self is a pseudo-personality, or persona, that masks the shamed-defective self while allowing the person to stay in relationship with others. The most common forms of the false self are characterized by a pleasant exterior but an unconnectedness with others and a preoccupation with self-protection. The person often has studied mannerisms and self-conscious posturing, and in exaggerated form may act flamboyant, effeminate and "campy." But in most cases, especially for the non-gay homosexual who comes to therapy seeking change, the false self takes the form of a muted, self-effacing, nonspontaneous and shy manner. The overall effect is an inhibition of the full personality.

Characterized by defensiveness and standoffishness, this false self maintains a "curtain of anxiety" restricting the man's ability to relate to others, especially other men. As a way of being in the world, it is a nonfeeling mode – a pretense, a place of hiding. All of this affects the man's attitude, mood, thoughts and feelings. More than an isolated psychological phenomenon, it consumes him, and his entire personhood is constricted into a narrow and limiting posture. All behavior must be designed, lives must be arranged, and relationships kept shallow – all for the sake of avoiding shame. The false self is a virtual straitjacket placed over his authentic spontaneity and natural vitality, forcing the containment of all spontaneous expression.

The true self, on the other hand, is the "posture" or stance through which the man feels and authentically expresses to others his true emotions. Central to reparative therapy is assisting the client to transition from the false self to the true gendered self.

Styles of the false self include:

1. *Passive-compliant (AKA the nice guy)*. The nice guy is by far the most common form of false self. It is an outgrowth of the "good little boy" of childhood. We see someone who is easygoing, never confrontational, avoids upsetting others and seeks peace at all costs. "I know how to take care of people's needs, but I don't know how to let people know my own needs. I do what I think I'm supposed to, but then I feel cheated. Then I get hurt and disgusted and disengage from relationships, and don't even realize it."

2. *The theatrical entertainer.* The less common style – theatrical enter-

tainer – is outgoing and exhibitionistic; the person who adopts it has to keep the conversation going and keep everybody "happy" (with him). Anything less than enthusiastic approval from others is interpreted as personal rejection. *I have to be Mr. Personality, Mr. Showboat all the time. How am I appearing? What are they thinking of me? Do they like me? Do they dislike me?* The theatrical entertainer appears to have a strength, energy and vitality. But a closer look reveals a forced and pressured animation, a shallow intensity that is actually driven by anxiety and ultimately it exhausts him.

3. *The outrageous, hyper-feminine character.* The man who adopts the hyper-feminine style is likely to be seen within the gay community at gay-pride parades, flaunting his feminine side. His style is outlandish; he enjoys an "in your face" violation of social norms. He is the drag queen who affronts sensibilities with an insulting and ridiculous caricature of femininity. Gratification for this false self is found in shocking others.

4. *The angry activist, hyper-masculine character.* The angry hyper-masculine character assaults political and social norms, is confrontational, combative, pugnacious, joining militant gay-activist groups, which become his new family.

The false self will manifest itself in our clients' relationships with both men and women. With men, he uses the false self as an attempt to sidestep mutuality and competition, and avoid direct, adult-adult communication. Most clients will admit, "I'm afraid to show myself to men." With women the false self usually operates to keep them at bay, to maintain a safe distance, and the fear is that they will be smothered and engulfed by him. With men the fear is of not getting enough attention; with women it's getting too much attention.

An imposter. The man living through the false self is encased in a static role, not fully alive. He is an imposter, even to himself. Held captive by the demands of others, he suffers from chronic irritability, resentment and hidden hostility. At the root of the matter is a trust issue: because a fundamental trust was violated in early childhood, he now remains uninvested in relationships. He either avoids others due to his distrust of their motives or places an indiscriminate trust in some people, indulging in indiscreet self-disclosure.

His anticipation of shame leaves him mired in a chronic state of emptiness, loneliness and dissatisfaction. Living with the underlying fear of abandonment-annihilation, he carries on a dissociated, alienated and pessimistic existence. One man described it this way:

> My identity comes from living the expectations of other people. I feel used, tired and drained. It's like I'm nonexistent, empty and have no purpose – no grounding. I have no home, no place to belong. I fall asleep during the daytime just to find an escape.
>
> I'd like to scream, to tear down the walls that bind me ... but what walls? I don't even see walls, just empty, dark space inside. I *am* that dark space.

As we have seen, homosexuality is truly an attachment problem. Since early childhood, the man with SSA has longed to feel whole and understood, with a secure place of belonging.

Signs of the True Self Versus the False Self

Table 5.1 reveals the general distinctions between the true self and the false self.

Throughout childhood, the boy's potential to develop his true gendered self has remained smothered beneath his familiar false self of the good little boy. He will not allow himself to feel the hidden grief that is inhibiting the expression of his anger and sadness. As he grows up, homosexuality appears as a narcissistic reparation to bridge the shame-induced split that has separated him from his own masculine ambitions.

Only by fully experiencing the two innate affects of sadness and anger in the present can the client begin to grieve and to heal. Overcoming this blockage is one of the formidable challenges of successful treatment.

Table 5.1 Signs of the True Self Versus the False Self

TRUE SELF	FALSE SELF
Within Self	
Masculine	Unmasculine
Adequate, on par	Feels inferior, inadequate
Secure, confident, capable	Insecure, unconfident, incapable
Experiencing authentic emotions	Emotionally dead or, alternatively, hyperactive
Energized	Depleted
At home in body	Body is object
Physical confidence	Anxious clumsiness
Feeling empowered, autonomous	Feeling controlled by others
Accept imperfections	Perfectionistic
Active, decisive	Passive
Trusting	Defensive posture
Creative	
With Others	
Attached	Detached
Outgoing	Withdrawn
Spontaneous	Overcontrolled, inhibited, "frozen"
Forgiving, accepting	Retaliatory, resentful
Genuine, authentic	Role playing, theatrical
Seeks out others	Avoidant
Humility	Self-dramatization
Aware of others	Constricted awareness
Assertive, expressive	Nonassertive, inhibited
Mature in relationships	Immature in relationship
Respectful of others' power	Resentful of others in power
Empowered	A victim
Integrated; open	Double life; secretive
Rapport with opposite gender	Misunderstanding of opposite gender
Sees other men as like self	Pulled by mystique of other men
NO HOMOSEXUALITY:	HOMOSEXUALITY:
"Homosexuality does not come up for me. I can willfully visualize it—but it doesn't have that compelling quality."	"I'm in that whole gay mindset. Sexual attraction to guys preoccupies and dominates my entire outlook."

PART TWO

Treatment: Affect-Focused Therapy

CHAPTER 6

The Primacy of Affect

Recent advances in psychotherapy have focused on the central importance of affect in the therapeutic process. Emotional disregulation, most often in the form of shame, prompts the client to seek relief in homosexual enactment. Same-sex behavior is used as an attempt at affect regulation in response to attachment trauma. It is through these same emotional and somatic pathways that we approach the process of attachment reconstruction.

There is a powerful affective expansion when the man allows himself to be "seen" by the therapist while sitting in the shame. Healing moments occur when the client feels "unbearable" affect while at the same moment experiencing the support of the therapist.

Looking to the pioneering research of Davanloo (1978), which was further developed by Neborsky (2004), Coughlin Della Selva (1996), Alpert (2001), and Fosha (2000), we have adapted an application of these clinicians' programs of affect-focused therapy (AFT). Indeed, our long-time work with homosexually-oriented men has confirmed that AFT produces the quickest results toward the resolution of same-sex attraction.

AFT was developed out of prior research that examined primates' mother-infant bonding. It gained further empirical support from attachment theory and mother-child studies in humans tracing back to John Bowlby. Drawing from Bowlby and others in the field, AFT practitioners now view much of the pathology presented by clients to be a result of attachment loss, with the goal of therapy being attachment reconstruction.

The particular meeting place of reparative therapy and AFT lies in our view that homosexuality is fundamentally an attachment problem. We see most same-sex behavior as an attempt to repair an insecure attachment to the father. Homosexual activity, fantasy and ideation compensates for the failure of this attachment bond.

But we do not reduce this phenomenon solely to father-son attachment failure; in fact, we believe that the deficit in attachment may well have begun, for some clients, with problems in mother-son attunement. The boy's earlier defense of dissociation against a disregulating maternal style has, in such cases, laid the foundation for later difficulties when he encounters a father with a weak or hostile paternal style.

Consequently, the effectiveness of reparative therapy is increased by use of techniques that explore early mother-son attachment problems. Thus our treatment process has moved away from traditional attempts at resolving intrapsychic conflict and turned greater focus on affect regulation, with the therapist as affect-regulation facilitator.

In the final analysis it is interpersonal rapport that characterizes our deepest humanity and determines our internal equilibrium. The quintessential model of this rapport is the "double loop," a powerful therapeutic achievement between client and therapist.

A Radical Therapeutic Resonance

Because the mother-child bond molds our earliest sense of self and shapes and refines our character, therapy must inevitably revisit that attachment; therefore, AFT focuses on the way we attach, detach and reattach.

Utilizing AFT techniques, the reparative therapist attempts to evoke the client's expression of innate affects and to broadly expand his somatic awareness. Affective expansion has been shown to occur when there is a radical level of client-therapist resonance. Therefore the therapist must be fully emotionally present in order to elicit and deeply share the client's visceral experience – emotionally engaging him with an empathy and moment-to-moment accurate attunement that is far beyond, and even contradictory to, the traditional psychotherapeutic approach.

As trust and confidence build within their exchange, the client begins to feel confident enough to experience an authentic exchange with other men. From there, he can begin to more authentically engage women.

Neurophysiological Research

All interpersonal communication has a neurobiological impact, either corrective or harmful. Affects are the signal transmitters of human relations that connect the person with his emotional environment. Supportive evidence is strong for understanding the therapeutic alliance as an "affective correcting experience" (Schore, 1991, 2003; Stern, 2002; Siegel, 2002). Recognizing that this experience is the essential force for therapeutic change, treatment focuses on the removal of blocks that disconnect the client from his core feelings.

The flow of affect is determined by attachment. Traditional psychodynamic concepts such as "internalized objects" are metaphors for this biologically based phenomenon of neurological transmission. What we call "internalization of the object," for example, is actually a body-held memory, a conditioned affective response.

Each person's neurological structure is designed to be synchronized with other persons' neurological structures. Stern (2002) reminds us that our brains were designed to lock in with other brains. But human attachments can break down (as illustrated by the double bind) and then reconnect (through the double loop). Interruptions of affect – through anxiety, shame or fear – disconnect the person from his emotional environment and cause disregulation or shutdown.

The opposite emotional state, an affective "turning on" or openness, is the goal of reparative therapy. This means openness first to a male therapist, then to other men and finally to women.

Laying down new neurological pathways. In his work on the interpersonal neurobiology of the developing mind, Daniel Siegel explains how the therapeutic relationship not only corrects the interrupted flow of affect but actually creates new neurological pathways to promote this new flow. This "new flow" of neurotransmitters may be what is happening on a biological plane in the traditional psychodynamic model of conflict resolution.

This same physiological understanding of therapeutic change is the basis for EMDR therapy (see appendix).

Also compatible with this concept is dual-brain psychology (Schiffer, 1998), which locates affective activity in the right brain and cognitive activity in the left brain. The right brain is not only the source of affect, Schore says, but is also the locus of the unconscious.

In our own use of AFT the therapist maintains empathic attunement in the working alliance to facilitate unification of the two brain hemispheres. In so doing, the therapist metaphorically embeds himself between the client's right brain and his left brain.

Attunement changes brain structure. Traumatic malattunement, the inevitable consequence of the double bind, creates shame, and shame maintains detachment from the unified self. In contrast, attunement with the therapist in the working alliance (a consequence of the double loop experience) resolves this barrier of shame and fosters self-reattachment.

Through connectedness with the therapist, the client allows himself to feel the disturbing bodily sensations that are associated with his painful early experiences. Healing moments occur when the client can feel what seems to be unbearable core feeling, while at the same moment experiencing the care and support of the therapist.

Thus, in a delicate process of interactive repair, their attuned relationship actually changes the neurological structure of the brain.

The Double Loop and the Transformative Moment

The double loop is a process of attunement that unifies the client with himself, then unifies him with others. Interpersonal attunement (or malattunement) determines our intrapsychic relationship with ourselves, and this attunement with another person leads back to greater attunement with self. For the client who grew up in the narcissistic family, early trauma from the parental double bind has created an internal, attunement split.

Forming the double loop is not a science; there is inevitably a "sloppy, hit-or-miss" quality to all such intimate interpersonal exchange (Stern, 2002). This makes the formation of the double loop not a mere technical endeavor but a uniquely human event between two people in time, with a sort of mystical or transpersonal quality with a larger-than-life sense to it. When the client drops his usual defenses and allows such an attuned exchange to occur, we see a transformative depth of shared emotionality that permits reintegration of the formerly split-off (shamed) aspects of the client's self.

The most powerful change occurs when the client who is emotionally present in the double loop reexperiences an early trauma. At such intense times – when all that exists for both client and therapist is the here and now – we observe this transformative moment of *reattachment with self* through the medium of the other.

Only after many such self-reattachment experiences do we move on to the next phase – the cognitive making sense of one's feelings, also known as the "narrative reconstruction process."

From Anxiety to Spontaneity

Affect-focused therapy rapidly accelerates the client's encounter with his fear-filled emotional life. The therapist encourages him to feel and express his anxiety-provoking feelings, while at the same time supporting him in maintaining their interpersonal contact. Toleration of previously unbearable affect is possible because of that emotional rapport.

Through the double loop experience the client learns that painful emotions are not intolerable in themselves, but rather that *it was the early sense of parental abandonment associated with those emotions that has actually rendered them intolerable.*

When the client integrates these once negative-seeming affects, he experiences a surprising eruption of spontaneity, authenticity, vitality and self-integrity – all of which is prompted by the restructuring of the true self. This restructuring is expressed as a greater outflow of energy in relating to others and less preoccupation with oneself. With the emergence of the true self we gradually see the establishment of new, far more authentic relationships.

The newest forms of AFT challenge the therapist to enter even deeper dimensions of attunement and caring (see Alpert's collaborative model, and especially Fosha's). It is at these deepest levels of attunement that AFT opens the way for the next step of the process, which is grief work.

Therapeutic grief work is approached through two pathways: anger and sadness. Here, the client confronts the profoundly disturbing feelings associated with the attachment loss.

Sequence of Attachment Loss

The child's response to parental attachment loss takes place in sequential phases: first protest, then despair and finally detachment (see Bowlby). In the final stage (detachment), the parent is actively avoided by the child and is treated like a stranger. This antipathy of the child toward the same-sex parent (commonly reported by fathers of homosexuals and by homosexual men themselves) is the phenomenon that Andy Comiskey, founder of an ex-gay ministry, has described as his "unnatural indifference" toward his own father.

This dismissal of the father as "unimportant" is a thin, veneer-like defense for the unexpressed anger and sadness that is regularly encountered in grief work.

Shame: Being Cut Out of the Herd

The drive for attachment is rooted in a biologically based survival instinct. Shame inducement by the parent prompts the dread of annihilation, necessitating the child's compromise of fundamental aspects of the self – if necessary, identification with his own gender. This process lays the foundation for the most common form of homosexuality, wherein we see a fundamental disavowal of gender attachment, later resulting in the drive for homoerotic reparation.

"Neurobiologically…humiliation…[is] a survival issue; the evolutionary equivalent of being cut out of the herd," says Francine Shapiro (2001, p. 113). So when a person is shamed for his feelings, those feelings become so unbearable that he cannot allow himself to own them – even to feel them.

Insight as a Sudden Awakening

Insight is "the linking up of two formerly separate neural networks." Shapiro (2001) explains it as "I knew 'this' and I knew 'that,' but I never, until now, saw the connection between 'this' and 'that'" (p. 122).

Karl Bühler's (1990) "Aha!" experience of insight is similar. This is not just a cognitive but an embodied phenomenon. We see evidence of this phenomenon in the posture of the person who has just recalled something; there is a subtle but unmistakable jolt or shock reaction, as if the person is suddenly waking up. We see this "aha!" affective shift in the scenario preceding homosexual enactment, when the client recalls the shame moment that destabilized his assertive state.

Sublime Attunement as Cocreation

When the child goes to the parent in distress and the parent reacts with either disregard or exaggerated fright, the child's affective disorganization increases. With the mother ignoring or overreacting to his distress – failing to accurately mirror his internal experience – he becomes emotionally isolated.

When affect-focused therapy functions at its best, this affective disorganization is gradually corrected. With the therapist who is capable of subtle, highly nuanced communication, there is an experience of sublime attunement. Therapist and client share an implicit knowledge – that nonverbal, pre-explicit experience that occurs between two people in the recognition that *I* know that *you* know that *I* know.

In many hours of analyzing video recordings of actual psychotherapy sessions at my clinic, I have seen how this subtle synchronicity emerges between client and therapist, with each person eventually having the sense of what the other is trying to express. Stern (2002) offers the example of two people kissing: the speed, direction, angle of approach – all perfectly coordinated for a "soft landing" (without crashing teeth) – is a miracle of psychic intimacy with "maximal complexity" of thinking, intending and then doing. He says it simply: "Our minds are not created alone; they are co-created. Our nervous system is ready to be taught by other peoples' nervous systems, which transforms us." Indeed, psychotherapy offers a second opportunity to integrate one's emotional life through actual neurological changes in the brain.

In attempting to explain how this therapeutic "second opportunity" works through the model of sublime attunement, Stern speaks of the importance of setting the correct tempo for "moving along" – the unspoken regulation of the rhythm and intensity of the back-and-forth between two people.

Stern also notes the importance of intermittent "field regulation." This is the assessment of the other's receptivity with questions such as, "What's actually happening between us right now?" He is particularly interested in what he calls "*now* moments," when the entire frame of the picture alters, zooming in on two people as they are pulled into the present moment, experiencing an intense "existential presentness." These "*now* moments" contain a heightened anxiety and the sense that somehow "this moment is important," either for good or ill in the relationship.

Personal exposure and vulnerability are a basic part of these moments; we see an excitement, a recognition of each other on a deeper level and perhaps a slight, embarrassed smile that recognizes this sometimes-awkward vulnerability and intimate exposure. Such moments, which Martin Buber calls "moments of meeting," cannot be forced; but as therapists we can certainly, as Stern says, be ready to coax such opportunities into existence.

Stern's description of the textured aspects of these central moments constitutes our double loop.

Two Binary Affects: Assertion Versus Shame

AFT helps us distinguish the basic "on" (attaching) affects versus the "off" (detaching) affects. The essential "off" (detaching) affect is associated with the self-state of shame. The essential "on" (attaching) affect is associated with the self-state of assertion. This fundamental open-closed distinction, described by Fosha as the "green signal" versus the "red signal," is equivalent to the sympathetic versus the parasympathetic neurological response.

Making the same distinction but in different words, Schore (2003) identifies the attaching affects as openness and attunement, which are in contrast to the "freeze" (closed) response. This freeze response is much like reparative therapy's shame – the consequence of the boy's feeling humiliated for his masculine gestures.

Clients have expressed this *attaching-detaching* affective shift as the difference between

- *exploding* and *imploding*
- *heart open* and *heart closed*

- *inflated* and *deflated*
- *expansive* and *constrictive*

Assertion and shame have physiological substrata in the autonomic nervous system. The autonomic nervous system has two coordinating systems, the sympathetic nervous system and the parasympathetic nervous system. The sympathic nervous system generates responsiveness, openness and connectedness, while the parasympathic nervous system conveys a shutdown and inhibited state. In the shame state (similar to Fosha's "red signal" affect), we see the physiological equivalent of the parasympathetic (shutdown) response. The sympathetic response, on the other hand, corresponds with the return to connectedness. Reparative therapy is focused on shifting the client from the inhibitory "shutdown" state of shame and into the vitality state of assertion. It is in the state of sympathetic response or connectedness that one learns about oneself. This state becomes possible when the client overcomes the shame posture and his shutdown, emotional deadness.

These vitality and inhibitory affects are illustrated by the "pike phenomenon" (Wolverton, 2005). In an experiment a pike fish is placed in a tank with live minnows. The pike immediately begins eating all the minnows it sees. Then an invisible glass cylinder is placed over the pike, separating it from the minnows. Any further attempts to eat the minnows result in the pike hitting its nose on the glass cylinder, causing it pain. The cylinder is then removed, but the pike, anticipating pain, makes no more attempt to eat the minnows. The vitality response has been lost and the inhibitory response is substituted.

The pike phenomenon illustrates a conditioned response that inhibits healthy assertion. For our clients, we see an anticipation of shame for their gender assertion. Anticipatory shame represents a somatic flashback, which switches the body into a defensive shutdown mode. This shutdown (shamed) state is a defense against the pain of traumatic loss.

Emotional Shutdown on a Biological Level

It is sometimes helpful to explain to the client that his shutdown is actually a *physiological, bodily* reaction. This helps him observe his own bodily shifts as they occur in the moment. Developing a self-observant stance can increase the client's ego strength as he notices his body (not his conscious self but his body) shift to the shutdown mode. Teaching the client to observe his own bodily response is similar to EMDR's repeated instruction to the client to "go back to" and then "let go of" and then "go back to" the traumatic image (see appendix) over and over.

Another term for the shame moment is the "freeze response," in which the person loses his somatic vitality, with the body becoming rigid and stiff.

In dissociation there is a "segmentation of minds," each possessing its own cluster of thoughts, feelings and memories (Jung) which are held in the body. When someone is "in one mind" (a cluster of embodied memories), it is hard for him to recall the other "mind," and if the other mind is recalled (i.e., felt in the body), then it has already left the first mind. For example, when we have a quarrel with a friend, our hurt and anger make it difficult to recall, on a feeling level, anything pleasant about him or her. When we resolve the dispute, it is hard to "recall" what we disliked about the friend.

A client reported going on a weekend trip where he was camping and shooting with his friends. This experience put him into the assertion state, where he couldn't recall the other "mind" of homosexual temptation. A week later, when he was back into the shame state, the opposite occurred: he was preoccupied with homoerotic fantasies and couldn't recall the mindset of assertion.

Shame Posture Versus the Assertive State

Reparative therapy methodically examines the self-states with the client, especially regarding the "scenario preceding homosexual enactment" (see chaps. 12–13). The simultaneous experience of feeling shame in the body and the acceptance and understanding of the attuned therapist works to diminish the physiological charge of shame.

When clients are in the assertive stance, they can vaguely recall but cannot intensely feel their homoerotic attractions. When they shift to the shame posture, they cannot recall what it was like *not* to have compelling homoerotic feelings.

Like all other self-states, shame has an evolutionary survival function.

(Shame, it should be noted, is not the same as guilt. Guilt results from a negative judgment of one's own behavior, while shame is a basic physiological response.) A child will be shamed – which is to say, threatened by expulsion from the pack – for behaviors that risk the stability and survival of the group.

The self-state of shame brings to mind the work of Freud's mentor, Pierre Janet, known as the father of dissociation. Janet laid the foundation for Freud's later work on hysteria, where past events, when held outside of consciousness, still retain an influence on present behavior. The shame moment is also related to the Freudian concept of dissociation, which is triggered when the person anticipates a recurrence of some past trauma. Dissociation represents the mind's attempt to block out traumatic childhood memories that still, on an unconscious level, feel overwhelmingly threatening.

Laying Down New Neurological Pathways

The child's affective development takes place in three critical phases of *attunement, misattunement* and *reattunement.*

Through the sequencing of these three critical phases the child learns how to tolerate distress levels while simultaneously maintaining contact (attunement) with the parent. At intolerable levels of excitement, the infant breaks contact (misattunement), and when the level of arousal reduces back down to a tolerable range, he reattunes with the parent. Through this process the child is able to increase his capacity to tolerate emotional distress.

Memory is a psycho-physiological phenomenon. That is, it is not only cognitive but also somatic – a trauma that is stored in the body. Schore (1996) believes that the therapeutic relationship actually reencodes the synaptic connections of the memory system. Therapeutic success would mean that new, positive neurological pathways would be laid down on top of the old, traumatic neurological memories.

Somatic Shift Leads to New Meaning

Reparative therapy focuses on body work because we understand the unconscious mind to hold a buried "body memory" that operates without cognitive awareness. The body does not deceive us, but the mind can do so. Freud summarized the goal of psychoanalysis as, "Where 'id' was, there ego shall be" (1933). He meant that unconscious, irrational impulses are replaced with self-awareness (insight) and rationality.

We may revise this dictum to propose that *where the somatic shift is, there new meaning shall be.* The mind gives new understanding to embodied experiences. For example, the gay-identified man says: "My inherent gayness determines my sexual arousal to an attractive male. Such attractions are normal and natural for me." For him, an attractive male is associated with sexual gratification, and he comes to believe that such feelings authentically define him.

However, the non-gay homosexual has the same somatic reaction to the same attractive man, but his internal narrative is quite different. He says: "My assertive state or shame state determines my sexual arousal to an attractive man. I'm attracted to that man because he possesses qualities of masculinity that I feel are lacking right now within myself. This attraction is not part of my deepest identity." He then asks: "How am I feeling about myself right now that makes me susceptible to this sexual response? And what can I do to change that?"

How the gay-identified man and the non-gay homosexual interpret and respond to their body awareness is the essential difference between them. What the gay-identified man takes at face value, the non-gay homosexually oriented man instead chooses to question. The gay man believes this attraction is about another man who is "out there" and is reflective of his true self-identity. But the non-gay SSA man uses this attraction as a catalyst to look within.

CHAPTER 7

The Body

My body is my inner compass. It tells me what's going on – where
I'm at in a given situation – and my true attitude about things.

⊷

Only a fool cannot feel.

— OLD HEBREW SAYING

⊷

When I was young, this thing [homosexuality] got
into the middle of me, and stayed there.

All emotions are felt in the body. Because homosexuality is symptomatic of gender-related trauma, reparative therapy must target the trauma that is being held in the body and remembered.

The sympathetic nervous system (SNS) and the parasympathetic nervous system (PNS) are the neuro-storehouses where shame and assertion are held. Stress is associated with shame, and relaxation/free response is associated with assertion. We have found it helpful to explain these shifts of the nervous system to our clients, while encouraging their ongoing observation of these changes in themselves from one mode to the other.

These neurological shifts prompt a corresponding shift in one's state of mind. Most clients report that when they are in the assertive state, they cannot imagine homosexual enactment. Conversely, when in the shame state (and the subsequent mood of the gray zone), they can think of nothing else, and homosexual enactment becomes an obsession.

The Double Bind: Learning to Distrust Visceral Communication

Within the triadic-narcissistic family that we see so often in our clients' histories, there is a characteristic chaotic communication style, where the child is left in a state of internal discord because the words of the parents' messages are inconsistent with the way those messages are conveyed. There is a disconnect between content (the subject matter, received by the left brain) and process (the unspoken, implicit message that is registered by the recipient in the right hemisphere of the brain).

In the double bind situation, in which content and process are at odds, the mind has difficulty making sense of the contradictory message felt in the body. The right brain is more directly connected to the body. Thus the victim of the double bind feels bodily sensations that he cannot quite cognitively grasp. These sensations may be vague, but they ultimately do not match the words he is hearing.

At such moments the child becomes confused, disoriented and then numb, unsure which message to believe. The result is that he begins to ignore the visceral impact of human communication. He learns not to listen to his own feelings. This lesson is taught through negative reinforcement by the parents, in the form of explicit or implicit disapproval when the child responds not to the *content* but to the *process* part of the message. Consequently, he absorbs the message that he cannot really trust his gut. One client told me, "I know I'm in a double bind when the words sound nice, but my mind feels disjointed. I'll feel 'out of order' in my head. Despite those nice words, I'll be having very different feelings – sad, hurt, angry, left out, shunned and confused."

The result for the client is a disempowering moment that shifts him from vitality to paralysis, and from assertion into shame. For many men the only recourse against such a discordant message is to internalize the shame-based distortions he feels as a result of such communication. In therapy he must now learn to respectfully attend to his body and express his affective response to the communicator. When he is gradually sensitized to the messages coming from his body, he is able to recognize these double bind situations as they arise. This helps him to avoid personal disempowerment. The destabilizing moment – the result of a double bind message – becomes, whenever it is not carefully attended to, a disempowering moment which triggers relapse into the shame self-state, the state which leaves him vulnerable to homosexual enactment.

The Embodied Shift

The phenomenon of an "embodied shift" is experienced internally, yet it also is an observable phenomenon. The trained therapist will note the moment when the client shifts from the false self into the assertive stance (the true self). The change is immediate and is evidenced not only in attitude and mood but in posture, facial expression and vocal resonance.

After his shift to the assertive stance, the client appears calm, centered and self-possessed; he expresses himself with confidence.

Many of our clients complain that they do not know where they stand with other people; their inner compass of perception and emotions is out of balance. Here we see the importance of body work, because it sensitizes the client to a cognitive awareness of the destabilizing moment: the assertion-shame conflict imposed through conflictual communication.

For the typical client at the start of therapy, the task of actually identifying the double bind at the same moment it occurs is difficult if not impossible. But in time he learns to rely on his body to tell him what is happening. Body work makes it possible for the client to identify his visceral reactions to interpersonal conflict. Specifically, he learns to identify embodied cues during his affective shift away from the assertive stance.

This body awareness is vital because it cuts through the manipulations of others, pushes the client past the anxiety of anticipated rejection and enables him to move into the assertive stance before he slips back down into shame.

After successful body work, one client reported, "I've learned that my body is my inner compass. It assesses the situation and my position in it. The lesson is that I can't just listen to words. I have to keep myself continually attuned to the message my body is giving me."

Definition of terms. The definitions of *affect, emotion, sensation* and *feelings* are often confused. In ordinary use, these terms are interchangeable. Nathanson (1992), however, offers us a useful distinction:

- *Affect* is the biological aspect of *feelings* and *sensations*, which are synonymous. Affect is what happens through the autonomic nervous system – changes in breathing, heart rate and so forth.

- *Feelings* and *sensations* are expressed through the language of *emotions*. They represent the internal or subjective experience of affect – butterflies, queasy stomach, energy in arms, squeezing throat, needles in shoulders, heavy weight in chest.

- *Emotions* are words that we use to describe the *sensations* and *feelings* of the bodily *affects* – such as anger, sadness, fear.

Sometimes we encounter obstacles to body work in the form of a problem in recognizing and naming what the body is telling us. Common words that name emotions may not accurately represent the body's message. Therefore, words that describe emotion should be "grounded" in bodily sensations/ feelings. For example,

CLIENT   I feel anger.
THERAPIST   Yes. How do you feel that anger now?
CLIENT   A rising heat in my chest.

By returning to his feelings/sensations, the client develops the skill of more directly reading his body's message, an ability helpful not only in the session but as a skill for everyday life.

The innate affects. The diagram on page 142 offers a very general "map" of embodied affect, within which are the many idiosyncratic variations for each client. For example, for some men vulnerability is felt as a focused pain under the left ribs. For others, it is a tingling tickle around the chest. While an ache or pain in the head is generally regarded as a defense of intellectualization, for some men sensations in the head actually reveal anger. These anger sensations radiate to the head through their clenched jaws.

In the final analysis, while generalizations can be made, the therapist will need to develop special sensitivity to learn the body language of each client and then to teach the client how to recognize it himself. As one thirty-two-year-old man said, "I lost my ability to understand what I was feeling. Now I'm renaming what I'm feeling inside – in fact, naming things I never knew."

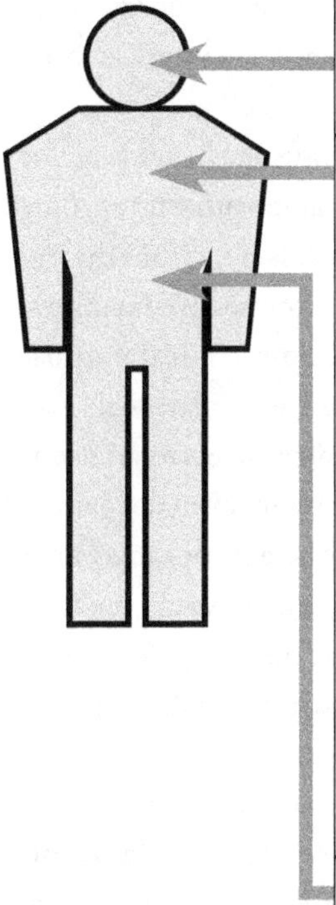

Location	Sensation	Affect
Head	Pain, ache, tightness, pressure	
Center Chest heart area	Tight, gripping, clenching, sharp stabbing pain	Fear
	Energy surging up and out to shoulders, arms, hands, legs, feet	Anger
	Dropping, weighted, heavy, hollow, empty, throat-pressure	Sadness
	Mental state: dazed, stunned, confused *Body posture:* head dropping, chin down, chest caved in, shoulders rolled inward, collapsed, curled up, turned inward, fetal posture	Shame
Abdomen	Queasy, jittery, "butterflies," nausea	Anxiety

Figure 7.1. Body language

The Four Negative Affects

The four innate affects that we will be focusing on are most often felt in the chest, solar plexus and heart area. We adopt the affective systems described by Tomkins (1981, 1991) and developed by Nathanson (1992). These terms offer the client a wide understanding of his affective experience. Their manifestations may range from mild to extreme.

1. *Fear/terror.* This is a feeling of tightness, gripping, clenching, clamping down, a sharp, stabbing pain, or "a tight fishing line around my chest." In body work, fear is described by the client as something happening inside that feels like "too much, too fast." When the client remains focused for awhile on this fear sensation, he may shift into shame/humiliation or else break through to anger/rage or distress/anguish, which are the interweaving pathways that offer an entry into grief work.

2. *Anger/rage.* This is a rising up and pushing out of energy, which radiates and extends to the shoulders, arms and hands. An impulse to kick is also an expression of anger.

3. *Distress/anguish.* This is a pulling-down feeling or a heaviness, with a dropping or weighted sensation, which is associated with a lump, block or tightness in the throat. Or it can be moisture/pressure within the eyes. Distress/anguish was described by one client as "an oppressive metal vest – but it's under my skin, and I can't take it off." For our clinical purposes we understand distress/anguish to be a consequence of relational loss.

Anger/rage and distress/anguish are the key entry affects to grief work, alternating from one to the other as the client moves into even deeper grief. The therapist should be mindful that these affects be appropriately attributed and not reversed in a self-defeating manner, which would mean distress/anguish for the other person, with anger/rage turned against the self.

4. *Shame/humiliation.* This feeling is identified as a shrinking, crunching, collapsing in the center of the chest; a caving in or a collapse into a void at the solar plexus. As one man said, "My shoulders are rolling in to my chest; I'm curling inward." Another man described it as "a balloon deflating inside my body.... The air is being pressed out of my chest." This embodied experience of shame has also been described this way: "My head is drooping like a plant wilting forward, needing to be watered."

The Two Positive Affects

Besides the four negative affects described above, we include two of Tomkins's (1982) positive affects, explained by Nathanson (1992). These innate affects are:

1. *Enjoyment/joy.* This is felt from the center of the chest as energy radiating forward, upward and out. The person feels open, filled up, expansive, solid and centered. Joy is often associated with the double-loop experience, which is accompanied by a feeling of deep emotional resonance with the other person. It is characterized by relaxation, a sense of relational connectedness, a calm centeredness within, a "lightness" or a burst of jump-up-and-do-it energy.

2. *Interest/excitement.* The face takes on the attitude of rapt attention and focused concentration on something (a feeling or idea). There is a

pleasurable increase in neural firing and a feeling of healthy pride and competence/pleasure.

These two positive affects are more frequently encountered toward the latter part of treatment when the client has begun to stay in his assertive self-state for longer periods of time. To simplify Nathanson's terminology for our own purposes, we will proceed using the following terms:

Table 7.1 Four Negative and Two Positive Innate Affects

The Four Negative Affects	The Two Positive Affects
Fear/terror → fear	Enjoyment/joy → joy
Anger/rage → anger	Interest/excitement → excitement
Distress/anguish → sadness	
Shame/humiliation → shame	

Besides the affects we address, there is one more innate affect – disgust – which is rarely addressed within the context of reparative therapy. However, clients will sometimes report it. One such example is from a thirty-eight-year-old architect who had long felt a strong aversion to the female body. He traced this disgust back to a memory, when he was about five years old, of being forced to have oral-vaginal sexual contact with his teenage sister. While there were other factors contributing to his homosexual problem, this memory, with its associated feeling of aversion and a resulting defensive anger toward all females, proved to be a significant obstacle to his heterosexual development.

Anxiety is one of the first feelings to emerge in body work. This is a reaction to some unconscious threat and is most often identified in the abdomen as a sensation of being queasy or jittery, with a sense of nausea or butterflies in the stomach. Focusing directly on the client's anxiety is usually counterproductive, as the anxiety may then become paralyzing. Rather, we try to sidestep anxiety with a phrase such as: "Let's see what feelings are behind your anxiety," or "What might be a deeper feeling?" Anxiety signals the emerging awareness of deep and conflicted innate affects which, when acknowledged, usually express themselves in fear.

Clients often report feeling anxiety just before they access some form of unacceptable truth. It is not the associated emotions per se that are unacceptable to feel, but the underlying, unbearable sense of annihilation-abandonment that the person cannot allow himself to acknowledge and reexperience.

In childhood, clients anticipate abandonment by loved ones whenever they feel and express their natural but unacceptable emotions. As one client explained:

> My folks could not tolerate my getting upset. I became too weird for them. We kids weren't supposed to have problems. Only they could be upset, because they were the adults. We got the message to keep our negative feelings inside us.

Clients' Use of Imagery and Spontaneous Pictures

In doing body work, the client may use images or pictures to describe internal states, such as, "My heart is dry and dusty," or "There is a black cannonball in my stomach." Unlike cognitions, which lead the client farther away from his feelings, these images are not detours away from affects but instead serve as bridging devices toward feelings and sensations. As with dreams, these spontaneous and primal creations often lead toward even deeper affect. The therapist may ask, "OK, so tell me, what does dry and dusty feel like?" or "How does that black cannonball feel inside you right now?"

Common Mislabelings

In body work, oftentimes there will be a mislabeling of the sensations.

Fear-anger conflict. When feeling this conflict, some men describe an unusual feeling of sharp pain – such as blades, knives or spikes stuck deep into the upper shoulders, lower neck and back. There is a tension between the impulse to release muscular tension and the impulse to constrict the muscles and hold back. As with isometric exercises, the result is a painful aching deep in the muscle tissue. After he moves beyond the fear-anger conflict down to a deeper level, the client then typically shifts into sadness and, finally, into grief.

Fear or anxiety? We sometimes need to help the client distinguish clearly between fear and anxiety. Fear springs directly from the awareness of a threatening object. With anxiety, the source is some internal, unconscious dread.

Sadness or shame? While sadness and shame are often evidenced at the same time, the distinction between them is important for the client to understand. Sadness is about something having been taken away. Shame involves a loss of self, that is, a self-diminishment or self-depletion.

Shame Need Not Be Intensified

While most feelings are worked through by confronting them, shame does not seem to be released by intensifying the feeling. What seems to alleviate it is not a direct confrontation but a surrendering or releasing of it. Shame slowly but surely evaporates when the person is able to feel and express it while at the same time experiencing close attunement with another person. In relationship with the therapist the client cannot experience both shame and acceptance in the same moment.

An Attitude of Respectful Attentiveness

When doing body work the therapist sets the tone by being slow, deliberate and calmly attentive. He conveys his curiosity, interest and concern for what is happening inside the client. This attitude is similar to what is aimed for in "mindful meditation" (Siegel, 2007), referred to as COAL (curiosity, openness, acceptance and love).

The therapist's patient yet serious interest conveys the unspoken message, Your emotional responses are not irrelevant or crazy. What goes on inside of you matters. This message is quite the opposite of the parental message given to the child of the triadic-narcissistic family, which was, What matters most is how *you* affect *us*. As the therapist communicates this implicit message of caring and attunement, the client gradually begins to experience and respect his inner compass, reflected in his body, of the interior world that he is now coming to know and accept.

CHAPTER 8

Reparative Body Work

The Concept of the Two-Triangle Sequence

Having reviewed the core and secondary affects and their corresponding embodied feelings, I will now detail the process of body work. This
technique was adapted by our clinic for our client population, whose
primary defense is emotional detachment (dissociation).

Passive-avoidant, emotionally unreachable men are the most problematic cases presented by our therapists in case supervision (sometimes
called "Teflon" or "jellyfish" clients), and previously, we had great difficulty
reaching them through standard therapeutic interventions. In spite of their
conscious desire to change, these men are highly resistant to accessing their
feelings. Most of them, it seemed, had learned to defend against emotional
vulnerability as a result of their childhood shame traumas.

We had previously used the intensive body work technique of intensive short-term dynamic psychotherapy (ISTDP), but its confrontational
approach – pressure and challenge designed to "create an intrapsychic
crisis leading to psychic disequilibrium in patients" (Coughlin Della
Selva, 1996, p. 68) – did not work well with our population, which is
highly shame-sensitive and distrustful of techniques that feel in any way
manipulative.

But when we modified the classic ISTDP model for use with our men,
a modified, gentler version of body work became our clinic's modality of
choice. (*Body work does not, I reemphasize, involve any physical touch.*)

Abreactive and emotive therapies focus primarily on catharsis and emotional release but often lack cognitive integration. By adopting the approach of ISTDP, reparative body work is particularly productive because it requires powerful emotive/affective work, which is then followed by narrative reconstruction (i.e., "meaning transformation").

Not every session calls for body work, but once client and therapist have decided on it, the two-triangle sequence should be carried out to its end. The two triangles are taken from Menninger's (1958) "triangle of insight" and Malan's (1979) "triangle of significant others," and were later redesigned for affect-release work.

The Session Sequence: A Brief Overview

The *triangle of containment* is designed to keep the client "contained" within the three points of the triangle – the identified conflict (IC), the therapist, and his own body-based feelings and impulses. At the same time we work to extinguish the anxiety and defenses that block the affective breakthrough that opens the client to the triangle of persons and meaning transformation (see fig. 8.1).

The *triangle of persons* gives understanding to the emerging emotions and impulses as they relate to past (P) and current (C) relationships, including the client-therapist relationship. (The triangle of containment

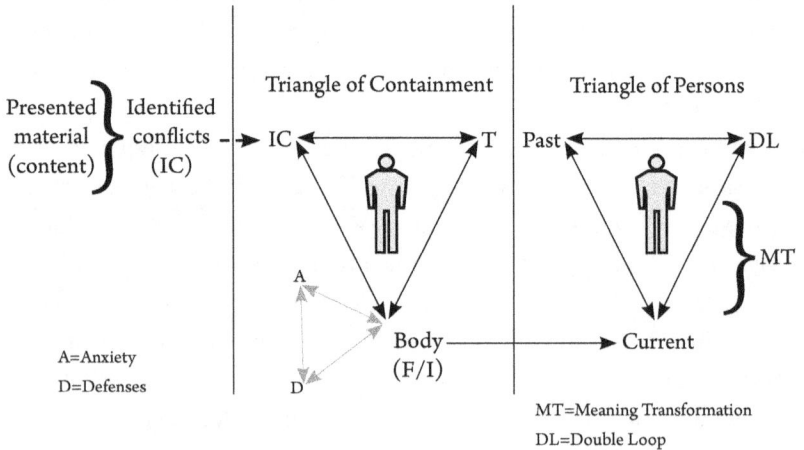

Figure 8.1 Session sequence

is adapted from ISTDP's "triangle of conflict," which originated with Menninger [1958]. Menninger identified the intrapsychic barriers preventing the client from penetrating his feelings and impulses about a threatening issue.)

At any one time during this session sequence the client will be at one of the three corners of the triangle as the therapist attempts to direct him to his feelings and impulses about the conflict (F/I). (In the original ISTDP model, the corner of the second triangle is "transference," in which the client is confronted with his transference projections; with an emphasis on the "working alliance," however, we substitute the one-dimensional aspects of transference for the complete, dyadic engagement of the double loop.)

Our therapeutic aim is to link all three points of both triangles, avoiding anxiety and defenses in each session, and to do so repeatedly during the course of treatment.

Systematic Desensitization

Reparative body work can be viewed as a method of systematic desensitization to emotional phobias (see McCullough et al., 2003). But in a more comprehensive understanding, the goal for the client is the "corrective emotional experience," which is to say, to learn to feel and express intolerable emotions while experiencing the therapist's attunement. Through this process the client experiences reparation of parental malattunement and gains greater self-compassion.

The inexperienced therapist will at first feel uncomfortable structuring the session to hold the client at a level of significant distress. But with continued practice the therapist's discomfort will be mitigated by the evident benefits to the client and particularly by the fast-forward momentum of treatment.

Body work is intended to evoke both emotional and cognitive reexperiencing of past trauma, that is, the shame moment. To accomplish this the interventions are necessarily uncomfortable and challenging. The client must be enabled to move past his anxiety and abandon his defenses in order to fully feel and express the emotions and impulses that will lead to an innate affect. The result is a psychic restructuring, often accompanied by an observable phenomenon called the "felt shift" of affective expansion.

In the first session the client needs to understand from the outset that body work is usually the best modality to fast-forward the healing process. At the same time he can choose not to engage in this or any other such approach if he wishes. He must always feel in control of the session, never being pushed to agree to something that feels uncomfortable.

The therapist should allow the client a trial session to experiment and see how body work feels for him. For example, the therapist may explain, "At times, we will be using a method to focus you on your feelings. I'll ask you to pay attention to your bodily sensation as a way of understanding yourself. I may seem rigid when I try to focus you narrowly at times, and it will take some getting used to."

The suggestion to use body work may arouse considerable apprehension in the client since the fear of emotional vulnerability is common to homosexual men. Yet surprisingly, I have found many clients quite open – even eager – to try something that promises significant progress.

The trial session provides the opportunity to evaluate the client's defensive or cooperative response, to test his ego strength and to determine whether or not he can actually handle this modality as part of the therapy. During the trial session the therapist explains that although psychotherapy is a supportive experience, it must also include some challenges. The client should be informed that he will be asked "feeling questions" in the "here and now."

For the apprehensive client frequent but shallow attempts with incremental steps may work best. For such a client the old rule applies best: Go slow to go fast.

Men with unwanted homosexuality evidence defensive strategies whenever they anticipate shame and humiliation. Therefore, body work should never be attempted in a manner that is too threatening. For the client who cannot identify feelings, it may be best for the therapist to back off from direct pressure and allow the client to express himself as he can. As the client speaks, the therapist listens for any indication of feelings, including gestures, posture, intonation or facial expression, and brings attention to that behavior, gently suggesting a feeling that may be under the surface. The therapist attempts to amplify whatever he infers the client is feeling. Then through the therapist's successive approximations, the client begins to familiarize himself with his own emotional life.

Through his attunement the therapist may become aware of the client's feelings before the client senses them himself. The therapist may say, "I can see what's happening now, I can sense what you're feeling. How would you describe it?" or "Stay with that feeling, it's important to feel that now." While maintaining the focus the therapist is also offering supportive comments as well: "You're doing a good job staying connected to what's inside. I know it's difficult, but I can see you working hard at this."

At times the client will become unfocused and bogged down with multiple or contradictory sensations such as, "I feel tightness in my chest and sinking in my stomach" or "I feel tension in my shoulders and energy in my arms." At such times it may be helpful to offer a choice; "Which one do you feel the most strongly right now?" "Of the two, which one is most intense?"

Counterindications to reparative body work. The therapist may identify some clients who show symptoms counterindicative to body work. These are symptoms of high anxiety such as hyperventilation, dizziness, disorientation, fragmented thinking, paranoia or a display of other regressive defenses.

When we see intense anxieties and fear about uncovering feelings, we understand that they are based on the terrifying apprehension of being shamed to the infantile level of annihilation-abandonment. His earliest experiences may have convinced him that if expressed, authentic feelings would lead to parental rejection and a sense of profound emptiness and unworthiness. Body work is designed to evoke this threatening affect, but is linked with the experience of emotional closeness with the therapist.

Our clinic's approach encourages clients to stay in contact with the therapist as he moves into deeper feelings. The therapist is constantly monitoring the working alliance: "Are you feeling connected to me as you are feeling these bodily sensations?" "As you go deeper, how are you feeling?"

Session sequence. The session progresses as follows:

Presented Material → Identified Conflict → Conflict Moment →
First Triangle → Second Triangle → Meaning Transformation

When the client begins the session with a report about the previous week's event, we may view this as simply the opening to more important work, but we need to listen respectfully and appreciate his need to tell his story. From this presented material, the therapist gradually attempts to synthesize an identified conflict (IC). For clients who grew up in the triadic-narcissistic family, being heard by a "significant other" with patience and attentiveness remains a vitally important relational experience.

Identifying the problem. It is often difficult for the client to identify any particular conflict since he tends to view himself through others' expectations of him. His chronic anticipatory shame posture distorts his ability to see what he is realistically entitled to. Consequently, his attempt to identify a conflict is often vague, indirect and implicit. The therapist must therefore focus him on his needs and try to crystallize the moment of conflict, pushing the client beyond his vagueness, generalities and role as a helpless complainer to actively "own" the challenges he faces.

Clients may indirectly report a conflict, with words such as, "I felt awkward, uncomfortable, out-of-place." We may hear a vague expression of anger or hurt, with the client saying something like, "I felt annoyed, frustrated, bothered, irritated." His inability to assess a situation clearly may also suggest a conflict: "I don't know what was going on with me. I just felt confused, surprised, bewildered, stunned."

The therapist should not settle for vague or indirect reporting of an incident, but encourage clear identification of the embedded conflict. "What do you mean? What 'annoys, bothers, upsets' you?" Eventually, the client's attention must be focused on his bodily feelings.

What do you want? Our client will easily lose focus on what he wants and needs. A question we must ask repeatedly and in various times during the session (a question typically not asked of the client by his family of origin) is, "Tell me, what is it you want here, in this situation?" The sort of passive-detached attitude we often see is described by one man as, "My attitude toward life is 'I'm not registered for class – I'm just auditing.'" Disconnectedness, alienation and passivity, for many men, have become a lifestyle. We therefore work to shift the client from being a passive recipient (or helpless victim) into an active participant in every session, with questions such as, "What do you want to work on today?"

The therapist may come alongside the client and suggest he enter deeper into his vague feelings. "As I'm listening to you describe your boss,

I'm hearing some intense feelings. I'm wondering if we can explore your deeper feelings" or "You say your mother 'annoys' you. Can we see what is behind that word 'annoys'?"

When the identified conflict has been defined to both therapist and client's satisfaction, the therapist then invites the client to do body work. The client's agreement to this step will mark his entry into the triangle of containment. Client and therapist focus together on his embodied experience *in the present* about the past conflict.

Directing the client away from his defenses (D) and anxiety (A) and encouraging him to be attendant to his bodily feelings/impulses (F/I), the therapist moves the client toward ever fuller expression of a deeper affect: fear, sadness, anger, grief and so on. To accomplish this the therapist must shift to a more rigid stance, holding the client to the protocol. His pace must be slow and deliberate, conveying respect and value for the client's gradual attempts to identify his feelings, and conveying an attitude opposite to many parents' disqualifying, dismissive, judgmental or indifferent response to his unfolding interior experience.

When the client fully experiences and expresses his present feelings and impulses, he is then directed to the triangle of persons, making links between his current (C) and past (P) relationship(s). This is the time when he is affectively most open to making such cognitive links.

The last corner of the second triangle considers the client-therapist relationship within the context of their work together. Here, the therapist attempts to connect the identified core feeling to all the points (persons) in the triangle of persons.

Finally, client and therapist will explore the client's new understandings of the original identified conflict. Throughout the session sequence, the therapist is ever mindful of and monitoring the working alliance.

From identified conflict to conflict moment. We might say that the distinction between the "identified conflict" and the "conflict moment" is the difference between a video clip and a photo snapshot.

To make this distinction, we have found it helpful to focus on the key moment within the conflict situation: that "snapshot within the video clip" that contains the strongest feeling. It has been our experience that once the larger conflict has been identified, the actual conflict moment is quickly recalled. This snapshot contains the most intense bodily discomfort and best serves as entrée into the first triangle. The client is encouraged to feel *now* the feelings that occurred then: "What is it like for you *right now* to recall that moment? What are you feeling now, *in your body*, as you tell me about that conflict?"

Here are three examples:

1. *Identified conflict.* "My boss takes advantage of me. He expects me to do whatever he wants at any time. Last week he asked me to work overtime just as I was about to go home for the day."

Conflict moment. "I was standing at my desk, my car keys in my hand and he was standing in the doorway."

2. *Identified conflict.* "My problem is relating to the guys at work. I tried to practice what you told me to do during coffee break. I forced myself to talk to a few of them standing around, but I felt very uncomfortable. They seemed unfriendly."

Conflict moment. "I'm in the middle of the room and they seem separate from me, like there's a space between them and me. And one guy, Tony, is looking at me like 'What do *you* want?'"

3. *Identified conflict:* "My mother annoys me. She has no consideration for my life. Last night she asked me to pick up her prescription, but it could have waited until the next day."

Conflict moment: "I was just calling to see how she was feeling and suddenly she says, 'Oh, I need my medicine right *now*!' I was standing in the kitchen with the phone in my hand."

Once the conflict is identified, it is unproductive to further discuss the event itself; rather, the therapist remains focused on the feelings/impulses that exist about it in the present moment.

The conflict moment itself, when clearly identified, gives a visual context to the ensuing body work. Defenses that arise against the body work can then be challenged by recalling the client's own descriptive words for the conflict moment.

The Working Alliance

In response to our client population's particular difficulty with trust issues, reparative therapy gives special importance to the working alliance. Only through the working alliance can the therapist offer a corrective experience to his client's past emotional betrayals. That a salient man may truly have his best interest at heart is often a hope too difficult to sustain. Through a trusting relationship with a same-sex therapist, he can begin to surrender his posture of anticipatory shame.

The working alliance can be viewed both within the wider context of the entire course of therapy and within the narrower context of the individual sessions. A good definition of the working alliance within the overall treatment is that the therapist and client together agree on goals and objectives as defined by the client. Within each individual session the working alliance is then regularly reaffirmed by having the client choose the identified conflict; that is, the therapist may clarify, "So we agree that this is a problem that you would like to work on for yourself today."

Talking About the Relationship

Recent studies of therapeutic efficacy reveal the importance of "talking about us." Time spent in mutual discussion of the therapeutic relationship is invariably well spent. Connectedness with the therapist should be established early on and maintained as the foundation for countering upcoming defenses against painful affects. We must "bring into the room" (consider and discuss) any moments of misunderstanding which hinder the client's deactivation of his shame-based defenses.

Dialogue involving mutual understanding is important, that is, commenting on and expressing personal experiences, such as asking, "How we are getting along?" "How is this working for you?" "Is what we are doing helpful?" "Do you feel that I understand you?" Such questioning helps him to process and integrate any secret doubts. And rather than just reacting to split-off aspects of the self, the client is encouraged to verbalize his affective experiences to the therapist so that he can gain intrapsychic integration of them.

Reparative therapy requires the working alliance to function within a very small circle, an intimate psychological space. Stylistically, it is up-close, face-to-face, eye-to-eye. Within this small theater there are only four parameters; it's simply "*You* and *me, here* and *now.*"

As client and therapist assess how they, as a team, are working toward the client's defined goals, they continue to monitor the working alliance. Ever mindful of the central importance of the working alliance, we move beyond classic psychoanalysis's one-sided analysis of the transference into a mutual examination of the relationship, encouraging the client to take an egalitarian role in his own therapy. The optimal outcome of this analysis is the double loop.

Addressing the transference. An analysis of the transference remains an important part of therapy. How the client projects conflicted and painful past relationships onto the therapist is a central feature of treatment and provides a powerful (if often painfully challenging) opportunity to move the growth process forward.

The two-triangle sequence offers a special opportunity to address the transference (see fig. 8.1 on p. 149, third corner of the second triangle). Following a discussion of past and current figures in the client's life, the therapist then inquires as to how he, the therapist, may evoke similar feelings in the client: "You felt intimidated by your boss, which prompted you to recall feeling intimidated by your older brother. I'm wondering if you sometimes feel intimidated by me?"

This inquiry is an opportunity for a more focused look at the working alliance using the P → C link as a starting point, and may go beyond the narrow P → C comparison to consider any aspect of the therapeutic relationship.

In classic ISTDP the therapist looks at the client's projection onto him. Our adaptation extends this into an interactive exchange where the therapist personally responds. Both men look at how they may have contributed to a transference projection, with such projections being resolved through the double loop.

The often-found narcissistic features associated with our client population require the therapist to maintain exquisite attunement with any interaction that could provoke narcissistic injury. Malattunement on the part of the therapist could prompt the client to turn the therapist into a bad object: "You don't understand me, you can't/won't understand me."

The client's negative feelings about the therapist, no matter how indirectly expressed, should be addressed as an immediate order of business. This is similar to the old psychoanalytic rule (although not as egalitarian):

"First, address the resistance." To do so early on is to avoid any later and possibly insurmountable difficulties. I ask the client, "How are you feeling *here* with me *now*?" Only after the client has fully articulated any negative feelings, including his projections on the therapist, should the therapist examine and articulate his own reactions to the client: "Let me tell you how I see you right now, what I'm feeling about you."

Countertransference. The novice therapist who is new to body work may find himself feeling uneasy about pushing the client into uncomfortable feelings and sensations. As helpers professionally committed to the alleviation of human suffering, we sometimes find it difficult to actively evoke, then hold the client in a state that can be one of intense emotional discomfort. Meanwhile, beneath his own discomfort, the therapist may encounter unresolved issues from his own past. These unresolved personal losses may compromise the effect of the body work he does with his clients.

In training reparative therapists, we tell them, "Assess your countertransference issues if you find yourself excusing the client from doing his body work."

The therapist should keep in mind that he is not *inflicting* but rather *eliciting* repressed painful experiences, so that the client may move to self-understanding. He plays a vital role in that he is a key person in the client's life who can respect and affirm his right to feel, express and work through his pain.

Naturally, many therapists are more comfortable focusing on feelings about outside figures, neglecting the subject of the client's feelings for the therapist. Addressing those feelings, especially negative ones, typically evokes anxiety within the therapist, thus contributing to his unconscious collusion with the client in avoiding the discussion. Over time, however, unaddressed negative transference and countertransference will contribute to increasing difficulties.

During body work, the therapist must make many moment-to-moment decisions: to elicit, to support, to challenge or just to wait. When the client pauses or is tentative, the therapist conveys an attitude of patient waiting, but also indicates attentive anticipation, as if trusting that the client is on the brink of moving to deeper feelings.

For the client who, in childhood, rarely had his true feelings recognized and appreciated, the therapist must model high regard for the client's personal experience. His tone must mirror the client's affect and convey deep appreciation for his interior perception. He shows his respect not simply by hearing but also by repeating and amplifying the client's words in robust form, echoing the tentative expression of his subjective experience with understanding and clear esteem.

Penetration into his deeper feelings creates for the client a sort of altered state, a suspension in the present moment. While in this disoriented and vulnerable state, he must have a safe holding environment that allows him to weave together the frayed affective threads.

Many sessions end with a conversation like the following:

CLIENT   I probably told you about the most repulsive part of myself. I don't even know how you could stand to listen to me.

THERAPIST   I feel privileged that you shared these painful and shameful aspects of yourself. I can understand how difficult this has been for you. I admire how you've been so honest with me.

CLIENT   Well, thanks... I appreciate your understanding.

An ideal conceptualization of the working alliance would be a continual double looping – the back and forth and back again of the client's disclosure met with the therapist's acceptance, encouragement and attunement met with the client's expression of his experience of that attunement met with further disclosure.

Collaborative approach offers empowerment. Sometimes the client is following his affects and expressing his feelings and bodily sensations, but then suddenly he takes a defensive detour (such as an intellectualization or a return to a discussion of content). One quick maneuver that is effective in neutralizing this defense is the "dismissive strategy," where the therapist simply ignores and overrides the defense, returning the client's attention to his most recently expressed feeling. This may succeed in getting him quickly back on track. But if he offers continued resistance, then the collaborative strategy may be required.

The collaborative approach, with its open dialogue about obstacles, involves the therapist pointing out the client's defenses and contrasting them with his most recently expressed feeling: "This is what I see you doing, which I don't think is helpful to you."

The therapist may then offer a choice: "Either we can continue to [naming defense] as you are doing now, or we can return to [naming most recently expressed feeling]. I believe [naming the feeling] to be important to look at, but if you don't want to do that now, we can do something else. So what would you like us to do?" Or "This is my thought about what we should do now, but what you think is best for you?" Addressing blocks through this collaborative approach is essential for our clients, who typically feel disempowered in relationships.

Triangle of Containment

The triangle of containment (see fig. 8.1 on page 146) consists of restricting the client's focus of attention on three points: (1) the identified conflict, (2) his body and (3) contact with the therapist.

The therapist's goal is to move the client away from anxiety (A) and defenses (D) to deeper-level feelings and impulses (F/I). The goal of this phase is to neutralize the client's anxiety and help him drop his defenses in order to deepen and then express a core feeling regarding the conflict. This is done while maintaining emotional connection with the therapist.

Resistance in the form of anxiety and defenses blocks the client from working through painful feelings and impulses, and also blocks connectedness between himself and the therapist. Conversely, when there is an unblocking of anxiety and defenses, this is immediately experienced by the client as connecting him with both himself and the therapist. This connectedness is later consciously explored and verbalized in the double loop (third corner, second triangle).

Common defenses (D). Defenses take many forms: evasiveness, rumination, obsessiveness, intellectualization (expressing ideas instead of feeling feelings) and self-defeating ideation. More generic and subtle defenses include vagueness, lack of focus, unconnectedness or shallow contact, generalized complaints, helplessness, inability to feel and express anything, and continual flat affect.

The defenses most commonly seen in reparative therapy are those associated with narcissistic personality types, particularly overdramatization, theatricality, and self-pity. In addition, clients with the more narcissistic personality features may display brittle defensiveness, object splitting, feeling slighted or insulted, and feeling hopelessly misunderstood.

The therapist's task is to identify these defenses and repeatedly point out (but not interpret) them to his client as they arise. The intent is to gently but firmly return him back to his feelings/impulses.

It is helpful to name defenses in ways the client can understand: "You're changing subjects." A catchy phrase for the identified defense can be helpful, for example, "You're acting helpless," "You're going numb," "You're acting scared," "You're going into your head." As the therapist repeatedly names these defenses, the client can more quickly identify them as they come up.

In a tone conveying his active concern, the therapist points out the realistic consequences of holding onto these defenses. The self-defeating consequences are clearly but compassionately presented. In a gentle yet confronting manner, he may ask, "How long have you been doing this to yourself? And at what cost?" With sufficient positive transference, the client will begin to surrender his defenses and join in the working alliance.

As a result of the conflict between his defenses and the working alliance, the client slowly disidentifies from his defenses, aligning himself ever deeper with the therapist. In this way the defenses gradually become ego-dystonic. As both therapist and client work together in separating and naming those defenses, the client will eventually abandon them. As they work the triangle, the client develops trust, deepens the transference and further surrenders those blocks to his progress.

There are two general categories of defenses encountered in body work: *intrapsychic* defenses and *interpersonal* defenses (Coughlin Della Selva, 1996). Characteristics of each include:

1. *Intrapsychic Defenses*

    • intellectualization

    • rationalization

    • deflection

    • minimization

    • introjection

- displacement

- helplessness

- reaction formation

The more regressive intrapsychic defenses (indicating greater impairment of ego functioning) include:

- projection

- argumentativeness

- somaticization

- denial

- behavioral enactment

- discharge of impulse

2. *Interpersonal Defenses*

In addition to the intrapsychic defenses there are the interpersonal ones, what Davanloo (1995) calls "tactical defenses." These fall into two categories; verbal and nonverbal.

2.1. Verbal Tactical Defenses

- vagueness

- generalities

- contradicting statements

- sarcasm

- excessive verbiage (making dialogue impossible)

- diversification (jumping from topic to topic)

2.2. Nonverbal Tactical Defenses

- avoidance of eye contact

- smiling and giggling

- weepiness

- air of detachment

- arms/legs crossed

Anxiety (A). The second category of resistance is anxiety, defined as a physiological reaction regarding a threat to the sense of self. Anxiety symptoms include headaches, increased heart rate, sweating, dry mouth, numbness and disturbed breathing. When anxious, the more fragile clients will experience cognitive disruption, disorientation, losing track of thoughts, scattered or foggy thinking, dissociation, depersonalization, heightened sensory awareness, inability to stay focused, feelings of dizziness, and difficulty in formulating and expressing their ideas.

Normal or "entry level" anxiety (typically located in the abdominal area) usually serves as a prelude to core feelings. These sensations include what the client may describe as feeling jittery, flip-flops, queasy, butterflies or knots. These anxieties or pre-emotions will give way to authentic or core feelings located in the chest area. Among those authentic feelings in the chest area we often see fear that gives way to anger or sadness and, later, grief.

Thus the sequence we see is anxiety → fear → anger/sadness → grief.

More serious anxiety symptoms include vasomotor changes, musculoskeletal disturbances, trembling, paralysis, increased sweating, sense of impending danger, bodily tension, hypervigilance, and apprehensive self-absorption. Psychosomatic symptoms include preoccupation with the body, feeling weak, sick or experiencing vague physical symptoms. Anxiety can involve mental disorganization, foggy thinking or numbness in the head. Physically the client may experience pressure or tension in the pit of the stomach or tension in the striated muscles.

The therapist must determine the client's ability to tolerate these symptoms, since intense or overwhelming anxiety symptoms indicate that he is unready for body work. In such cases, client and therapist may need to slow down and develop a stronger working alliance, or lay the foundation with other preparatory work.

A method developed by Davanloo (1995) to dispel anxiety is to have the client identify the form in which he expresses his anxiety: "Let's see how your body 'signals' anxiety to you." In doing so, the client takes a detached observation of his symptoms, which diminishes their intensity. Identifying the physical sensations as anxiety offers the client a sense of mastery, leading to eventual awareness of his core feelings.

Another effective method is to shift the client's attention away from his anxiety by suggesting further exploration. For example, "Let's see what might be behind that" or "Where does that lead us?"

Feelings/impulses (F/I).

1. Fear. As the client moves beyond anxiety (abdomen area) he touches on core feelings typically felt in the chest/upper torso. There, he may first encounter fear. Experienced as a gripping, clenching, squeezing feeling, fear may be further described as "constricting wires, cables or straps" tied around the upper chest area. Sometimes the client's sensation of fear is described as a tight knot or hard ball at the solar plexus or center chest.

If attended to, fear will usually release to either anger or sadness (loss).

2. Anger. Inevitably, along the course of tracking feelings, anger will be encountered, at which time the therapist is advised to follow through by encouraging the client to express the anger. The therapist should be quick to point out any evidence of anger impulses, such as a jerking or thrashing outward of extremities. The clenching of the jaw or fists also should be pointed out. It is also critical that both client and therapist identify the object (person) toward whom the anger is directed. Anger toward self is self-defeating and shame-evoking.

We have found it is helpful for the client who is conflicted between anger and guilt to distinguish between the "good part" and "bad part" of the other (mother, father, etc.). The therapist may explain, "I know _____ loved you, but there was this other side where he/she did _____ to you, which really hurt you," and the like.

It may sometimes be appropriate to utilize a *scenario of violence.* This visualization method helps the client access the depths of his anger and facilitate its embodied expression. By employing visual techniques to create this scenario, he is encouraged to play out the imagined scene in detail to completion. While reminding the client that this is only a fantasy, that in fact he does not really want to (and he should not) engage in violent behavior, the therapist may ask, "What kind of a scenario would release your anger?"

As the client visualizes violence against someone in the fantasy, he is encouraged to detail the scene: "Where does this take place?" "How do you punch him? With your left hand or right hand?" "Is he fighting back?" "What is his facial expression?"

A fantasy scenario may be utilized to evoke tension and muscle activity in the chest, shoulders, arms, hands and legs. The somatic region where most people feel their anger is in the striated muscles (i.e., the striking muscles).

However, anger work does not encourage emotional outbursts, high emotionality or theatrics, since screams and shouting are sometimes exhibitionistic defenses against authentic anger. We want anger to be fully felt and expressed within the body, yet contained. This scenario of violence should be continued until there is no more bodily-felt anger.

The expression of intense anger is a transformative process that many therapists have difficulty tolerating. It is necessary for the therapist to monitor his own discomfort so that the client is free to express his anger.

Anger, when focused, intensified and fully expressed, leads to an affective shift. Coughlin Della Selva (1996), Davanloo (1995) and other clinicians report that successful completion of the violent fantasy often ends in remorse and regret, with feelings of hollowness, emptiness and a void in the chest and in the heart area, followed by an integrative phase of compassion and love.

It is sometimes easier for the client to get *angry at the therapist* than to direct the anger toward a significant figure in his family life (usually a parent). Still, he may need to enact a "scenario of violence" toward the therapist before he can address his anger at a significant other.

At this point, aware of his own countertransference reaction, the therapist needs to permit the client to experience and express his anger toward him: "How do you experience that anger toward me right now?" "If you had the freedom to do violence toward me, how would you do it? What would you do right now?"

It is understandably difficult for the therapist to remain empathetically attuned while the client is expressing murderous rage toward him. Resisting his own discomfort, the therapist should try to refrain from premature interpretation or reassurance. Rather, the task is to allow the client to project his anger onto the therapist, while the therapist contains his own tension and discomfort. Most often, this anger is followed by expressions of guilt, shame or remorse. The therapist should reassure the client that his expression of anger did not affect his care, concern or commitment to him.

3. *Sadness*. Rather than moving from fear into anger, the client may move to sadness, usually felt as a dropping, sinking, heavy feeling in his center-lower chest (sometimes upper abdomen). As with anger, it is important for both client and therapist to be clear about the person toward whom the sadness is directed, because sadness for another rather than sadness for oneself only serves to in intensify the shame.

Anger and sadness often go back and forth, with one emotion moving into the other. Sudden shifts between the two may confuse or discourage the client, but the therapist should supportively encourage expression of whichever emotion is most strongly felt in the moment, since one supports and leads to the other. Together these two emotions lead the client to grief work.

Daryl, an eighteen-year-old college student, receives about three phone calls per day from his mother, from whom he has had great difficulty disentangling himself. Throughout many sessions, Daryl *alternated between fear and anger* toward his mother, sometimes confusing sadness for her with sadness for himself.

CLIENT	My mom was talking to me the other day and she said, "Oh, Daryl, you are my best friend."
THERAPIST	How did that feel?
CLIENT	Weird.
THERAPIST	Do you want to do body work on this?
CLIENT	Sure.
THERAPIST	(*repeats Daryl's mother's words*) "Daryl, you are my best friend." What comes up?
CLIENT	An awkward feeling. Tense. I know it's not right.
THERAPIST	But that's a thought.
CLIENT	Well, disgust.
THERAPIST	Where?
CLIENT	In the stomach. Yeah – an uneasy feeling in my stomach. (*after a moment*) I feel sorry for her, though.

THERAPIST	So what's that feeling?
CLIENT	Tightness in the chest.
THERAPIST	Stay with that.
CLIENT	I feel sorry for her loneliness. I do want her to have a best friend, but I know it shouldn't be me. But it's hard for me to say, "Mom, I can't be your best friend" because I want her to be happy.
THERAPIST	Sure you do. What's the feeling?
CLIENT	That it's not healthy.
THERAPIST	But the feeling?
CLIENT	In the stomach. I feel a tension...
THERAPIST	Where else?
CLIENT	Hands and feet.
THERAPIST	Stay with it.
CLIENT	Fidgety...
THERAPIST	Yeah. And where's "fidgety"?
CLIENT	In my arms and legs. (*feet are twitching back and forth*)
THERAPIST	I can see that.
CLIENT	And in my fingers. (*closing and opening fingers*)
THERAPIST	So, what do you think you are feeling?
CLIENT	Frustration. Irritation.
THERAPIST	What's the emotion word?
CLIENT	Maybe anger?
THERAPIST	Not sure? Try to picture her face. What would you say to her?
CLIENT	"But Mom, I can't be your best friend!"
THERAPIST	Where do you feel that?
CLIENT	In my hands and feet.
THERAPIST	Good. Can you feel it from your chest?
CLIENT	(*considering, then slowly nodding*)
THERAPIST	What's the feeling in the chest?
CLIENT	Tingliness. A surge.
THERAPIST	OK, so tell her from that place – from your chest.
CLIENT	(*more forcefully*) "Mom, I can't be your best friend. I don't want to be your best friend. It's not good for me!"

4. *Grief.* The expression of sadness and anger eventually moves the client into bereavement (grief), which is more of a self-state than an affect, imparting a broad feeling of devastating void and utter loss. Grief usually follows from sadness as the heavy-weighted feeling becomes an empty hollowness in the chest. As he goes yet deeper, grief spreads and seems even more pervasive, leaving him feeling suspended in time.

Grief work is a necessary phase for the completion of reparative therapy, although the depth and extent of this work is determined by variations in each individual case (see part three).

The overlooked impulse (I). While most of our attention is on the F (feelings) of F/I, there is another aspect to consider: the impulse (I), which is too often overlooked if the therapist is not attending to the client's subtle bodily shifts. The therapist should be mindful of any unexpected gestures or behaviors and appropriately point them out as suggestive of deeper feelings: "I noticed that you just slumped your shoulders" (shame); "I can see you moving your legs" (anger); "Look at how you are tightening your fists" (anger); "Your facial expression seems flat, and your eyes look downcast" (sadness). Reflecting back to the client his slight bodily shifts will serve to enhance his sense that his feelings and reactions are valid.

Triangle of Persons

The second triangle, the "triangle of persons" (Malan, 1979), is a cognitive process that follows after the client has experienced an innate affect. The basic rule is: *First affect, then insight.* To attempt insight before release of affect only reinforces intellectualization. As it is said, "First he undergoes, then he knows."

The triangle of persons (see fig. 8.1 on p. 146) represents the client's three core relationships: significant persons in his past (P), in the current life (C), and now the therapist (DL).

The first triangle questions are Where? (where in the body) and What? (what does it feel like in the body?), while the second triangle questions are Who? and When? (in the past) and Why? (self-motivation).

When it has been determined that the client has experienced and expressed F/I to the level of a core feeling, then the therapist moves the client's attention to the triangle of persons. Factors that determine when to shift to the second triangle include time constraints and the client's capacity for going deeper into feelings and impulses, at least for that session.

The lowering of defenses and the release of feelings and impulses facilitate affectively based cognitive links between his past (P) and current (C) relationships. "As you're feeling _____, I'm wondering if there was a time in your past when you had this same feeling?" or "I wonder if someone else in your past created that same feeling in you?" Even though this is a cognitive inquiry, the link from P to C is actually through an embodied memory. This recall to the past person necessitates the accessing of an embodied memory, which is then made cognitively understandable through comparison. What follows recall of this memory is not just an intellectual insight, but a *felt* insight, akin to the Aha experience of Karl Bühler (1990).

It is the addition of insight into the triangle of persons, offered at the time of affective expansion, which makes body work more than a mere abreaction (emotional catharsis or body-tension release). Thus after the emotional breakthrough and release of affect, there is a discussion of the historical context of understanding.

Double looping. In the original intensive short-term dynamic psychotherapy (ISTDP) model, the third corner of the second triangle is T (transference), which confronts the patient with his transference projections. Rather than confrontation/interpretation, our "kinder, gentler" version addresses the transference within the context of the double loop. This two-way exchange accommodates our client's sensitivity to shame reactions. In addition, during the double loop, the therapist models authentic vulnerability and offers an opportunity for the client to experience moments of intimacy.

The therapist initiates the double loop experience by beginning in the same way as the ISTDP approach. The common theme linking C to P is now applied to T. The therapist may ask: "Both your boss (C) and your father (P) intimidated you; I wonder if sometimes I have that intimidating effect on you?" or "We noticed that your wife (C) and your mother (P) elicit in you a compliant, 'nice guy' role. Do you think that false self emerges in our relationship as well?"

From T to DL. From this investigation of T (transference) within the context of the P-C (past-current) link, the therapist may move deeper into the DL (double loop). The therapist may ask, "How did you feel about me [my work with you] during this period of time? Did you feel I understood you? What could I have done differently? How better could I have helped you? How does it feel to be understood by me? Did we work well together?" These questions are designed to encourage open "discussion about us," leading to a conscious experience of the intimate sharing which has taken place.

Therapist as compared to others in client's life. To facilitate the double loop experience, the therapist may encourage the client to compare his experience with him to others in his life, past or present. "Has there ever been anyone else with whom you felt this level of understanding?" "Have you ever shared this depth of [information, vulnerability, exposure, painful memory, etc.] with anyone else?" Asking the client to articulate his experience of acceptance fosters cognitive ownership and reinforces the experience.

Meaning transformation (MT). In the meaning transformation phase of the session sequence, the therapist encourages the client to articulate the significance of the session thus far. Reminding him of his original identified conflict, the therapist asks what he has learned from the session sequence. "We started with _____ [repeat the identified conflict]. What have you learned [accomplished, gained, discovered, realized] about yourself?"

The final 7–10 minutes for single (45-min.) sessions or 15–20 minutes for double (hour-and-a-half) sessions should be spent on the exploration of such questions as, What will you take away today? What do you understand about yourself? What have you gotten out of all this? What stands out for you as being helpful in this session?

To encourage the client to explore and own his feelings, the therapist cognitively reinforces his embodied experiences. This is particularly important for our client population that denies their personal power and self-determination. When the client has said all that he can about what he has learned, the therapist may reinforce, supplement and expand on those hesitant insights.

This phase offers the client the opportunity to create a meaningful narrative of his experience. In so doing, he sees more closely how he perpetuates his self-defeating patterns of behavior. Often these maladaptive behaviors represent illusions and distortions that need to be faced realistically and eventually abandoned.

Distortions of reality. Unrecognized fears compel the client to create illusions and distortions of reality. These, in turn, will cause a faulty writing of his autobiography. These adaptational defenses that worked during childhood are now, in adulthood, maladaptive and self-defeating. In the process of recognizing and uprooting these defenses, the client exchanges this symptomatic behavior for a more realistic perception of himself and others.

We ask the client, "How has your body work informed your original identified conflict?" This question reinforces his awareness that all the functions of the brain are mediated through the body. It is the body that mediates between the brain and the world. An altered bodily response to an object will alter the cognitive meaning of that object. Body work regarding the identified conflict often leads to the insight that in fact it is not a conflict at all.

Further, not only is the meaning of the object of conflict transformed, but in the larger context, the split-off and "problematic" part of the self is also transformed in relation to that object. A felt shift about the object cannot happen except within the larger context of the narrative self: "I experience that part of me differently now, because I see the conflict in a different way."

Authenticity and vitality. An embodied shift regarding the original object of conflict prompts a meaning transformation regarding that object. The new narrative is more comprehensive – not only acknowledging the actual facts (of the original conflict) but also broadening to take in the larger context of one's life. From this perspective of personal truth, the client comes to feel that, at last, it all makes sense. From this Gestalt or totality-of-the-person shift, there emerges a sense of authenticity and vitality. "Isn't that what we mean by insight," says Shapiro (Solomon et al., 2001), "two neural networks linking up? The earlier information from childhood now links up with mature understanding." At this time, Shapiro says, we see changes "on a facial level, a full body level, an emotional level, and an insight level. It's simply two networks linking up" (p. 122).

Accompanying this alteration is a focused and heightened sense of self-awareness, with an inner calm and greater certainty. No longer preoccupied with the past, the client begins talking about his present and future. He may speak about his long-term plans or just the immediate future: "I'm looking forward to today. I want to slow down, go for a walk, enjoy the day."

Although our therapy is essentially secular, the client may see his life from a religious perspective, which contributes to his now-expanding outlook. The client may now see God's guiding hand in the changes that occur in his life, along with other blessings and gifts not previously recognized. Thus it is from a sense of deep gratitude and humility that he feels a prompting to reach out to help other people – often men with similar struggles.

Adherence to Session Sequence

The two-triangle sequence has been developed and refined over many years to become, in our view, a highly effective method of therapeutic change. As much as possible the training therapist is encouraged to follow the sequence closely. However, the question may arise, how closely should it be followed?

The basic rule is: We should be willing to compromise the session sequence to follow the clients' affect. It is the pursuit of affective expression that produces therapeutic insight. To dismiss spontaneous-feeling expression for the sake of "the model" is to be the "bad parent" who pursues his own agenda rather than attuning to the child's (client's) own needs.

Following the affect. In this example, the therapist is working the triangles and attempts to move from (F/I) to (P), but the client suddenly makes available the opportunity to double loop. Allowing the client to take the lead, the therapist wisely compromises the orthodox two-triangle sequence and follows the client's affective response. The client is thus able to express his deep needs for masculine affirmation and to feel heard and understood in the process.

CLIENT   Last Wednesday night I went to my usual spot.
THERAPIST   What's that?
CLIENT   (*hesitantly*) The bathhouse. (*sigh*) Whenever I act out, the

next day I feel this lowered esteem. I'm not good at my job the next day.

THERAPIST   (*identifying the conflict*) So, you're talking about the conflict you felt as a result of your acting out; that it affects your self-esteem and your work.

CLIENT   (*nods*)

THERAPIST   Do you want to address that, John?

CLIENT   I guess. OK.

THERAPIST   All right.

CLIENT   (*client nods, waits*)

THERAPIST   OK. Can you recall a moment when you felt that lowered self-esteem most intensely?

CLIENT   Yeah, when I woke up and had to go to work, I didn't want to get out of bed, didn't want to move.

THERAPIST   (*softly*) So, when you say that, what does it bring up for you?

CLIENT   Hmm...fear, sadness and shame.

THERAPIST   (*nods*) Are you feeling these feelings now?

CLIENT   Um...I'm certainly feeling some of them, yes.

THERAPIST   Let's focus in on that.

CLIENT   OK.

THERAPIST   (*waiting*) What exactly is it that you're feeling now?

CLIENT   (*considers*) Well, fear. Certainly...that's what I'm experiencing, yes.

THERAPIST   How is that for you?

CLIENT   I feel shaky...My stomach is churning. I feel a lot of anxiety...tense. (*long pause, then blurts out*) Actually, I just feel lost.

THERAPIST   So the fear – for you – moves into the feeling of "lost"?

CLIENT   (*nods*)

THERAPIST   (*gently*) OK, John...How does "lost" feel in your body?

CLIENT   Um, a heavy sinking.

THERAPIST   Where?

CLIENT   Here. (*pointing to upper stomach*)

THERAPIST   So that's "feeling lost"?

CLIENT   (*nodding*) Hmm...lost, yeah. Sadness.

THERAPIST   Can you feel that sadness now?

CLIENT   (*nodding*)

THERAPIST   (*returning him to the body*) Where in your body, John, do you feel that?

CLIENT   In its heavy weight.

THERAPIST   Sure, heavy in your body. I can see that...you look uncomfortable. Burdened down...

CLIENT   And tenseness.

THERAPIST   Can you give me an idea where?

CLIENT   Ah, like a lump in the throat.

[A lump in throat generally represents holding back crying; the lump is constriction.]

THERAPIST   OK. Lump in throat.

CLIENT   Yeah.

THERAPIST   (*softly*) So the heavy tension in your body leads to feeling that lump in your throat. Tell me, John, are you actually feeling that now?

CLIENT   Yes.

THERAPIST   (moves to second triangle) OK, can you think of another time when you've felt very much like you feel now?

[Client is obviously in conflict, and after considerable hesitation, shifts away from the therapist's question about his past and addresses his present feelings for the therapist.]

CLIENT   Um. (*long pause, heavy sigh*) Nothing is coming to mind. I'm sure I've felt this before.

THERAPIST   (*noticing an impulse*) You let out a big, heavy sigh there. What was that saying?

CLIENT   Well, to be truthful, you are making me feel deep sadness because what you're giving me now is what I'm really looking for – acceptance and affirmation from a man.

THERAPIST   Yes. Tell me about what's happening.

CLIENT   It's real hard. I don't know how to take the nurturing, and to be truthful, I've never felt anything other than a patient-shrink relationship in my previous therapies, and no one who I really felt safe with. But when somebody's really safe and nurturing... I just don't know what to do with it.

THERAPIST (*softly*) OK. Let's stay right there with that. A really, really important question. How do you feel in your heart as we're talking?

CLIENT Um... I feel a little bit of warmth.

THERAPIST (*nodding slowly*) OK.

CLIENT And some sadness, too, because Tuesday night, I went out to find just this. Of course, I didn't find it there.

THERAPIST What's the "this" you were looking to find?

CLIENT Someone to affirm me, to appreciate me, to pay attention to me. Someone who has the confidence – like they're not lost, they know what they're doing.

THERAPIST (*gently*) How does it feel when I accept those parts of you that are insecure... sad? In your heart, how does it feel?

CLIENT Um... I just feel... tears.

THERAPIST (*gently*) Tears?

CLIENT Watering around the eyes.

THERAPIST Sure. So when you feel someone [distancing use of the impersonal "someone," rather than "I," but using client's own words] being nurturing toward you, you have these physical feelings that go with that, and you're saying to me you have some tears and wetness in your eyes.

CLIENT Yeah.

THERAPIST And how do you feel about talking to me about this? You're feeling OK about expressing this?

CLIENT Yeah.

THERAPIST Good, because I think it's really wonderful that you're connecting with that deeper part of yourself and expressing who you are. (waiting) And when I say these words to you, what do you feel?

CLIENT Um... I want to... I think immediately of the photo my grandmother has of me in her living room – I look kind of like a woman, so that I think that's not entirely who I am. I

	mean... I just don't *like* how I am. I'm soft, I'm overweight, kind of effeminate – so when you say that you accept me for exactly who I am... um... (*falls silent*)
THERAPIST	(*waits*) "When I accept you"... then you...?
CLIENT	I just immediately start thinking about all the things I dislike about myself. I'm not really interested in sports, I'm more interested in art. That makes me not feel like a man. I got that message from my dad; I'm different. And I don't like that I have so much anxiety and fear. I don't like how I act; I don't think it's manly. And I'm afraid of how I'm coming across.
THERAPIST	How does that feel now as you tell me these things?
CLIENT	It feels good that I can just say that.
THERAPIST	And that I can hear it? And accept it. That this is who you are... and that that's OK.
CLIENT	Yeah. That you can just sit here and just hear that.

In this session we saw the therapist follow the client's affective response, which – although following it was the right thing to do in this instance – disrupted the session sequence. In such situations the therapist should try to return later to complete the remaining steps of the sequence.

CHAPTER 9

Reparative Body Work
Working the Two-Triangle Sequence

I've "recoiled" from the part of me that would have come to
me from my father, and so I fall back into the fantasyland
which prevents me from being an adult man.

In chapter eight I detailed the two-triangle sequence. The following illustrations reveal how this sequence is applied toward the goal of returning
the client to the feeling memories that are stored in the body, sensitizing
him to better recognize his own "bodily knowing" and connecting those
feelings with sources in the past. At the same time, through an attuned
relationship with the therapist, the client grows in the ability to relate with
authenticity and mutuality to other men.

Bill's Disappointment

This session begins with the client offering vague and unfocused complaints. The therapist tries to identify a conflict so they can enter the first
triangle. For a long time the session seems to go nowhere.

This transcript illustrates the difficulty of moving some clients past
their defenses and into their feelings.

CLIENT   My week went OK, but I was feeling kind of down.
THERAPIST   OK. So this whole week you've been feeling depressed...
            kind of down.

CLIENT	Not the whole week.
THERAPIST	Some of the week.
CLIENT	Yeah, just some of it.
THERAPIST	(*nods*) OK. Bill, let's see if we can find out where this started – where this (uses client's own words) feeling of "down" came from, shall we?
CLIENT	Well, I'm not feeling that "down" right now.
THERAPIST	OK, so what are you feeling?
CLIENT	(*shrugs*)
THERAPIST	Let's go to your feelings.
CLIENT	Well, I was feeling bad when I woke up this morning.
THERAPIST	You woke up feeling sad this morning. What was going on?
CLIENT	Nothing.
THERAPIST	You just woke up sad.
CLIENT	I just woke up and I didn't want to get out of bed.
THERAPIST	Were you anticipating something today?
CLIENT	No, I had the day off, so it was supposed to be a good day but...
THERAPIST	OK. Maybe, then... something yesterday? (pauses, waits)
CLIENT	Yesterday I talked to my friend, Pete.
THERAPIST	He's your best friend, isn't he?
CLIENT	I thought so.
THERAPIST	Oh? (suspects they are approaching an identified conflict)
CLIENT	Well, we were supposed to go on a hike Saturday. Then yesterday he called to say he couldn't go because his wife wants him to do this "family thing." So he said he couldn't do it after all, and I said, (*spoken in self-mocking, singsong, cheery voice*), "That's OK, it's no big deal."
THERAPIST	You're making fun of yourself. But it wasn't OK at all.
CLIENT	(*suddenly serious*) No, it wasn't.

[Therapist identifies conflict and proposes body work.]

THERAPIST	So this was a conflict for you. (*pauses, waits*) Should we go into the feelings about that?
CLIENT	(*shrugging shoulders*) Yeah. I guess.

THERAPIST OK. (*focusing on the conflict moment*) Let's recall that moment. Was it by phone?

CLIENT (*nodding*)

THERAPIST Let's go to that moment. What's the feeling?

CLIENT (*silent*)

THERAPIST What was happening inside?

CLIENT I didn't feel anything... You know what I felt? I just felt numb.

THERAPIST OK. You felt nothing, just numb.

CLIENT Right... So I'm talking to him and my voice is like, I can tell, this fakey thing like my mom used to do. I hate when I do that. (*uses singsong cheery voice again*) "It's OK. Catch you next Saturday."

THERAPIST So, on the outside it was, "That's OK," but on the inside, it was just "numb."

CLIENT (*sadly*) Yeah.

THERAPIST Let's try to go to what was going on inside you at that moment, OK? Try to go to that feeling right now.

CLIENT (*long silence*)

THERAPIST Let's try right now to go to how you felt when you hung up the phone. Can you feel that numb feeling you felt?

[Sensing client is having difficulty recalling his feeling, therapist attempts to re-create the emotional situation. This is a technical error. Once the conflict is identified, he should stay in the first triangle, namely, the client's feeling or his defense against the feeling.]

THERAPIST Going back to that phone call... Pete has just cancelled the hike with you; his wife wants him to do something. You feel disappointment but say, "That's OK." You hang up. Shall we go to that?

CLIENT I remember sitting on the couch after I hung up the phone and I just stared at the floor.

THERAPIST Try to feel what you were feeling then as you're sitting on the couch looking at the floor. What was going on inside your body?

CLIENT	Sad.
THERAPIST	You felt the sadness. (*softly*) There was a sadness, wasn't there?
CLIENT	God, it was really sad.
THERAPIST	Can you feel that feeling of sadness now?
CLIENT	(*slowly nods*) Yeah, here in my chest.
THERAPIST	Tell me what you are feeling in your chest right now. Stay with that feeling right now.
CLIENT	Down. I just feel totally down.

[Therapist goes beneath emotions to feelings/sensations.]

THERAPIST	What's the feeling in your chest with that?
CLIENT	Heavy...like a weight.
THERAPIST	Yeah. Let's just sit with that heavy weight in your chest.
CLIENT	(*moves away from feelings back to defense of "nothing"*) I don't feel it right now.
THERAPIST	What do you feel right now?
CLIENT	Nothing.
THERAPIST	You feel nothing.
CLIENT	Not really anything right now.

[Client's resistance prompts therapist's concern, and fearing he might be pushing too hard, he slows down to reduce the stress and reassure.]

THERAPIST	Let's just sit with that for a minute. OK? (*softly*) Let's just sit here and stay for a moment with the "nothing" and let's see if it takes us anywhere.
CLIENT	(*still and silent*)

[Therapist senses deeper resistance and decides to use the collaborative method.]

THERAPIST	(*softly*) Listen, Bill, we don't have to do this. We can talk about something else today. What do you think? (*pause*) Or shall we go back to "nothing"?
CLIENT	(*slowly nodding, after some time*) OK. Well...it just feels completely empty.
THERAPIST	You feel empty.

CLIENT   Empty. Yeah.

THERAPIST   Mm…Where do you feel that empty right now?

CLIENT   Kind of like, below my chest.

THERAPIST   (*gently*) Where?

CLIENT   Right there in the middle.

THERAPIST   In the middle of your chest.

CLIENT   Yeah, just kind of hollow.

THERAPIST   "Hollow." Yeah, let's stay with that. We're going from nothing to empty, an "empty feeling" in your chest, to that "hollow."

CLIENT   But I can't just make my feelings come out…(*frustrated*) I'm saying I just can't conjure up a feeling.

THERAPIST   (*correcting himself, returning to collaborative posture*) Of course you can't. This is not easy. We don't have to do this right now, but we might have an opportunity to learn something here if we give it a try.

CLIENT   (*nods*)

THERAPIST   (*gently*) Shall we move nice and slowly, and try again?

CLIENT   (*shoulders relax, takes deep breath, pauses*) Actually…it's that I can't tell if it's just "empty," or if it's this whole kind of thing where something actually wants to come out.

THERAPIST   Stay with that "something that wants to come out."

CLIENT   I feel it in my eyes, feels like, moist in my eyes. Like something wants to come out of my chest.

THERAPIST   So what do you feel more strongly right now, moisture in your eyes or something wanting to come out of your chest?

CLIENT   (*immediately*) My chest.

THERAPIST   How does it feel?

CLIENT   (*sighs*) I just feel so let down.

THERAPIST   And the feeling in your body?

CLIENT   Heavy in my chest, like a weight. (motionless for a while)

THERAPIST   I'm seeing some tearing up also, aren't I?

CLIENT   (*softly*) Yeah. This is very old stuff. Very old stuff.

[Perhaps prompted by the insistence that this is "old stuff" and sensing Bill has gone deeply enough for this session, not wanting to pressure him further, the therapist moves to second triangle.]

THERAPIST   Bill, have you ever had that same kind of heavy weightiness in your chest, the same kind of tearful feeling around the eyes? Does that evoke something from your past?

CLIENT   Yeah. A lot of different things. But the time that sticks out really, really clear right now is when I was like seven or eight and I had this friend Tim.... He lived down the street and he said that I could go with his family to Disneyland, because they were going to go in a week or something, and then...

THERAPIST   You were looking forward to that.

CLIENT   Sure.

THERAPIST   Was Tim a good friend of yours?

CLIENT   Yeah, I was looking forward to it not because of Disneyland – I had been there a lot – but because I liked Tim. Tim was really cool, and then like a week before we were supposed to go, Tim and I got into a fight about whether we should bring another friend of his, Jack, a guy I didn't like. Then, like the next day, Tim said that he wasn't going to take me with him, he was going to take this other guy Jack instead because I was a "loser" or a "creep" or something.

THERAPIST   (not dwelling in the details of the story, decides to go straight for the feelings) What was the feeling that you felt?

CLIENT   The same thing.

THERAPIST   The same feeling. What's that same feeling in your body between when Pete didn't go with you, and when Tim called you a loser. What is that feeling in your body?

CLIENT   Sad. Painful. Disappointment. Right here in my chest. And also the other feeling is the numb feeling, because I remember like it was yesterday. I remember when he told me that. I recall that I just froze. I just stood there completely numb, frozen. (*sighs deeply*) Oh, man. It was in that same cheery voice, I said to Tim, "That's OK." I can't believe I did that, acted so cheery. "That's OK." Then I went home and I cried, like for the whole afternoon. My mom kept going, "What's wrong?" I said, "Nothing."

THERAPIST   (*gently*) So you're really into that feeling now. (*reviews and reinforces the link between the present and the past*) Both those friends disappointed you, painfully disappointed you, creating those same feelings inside. (*moving to DL*) Let me ask you, Bill, (*gently*) do you feel like I understand what that feels like for you, that I understand what you are feeling right now, in this moment?

CLIENT (*head bent, slowly nodding*) Yeah, I do.

THERAPIST OK. Because when you were a kid – we've talked about this before – about how you felt alone, lonely...like nobody understood what you were going through. Do you feel like I understand what is happening to you right now, with Pete, at least?

CLIENT Yeah, I think you do. It feels good. I never told anybody that. My mom and my grandma kept asking. I never told her, or my mom. I just made up some lie to them about why I wasn't going. It feels really good to have somebody hear that.

THERAPIST (*returning to double loop*) So, how does it feel right now between you and me...right now.

CLIENT (*looking up, direct eye contact*) Good. Like you understand.

THERAPIST And how does feeling understood by me feel right now for you?

CLIENT (*deep sigh, relaxes*) It's a feeling of comfort...warm, accepted.

THERAPIST (*nodding*)

CLIENT Yeah, it feels warm and calm. (*considers*)...I can feel the tightness in my throat relaxing...it feels good.

THERAPIST (*nods*) Yes...I can see that.

CLIENT The hard knot in my chest has softened up. (*touches his solar plexus*)

THERAPIST OK...

CLIENT (*sinks down deeply in his chair*) and I just feel kind of (*takes a deep breath*) calmer, quieter.

THERAPIST It's great for me to see you push through and make this contact, which I'm feeling for us now.

[After some quiet moments of sitting with the feelings, there is a brief discussion of another matter, then the therapist moves to MT.]

THERAPIST So what did we accomplish today? What did we learn?

CLIENT   (*reflecting*) Well...it brings back a lot of those old memories of when my dad was never around...I was feeling left out at school. I remember now what she'd do. (*speaks in a mocking tone*) "Oh, honey, forget those boys! C'mon, let's go shopping," or...she'd say something like that. I know she wanted to help me somehow,...but she never really understood what it was that I was looking for. (*deep sigh*)... Or what it was that I didn't have.

Carl's Home Visit

This twenty-two-year-old student begins with a superficial review of his week. The therapist tries a bit too hard to bring the client into body work. Not surprisingly, the client offers repeated resistance, and the session at first takes a negative turn.

CLIENT   I went home this last weekend – something I don't do very often. They bug the s—t out of me.

THERAPIST You mean your parents?

CLIENT   Yeah, they give me a hard time, and when I go home, every time when I go home, my mom just crawls up into me, she's always asking me all these questions, wanting to know who my friends are, what am I doing, how are my grades,...have I been taking my medication.

THERAPIST As soon as you walk in?

CLIENT   Yeah, it's like, I mean, I barely have time to put my keys down, and she's just right into me. "You haven't been smoking, have you? Are you making friends? Have you been wearing your glasses?" I'm just sick of her questions.

[Therapist identifies the conflict – unexpressed anger – and after some moments of further discussion, decides to enter the first triangle; introduces body work.]

THERAPIST So, let's do some deeper work here, OK? (*focusing on the conflict moment*) OK, so you walk in the door and before you can even sit down, she's in your face?

CLIENT   Yeah.

THERAPIST	What were you feeling inside your body?
CLIENT	I ignored her. I was annoyed. It doesn't do any good.
THERAPIST	Yeah, but how were you feeling inside your body?
CLIENT	Nothing. I mean, there's nothing more to do with her. She doesn't understand. You can't talk to a woman like that.
THERAPIST	How are you feeling when you visualize coming home? You haven't even put your keys down, you're tired, and your mother doesn't seem to notice that. She just starts in with the questions.
CLIENT	Well, I mean I don't feel hardly anything. I was just telling you the story.
THERAPIST	That's fine, but what was the feeling? I heard some strong feelings. Some anger. Some frustration. Let's go to that.
CLIENT	(looks perplexed)
THERAPIST	(softly, cautiously) What are you feeling right now? Right now how do you feel when you think about that visit to your parents?
CLIENT	About my mom? I guess I feel a little nauseous.
THERAPIST	You're feeling nauseous right now. Stay with that. Where you do feel the nausea?
CLIENT	In my stomach. My throat and stomach.
THERAPIST	(attempts to focus the client) Carl, where do you feel it more strongly, in your throat or in your stomach? Which one is the strongest right now for you?
CLIENT	(agitated) In my stomach.
THERAPIST	What are you feeling?
CLIENT	I don't see what this is about ... you're not my mom.

[Therapist does not attempt corroborative response but the quick dismissive strategy. In this case it briefly succeeds in helping the client move ahead.]

THERAPIST	I know I'm not your mom. (they sit together in a few moments of quiet) But shall we go back to that nausea in your throat and stomach?
CLIENT	(considers, then seems to relax) OK. So I've just come home.

	(*reflects for a while*) In my stomach I feel jittery. I feel like a tingling, a little queasy I guess. When she starts asking me questions about...
THERAPIST	(*dismissive strategy*) Yeah, I understand, but right now, stay with your body. Go back to "My stomach is tingly and queasy."
CLIENT	OK... tingly, queasy, it just feels like my stomach is doing backflips.
THERAPIST	Stay with the nervous. Let's see what's behind those feelings in your stomach.
CLIENT	Like underneath it?
THERAPIST	Exactly underneath it, stay with that.
CLIENT	Well, I'm mad at her.
THERAPIST	You're feeling mad. Where do you feel the mad? Where in your body?
CLIENT	Like it was in my stomach, but it's also like my arm, my shoulders. I'm thinking about the way that she talked to me, the look that she has and it enrages me. I just want to punch her. (*swings his arm*)
THERAPIST	(*acknowledging his impulse*) Yeah. You took a swing. Stay with that. That's important, Carl.
CLIENT	(*becomes thoughtful*) I can see the look in her eyes.
THERAPIST	What are you feeling right now as you're seeing her? What are you feeling in your body?
CLIENT	(*sighs*) My heart's beating faster. I'm starting to feel hot. I want to take off my coat or something.
THERAPIST	Carl, I want to tell you something. You say you're mad but you don't sound mad right now. Sit with it for a minute; see if you can really go into that "mad." You're telling me you're feeling it. I don't want you to just tell me about it... I want you to feel it.
CLIENT	(*pauses*) OK. I feel it in my chest.
THERAPIST	What in you chest do you feel?
CLIENT	I feel my heart speeding up. I feel my chest muscles tight and burning.
THERAPIST	Do you visualize her?

CLIENT   (*nods*) Yeah. I can see her right in my face…I see that face, I see those sad eyes. I see that manipulation that she likes to do to me, and she's always just looking at me, and God, I'm… (*client is now clenching his fists*)

THERAPIST   You see her face this time. You can see her eyes.

CLIENT   Yes.

THERAPIST   (*pause*) What's the feeling in the body?

CLIENT   Explosion. I want to explode. I want to scream at her, "Leave me alone!

[Client continues to yell at mother for some moments as therapist supports him.]

[Therapist decides to move to second triangle.]

THERAPIST   Let me ask you, have you felt this same kind of anger before? Can you remember a time in the past, this same kind of anger? Stay with that same feeling.

CLIENT   (*after a moment, speaks softly*) I used to feel this way a lot. In fact, I felt this way all the time.

THERAPIST   With her?

CLIENT   Yeah, with her, but what's coming to mind is when I was in junior high. I was in ninth grade and I would want to play ball with the guys or something and they would call me a sissy and a fag and all these stupid things and there was nothing I could do at that point.

THERAPIST   OK. I want to hear about junior high school. What would they do?

CLIENT   They would make fun of me when I would try to play sports.

THERAPIST   Like a group of boys?

CLIENT   Yeah, the popular kids. They would make fun of me when I would try to throw a baseball. And if I didn't play, they would call me names: faggot…klutz, loser. There was nothing I could do.

THERAPIST   And what's the feeling?

CLIENT   I was totally pissed, trapped.

THERAPIST   "Trapped"... Stay with that. Can you to feel that feeling right now that you felt when you were in ninth grade?

CLIENT   You're starting to irritate me a little bit. You're asking questions like my mom asked me questions all the time.

[Therapist drops his intensive work agenda and shifts to addressing the working alliance, particularly the client's irritation.]

THERAPIST   Fair enough. Be absolutely frank with me now, OK? So how are you feeling about me right now?

CLIENT   I feel like you're pressuring me.

THERAPIST   Which I am...

CLIENT   Well, it makes me mad. I don't see the purpose of trying to feel all these feelings. I just want some solutions to help me deal with my parents and my brother.

[This breach in the working alliance creates a new identified conflict which suddenly supersedes the previous identified conflict, returning them to the first triangle.]

THERAPIST   OK. Let's look at that. So, let's go back to how you're feeling about me right now.

CLIENT   (*pause*) I'm feeling frustrated.

THERAPIST   Stay with the feeling... You're frustrated, irritated... mad!

CLIENT   (*angrily*) I want help, and you're not telling me how to deal with them.

THERAPIST   (*a double bind, so therapist moves to double loop*) In fact, I'm frustrating you like your mother does.

CLIENT   (*nods*)

THERAPIST   I'm hitting you with so many questions... you're feeling tense and angry.

CLIENT   (*shrugs*) A little.

THERAPIST   But you can tell me about it. You are telling me right now that I'm frustrating you. (*pauses, looks directly at client*) And I'm hearing your frustration toward me.

[Client and therapist look eye-to-eye for some moments.]

THERAPIST	Do you feel like I'm hearing you?
CLIENT	(*softly*) Yeah. (*pauses, sits back in chair*) I'm feeling calmer. I'm feeling like a weight was lifted off my shoulders.
THERAPIST	Do you feel like I understood you?
CLIENT	Yeah. You heard me. I feel like you understood me. You know, I don't usually tell people that I'm mad at them right to their face.
THERAPIST	It was good you could let me see that.
CLIENT	I feel good.
THERAPIST	Yeah. I feel good about that too. You need to feel free to do that with me. (*after some moments, moves to MT*) Carl, what did we accomplish for you today? You started with a home visit and anger at your mom. Where did that take us?
CLIENT	Well, I felt the anger! That's new! (*reflecting further*) And I got mad at you.
THERAPIST	And...
CLIENT	And I told you about it. (*smiles*) That felt good.

Dave's Infatuation

Twenty-eight-year-old David discusses his feelings for coworker Bob. David is trying to sort out the experience of feeling warmth and affection for another man, without those feelings being eroticized.

CLIENT	I had seen him around the office for a while. I'll admit, I was a little attracted to him. Unexpectedly we sat at the same table in the cafeteria and I felt like we had this immediate connection. He seemed just real friendly toward me. It felt so comfortable, like there was nothing wrong with it, know what I mean? It wasn't sexual or anything like that. It was such a great experience. I can't even explain it. I've got to tell you, I spent the weekend thinking about him.

[Identifying the conflict moment but not hearing a conflict, therapist suspects deeper feelings.]

THERAPIST	What were the feelings for Bob as you were sitting with him in the cafeteria?

CLIENT　　　It was exciting, like "I want it all now. I want I fast. I want it now."

THERAPIST　(*amplifies reaction to encourage greater affective expression*) Yes... "Exciting! Wow!" (*with empathy*) Because this is a new and exciting opportunity for you. A chance for a real connection.

CLIENT　　　Yeah. It was just a great experience. It was totally unbelievable. I said to myself, *This is what we've been talking about here in therapy.* You know – how good it is when you get the right connection going on – and I left there thinking, *I could die right now and be happy.* That's how good I felt. I said I *could* because I don't think this will ever happen again in my life, you know?

THERAPIST　Totally enchanted.

CLIENT　　　I was! I was totally enchanted, and the coolest part is that there was nothing gay or flirtatious about it.

THERAPIST　(*reinforces his earlier distinction*) Or sexual.

CLIENT　　　Or sexual. It was so awesome. So real.

THERAPIST　This is a new and very important person in your life.

CLIENT　　　Right, and he was like so totally, you know... We had good eye contact and everything. He was just like, "right there," and it helped me because I was struggling at first telling him about myself, but then he just kind of brought it out of me.

THERAPIST　(*trying to identify conflict*) OK, I'm glad to hear this, but is there a problem with this new friendship?

CLIENT　　　Well, I was literally obsessed all weekend long. I was in an emotional heap over it. Immediately on the way home I started trying to disconnect from it because I thought, this feels too darn good! I can't accept this.

THERAPIST　(*attempts to identify the conflict*) OK, so what's the conflict?

CLIENT　　　I'm totally overwhelmed by my feelings.

THERAPIST　Let's try to separate them out. What's the conflict?

CLIENT　　　It's like I want to be with *just* him. And always that's what's so, uh, unhealthy about me.

THERAPIST   You're judging yourself. Let's forget that. Let's just go to your feelings.

CLIENT   I want to be with him.

THERAPIST   What do you feel inside of you?

CLIENT   Love ... and fear.

THERAPIST   Right. Which one do you feel more intensely right now?

CLIENT   Love.

THERAPIST   Where do you feel the love?

CLIENT   I feel the love in my heart.

THERAPIST   Do you feel it right now? At this moment?

CLIENT   (*considers*) Yeah. I do.

THERAPIST   Can you allow yourself to *really* feel that love right now?

CLIENT   Yeah.

THERAPIST   Tell me what that love feels like.

CLIENT   Well, it feels reassuring, comforting.

THERAPIST   Those are ideas. Let's go to your body. How in your body does the love feel?

CLIENT   Well ... it feels like the swelling of my heart.

THERAPIST   Yes.

CLIENT   A fullness ... (*softly*) a total fullness of heart.

THERAPIST   (*gently*) Can you just stay with that? Allow yourself to feel that fullness of love for him?

CLIENT   (*softly*) Yes. Yes.

THERAPIST   Let's stay there. Just let yourself feel it. That love ...

CLIENT   It hurts, man.

THERAPIST   It hurts?

CLIENT   It gives me a headache.

THERAPIST   Does it have an actual pain to it?

CLIENT   Yeah, I'm afraid of it.

THERAPIST   You're afraid of it?

CLIENT   I'm afraid of feeling that much love for someone, for another guy.

THERAPIST   So this love you're feeling goes to feeling afraid?

CLIENT   (*thoughtfully*) Yes. It does.

THERAPIST   Tell me what else you're feeling.

CLIENT	My head's pounding right now.
THERAPIST	(*spoken with understanding*) Sure. So you're in conflict.
CLIENT	Yeah. I'm afraid.
THERAPIST	So you're feeling a conflict between love and fear. Stay with those two feelings. Go there and just sit with those conflicting feelings. (*gently*) Which one would you say is stronger?
CLIENT	(*after some moments*) Well... fear.
THERAPIST	So it's more fear. Tell me how you feel fear in your body right now.
CLIENT	(*silence*)
THERAPIST	(*speaking softly*) Stay with the fear. The feeling it gives you inside.
CLIENT	Like I just want to run.
THERAPIST	(*nods*) That's right. Run away...
CLIENT	And I want to just get away.
THERAPIST	That's right. What's the feeling? Stay with the feeling. (*moving from emotions to bodily feelings*) How do you feel the fear?
CLIENT	In my body.
THERAPIST	Yeah, where exactly?
CLIENT	(*pause*) In my chest.
THERAPIST	How does that fear in your chest feel?
CLIENT	Like a tightness, constriction.
THERAPIST	Where?
CLIENT	Right across here. (*gestures across his chest*)
THERAPIST	Stay with your feeling now. Sit with it.
CLIENT	There's sadness. It's weird. I feel really sad about it.
THERAPIST	Stay with the sadness. Allow yourself to feel that sadness right now. *Really feel it.* How do you feel in your body?
CLIENT	(*closes eyes, considers for a moment*) I feel it in my heart, and in my head.
THERAPIST	Right. Stay with the sadness right now. Let's stay with that. Just allow yourself to sit with that sadness. And how it really feels.
CLIENT	(*suddenly*) I'm afraid he's going to reject me.
THERAPIST	But that's an idea. What's the feeling behind that idea?

CLIENT   Fear.

THERAPIST   (*gently*) It kind of goes back and forth between fear and sadness, doesn't it?

CLIENT   It does. (*with increased agitation*) But I want to be so close to him that it would overwhelm him if he knew how close I want to be. Besides, that kind of relationship isn't right. It isn't healthy... I know that. I've learned that. (*shakes his head*) And it would end up destroying the good thing we've got right now...

THERAPIST   (*nods*) Of course, your fear of rejection is realistic. He probably won't want the intimate and exclusive friendship you're hoping for. That's the reality. So I understand the fear and sadness you have about that.

CLIENT   (*nods*) Yes.

THERAPIST   But besides the reality of this situation, let's look at your intense reaction to anticipated rejection, your intense fear.

CLIENT   OK...

THERAPIST   Let's go back to your feelings. Right now you're feeling fear and sadness.

CLIENT   (*nods*) Right. That's totally right.

THERAPIST   Let's stay with these feelings and let's see what comes out. Let's sit quiet for a minute.

CLIENT   (*calming*) OK. (*pause*)

THERAPIST   What do you feel in your body?

CLIENT   I feel nervousness.

THERAPIST   Hmm...

CLIENT   I feel shaky inside. I feel actually *scared to death.*

THERAPIST   (*nods*) You feel scared in your body.

CLIENT   Yeah.

THERAPIST   How in your body do you feel scared right now?

CLIENT   My insides are shaky, and my head – I have a headache right now, it's pounding.

THERAPIST   (*quick dismissive strategy*) But you're afraid.

CLIENT   Yeah. I'm afraid that he won't love me in return.

THERAPIST   Exactly. That you're going to lose him.

CLIENT   Yes. I'm going to lose him.

THERAPIST   That you're going to turn him away.

CLIENT   Right. I'm going to turn him away. That's exactly right.

THERAPIST   And what's the feeling?

CLIENT   Sad. Really sad. (*becoming physically rigid*)

[Therapist decides Dave has gotten as deeply into his sadness as possible for now. Moves to second triangle.]

THERAPIST   Dave, (*spoken gently*) does this really sad feeling right now remind you of something from the past?

CLIENT   (*immediately*) Yeah, totally.

THERAPIST   What's that?

CLIENT   My father.

THERAPIST   You recall your father here...

CLIENT   Yeah. He *did* turn me away.

THERAPIST   Do you have a particular memory?

CLIENT   It's always the same one. It comes to mind when things like this happen to me.

THERAPIST   Which is?

CLIENT   When he just devastated me with what he said.

[This is not an unusual phenomenon, when the body so closely links C (current person) and P (past person), that the client's narrative slides quickly into the past.]

THERAPIST   Your father?

CLIENT   Yeah.

THERAPIST   When you were a kid?

CLIENT   Yeah.

THERAPIST   What's the memory?

CLIENT   The memory. There was a family gathering going. I think it was Thanksgiving, and he is yelling at me not to hang out with my aunt and my grandma, to be a man. That's the memory.

THERAPIST   He scolded you when you were a kid?

CLIENT   Yeah, in front of all those people. I guess the women were

standing there in the kitchen, and I just felt more comfortable with them. I'm just a little, little kid...

THERAPIST   How old?

CLIENT   (*pause*) Maybe five.

THERAPIST   Five!

CLIENT   Yeah. He was screaming. I remember his face, all screwed
up, his eyes bulging. (*pause*) I can just picture it.

THERAPIST   How did you feel?

CLIENT   (*slowly, stiffly, looking straight ahead, describes the quintessential shame moment*) Petrified. Stunned. I couldn't move.
I became numb. (*quiet for a while*) I was a nothing.

THERAPIST   (*after a moment*) Then what happened?

CLIENT   I don't know. Then somebody said something like "Let's go
play poker." I mean, this is just one of many, many incidents,
but this stands out in my mind.

THERAPIST   (*reinforcing P-C*) And now you're anticipating that Bob is
going to turn on you, reject you?

CLIENT   Right. He's going to see that I'm a pain in the a— or something, that I'm gonna annoy him or something. Want too
much of him.

THERAPIST   And you'll be left devastated again.

CLIENT   Right.

[Client goes deeper into his fears of rejection, then the session time has
come to a close.]

THERAPIST   (*moving to DL*) How did you feel about our connection this
session? You exposed some insecurities with me.

CLIENT   Yeah. I guess I sounded like a little girl.

THERAPIST   (*gently*) Do you feel, right now, that I understood you?

CLIENT   Yes... But in some ways, I don't know if you can – if you can
really relate.

THERAPIST   Infatuation is universal. We all know the feeling. It's exciting,
it takes your breath away, it overwhelms you... (nodding)
like you and the other person are the only two people in
the world...

CLIENT	Yes...
THERAPIST	But what do you mean, you were a "little girl"?
CLIENT	I sounded "over the top," like, star struck, idolizing.
THERAPIST	So that means I would feel critical of you?
CLIENT	I don't know, I just... I don't like losing control. (*thoughtful silence*) But as to whether you understand, yes, I do think you're trying. That's important for me.

[This could have been explored, but the therapist moves to MT.]

THERAPIST	This has been a hard session for you, Dave. This friendship with Bob opened up a lot of confusing and painful and frightening feelings. How do you sort out all that came out from inside you today?
CLIENT	Well, Bob has the power to make me into a nothing. I tried to put the whole thing out of my mind.
THERAPIST	What whole thing?
CLIENT	The conflict about my feelings of love and fear.
THERAPIST	The conflict that you tried to put out of your mind was those feelings of love and fear, of loss of love. You want to be loved – you want to get that healing, that bonding relationship – but you're also afraid because your experience with your father taught you that you really don't deserve this kind of closeness and understanding with a man. You anticipate rejection. You expect to be hurt.
CLIENT	Right.
THERAPIST	Your experience of your dad so shamed you – made you feel so rejected – that now you're anticipating that same treatment whenever you get close to another man.
CLIENT	(*nods*) Yes.
THERAPIST	Let me tell you what I thought was meaningful. You used some judgmental terms for those loving feelings. You said it's "too much," it's "weird," it's "abnormal."
CLIENT	Right.
THERAPIST	What was that about?
CLIENT	Self-protection.

THERAPIST	Sure. But where do you go from here with your friend?
CLIENT	Well, I'm still scared.
THERAPIST	Sure. But how do you want to proceed?
CLIENT	To take it easy, I guess, one step at a time. But it always brings up those deeper feelings and I want to run away.
THERAPIST	Exactly. You've got to watch the way you sabotage that friendship. Look at the way you anticipate and then actually initiate the destruction of the relationship by anticipating his rejection. We need to look at that pattern of intense infatuations and how this distracts you from forming reality-based friendships.
CLIENT	I know. I don't know what to do about him...
THERAPIST	Yes, that's still a concern. We haven't figured that out yet. We've got to work on finding ways for you to build accurate perceptions of what other men can realistically offer you.
CLIENT	(nods)
THERAPIST	Love...Fear...
CLIENT	(as if waking up from a dream) Yeah...fear. No...not fear...devastation. Like, death.
THERAPIST	That's the fear connection between Bob and Dad. What about the love connection?
CLIENT	There isn't any...I never got that from Dad.
THERAPIST	But did you want it?
CLIENT	You know what? (shakes his head bitterly) I don't remember ever having even wanted Dad's love.

Having been in therapy for only two months, Dave still could not recall ever having desired his father's love. Some men's longings, like Dave's, are so deeply buried under layers of hurt that they cannot recall any time in their lives when they actually desired a close relationship with their fathers.

Over time, the client's deepening attachment to the therapist may awaken his repressed desires for paternal love. In fact, months later, Dave was finally able to recall specific memories of wanting his father to show interest and pride in him. He remembered that his father used to put little notes of encouragement in his lunchbox when he was about to take an exam, and he admitted that he had actually longed for a more personal, one-on-one kind of encouragement.

By opening himself up to fully grieving the loss of his father's love, Dave was able to reexperience the source of his anticipatory fears of masculine rejection. Over several months of sessions, his infatuations diminished and his circle of realistic male friendships grew.

Michael's Temptation

Sixteen-year-old Michael begins his session by reporting homosexual feelings resulting from physical proximity to a teenage friend.

CLIENT   So when we were together, I felt this affection, this sexual sensation with Adam, but it also made me feel uncomfortable, like "this is weird."

THERAPIST   (*attempting to identify the conflict moment*) So his body is pressed against yours as you were sitting together on the bench outside of school.

CLIENT   Part of me liked it, and part of me said, "Michael, that's not where you want to go."

THERAPIST   OK. Stay with that moment of opposing feelings. Shall we explore what is behind it?

CLIENT   Yes.

THERAPIST   OK, how did it feel?

CLIENT   I liked being touched. I was being cared for even though it wasn't the right way. I felt like I was connecting with a guy.

THERAPIST   Let's go to the feeling of "cared for," that feeling of "connected." Let's focus in on those feelings, because that's what the pull was, wasn't it?

CLIENT   Yes … it really wasn't like I was getting an erection or anything. That's not what I was feeling.

THERAPIST   Uh-huh. And what were you experiencing?

CLIENT   It feels like I like being cared for.

THERAPIST   Let's go to that feeling of "being cared for." Let's focus on what that appeal was for you. What was so attractive about that? Even now, when you think about it, what do you feel in your body as you recall that moment?

CLIENT   As usual, I feel mostly a rejection of the feeling. I'm trying to knock it down.

THERAPIST   That's right, you're fighting it, but let's put that aside. Let's put aside the rejection. Instead, let's go to the feeling of "cared for" and "connected." These are the feelings that motivated you, that appealed to you.

CLIENT   I just want to be wrapped up and held, and just hugged. Just a desire for affection any way that I can get it.

THERAPIST   Sure. Pay attention to your body right now as you say "being wrapped up and held," feeling "connected" and "cared for." Feel the connection. How does it feel?

CLIENT   (*pause*) It feels good.

THERAPIST   Tell me more how it feels good to you right now.

CLIENT   It's like a relaxation, like "this is what I want."

THERAPIST   Go to the feeling. What do you feel in your body as you say that? What is that "relaxation"?

CLIENT   It just makes me feel more whole. I feel comfort. There's a satisfaction in that I'm cared for and approved of.

THERAPIST   How does that feel right now as you talk about that?

CLIENT   The stomach unclenches... relaxes.

THERAPIST   Can you feel your stomach relaxing?

CLIENT   Yes. I get so caught up in trying not to feel something that I forget that I'm feeling this.

THERAPIST   That's right. Go to the feeling, that desire of affection. What is that feeling of being wrapped up and held? Do you feel something other than that relaxation in your stomach?

CLIENT   I feel hunger for it.

THERAPIST   Tell me about how you feel the hunger.

CLIENT   It's at the pit of my stomach. It's a pulling.

THERAPIST   Stay with that. That pulling at the bottom of your stomach.

CLIENT   I've not been aware of feeling that for a long time, but I feel it now. It's this feeling of "I can't trust it because I know it will hurt me."

THERAPIST   Uh-huh.

CLIENT   I just want to clamp it off. But if I could have it...then it would just be like receiving something that just fills up the whole body.

THERAPIST   What does that feel like right now as you say this? What's the body sensation right now?

CLIENT   It feels like eating a big meal when you're so hungry, and it fills up your whole body.

THERAPIST   That's right. And you're feeling that right now, aren't you?

CLIENT   And I want that!

THERAPIST   Yes! What's the feeling in your body when you say, "I want that?"

CLIENT   It's that yearning...it's just an aching kind of hunger.

[Avoiding discussion of the meaning of the feeling, which will be done in a later session, the therapist stays with the feeling. At the same time, the therapist must fully acknowledge and respect the client's powerful needs and desires. This may well be one of the first strong love experiences of his life, and the basic emotional need from which it arises – for masculine understanding, affirmation and approval – is deep, genuine and healthy.][1]

THERAPIST   Where do you feel that yearning and that aching hunger?

CLIENT   In the stomach...Expressing it right now says it's OK to want what you're wanting, and that's a relief, instead of clamping it all back down.

[Client already feels the benefits of expressing the shame he feels for feeling his authentic needs. The therapist could seize this opportunity to double loop but instead attempts to go deeper into feelings.]

THERAPIST   That's right. Stay with the feeling. How do you feel that yearning in your body?

CLIENT   I don't know if I can go any further. It's a slight aching in the stomach. There's a slight tension in my heart.

THERAPIST   Stay with your body and your feeling.

CLIENT   It just makes me sad. I feel that in the chest area.

THERAPIST   Stay with that. Tell me how you're feeling that sadness in your chest area right now.

CLIENT   A desire for some kind of resolution...oh, why do I hate doing this so much?

THERAPIST   (*quick dismissive strategy*) We can talk about that later. I know this is hard, but stay with it. Go to your heart, pay attention and see what you feel with that sadness at the center of your heart.

CLIENT   I feel a kind of emptiness.

THERAPIST   Let's go to that emptiness and put words to that empty feeling that you're feeling right now.

CLIENT   It's a feeling of...that I don't really matter. I'm a nothing.

THERAPIST   Let's go into that. Let's stay with that empty feeling in your heart of not really mattering.

CLIENT   The feeling just takes away my will to even, like, move. I don't know what it is.

THERAPIST   Let's not worry about what it is or its causes. Let's just go deeper into that sad, empty feeling of not really mattering.

[Client is entering grief work.]

CLIENT   That feeling of not mattering and not feeling important just sucks the life out of me. It's like a hole in my heart. Like a huge sinkhole.

THERAPIST   Stay with that. This is a very painful feeling, but you're there now. (*moves to the second triangle*) Have you had a feeling like this before? Can you recall a time?

CLIENT   Oh, yes.

THERAPIST   Which one comes to mind?

CLIENT   Something from grade school. I was probably in fourth grade. It was just a joke, but it wasn't funny to me. A kid a little younger than me would say, "Oh jump up and down for us again, Michael...dance!"

THERAPIST   And tell me about that feeling.

CLIENT   The feeling was of being squashed, of being crushed. And everybody else would laugh.

THERAPIST   And it was a devastating feeling, wasn't it? You can really feel it now.

CLIENT   It was rejection, and almost like being exiled. That was what
                my whole school experience was like.

[After some further discussions, therapist moves to MT.]

THERAPIST   Michael, let's look at what we're doing here. What have you
                accomplished for yourself?

CLIENT   Well, I was talking about sitting next to Adam on the bench.
                And I felt a lot of conflict about that.

THERAPIST   (*leading*) But what was the feeling under the conflict?

CLIENT   A real need for comfort, that aching hunger. That neediness.

THERAPIST   (*leading*) And what was that empty sadness about?

CLIENT   That it goes to my grade school years.

THERAPIST   (*waiting, nodding, expectantly*) And...

CLIENT   (*as if startled awake by the obvious expectation*) Uh... I always
                felt needy and hungry. That's what Adam could give me, but
                it wasn't sexual, what I wanted.

THERAPIST   (*stating the unspoken obvious*) So it felt kinda sexual to you,
                but you know it wasn't really about sex.

CLIENT   Yes.

THERAPIST   When we look at it, we see it goes to an emotional need, that
                "cared for" feeling, that connection, "wanting to be wrapped
                up and held." It's a good, relaxed feeling: "This is what you
                want." It gives you a feeling of comfort; it makes you feel
                whole. Your stomach relaxes when you think of it. "I just
                want it." And as you go deep into that, you go to a yearning,
                an aching, a hunger. Right?

CLIENT   Yes.

THERAPIST   And then it leads you to this sad feeling, deep in your heart:
                "I really don't matter." Now it's no longer sexual, it's no longer
                what you want from this guy emotionally, but eventually,
                you go back to "something empty inside of me – that I'm
                not really mattering. A lacking of personal importance. A
                hole in my heart." And that's a feeling that you've been
                carrying within yourself for so many years in school when
                they would joke about you, and everybody would laugh.
                You were feeling squashed and crushed. Do you see that?

[This exemplifies the importance of the therapist taking notes of the client's actual words and relaying them back during the meaning transformation (MT) phase to underscore the client's exact experience. Further, the therapist is demonstrating that the client's experience is important, worthy of notetaking and repeating.]

CLIENT   Yes. That's how I felt.

THERAPIST   (*looking at his watch*) Michael, we got into some deep feelings today. We have to stop now and continue next week.

CLIENT   Yes.

[Therapist moves to DL.]

THERAPIST   What's important, Michael, is that you're sharing that with me right now. You're able to go to that feeling and talk to me about it. Do you feel like I understand you?

CLIENT   Yes. But at first I didn't want to do it. To go to those feelings.

THERAPIST   I know you didn't want to do it.

CLIENT   Well, I don't know why... But, I mean, it makes me feel better. I kind of feel stronger when I'm understood, and you don't have to fear about being rejected when you are understood.

THERAPIST   (*nods*)

CLIENT   I've always been afraid that the more you understand me, the less likely that you're going to like me.

THERAPIST   What you just said is very important. "I feel stronger when I'm understood."

CLIENT   (*nods*)

THERAPIST   How do you feel about me right now?

CLIENT   Good. (*sits up in chair*) Um, I feel relieved, and I feel just... well, getting that caring matters to me.

THERAPIST   That I have seen and understood you, as you say... (*client nods*) and that I do not reject you. That I understand these painful experiences, that I hear them, that I'm with you on them.

CLIENT   Yes. That's significant to me. I have to remind myself of that.

	I forget it. I always assume that if somebody really knows me, they won't like me.
THERAPIST	Of course, of course you forget it. Because, whenever you get in touch with that shame or that emptiness or that feeling of not belonging, of not mattering, you just believe that if people see that, they'll reject you.
CLIENT	I've been disappointed about myself. I feel shame before the Lord. I'm still having trouble accepting forgiveness.
THERAPIST	Yes. Yes. So one of the things you're doing is you're continuing to be critical of yourself, to condemn yourself.
CLIENT	Yes. And I know that isn't right. I have to accept forgiveness.
THERAPIST	(*long pause as they sit together in silence*) This was very hard for you to do, what you just did in this last half-hour. To push past the shame and the self-rejection.
CLIENT	It was like a huge wall in my heart that I could feel just pressing against me.
THERAPIST	That's right. Absolutely.
CLIENT	(*nods*) And to try to lay that shame aside is one of the hardest, hardest things you could ask me to do.

The challenge of the two-triangle sequence is to slowly reconnect the client to his disowned emotions through the medium of the body. He is encouraged to feel and expose the split-off (shamed) parts of himself while maintaining intimate contact with the psychotherapist, who returns him again and again to his own interior experience.

This frightening but healing experience of "sitting in the shame" while at the same time receiving the therapist's acceptance slowly expanded for Michael as he allowed himself to seek out other men in his life. He discovered salient men in his church group who could help fill the lifelong divide between himself and other males. In time, the "shame gap" between him and other boys – which he had attempted to bridge with eroticization – began to be filled up in healthier ways.

CHAPTER 10

The Double Bind

The double bind is the classic disempowering mechanism operating within the triadic-narcissistic family. This mechanism occurs when the explicit message (the words) are in contradiction to the nonverbal or implicit message. The person's cognitive function picks up the verbal message while his body registers the contradictory implicit message. Nonverbal messages are conveyed through facial expression, vocal tone and gestures.

If the child listens to the parents' words but denies his own affective bodily response to what he is hearing, he maintains their acceptance. But if he follows his affective response and does not listen to (i.e., believe) his parents' message (thus maintaining contact with his own internal reality), he is shamed.

As the recipient of this paradoxical message, he is prevented from stepping outside the frame of the message due to the dependency built into the relationship. He cannot say anything about the paradox because he will feel punished for his perception.

Characteristics of the Double Bind
In adapting the concept of the double bind to reparative therapy, we see a source for the anticipatory shame posture that is so characteristic of the homosexual client. The double bind fosters the disintegration or "dis-integrity" of the mind-body connection that we see almost universally in our client population.

Disconnection from affective life. The destructive result of double bind communication is in the broad damage done to the recipient's affective life. He learns to distrust his interior perceptions and becomes prone to shame-infused shutdowns of emotional relations.

Bateson et al. (1956) was the first to describe the double bind structure of paradoxical communication. He offers this example: one person asserts something to another, then he asserts something about his own assertion, but these two assertions are mutually exclusive – and the unspoken message is that the other person must not comment on (or even recognize) the obvious paradox.

We view this double bind communication as creating both an intra-psychic split (cognitive left brain from affective right brain) and an inter-personal split (self from other). The person learns to distrust his feelings, and interpersonal communication in general.

Experiencing the double bind. The experience of the double bind begins with the victim feeling an immediate, fearful or uneasy sensation. Something is suddenly wrong; some sort of injustice has happened, but he is confused about what it is. He not only feels confused but also angry. Yet he does not express his anger because of the fear and self-doubt which paralyze him.

Intrapsychic and interpersonal blocks

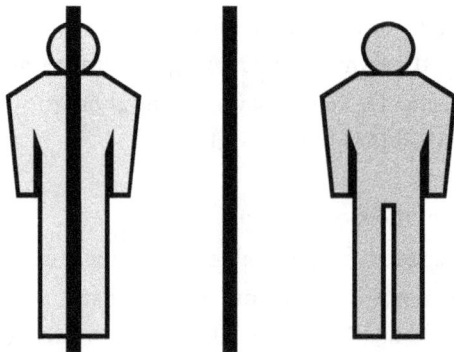

Figure 10.1 The double bind

One man said, "During those moments of double bind communication, I feel angry and unsure about what's happening, and I don't know what to say. I'm not really sure if the problem is with me, or if it's something the other guy did to me." But even though his mind is confused, his body, which feels anger, "knows" the true message of the communication.

The victim senses that "something that is happening feels wrong, but I don't know what it is," or "there is something happening that makes me feel _____ [sad, angry, disappointed, hurt, diminished, left out, etc.], but I can't identify exactly why I feel that way."

Clues to indicate that one is in a double bind situation are

- when a person feels "bad" about an interaction but does not know why

- when a person feels some sort of injustice but can't articulate it

- when a person feels frustrated but can't actually see the contradiction that is causing the frustration

A habitual expectation about human relations. Many writers have noted another insidious feature of the double bind, which is particularly relevant to our client population: when repeated consistently over long periods of time, it becomes a "habitual and autonomous expectation about human relations and the world at large, an expectation that does not require further reinforcement" (Watzlawick et al., 1967, p. 215). Over the long term the person develops a hypersensitivity to restimulation of the same inhibition.

The crazy-making nature of this type of family communication was conveyed by one client this way: "I'll get these messages; I'm not dreaming them up! They're coming from my parents. But when I say something about it, they deny that they're there. So what do they want from me? I just don't care any more. I give up."

When the experience is generalized into a negative expectation about relationships, the victim of the double bind learns to ignore his bodily response to any implicit (process) message. He is taught to be suspicious of anything he intuits through the other person's tone, timing, posture and facial expression (i.e., what is really going on) and instead to respond to and comply with just the explicit (content) message.

The third element in the double bind situation is the unspoken rule

1. *Self.* Feels and expresses
   authentic needs to other

2. *Other.* Responds with punishment.
   (ignore, discount, criticism, etc.)

3. *Self.* Responds to punishment (sadness,
   anger, hurt, disappointment, etc.)

4. *Other.* Responds to response
   with further punishment

5. *Result.*
   1. Internalizes negative introject, *shamed*
   2. Abandons authentic needs
   3. Split off from self and other

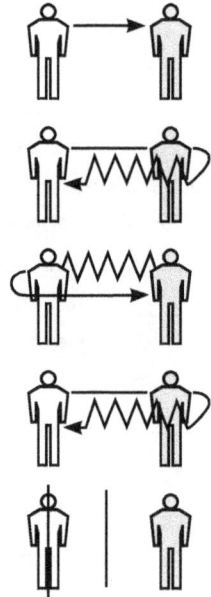

Figure 10.2 The double bind message

that the victim cannot disengage from the communication. His role is to participate in the game. When he is receiving two messages at once, the relationship does not permit him to comment on the paradox, for implicit to this system is an unspoken taboo against exposing the contradiction. An autonomous adult has the power to refuse to participate, thus terminating the double bind communication, but the child within the narcissistic family has no such choice.

Teaching the client to refuse to participate. Healthy reintegration of the self requires that the conscious mind now becomes attuned to one's own bodily response of what is actually going on, at the moment it is happening.

It is critical to teach the client how he can survive this affective-destabilizing communication style without compromising his internal truth. If he compromises his actual perception of the incident, he will be propelled from assertion into shame.

Here is our model of the double bind message:

Self. Communicates an expression of authentic needs to other.

Other. Responds overtly (through words) with a situationally acceptable message, while conveying a covert (unspoken) message through facial expression, vocal tone or body posture that is negative (i.e., contradictory, critical or diminishing of the person).

Self. (1) Cognitively (left brain) accepts the overt, situationally acceptable message, yet the body (right brain) "feels" the covert message. (2) Through negative reinforcement the person has been taught and now believes that it is not possible to comment on this contradiction.

Result. The embodied reaction to the implicit message prompts (1) a shamed self-state response, (2) a negative message about the self internalized into self-identity, (3) an intrapsychic split within the self (cognitive splitting off from the affective) and an interpersonal split (from the person who conveyed the message).

Double Bind in the Triadic-Narcissistic Family

The goal of reparative therapy is to resensitize the client to his bodily response so that he may know his inner truth. Through the therapist's modeling and encouragement, the client becomes reacquainted with his "bodily knowing" so that he can trust that knowing in moments of contradictory communication.

One of our clients described his family's communication style, where overt content and implicit message were often contradictory, as follows:

What stands out most for me about the communication in my family was that my mother always says she wants me to be independent – to be a man and seek a woman, have a family – yet she has always signaled a deep sadness to me about the idea that I might actually leave her.

When I told her about Sara [his new girlfriend] she tried to put on her "happy face," but I heard the tears that she was keeping me from seeing. When I picture her face, I just feel a huge guilt and shame in my body, and I feel responsible for her sadness and her loneliness.

The transcript below illustrates how the recipient of a conflictual message often has difficulty identifying exactly what it was that he picked up in the person's voice:

CLIENT   I went on my first date Friday night and felt good about it. I had a good time with the girl; we went to a play – we both like Shakespeare – and we really clicked together. My mother called Saturday morning, like she always does, and she said, "I called last night, and no one answered. Where were you last night?" I felt proud to tell her that I went on a date with a girl that I really liked. "Really..." she said. That's what she said – "Really?" and I felt my stomach sink. I know she didn't like the idea.

THERAPIST How could you tell? Your mother only said, "Really."

CLIENT   I know her. I could tell it in her voice that she was...sad or...disappointed or something. But then she followed up by saying, "That's nice."

THERAPIST (*curious*) But what exactly was it in the voice?

CLIENT   I don't know. Maybe it was her tone or the sudden drop in her voice, or maybe it was the way her voice suddenly became distant. Even though she said "That's nice," I didn't believe it. I started the phone call happy and optimistic, wanting to share my joy with her, and instead I hung up feeling kind of guilty and down.

From my experience with clients such as this man, if the conversation between him and his mother had remained unanalyzed, the unspoken – yet still powerful – disapproval he heard in his mother's voice would eventually cause him to have doubts about the relationship with the girl he was dating. The doubts would be generated by his shame-based distortions and false-negative perceptions.

Embodied Experience of the Double Bind

Assisting the client to effectively counter the double bind necessitates the therapeutic use of body work. The embodied experience of the double bind is felt primarily in the chest area, first as a quick jolt, followed by a gripping tightness (fear), followed by a lower-chest sinking or dropping sensation (sadness). The client may also recognize a distant, fleeting surge of energy rising in his upper chest and shoulders, or in his arms. This is an anger response, a boundary-setting emotion, but it is quickly repressed. Rather, anger should be felt, expressed and actively encouraged since anger is the way out of the double bind.

The client must learn to identify the double bind in the exact moment that it is occurring. The therapist teaches him how to recognize such a situation, listen sensitively to his bodily responses and eventually learn to speak from them.

CHAPTER 11

The Double Loop

I "become" through my relation to the Thou.... All real living is meeting.

– MARTIN BUBER

We create each other.

– GEORG WILHELM FRIEDRICH HEGEL

So wonderful in your eyes I see myself becoming.

– F. HEBBELS

The central healing process of reparative therapy is the *double loop*. In this process, an accurately attuned, empathic therapist stands alongside the client while he reexperiences the shame moments that have split him apart from himself.

Several recent neurobiological studies have opened a window into this process of psychic reintegration. These findings suggest that the psychodynamic view of the division of the mind into unconscious-conscious, repressed-unrepressed, affective-cognitive is anatomically represented by the division of right brain–left brain activity.

Those two parts of the self, when traumatically severed, are brought back into unity through the double loop experience facilitated by body work.

This new neurological discovery tells us nothing radically different, of course, from what good psychoanalysts have known for more than fifty years. But what is important is that we now have a body of data from neurobiology which confirms how this critical aspect of therapy actually works.

One of the most important messages of the double loop experience is that *it assures our clients that a deeply felt emotional connection with another man is not "gay,"* and that feelings of warmth and closeness need not be experienced as erotic.

The Origins of the Split Mind

The origins of the traumatic severing of the mind (i.e., the childhood trauma) are particularly evident in the paradoxical communication style of the double bind. The double bind creates two schisms: the first within the self (intrapsychic) and the second between self and others (interpersonal).

We use the double loop to undo the trauma and link the person back to himself and others. Stated simply: *the double loop repairs the double bind.*

Double loop.

Self. Communicates an expression of authentic needs to other.

Other. Responds with an integrative self-expression of understanding, support and affirmation.

Self. Receives the integrated message.

Result. The person's embodied reaction to the unified message prompts an assertive self-state response, and the affirmative message is internalized into self-identity. There is an intrapsychic integration (the cognitive dimension comes into harmony with the affective) and an interpersonal integration (with the other).

Our double loop model proposes that the healing occurs when two events happen at the same time: *the interpersonal loop* and *the intrapsychic loop.*

The Session Sequence

The quintessential moment of the double loop is built on gradually established rapport between client and therapist.

As the session opens, the therapist begins by responding to the client's verbal reports. He attempts to establish the double loop by conveying his respect, empathy and attuned caring, thus validating the client's expression of his personal experience. The therapist encourages him to attend to and feel his own embodied experiences, in the same moment that he is describing them.

This simultaneous *feeling-describing* can be a challenge for clients in the early phases of therapy. Typically, their anxiety and defenses will cause them to shift their attention back and forth from content to feelings, and they will find it even more difficult to stay connected simultaneously to their feelings and the therapist.

There will be a gap of time between the client's emotions as they emerge and his contact with the therapist. One man expressed the task as "watching a train go by. By the time I tell you the feeling I have, it's already gone."

At critical moments of strong emotion the therapist should gently remind the client, "Try to stay in contact with me and with your feelings at the same time."

1. *Self.* Feels and expresses authentic needs to other

2. *Other.* Responds with affirmative attunement

3. *Self.* Receives affirmation (connected, secure, reassured, etc.)

4. *Self.*
   1. Abandons negative introject
   2. Integrates authentic needs
   3. Unification with self and others

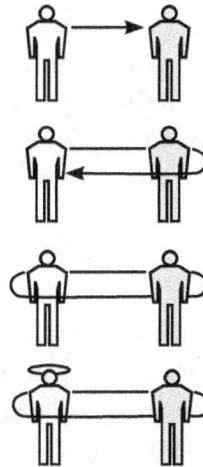

Figure 11.1 The double loop message

Client Therapist

F/I

F/I=Feelings/Impulses

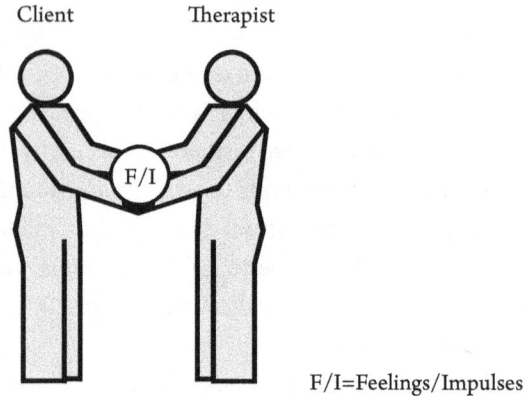

Figure 11.2 Double loop: Affective containment

Communication – putting into words one's feelings – is a cognitive act, but in this case it is also an act of trust that emotionally links the client to the therapist. Building a link between *thinking* and *feeling* will begin the process of unification between left and right brain hemispheres, between cognitive and affective, and between conscious and unconscious, all transmitted through the medium of the body.

This integration deepens as the therapist continues to offer his accurate empathy. Gradually, through accurate attunement and the establishment of the double loop, the therapist facilitates the client's discernment of his long-repressed affect.

At the completion of the double loop the client affectively receives the therapist's expression of respect and esteem, allowing himself to savor the experience of feeling understood. At its best this "intersubjective moment" is reminiscent of the earliest attunement between mother and child.

The Double Loop in the Dissipation of Shame

Shame splits the mind apart. The double loop unifies it. The double loop experience has shown itself to be the most effective tool for disempowering the inhibitory affect of shame. Unlike the other affects, shame dissipates not through more expansive expression but through simple exposure – a process for which the double loop is ideally suited.

The shame experience is the feeling of being unworthy of human contact, and so the protective impulse is to hide, to cover oneself and to

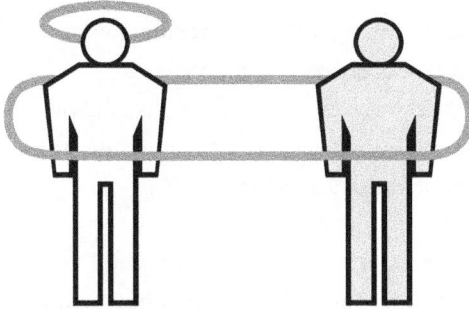

Figure 11.3 Double loop: Intrapsychic and interpersonal

cower in order to resist "expulsion from the pack." Internally, shame serves as an affective inhibitor, a shut-down state.

The therapeutic goal is for the client to remain in the shame (with all the feelings that surround and underlie it) while he simultaneously experiences emotional contact with an understanding and accepting therapist. Thus he allows himself to be "seen" while he "sits in the shame." This exposure brings about a process of shame release along with a general affective release, permitting the client to go deeper into core feelings.

Shame about shame. The process of affective expansion is accomplished through the positive transference and modeling. When the client first reveals a shame incident to the therapist, he often precedes it with apologies and excuses such as "This is gonna sound stupid." "I don't know why I'm even mentioning this." "It's no big deal; I don't know why this upset me." Such minimizing and apologetic introductory remarks reveal a deep embarrassment about his reaction. The therapist's empathetic response validates all the feelings, including the client's "shame about the shame."

When he surrenders his shame the client is able to fully feel his underlying anger (at the other) or his even deeper sadness (for himself).

Feeling shame in the presence of the therapist. When the client reveals a *past* – childhood or more recent – shame moment to the therapist, or a *present* shame moment in the therapeutic setting, we see an opportunity to double loop. The double loop experience and the dissipation of shame may then free the client to experience anger at the other and sadness for himself, two interactive aspects of grief work.

The following two transcripts illustrate therapist-client double looping regarding past shame and present shame.

Here, a forty-year-old client recalls a past shame moment from his childhood. After double looping in the shame state, he fluctuates between anger at the shamer and sadness for himself:

CLIENT   I can see where I was exactly, who I was with, where I was standing. I must have been about six, playing with some girls in the schoolyard. I was sitting on the ground laughing and having a good time and this older guy, the coach, walked over to me. The voice was fearsome; the look was stern. He said something like "Boys don't play with dolls – you need to play with the other boys. Come with me now," that sort of thing. He took me over to the boys, who were playing baseball.

THERAPIST   What is the feeling inside?

CLIENT   The feeling was, whatever I did was wrong and was exposed to the whole world. I was looking down at the ground hoping he would just go away. In situations like that I thought if I do nothing, if I just don't move, it might all pass, which only made it worse because I looked uncooperative. But I couldn't figure out what I did to deserve his anger. Why me?

THERAPIST   How does that feel... having the coach speak to you like that?

CLIENT   Crushed. Devastated.

THERAPIST   (*gently*) Let's stay with this; how it feels in the body.

CLIENT   I'm feeling weak, vulnerable, with a caved-in chest, and all tight around a hollow center. I'm just crushed, with the whole world weighted on top of me.

THERAPIST   (*nods*) Destroyed, crushed...

CLIENT   Suddenly I'm hyperaware of what's around me... It's like I'm no longer looking out onto the world, but it's reversed – people are staring back from the world directly at me. I'm stunned; everything goes into slow motion and goes deathly silent.

THERAPIST   What's the feeling inside?

CLIENT	Numb. No feeling. Like I'm frozen. I go into just feeling nothing.
THERAPIST	Try to stay with that "frozen" and stay connected to me.
CLIENT	(*shakes his head*) It's scary, I want to run and hide. I want to turn, or cover my face.
THERAPIST	(*leans forward*) Do you feel my understanding and acceptance of you in the moment, here and now – between you and me?
CLIENT	(*nods slowly; begins to visibly relax*)
THERAPIST	Try to allow yourself to really stay with your feelings of shame right now. To really express what that shame feels like.
CLIENT	(*long pause, as he attempts to center himself in his body*) OK... Well, I feel embarrassed, small, curled up, exposed, naked, heavy. (*pause*) There's a contraction of the rib cage...it's collapsed.
THERAPIST	OK...
CLIENT	(*pauses, considers*) It feels unfair. Why should this be happening?
THERAPIST	Let's just stay with those feelings in your body.
CLIENT	(*considers*) I'm also feeling anger now, resentment.
THERAPIST	The anger you felt then?
CLIENT	No. I didn't feel anger then. But I can feel the anger now toward that guy who treated that little kid that way.
THERAPIST	Stay with that anger now. How does that feel?
CLIENT	It's an energy. A force...
THERAPIST	Where?
CLIENT	Throughout. It radiates out from my center chest – out my arms, even to my fingertips. (*pauses, looking directly at the therapist*) I believe you also see the injustice, and that allows me to see the injustice in it.
THERAPIST	And that allows you to feel the *anger* about that injustice!
CLIENT	Yes!...Why should this have to happen? I'm angry to be in this situation. But at the same time I'm kind of scared to be angry...because I think they're right.

THERAPIST   Getting angry at yourself isn't going to help you. You were an innocent little child! Having a good time, just playing.

CLIENT   (*moving into sadness for himself*) I was just an innocent kid playing in the schoolyard... doing what felt normal... And he made me feel worthless... that guy who degraded me.

THERAPIST   That innocent little boy had no idea he was violating any social rules... He was just a child playing. (*long pause*) You seem more pensive... What's the feeling... now?

CLIENT   Sad.

THERAPIST   Yeah... And where inside?

CLIENT   My whole body feels heavy... Yeah, I truly feel sorry for that little kid.

[Several more minutes of discussion of the shaming event go by, and then the session time comes to an end.]

THERAPIST   Do you feel I was able to be with you on this?

CLIENT   (*looking up, slight smile*) Yeah, you were with me... You knew what that little kid... (*correcting himself*) what *I* felt like. But you didn't make it easy. Like, you didn't let me get away with much.

THERAPIST   Was that OK? I mean, was I not fair with you?

CLIENT   Oh, no. (*smiles*) You were fair, but you pushed me to go into those feelings – you were tough.

THERAPIST   What's the feeling for me right now?

CLIENT   (*looking in therapist's eyes*) Appreciation. Yeah.

THERAPIST   No problems?

CLIENT   No.

THERAPIST   This was hard work for you, reliving those moments and staying connected to me.

CLIENT   Yes.

THERAPIST   Can you feel my appreciation for what you did today?

CLIENT   Yeah. I can. (*nodding, direct eye contact*) I appreciate that. (*laughs*) That is, I appreciate your appreciating. (*laughs*)

Double looping about a past shame moment. In this second example of a past shame, the thirty-four-year-old client begins the session not sure about what he wants to discuss. As he attends to his bodily cues, a litany of past shame-infused events soon begins to unfold.

CLIENT   I don't know where to begin. Where do I go from here? What's my next step?

THERAPIST   Begin with your body. Just attend to what you're feeling inside…let your body tell you.

CLIENT   (*after a few moments*) There's a big blanket sitting on top of me. It's heavy. (*pausing to consider*) Like I can't move…it's paralyzing. (*acts as if having difficulty taking a deep breath*)

THERAPIST   What does that feel like?

CLIENT   It doesn't hurt, but I feel taped down, squeezed tight; like there's duct tape wrapped all around. (*gestures to chest area*)

THERAPIST   Yeah. Stay with that.

CLIENT   There is a frustration. I want to cry.

THERAPIST   Sure…of course you do. Where in the body does "crying" feel centered?

CLIENT   (*eyes tearing up, reddening*) Um, in my eyes. (*like a little boy, he points to his eyes with both index fingers*)

THERAPIST   (*gently*) Sure. (*waiting*) Sure…

CLIENT   And also on my side, right here. (*pointing to spot*) Like an arrow piercing my heart. Like it's stuck inside there. (*burrowing index finger into side of his rib*)

THERAPIST   (*nodding slowly, attentively*)

CLIENT   (*heavy sigh, as if having trouble breathing*) I feel so ashamed, so embarrassed.

THERAPIST   How does shame feel right now?

CLIENT   I feel it in my face. (*pointing to the entire area of his face*)

THERAPIST   (*nodding*) And you're feeling that now, no?

CLIENT   (*nods*) I feel like I want to hide my face. I feel ugly.

[Client moves to the second triangle, and therapist moves with him.]

CLIENT   That's how I always felt, ugly and skinny and weak. Everyone told me I was all of those things.

THERAPIST   Like who?

CLIENT   My parents.

THERAPIST	Your parents told you you were ugly?
CLIENT	Indirectly. My older brothers treated me like I was an embarrassment. They didn't want to be seen with me.

[Therapist attempts to double loop client's shame.]

THERAPIST	Arnie, how does "embarrassed, ashamed" feel now – with me, right in this moment?
CLIENT	I felt repulsive. I had it pounded into my head.
THERAPIST	(*moving client back into present*) Yeah...but can you feel the shame with me – right now, in this moment, right here?
CLIENT	(*under his breath*) I feel like I'd better run.
THERAPIST	(*a little surprised*) You want to run?
CLIENT	(*nodding slowly*)
THERAPIST	Like where, from here?
CLIENT	(*still slowly nodding*)
THERAPIST	What does that feel like, "running"?
CLIENT	Uh, a feeling of tension in my legs, my calves. (*reaching down and rubbing his calves*)
THERAPIST	Let's stay with this, Arnie. (*slowly, reassuringly*) Let's just stay with this for a while.
CLIENT	(*nodding slowly*) I remember there was this kid, Tommy, and doing...sexual stuff with him. You know, pulling down our pants and stuff. We were in his backyard, and his father walked out and said something to us, I don't remember. He told my father about it, but my father never said anything to me. (*shrugging his shoulders*)
THERAPIST	Arnie, (*looking seriously into his eyes*) how do you feel right now, telling me about this?
CLIENT	I want to shrink. I want to disappear. I feel very small.
THERAPIST	Let's stay with this. Tell me more, what's the feeling of "disappearing" feel like inside?
CLIENT	It's that feeling that's exactly opposite of when I have to look "powerful and in-charge" – that male mask I always have to put on.
THERAPIST	(*nodding slowly, looking into client's eyes*) Yeah.
CLIENT	(*eyes tearing up*) I'm hoping you won't hate me. (*crying*)

THERAPIST   I know this is hard.

CLIENT   (*continuing to sob, slowly composing himself, moving to thoughts of the past*) I remember being at a Christmas party. There was a group of girls. I was with them, and we were all laughing and... (*hesitant*) I felt (*voice softening*) ...like I was a girl. (*shrugging shoulders, wincing and then squirming*) I remember feeling like a girl.

[Therapist senses the client's need to tell his painful past. Therapist goes with him.]

THERAPIST   That was a difficult time.

CLIENT   That was about the time kids started calling me fag. Sissy or girlie, they would say. I remember trying so hard to be liked. I had a stack of academic awards from school in my room. I thought that if I only got good grades, then I mattered. There was this kid, Monty. I always wanted his attention. He was the opposite of me – good-looking, popular, athletic, tough and strong, people always wanted to be around him. But kids like him never sought me out. I was just so hungry to be accepted, to be wanted.

THERAPIST   (*attempting to return to "us"*) Arnie, have you ever told these events to anybody?

CLIENT   (*shaking his head*)

THERAPIST   What do you think my reaction is to your sharing these memories with me? (*looking into his eyes*) What do you think I'm seeing right now as I'm looking at you?

CLIENT   A broken man.

THERAPIST   Yes, a broken man trying to put himself together, facing some pretty awful memories and feelings and having the courage to face them... the courage to revisit the hurt. And the very real injustice.

CLIENT   (*nods, slightly smiles*)

THERAPIST   (*noticing his smile*) How are you feeling right now? (*waiting expectantly*)

CLIENT   Like you understand.

THERAPIST   (*gently*) This has been a difficult session for you today. You

were squirming, you were tearing up, there was a lot of discomfort. I've got to tell you what appreciation, admiration
I feel for what you have done for yourself today – revealing
things you've felt you had to keep buried inside. It really
hurt to do that.

CLIENT   (*long pause; slowly nods*)

THERAPIST   (*long pause*)

CLIENT   (*nods*) Yes…

THERAPIST   What are you feeling inside now as I am telling you my
                reaction to you?

CLIENT   (*heavy sigh, nodding*) Relieved. (*pause*) Yeah, I'm glad I told
                you, I've been carrying this around for twenty years.

THERAPIST   (*gently, slowly*) I'm feeling a connection between us right
                now, an understanding. Because we've gone into those
                feelings together. What do you feel about us right now?

CLIENT   (*cautiously*) Good. (*takes a deep breath*) Yes. (*another deep
                breath*) It feels good. I'm feeling better.

Double looping in a present shame moment. When he was a toddler,
twenty-five-year-old Jonathan had a medical condition that delayed his
growth. Many times left alone in the hospital, he was marked with memories of abandonment. His belief was that because his parents were helpless
to do anything about his damaged body, he was sent away from them.
Throughout childhood he was teased by his male peers for being frail.

He begins this session talking about Walt, his boyfriend, about whom
he feels intensely ambivalent.

CLIENT   I've been thinking about Walt.

THERAPIST   What about?

CLIENT   (*laughs nervously*) Like I want to have sex with him. (*nervous
                giggle*) Like… I wanna grab his d—k! (*then, with intense
                frustration*) I'm serious, I really am thinking a lot about him.

THERAPIST   Tell me about it. What exactly is sexual about Walt?

CLIENT   He's like a… a dad, and he really likes me.

THERAPIST   Let's go to your body now. Let's see what's there.

CLIENT   (*surprised, laughing*) My body! (*loud laugh*) I'm turned on!

THERAPIST   Yeah, I know. Let's stay with that: "He's like a dad, and he really likes me."

CLIENT   I want him to pick me up and hold me. (*long silence*)

THERAPIST   (*waits silently, then speaks softly*) What's happening?

CLIENT   I'm full of anxiety.

THERAPIST   OK. Where?

CLIENT   I don't know. (*pause, dismissive laugh*) I'm tired. I was up late last night.

THERAPIST   Sure. Stay with your body right now... Tired! Where do you feel tired?

CLIENT   My head feels heavy. (*a helpless, plaintive look*) Like I don't really want to do this.

[Therapist decides to use corroborative method.]

THERAPIST   OK. Listen. We can drop this. We don't need to get into your feelings for Walt right now. We can do whatever you want, but I think it would be really valuable for you to see what feelings are there for him.

CLIENT   I guess... OK.

THERAPIST   (*pauses, then speaks gently*) OK. What are your feelings for Walt? (*waits*)

CLIENT   (*heavy sigh, seems frustrated*) I just feel shame about (*self-conscious laugh*) talking about my homosexual feelings like this. (*shrugs helplessly*) I feel like a child who wants a father, and I'm embarrassed by it.

THERAPIST   You're being critical of yourself. You're condemning that little boy.

CLIENT   (*desperately*) I want it so badly. I'd do anything for him. I even imagine being totally vulnerable sexually with him.

THERAPIST   What's "vulnerable"?

CLIENT   I'm getting turned on thinking about it.

THERAPIST   What's the feeling?

CLIENT   Sexual! Like "hot"!

THERAPIST   Stay with it.

CLIENT   (*laughs, self-conscious*) I'm getting turned on just thinking he's gonna F—k me. He's gonna fill me. He loves me and he wants to fill me. Yeah, the whole idea feels totally sexual. There's something about...his hands; they're safe. They're not gonna hurt me. It doesn't feel degrading. He's a man and he's giving me something I need. His d—k. Like there's an acknowledgment of me. He's with me because I'm a man too...Not only that; I'm a man with these emotional needs right now. (*nervous laugh*) I'm feeling these strange feelings in my a—. It feels like a burning...enough to allow him to come into me...the gateway to allow him in.

THERAPIST   Yeah, and what are you feeling right now?

CLIENT   All over. I feel it all over my body.

THERAPIST   The feeling...

CLIENT   Feels good, my whole body. My head feels heavy. It feels so primal. I want that.

THERAPIST   That?

CLIENT   His masculinity. It's real. His penis is perfect. It's exaggerated. (*laughs self-consciously*) It's really long and thick. Almost nine inches long, it's ideal! Mine is not as big, also the shape is kind of crooked, not as perfect as it should be. God, if only I had Walt's d—k, I don't think I'd be having sex with a guy. I'd be wowing women. Sometimes I fantasize he is F—king a woman; that's such a turn-on to me. If I had the perfect d—k, then I'd be Walt, with the perfect d—k, F—king women. Sometimes I just want to hold it. (*slight laugh*) I don't know what to do with it. I just want to own it or something. This feeling is F—king strong. (*long pause, voice becomes shrill*) But it's terrifying because I don't want to keep doing and doing it, over and over, like this. But I have the need to pursue it.

THERAPIST   (*nods*) What's the feeling?

CLIENT   Oh s—t. It's because...it's a power drug.

THERAPIST   Yeah.

CLIENT   This is embarrassing.

THERAPIST   (*offhandedly*) What's embarrassing?

CLIENT	About sharing this.
THERAPIST	What about?
CLIENT	It makes me feel vulnerable, as vulnerable to you as I am to Walt.
THERAPIST	You're feeling embarrassed now?
CLIENT	(*squirming in chair*) Yeah, showing you how desperate I am is embarrassing. Like you can see right through me. You can see beneath to what I'm feeling.
THERAPIST	What's that? What's that feeling beneath?
CLIENT	Tortured.
THERAPIST	Is it about what I might be thinking of you?
CLIENT	(*nods*) ... That I'm weird.
THERAPIST	(*quietly, calmly*) Talk to me about how you feel, right now, in our connection together.
CLIENT	I'm reminded about how much I need it.
THERAPIST	It?
CLIENT	Sex. (*pause*)
THERAPIST	And...
CLIENT	And I feel inappropriate right now. (*giggle*) And you must think I'm (*laughs*) a crazy wacko! (*laughs*)
THERAPIST	Do you really think I'm seeing you as a crazy wacko?
CLIENT	(*suddenly serious*) No. (*heavy sigh, relaxes, shoulders drop*) I just find this stuff difficult to talk about.
THERAPIST	To *me*. Difficult to talk to *me*.
CLIENT	Yeah, I guess.
THERAPIST	Then to who?
CLIENT	Yeah, to you.
THERAPIST	(*long pause*) Do you feel I understand you? I mean, really – with compassion?
CLIENT	(*calming down further, looking at therapist directly*) Yes. I know you understand me. Who would better?
THERAPIST	I understand how important Walt and his d—k are to you. (*smile, half laugh*)
CLIENT	(*smiling, slight laugh*)
THERAPIST	I know how difficult that was to express, in such detail, those

	powerful feelings. That was not easy. Thanks for letting me see that part of you, Jonathan.
CLIENT	(*looks down*)
THERAPIST	Can you give me some eye contact here?
CLIENT	(*slowly looks up*) Yeah.
THERAPIST	How are you feeling right now?
CLIENT	I don't know.
THERAPIST	About my response to you right now … is there any feeling response?
CLIENT	I feel like you understand me.
THERAPIST	And how does that feel?
CLIENT	Good.
THERAPIST	Where is it "good"? Where inside?
CLIENT	(*searching, calm*) It's relief of the tightness in my chest …
THERAPIST	(*nods thoughtfully*)
CLIENT	Like a relief, a relaxation …

Not a time for interpretation. The double loop process does not take advantage of opportunities to offer interpretation – however tempting they may be. Interpretation is more effectively done after the double loop, during the final, meaning transformation phase.

In subsequent sessions Jonathan was able to see his obsession (as he admitted it to be) with Walt's penis as an envy response because of the defects he felt in his own body. This occurred when the therapist later took the opportunity to repeat Jonathan's own words; "God, if I had Walt's d—k, I don't think I'd be having sex with guys. I'd be wowing women."

Mindful of the rule "Where there is narcissism, there is shame," we see Jonathan shamefully acknowledging his narcissistic illusion of incorporating Walt's idealized penis and the masculine power it represented. Double looping with the therapist helped to expose and neutralize the underlying shame. By substituting self-compassion for self-criticism, as modeled by the therapist, Jonathan was gradually able to surrender his shame for the failure of his narcissistic illusion. Months later he was able to fully enter into the grief of the medical problems of his childhood. He also began to revisit the ways he had experienced parental abandonment.

CHAPTER 12

From Double Bind to Double Loop

Having defined the double bind and the double loop in chapters ten and eleven, I will now address their relevance within the therapeutic relationship.

From my clinical experience, those conflicts that most seriously threaten the continuation of treatment are situations in which the client experiences himself to be in a double bind regarding the therapist. These conflicts, often silently harbored and unexpressed, challenge the therapist to successfully "double loop the double bind."

In the course of therapy it is inevitable that at some point there will be misunderstandings that leave the client feeling hurt and frustrated. Past associations of abuse/neglect/malattunement and the resulting feelings of suspicion and powerlessness will resurface, distorting the therapist's intended message and leaving the client feeling angry and betrayed. The therapist's lack of accurate attunement, no matter how slight, may at any time be the catalyst for a serious breach.

The novice therapist may view the double looping process as unproductive; a time-out from "real" therapy, and may perceive efforts to repair a minor miscommunication as an interruption from addressing more pragmatic issues. But this is a mistake because the central healing process is the intersubjective experience of attunement, especially teaching the client to

Double Bind

Double Loop

1. *Self.* Feels and expresses authentic needs to other

Self   Other

2. *Other.* Responds with punishment (ignore, discount, criticize, etc.)

3. *Self.* Responds to punishment (sadness, anger, hurt, disappointment, etc.)

4. *Other.* Responds to response with further punishment

5. *Result.*
   • Internalizes negative introject, *shamed*
   • Abandons authentic needs
   • Split-off from self and others

1. *Self.* Feels and expresses authentic needs to other

Self   Other

2. *Other.* Responds with affirmative attunement

3. *Self.* Receives affirmation (connected, secure, reassured, etc.)

4. *Self.*
   • Abandons negative introject
   • Integrates authentic needs
   • Unification with self and others

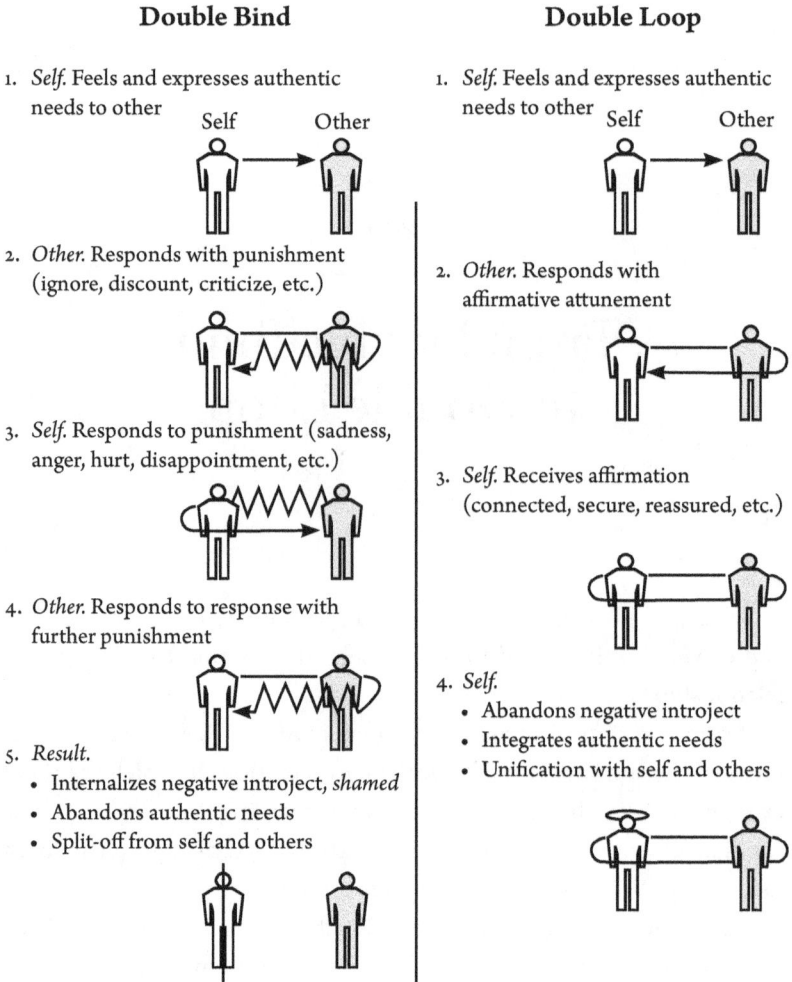

Figure 12.1 Double bind and double loop

openly express his feelings and then to reengage emotionally after a breach. Such an experience shows him that he can indeed negotiate the process of *attunement-misattunement-reattunement* and regain his lost trust.

These moments of reattunement are comparable to the mother-infant "repair" of emotional miscoordination, and represent the essence of treatment.

Eight Steps for Transforming a Double Bind into a Double Loop

1. Client's feelings are hurt by therapist. The therapist does something to hurt the client's feelings when his insensitive action or misconstrued remark evokes the client's hurt, anger, disappointment and sense of betrayal.

2. Client anticipates double bind. The client is negatively affected by the therapist's actions but is afraid to discuss it. He believes speaking up will only make matters worse – the therapist will manipulate him, prove him wrong or reject and overpower him. (This is the client's anticipatory shame.) The client fears that if he mentions the problem, the therapist will "think less of him" (e.g., perceive him as silly, foolish, too sensitive, "looking for trouble," "making a big deal out of nothing"). Thus the client anticipates being placed in a double bind.

3. Client inadequately expresses the conflict. Anticipating the double bind, the client "hedges his bets" by attempting to express his feelings maladaptively – either indirectly (through self-deprecating, passive-aggressive behavior or affective dissociation) or by overtly attacking, accusatory statements.

4. Therapist facilitates client's expression. The therapist encourages more open communication by coaxing and encouraging the client's full expression of his grievance. He must empathically attune to and accurately reflect the client's feelings. The therapist may say, "Oh, so when I said _____, it made you feel _____." Or "When I responded with _____, that gave you the feeling that I was feeling _____ toward you." The therapist expresses in his own words (rather than repeating back the client's way of saying it) what he believes was the client's experience at that moment of misunderstanding and what it must feel like for him now.

5. Therapist checks attunement. The therapist checks his attunement to the client to make sure that the client feels fully understood and empathized with in the present moment.

6. Client's embodied shift from double bind to double loop. The client's acceptance of the therapist's empathic response is seen in his embodied shift from tense/defensive to calm/softening. This is the moment when the double bind becomes the double loop. When he feels fully heard and understood, the client becomes more animated, expressive and "alive." He displays a clarity of expression and is more present, attentive, awake and alert. Even his posture shifts; he may sit up or lean forward. His facial expression will be more focused; his voice more resonant, deeper and have more "push." Very simply, he will abruptly "come into the room" and take on the assertive stance.

7. Therapist encourages the client's articulation of this shift. The therapist asks the client how he feels right now; this allows the client to consciously attend to the feeling of being understood. Client and therapist sit together in this experience. It is important to dwell fully in this attunement moment, allowing the client to fully savor the sense of being emotionally reconnected. Past emotional betrayals may have created resistance to owning what just happened. But encouraging him to verbalize his experience of feeling understood will facilitate the client's cognitive understanding and deepen the positive transference. The task of verbalization appears to "seal in" the double loop experience.

In a double-mirror metacommunication the experience is something like "I am seeing you, seeing me, seeing you, seeing me, seeing you…" The double loop thus ends with mutual understanding of the problematic situation, but more importantly, with an affective synchronicity. This synchronicity brings with it calm, security, peace and strength.

Some clients resist this step of the double loop – receiving attunement – by diminishing themselves or the therapist. The therapist needs to listen to the client's self-sabotaging efforts to accept another person's empathy. He might say, "My sense is you're making unimportant what just happened between us." "You seem not to be appreciating the good work you've just accomplished." The therapist expresses his full appreciation for the client's courage in taking such a risk, acknowledging how difficult it must have been for him to express his grievance when he anticipated further disapproval.

8. The therapist discloses his experience of the client. The therapist acknowledges his now-better understanding of the client; further, he explains that this problem and their ability to work through it together has deepened their mutual understanding. He encourages the client to share what this interaction had done for him (i.e., what he might have gained in the process).

9. [Optional last step] Therapist discloses his role in having created the double bind. We have found this step to be less important to the client, but more important for the therapist, who may feel the need to explain himself (or herself). The therapist offers his side of the problematic incident, disclosing his intent and motivation for the behavior that was perceived as hurtful. At this time he should acknowledge and humbly admit the ways he has contributed to the problem. This part of the double loop experience includes the client seeing the therapist not as perfect but more realistically as an ordinary, sometimes misattuned, and flawed human being.

Transcript Example of Steps to Transforming a Double Bind into a Double Loop

Step 1. The client's feelings are hurt by therapist. In the previous session Brian felt unfairly criticized by the therapist.

Step 2. The client anticipates a double bind. The session begins with Brian attempting to express his grievance but anticipating that the therapist will react critically.

Step 3. The client inadequately expresses the bind. Brian approaches the conflict in a very roundabout manner. Rambling on for a while, he indirectly suggests that perhaps he is to blame for the miscommunication.

CLIENT   In our last session I don't think that I communicated to you clearly. I was possibly too ambiguous. I wasn't even sure if I communicated because I was emotionally and physically exhausted. I had just come back from my grandmother's funeral. Anyway, one of your responses was that you linked this issue I had raised with some kind of assertion problem within me.

THERAPIST   *(caught off-guard, confused)* Yes...?

CLIENT   And the other issues I've got – and I didn't agree with – is that at first you tried to explain why you thought there was an assertion issue I had to deal with, and at some point in the conversation you got irritated at me and your actual words were, "I'm getting frustrated with you."

THERAPIST   (*begins to catch on*) Oh, OK.

CLIENT   And I recalled a while back you said to me, "The therapist should never lose his self-control however difficult the client might be. The therapist should just remain in control and not let his emotions come out in a way that's detrimental"... something like that.

Step 4. *Therapist facilitates client's expression.*

THERAPIST   Right. But I'm a little confused. Tell me clearly what you want to say. I really do want to understand what upset you.

CLIENT   What I want to say is, last week I felt you criticized me unfairly. What I had done as an assertion, you said was not an assertion.

THERAPIST   OK. So tell me how you feel now about it.

CLIENT   (*hesitating*) Well... OK. My feeling is (*finally blurting it out*) I'm angry with you.

THERAPIST   (*calmly, but revealing his concern*) Sure. (*nodding affirmatively*)

CLIENT   (*emboldened by the therapist's affirmation, nods, becomes more direct*) I'm angry. (*nodding seriously*) Yes. And I think this taps into probably something else: that you like being the one in authority. My sense is that you're trying to get the upper hand, but that's a bit too crude to say, but you like to be in control of the session, and if someone else is trying to control it, you sometimes sort of overpower it.

THERAPIST   (*correcting*) Overpower *you.*

CLIENT   Yes, *me.* At least that's my experience. And just one final point: I think there are times when you get irritated with me. I can hear it in the tone in your voice.

THERAPIST   Yes.

CLIENT   Maybe you have something to say and maybe you can give me your feedback?

THERAPIST   Let's see...so what I hear you saying is that I have a power issue and an inclination to take control over you, which clashes with what you're trying to express, which would be to express a view from your own perspective, yes?

CLIENT   (*nodding in agreement but still tense*)

THERAPIST   And so last session when we discussed the assertion issue, you experienced me as trying to pressure you into giving up your position and seeing things my way. And so that doesn't free you up to be yourself, and that doesn't give you a sense of assurance that I'm going to be completely understanding of what you're trying to tell me, and that makes you feel pressured in your relating to me. Is that correct?

CLIENT   (*anger dissipates*) Well, you're probably thinking I'm generalizing in every case. It's not like that all the time. It just happens every now and then.

THERAPIST   (*continuing to accurately reflect*) It just comes up every now and then.

CLIENT   Yeah. You get frustrated and impatient with me, I sense it in you.

Step 5. The therapist checks attunement.

THERAPIST   OK. (*slowly, thoughtfully*) Do you think I've got it correctly?

CLIENT   Sort of, yes...

THERAPIST   (*not settling for "sort of"*) But I'd really like to get it right. What am I not understanding?

CLIENT   Well, you said "pressured." I did not say "pressured" but "controlled."

THERAPIST   OK..."controlled." That's a different feeling, isn't it? Like "restricted, locked in"...OK.

CLIENT   (*nods*)

THERAPIST   (*waits*) OK. Do you think I've got it? Maybe there's more?

CLIENT   Yes, that's right. Just that sometimes, my hands feel tied.

THERAPIST   Can you tell me more about what that feeling is?

CLIENT   Well, first, I've got just one other point.

THERAPIST   Sure.

CLIENT   My mind is telling me that what you've said is sufficient now, and we can just leave it there – because you made it not only very clear you understand me, but you've gone beyond, when you said that you thought you handled it wrong. I thought you'd gone well beyond what I might have expected you to say, and I really do appreciate your humility on that.

THERAPIST   OK. Yes...

CLIENT   However, there is maybe some emotional stuff which I can't fully pin down that's making my mind ask another question. I'm thinking, "He said he acted wrong in that situation, but he never said sorry" and I'm thinking, *Is that necessary to ask?* But nevertheless there's something in me that's saying, *Why hasn't he said sorry?*

THERAPIST   OK, so do you feel like right now – when you check in with your body – do you feel the need to ask me to say, "I would appreciate it if you would say sorry?" I mean would that be your choice?

CLIENT   Yeah, because my body is still not feeling relaxed, even though in my mind I'm thinking it's been cleared up, but my body is still not feeling fully OK with it. Yet I know it's just a technicality that you have to say "sorry."

THERAPIST   So, in simple terms, your body is saying that you need to fully *feel* me being sorry, which requires those actual words even though your brain is saying, well, that's not necessary, he admitted to me he was wrong.

CLIENT   Yeah, exactly.

THERAPIST   Well, based upon our work together, which one do you think we must respect more: the body or the brain?

CLIENT   The body.

THERAPIST   Absolutely. So why don't you go with the body and put it into words and put it right out there, very directly, for me.

CLIENT   OK. (*hesitant*)

THERAPIST   Tell me, then, clearly: what do you want?

CLIENT   Well, I like what you said, but it doesn't feel very complete, and I think that you've been very humble, but you can be more humble by saying "Sorry." But maybe you don't want to say those exact words.

THERAPIST   OK, makes sense. So here we go, are you ready?

CLIENT   I'm ready. (*smiles*)

THERAPIST   (*spoken with sincerity*) Brian, I truly am sorry. I am sorry because I failed you.

CLIENT   OK.

THERAPIST   (*continuing*) I'm sorry because as your therapist – who should have been attuned to you, who should have been open to your experience, I allowed my frustration to get in the way, and my need, or whatever agenda it was at the moment, superseded my sensitivity to you. And you're here pursuing my help, and you're spending time and money to go to someone who can understand and tune-in to you. That's the most important thing. Rule number one is to really understand and tune-in to your client and his needs, and I failed you here, and for that I am genuinely sorry.

Step 6. Client's embodied shift from double bind to double loop.

CLIENT   (*visible embodied shift to calmness, softening*) Yeah. (*pauses, nodding slowly*) OK, thanks.

Step 7. The therapist encourages the client's articulation of shift.

THERAPIST   (*pausing for a minute or two*) So, tell me: how do you feel right now?... How does that feel to know that I really am sorry?

CLIENT   That was good. I liked that...

THERAPIST   And what's the feeling inside?

CLIENT   I feel completely relaxed. It was really important that we got through this.

THERAPIST   I understand. How do you feel about us right now?

CLIENT   The funny thing is that these disagreements between us are quite infrequent, but because of my past experiences my feelings can come into the present, so I feel like I might anticipate a future conversation like this, even though this conflict doesn't happen often.

THERAPIST   You're right. You've been sensitized to double binds and to people dominating you, and to the feeling that you're not allowed to defend yourself. That's why this talk is so important.

CLIENT   (*nods*)

THERAPIST   I want you to feel OK with me.

CLIENT   (*spontaneous positive association*) A few months ago you said something – we were talking about stuff and you said, I don't know what the words were – you said that we could talk as if we're really close friends although of course there is a professional boundary, and when I heard you say that, it changed my perception of you because until that point I felt the boundaries were even further back because of the professional role.

THERAPIST   And how does that make you feel now as you recall that?

CLIENT   Well, like, I value that you're telling me that.

THERAPIST   Yes, thanks... but the feeling, now?

CLIENT   It's good. Now I can be more relaxed, more myself with you.

THERAPIST   And the feeling inside...

CLIENT   More myself.

THERAPIST   That is exactly how I want you to feel with me. More like yourself.

CLIENT   When you said that, I understood better what you expect between yourself and the client.

THERAPIST   (*correcting*) Between *us*.

CLIENT   Yes, *us*.

Step 8. *Therapist discloses his experience of the client.*

THERAPIST   I feel like we've connected in a different way today. I feel like I've gotten to know you better. I see a clearer, more assertive side to you, which I like seeing.

CLIENT   (*smiles, nodding thoughtfully*) Yeah.

THERAPIST   (*looking at the clock*) Listen, it is about time for us to stop. So how are you doing?

CLIENT   Feeling good, thanks.

THERAPIST   Could you have raised this conflict between us six months ago or a year ago?

CLIENT   Oh, absolutely not!

THERAPIST   Great. I want to tell you that I appreciate what an accomplishment this was for you, and that I saw a strong, assertive side to you to today that I've never seen.

CLIENT   Yes. (*nodding*) I feel it was an accomplishment for me as well. And I'd like to say, I had never felt anything in my body particularly before, and since we've been doing body work, I've become open to it. Now it's really easy; I can feel a particular emotion, and before, I wouldn't have had any inkling of what I felt in my body. I really appreciate the way you've responded to what I've brought up, and my body is telling me that it's really changed very hugely the dynamic we have between us.

THERAPIST   I'm glad about that.

Step 9. Therapist discloses his role in creating the double bind.

THERAPIST   Brian, I'd also like to give you some feedback from my perspective. Maybe I should explain a frustration that I sometimes have. I sort of feel set up by you sometimes in that you will ask me a question, and I will answer, but my answer never seems good enough to you. It leads to another question, which I again try to answer, which leads on and on... I'm seeing clearly now that I need to identify those moments where I feel led on and on, and comment on them. And when that happens, that's my problem – it's not your problem, and I must look at why I get frustrated with you.

CLIENT   So are you saying that you haven't got something quite right?

THERAPIST   Yeah, absolutely.

CLIENT   I appreciate your humility.

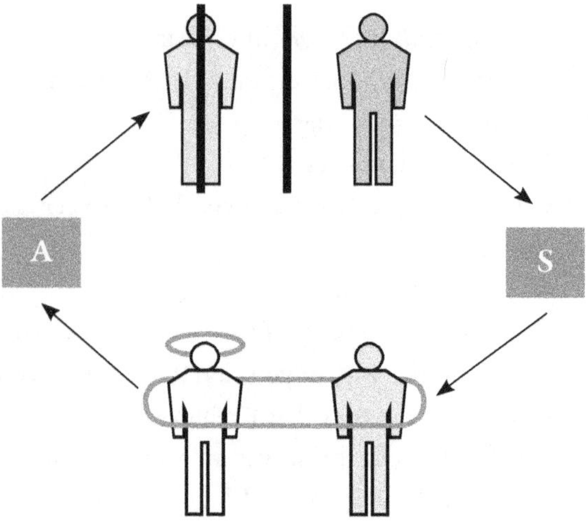

Body (Chest)
Double Loop: S → A = Open, expansive
Double Bind: A → S = Clenched, tight

Figure 12.2 Double looping the double bind

THERAPIST   If I get frustrated, then there's something wrong about me;
you're absolutely right ... and I think there's something about
our communicative style that brings up this argumentative
response in me, which I've got to watch; it's not good. But
it's very good that you can bring that up to me now, so that
we can look at it. You can remind me that I have to watch
that, because it doesn't serve you well. When I work with
a client ... (*correcting himself*) when I work with *you*, I have
to put that aside and just get totally into your experience.

Resistance to the Double Loop

When the client experiences a disappointment that he cannot openly
discuss, he may actually create a double bind.

He creates this no-win situation most often by devaluing himself (and
his ability to communicate) or the therapist (and his ability to care). He
blames the (now "inadequate") therapist, who has been made into a bad
object, with the idea that "you really don't want to [or cannot] understand

me." Or he might blame himself (the "shamed self") for not fulfilling the therapist's expectations: "I can't do what is necessary [express myself clearly, feel and describe my feelings] to be understood by you."

The client needs to understand that disagreements are a normal part of adult-adult communication, and specifically here, within the working alliance. These disagreements offer an important experiential lesson: that misunderstandings can lead to a new and deeper understanding.

Some clients re-create the double bind in anticipation of further hurt and betrayal. This is a mechanism for remaining isolated – a pattern of repeatedly pushing others away by creating a no-win situation with them.

We have found that the most common form of resistance to the therapist's efforts at double looping the double bind involves the client's creation of still another double bind. The creation of this double bind is built on the premise that the other person is wrong (e.g., defective, dishonest, judgmental, malicious, incompetent).

Obstacles that block the therapeutic relationship most often involve expectations (spoken and unspoken) within the working alliance, as with this client, Tom.

THERAPIST   Do you feel I'm with you on this issue?

CLIENT   Yeah, I think you understand.

THERAPIST   Not just "understand." Do you feel I'm on your side?

CLIENT   I think you have your own vision of what that means to be "with me" on this.

THERAPIST   How do you mean?

CLIENT   Well, (*hesitantly*) it's you who gets to set the limits on the relationship. For you, it's just a weekly session thing…

THERAPIST   Yeah…

CLIENT   I'm jealous. You can set the terms of the relationship, I can't.

THERAPIST   That's the truth, the undeniable truth that we have separate lives…I just want to be here in the best way I can for you during our time together each week. (*waiting for a response*) What do you think? (*waits*) Do you feel I'm doing that enough?

CLIENT   (*reluctantly*) Yeah. I guess so.

The session ends before there is time for their unreconciled difference to be explored, with the client's jealously of the therapist's private life unresolved.

Clients are motivated to create the resistance of the double bind whenever the "child within" believes the therapist will be like all the people in his life who have had the power to hurt and betray him. The power of the double bind lies precisely in the fact that it is not communicated. The client's fearful anticipation of it prevents him from expressing it. It is a learned defense from childhood that serves to protect him from unjust humiliation and is usually reflective of a repeated practice of pushing others away by creating a double bind. As such, it is a repetition compulsion.

Table 12.1 Two Ways Client Sabotages the Therapeutic Double Loop

	Failure to Communicate	Failure to Care
1. Devaluing of therapist	"You won't be able to understand me." "You don't know what it's like." "You've never been through this."	"You don't really care about me." "You're supposed to act as if you like me." "You're just doing your job."
2. Devaluing of self	"I can't express how I feel." "I don't know how to put words to what is happening inside."	"My feelings don't matter." "It won't make any difference." "My life won't change."

Joining with the Client on the Other Side of the Divide

The therapist should not attempt to resolve the double bind by simply explaining himself to the client. Offering emotional reassurance and trying to persuade with logic never helps and typically intensifies the defense.

The best approach is to join with the client in his feeling of being misunderstood, to stand with him in his double bind predicament and to empathize with his experience of being on the other side of a no-win barrier. Only by fully entering into the man's experience *as his ally* will the therapist succeed in overcoming the barriers created by hurt, anger and disappointment. That is the process that double loops the double bind.

CHAPTER 13

The Scenario
Preceding Homosexual Enactment

When I'm feeling shamed, then I'll want relief – some drug.
I'll keep on looking until I find something to lust after.

What actually takes place when our client moves into an episode of homosexual enactment? In this chapter I describe the function of the various self-states as they lead the client into an incident of unwanted same-sex behavior.

I will address the following self-states: (1) assertion, (2) shame, (3) the false self, (4) the gray zone and (5) homosexual enactment (HE).

The Empowerment Mode: A Birthright

The glory of God is man fully alive.

– St. Irenaeus

I can't go forward in life unless I begin with me getting more in touch with myself, becoming more assertive.

– thirty-four-year-old

It's really exciting to be who I was meant to be. This is the most important responsibility I have – to be myself.

– twenty-three-year-old

The man with the homosexual problem often holds the unconscious belief that he has little or no personal power. He believes that other people fail to take him seriously and do not respectfully hear him. The assertive state, on the other hand, is the healthy frame of mind where the client belongs. It is, as one man said simply, "my empowerment mode."

Assertion is the state from which is found the true gendered self. Assertion is part of a man's biologically rooted gender identity and is grounded in the basic human drive for self-mastery. In this stance the man feels calm, clear, centered, secure and strong, and he is able to influence the people around him.

When there is a consistency between inner needs and their exterior expression, he is able to grow in integrity, honesty, authenticity and self-possession. With a clarity and unity of his needs and desires, he lives in relational dignity and harmony. From the assertive stance we see spontaneous bursts of creativity, vitality, expressivity and joy.

Assertion of Self

- effective expression of authentic needs, wants and desires
- expression of true self
- spontaneous, vital, responsive, creative, gender-related
- able to express anger, a boundary-setting (self-protective) emotion
- *emotionally open*

Assertion is rooted in the biological drive to stay connected to the pack. But when assertion is blocked by shame, the damage to the personality is devastating. Many same-sex attracted men (SSA), having been shamed for their assertion, feel driven to find sexual partners who actually deepen and justify the shame:

> I want to have sex with guys that intimidate me, who make me feel uncertain about myself. I never have strong feelings for someone who is available, who consistently treats me well. I get bored with men like that – I lose respect for them.

When the man is living in a healthy assertive state, this drive to resolve intimidation through erotic acting out will disappear. He is able to enter into authentic and fully mutual exchanges with other men.

Developing a new life skill. Returning oneself to the assertive state requires practice and focus. As the client becomes better acquainted with it, he eventually finds it to be a place where he feels at home. One man described it this way: "Assertion is my birthright. It is an unoccupied dwelling, yet I own the deed. But I can't just stand there and look at it. I have to go in there and live. I have to take up residence."

Some clients have spontaneous recollections of a much earlier time of assertion when they remember being spontaneous and free, without the shackles of shame and the destructive, inhibitory social posture of the false self.

A qualifier on assertion. Homosexually oriented men are not necessarily nonassertive in all aspects of their lives. There are SSA men who are assertive (and very successful) in business affairs. Where we see the problem is in boundary issues in their private lives, particularly with their families of origin and in their intimate, personal relationships.

The men who come to us find that developing their assertion substantially helps them get out of the "gay mindset." By keeping their focus on developing mutuality and equality with other men, they see themselves as equal to other males – not sexual objects.

Shame

THERAPIST   As a boy, you were never allowed to be bad.
CLIENT   Bad? . . . I was never allowed to be real!

Shame

- anxiety about disapproval
- anticipation of rejection
- fear of disappointing, hurting, letting down other
- *emotionally closed*

Shame in different forms. In previous chapters of this book we have seen how, within our typical client's early environment, the fundamental drive to assert the true gendered self has been compromised. Men who grew up in the triadic-narcissistic family are burdened with the entire range of shutdown emotions, including fear, humiliation and anticipation of rejection.

This shame posture may be evidenced as a passive withdrawal and humiliation. But under the surface is a shame-driven, angry defiance, with an obstinate refusal to be emotionally dependent on another person.

In the service of assertion, anger can be a healthy reaction against a boundary violation by another person – a valid attempt to reestablish appropriate limits. But anger can also be used as a way of shutting out potentially healthy connections with people.

Anticipatory Shame

- often the problem is the client's *anticipation* of shame rather than shame itself
- client's need to understand his own expecting (anticipation) shame, and his being an active agent in creating the shame
- the body reacts (inhibitory affect) in the present as if it were the past (i.e., neurosis)

Anticipation of shame. As one client explained at the close of therapy, "For the first time in my life I'm not running away from myself. I'm feeling what it's like to *not* feel shame. It's amazing to walk around and not feel shame." We often see clients whose entire lives have been structured around the constriction caused by anticipatory shame. A forty-year-old man reflected:

> *Assertive*...that word is the exact opposite of what I am! I live my life always ready to meet with devastating disapproval. I'm tired of being nice. I often find myself in a down mood which was created by others' expectations of me. If people are displeased with me, I have to do something to make it better, because there's always a danger that someone will discover – once again – that I'm not loveable.

As therapy progresses, the client begins to realize that the assertion-shame conflicts that occur in his everyday life are usually not due to an outside shamer but rather to his own anticipation of shame, followed by his own inhibition of assertion.

Revisiting the shutdown moments. Beyond the original assertion-shame shutdown moments, when the client reflects back on his childhood, he often sees that it was not so much a particular shaming incident as *his anticipation of shame* that shut down his pursuit of masculine attachment. He lived with the constant expectation of humiliation for his attempts at assertion. By expecting to be shamed, he made himself the victim of a double bind, no-win situation, and in the classic model of neurosis, he re-creates his past experiences of childhood in his present relationships.

Only when he understands the paralyzing effect of anticipatory shame will the client begin to free himself from victim status. As he overcomes this chronic apprehension of disapproval and begins to authentically assert himself, he discovers homosexuality to be far less compelling:

> I remember, once, I had an argument with my mother about my college plans, and she tried to make me feel bad about not having settled on a college yet. She was intrusive and absolutely had to know – right then and there – what I was going to do with my life. My real feeling was anger, which I didn't express. I wish I had set boundaries about her intrusion and her disempowering demands.
>
> But I didn't, and that very same night, I sought out a homosexual encounter.
>
> I have learned that when I am in the assertive state, I am "myself." I do what is necessary to get my real needs met, without worrying too much about what others think. But when I feel weak and bad inside, then I look outside myself to other men for empowerment and comfort.

Precipitation of shame. Besides the *anticipation* of shame, we also see the client actively *precipitating* the shame, where he creates a shame situation as a form of self-punishment for his brief attempts at assertion.

One man who had struggled with gay fantasies during times of disempowerment told me about an incident that had happened recently. "We were helping this elderly lady with packing for a move," he said, "and I got to talking with her. She was wondering why I wasn't married yet. She says, 'A young man like you needs to meet a nice young lady. I'm going to help you find one!'"

He continued his story:

> My first feeling was elation at the hope of finding a girlfriend. I almost accepted her offer. I was anxious to be dating, and here was my chance. But then I thought about having to tell the girl about the homosexual fantasies I had struggled with in the past, and her being devastated. I pictured the humiliation of her going back to the old lady and saying, "Why did you set me up with a creep like *that?*" So I just kind of shrugged and told her I was too busy for dating.

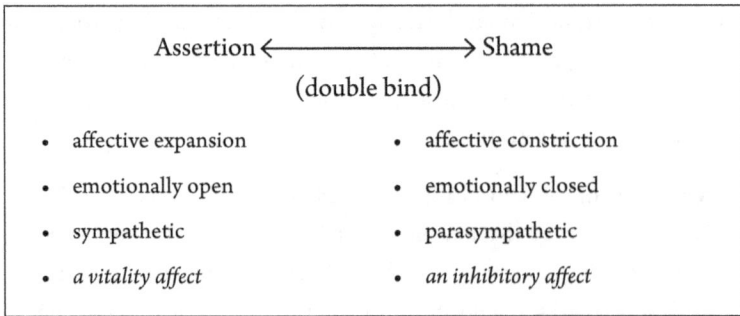

Assertion ←————————→ Shame
(double bind)

- affective expansion
- emotionally open
- sympathetic
- *a vitality affect*

- affective constriction
- emotionally closed
- parasympathetic
- *an inhibitory affect*

The assertion-shame conflict: Origins in the mother-son relationship. The assertion-shame conflict first presents itself in the boy's early attempts at gender self-assertion, which for many men was perceived by them as provoking a parent's displeasure. Typically, this conflict finds its earliest origins in the fear of displeasing or disappointing the mother, which places the boy in a position of ambivalence about his innate masculine strivings, and threatens the maternal attachment bond.

Psychoanalyst Charles Socarides (Socarides & Freedman, 2002) describes this as follows:

> No matter the form of homosexuality, I routinely find anxieties relating to the separation from the mother.... For all clients, the essential task is the elucidation of...fear of the loss of the object, fear of losing the object's love, and an undue sensitivity to approval or disapproval by the parents. (p. 23)

The boy with an insecure attachment to the mother will suffer most acutely when there is also a weak relationship with the father. When the father is in an ineffectual position within the family – for example, through disqualifying himself by his emotional detachment – the mother's influence becomes paramount. As one client said, "It was Mom's game or the abyss."

Later in life, the client who struggles with assertion-shame issues will likely reenact this conflict in his relationship with other women – perceiving his wife, if he marries, to be controlling and manipulative, and experiencing internal conflict each time he attempts to assert his true gendered self.

One man expressed his assertion-shame conflict as being "my fear of disapproval for staying in my truth." Another man, speaking of his present-day relationship with his mother, whose on-again, off-again attention had created a hostile dependency, described a dynamic that we often see within the narcissistic family: "My mother is in her own world, and she brings me in and out of it whenever she wishes."

Use of the False Self to Pacify the Shamers

In chapter two we discussed how the triadic-narcissistic family environment encourages the development of a false self. The false self develops in the type of early mother–son relationship where the boy has two choices: he can either be detached from himself and pleasing to his mother, or attempt to be self-possessed but risk emotional abandonment.

We will now consider the role played by this false self in the "scenario preceding homosexual enactment."

More than just a benign social role in compliance to environmental expectations, the false self is an internal, self-imposed straitjacket that shuts down the vitality affect of assertion. One client described his false self by saying, "I am in a body that is wearing a mask and a costume, and performing on stage."

The false self protects the person from the stress of the assertion-shame conflict, creating a shutdown zone. It is a façade – a staged and cultivated persona – a place of hiding that conceals the man's natural gendered vitality, stops his spontaneity and confines him in a role that is stiff and stylized.

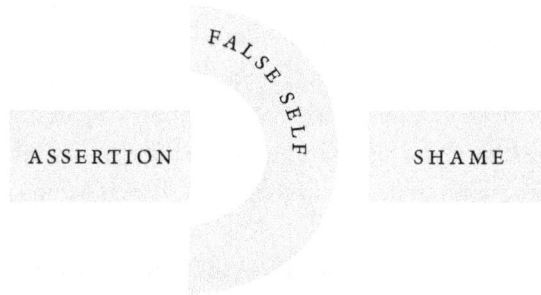

False Self:

- Function: Defense against *exterior* anticipatory shame

    Defense against *interior* anger and sadness

- Feature: Inhibited, pacifying, compliant

- Origin of the "good little boy"

Figure 13.1 The false self

In short, the false self blocks the personal power that would flow naturally from a life lived in the authentic self.

With its childhood origin in the role of the good little boy, this self-disqualifying stance serves as pacification toward future shamers. Clients have described their false self as follows:

> The only way I know how to make emotional connections is to give myself away, to give people what they want of me. It comes down to this: I'd rather be a "false something" than a "real nothing."

> I do what others want because I am afraid of disappointing them.

> I'm terrified of criticism. If I upset someone, it's the end of the world. I get disappointed in myself for disappointing others.

> I realize why I'm into service-type work. I've been serving others all my life, even when I was a child at home with my mother.

> My childhood survival strategy was to figure out what was wanted of me, and to give it; then I could feel OK. I still do that; I create relationships where I give up my power, which on some level, feels like what I actually deserve.

Relating in the false self makes relationships burdensome. Even though he appears to be engaged in his relational world, the man who lives in the false self is secretly detached, not only from others but also from himself. In Fosha's terms he is "dealing, but not feeling." The price for living behind this façade is a lifestyle of isolation.

Thirty-four-year-old client Mark, quoted later, was in several previous gay relationships that he found unsatisfying. After an initial euphoria about the other man, he would develop a hostile dependency. The inherent competitiveness that exists between any two same-sex people would inevitably surface, and he would soon want more from the relationship than he got. Finally – as with almost every gay couple – the relationship would become sexually open, and this would mark the beginning of the end.

Disillusioned and convinced that two men are inherently incompatible, Mark sought to explore his potential for a heterosexual relationship. At the time of the session recounted here, he had been dating a girl for six months. "I want to be authentic in the relationship, and stay connected to the woman," Mark said, but he soon found that the false self of the nice guy was posing a serious obstacle to that goal.

THERAPIST   When you think of Sara, what feelings do you have?

CLIENT   I feel obligated, annoyed and burdened. Sara keeps asking. "What's wrong?" But I don't know. The newness of the relationship just wore off, and now I feel left with the burden of execution. Somewhere along the line, I find myself just "checking out."

THERAPIST   Yes. Staying aloof, not being present to her...

CLIENT   I can't even stay present to myself. I get bored, it becomes no fun and I just want to run. Then I become a cold shell, and the more I get accused of that, the deeper into the shell I want to go. I have this ability to just keep going, to separate my feelings from my behavior. But I find myself tempted to duck out of the relationship and go back to a place where I feel safe... not harassed, molested or violated. But of course, that means I'll be alone again.

[After further discussion, the client acknowledged the self-defeating consequence of his false self.]

CLIENT	The gist of it is, I need to be present to Sara while I'm still present to myself.
THERAPIST	Yes. Not to feel drained by her.
CLIENT	My mother taught me to be present to her, to the exclusion of myself. It's a habit I've gotten into. But I can't put that on Sara. She doesn't deserve it. And I don't deserve that either.
THERAPIST	Having to stay in the "nice guy" persona is tiring – it wears on you. Feels inauthentic. The answer is to stay connected to your inner feelings and sensations and share them with her.
CLIENT	Yes. I've got to learn how to be with her and still stay in the same "real time" me.

Staying Stuck in the Gray Zone

When shame wins out over assertion, when the expectations of others compromise personal integrity, the result is the gray zone.

The gray zone was well described by Shakespeare, who understood the emotional paralysis that accompanies depression:

> In sooth, I know not why I am so sad;
> It wearies me; you say it wearies you;
> But how I caught it, found it, or came by it,
> What stuff 'tis made of, whereof it is born,
> I am to learn;
> And such a want-wit sadness makes of me,
> That I have much ado to know myself.
> (Shakespeare *The Merchant of Venice* 1.1.1)

The gray zone is triggered when significant others reject or a fail to respond to the client's vital affective expression, particularly his attempts at assertion, which propels him into the shame posture.

While shame refers to a shutdown self-state, the gray zone means "*staying* down." Like shame, it is an inhibitory self-state; however, it has a distinctly different feeling. It is a mood that is experienced as dull, flat and lifeless.

In actuality, the gray zone is not a self-state at all, because in it there

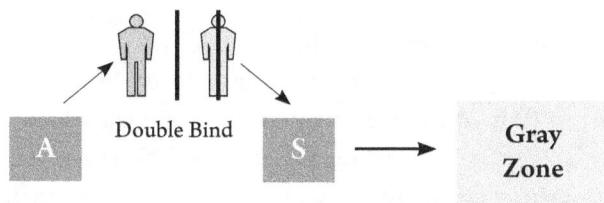

The Gray Zone, also known as

- the depressive position (Klein)
- lingering anaclitic depression (Schore)
- abandonment depression (Masterson)

Figure 13.2 The gray zone

is no felt sense of self. Nor is there an identifiable source for the distress. As clients say, "It's not about anything in particular." Psychodynamic literature would describe it as the "depressive position" (Melanie Klein); the "lingering anaclitic depression" (Schore); or "abandonment depression" (Masterson).

The gray zone is characterized by a pervasive state of disappointment, with vague and undefined frustrations, hurt feelings, and loneliness. It has been described by our clients as "feeling weak, inadequate, helpless, hopeless, powerless, isolated from myself and disconnected from others" or as "just a general feeling of blah."

While the gray zone has a quality of inconsolable brooding, in fact there is some indirect consolation for the helplessness: "I'm in the comfortable spot of indecision, at least." We see blaming of others, weepiness and a sense of victimization: "I feel totally empty, undervalued and disconnected. I don't care. I'm not inside my body. I'm not even here for me. Everyone has abandoned me, and so I abandon myself."

Among the words used by clients to describe their experience are "stuck," "helpless" and "smothered." They identify this petrified quality of this state as "encased," "engulfed" and "trapped." Another client described it as: "I'm in my own world where no one can join me, and there's no way out. It's an empty room, alone and desolate, my own personal pit."

Childhood origins of the gray zone. The gray zone could well be an affective memory of being trapped in the double bind, no-win situation.

Within the triadic-narcissistic family the child was made to feel shame for expressing feelings of abandonment-annihilation. We often hear comments such as, "My father made me ashamed of my sadness. If I cried, he would say, 'I'll give you something to cry about.'" Negative feelings were not supposed to be expressed. The anticipation of this bind often remains alive in adulthood. One man explained, "If I show any feelings of weakness, my friends will reject me. If I tell anyone how bad I feel, they will just go away from me."

Shame about expressing weakness prompts an entrenched hopelessness about the very nature of relationships. "No one can help me; my despair is too deep for anyone to reach. Nobody loves me enough me to hear me or understand me. I am truly alone." As an adult, such a man often finds himself reexperiencing the same numbness and deadness of primal grief and despair.

The gray zone versus grief. In some ways, the gray zone is an extension of childhood self-pity. It is a defensive maneuver against fully feeling real grief with all its sadness and anger. As one man said, "When I'm in this numb state, I don't have to feel sadness about this lonely kid inside me." In the gray zone there is no mind, no heart.

But while the gray zone is empty and meaningless and soulless, the state of true grief contains the vivid experience of self in relation to significant life events. When he is experiencing true grief, the client is feeling authentic feelings about real-life events.

Because grief and assertion are characterized by this deep self-awareness, it is in these two self-states – grief and assertion – that the person is enabled to grow.

Cynicism, masochism and negativity. Depression has often been said to be "anger turned inward." When a man has been shamed, anger is first felt toward the person who shamed him but then is turned back again against the self. Clients typically report that throughout the gray-zone experience they feel a pervasive self-anger. This anger is partly due to the man's self-hatred for being too weak to express anger directly to the shamer.

Not surprisingly, homosexual enactment is particularly attractive to the man who is mired in the gray zone because it releases – and justifies – some of the negative energy he feels against himself.

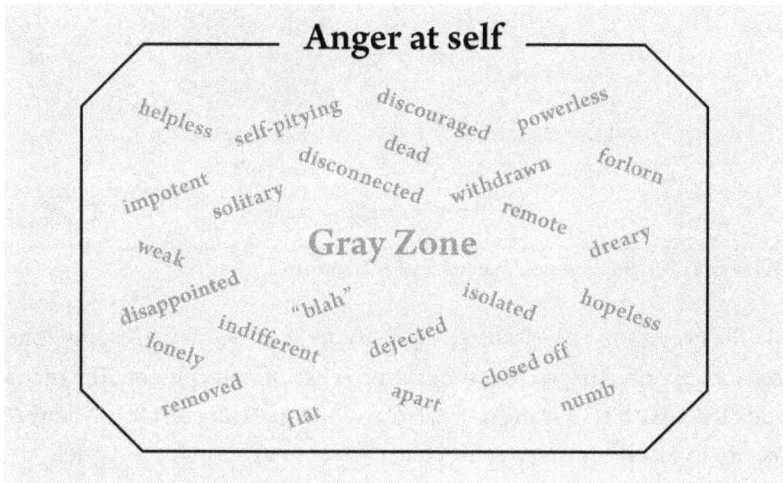

Figure 13.3 Emotions of the gray zone

The shamed person always knows, on some level, that he is not standing up for himself and is allowing himself to be victim. He knows that he has "wimped out" (some of the men say "weaned out") and has given away his rightful power. His self-hatred is expressed indirectly as cynicism and negativity about life and relationships, thus reinforcing his isolation.

In fact, what may appear to the therapist to be his inability to push against the paralyzing deadness in order to connect with others is, on some level, actually an unwillingness to do so, due to a desire to punish himself for having permitted himself to be a victim in the first place.

Being respected in the expression of anger. Many clients, perceiving as children that anger was unacceptable to their parents, say that it would provoke their parents' withdrawal, dismissive contempt, mockery or punishment.

> That's why, even today, I can't express anger – I feel stupid. I don't show it to anyone because I don't feel that it's valid. My mom made fun of me when I got angry, like I was being funny or silly or something. I would get enraged, and that was amusing to her.
>
> I don't have enough confidence to be able to show real masculine anger. I feel like I'm gonna look like a faggot or a girl ... [imitating high-pitched voice] "Oh, look at little 'gay Jason'; he's having a hissy fit!"

Gray Zone	$\longrightarrow$	HE

Hypo-Arousal   Hyper-Arousal

"Shut Down"   "Turn On"

HE=Homosexual Enactment

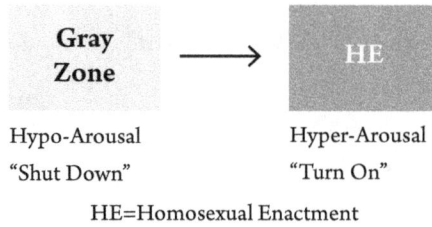

Figure 13.4 The gray zone and homosexual enactment

The gray zone as joylessness, ingratitude: A purgatory. The gray zone is a sort of purgatory with a suffocating sense of detachment. The man's body feels like it is shutting down, collapsing and caving in. He can neither rise up to assert himself nor descend deeper to experience real grief.

The deadening isolation may prompt a hyper-motor defensive reaction described as nervousness, tension, trembling and being on the edge of anger. This is neurologically reminiscent of the dying process, when the central nervous system is struggling to prevent impending annihilation.

Many men report this same state of flighty agitation before acting out homosexually. One man described it as "lots of energy I need to burn off" accompanied by a "panicked, fleeing" feeling. But agitation is not an effort at true assertion. True assertion contains a purposeful energy – not manic excitement – and is characterized by a focused engagement toward a self-chosen goal.

A Christian perspective. One Catholic client compared the gray zone to one of the "seven deadly sins": sloth. Sloth is defined as joylessness, ingratitude, indifference and apathy. In the Catholic tradition, "deadly sin" means capital sin – a sin that leads to other sins.

The sin of sloth encompasses more than mere "laziness"; it is a refusal to obey God's ordering of the world through the *right order of loves* – that is, loving the right things and in the right proportion. When humans stay in a state that is joyless, indifferent and ungrateful (the gray zone) one could say that they are trapped in sloth or deadening apathy.

Homosexual Enactment: A Pseudo-Solution

A quick and easy solution to the loneliness and deadness of the gray zone is found in homosexual enactment. The mere idea instantly shifts the client into a new self-state. As one man explained, "My mood changes instantly. There's a burst of energy, and it's exciting. Suddenly my isolation is gone, and I feel empowered."

The transition from gray zone to the idea of homosexual enactment typically happens as a quick impulse: "All of a sudden, I get the idea that I want to go act out. 'Why not? I'm entitled to feel good – to have sex – and find that "ideal guy" out there.' You know ... it's the same old fantasy."

Boredom and irritability leading to homosexual enactment. The man in this session was committed to his long-time marriage, but recently had been undergoing marital difficulty. As the session opens he reports that he has just impulsively contacted his old boyfriend, Jim. Through body work, he uncovers the feelings of the gray zone that preceded his impulse to act out:

CLIENT	I contacted Danny this week. (*long silence*)
THERAPIST	(*encouraging*) Tell me about it.
CLIENT	I just sent him an e-mail. "Is everything OK?" ... With everything that's been going on [i.e., the client's marital crisis] I knew contacting him could be disastrous ... but ... I wanted to do it anyway.
THERAPIST	What were the circumstances?
CLIENT	(*relaxing a bit*) Well, Jill was in the kitchen, and I was checking my e-mail and I just snatched the opportunity.
THERAPIST	Let's do some body work, OK?
CLIENT	OK.
THERAPIST	So, you're at your computer, what do you feel?
CLIENT	I'm at my laptop ... in the family room.
THERAPIST	And you want to instant-message Danny.
CLIENT	Yeah.
THERAPIST	So go to your body now.
CLIENT	(*considering*) Well, I feel it in my stomach ... at the bottom of my chest.
THERAPIST	(*reassuring*) OK, the bottom of your chest.
CLIENT	Yeah, also my head, my cheeks, sides of my face, eyes ... I just wanted to see what Danny's reaction was.
THERAPIST	Sure, but what's the feeling about that?

[Client seems temporarily lost. Therapist returns him to the conflict moment.]

THERAPIST   So, Jill's in the kitchen and you have this temptation . . . and . . .

CLIENT   I wanted to see what Danny's reaction was.

THERAPIST   Yeah. What's the feeling?

CLIENT   Tightness.

THERAPIST   Sure, . . . tightness, where?

CLIENT   (*thoughtfully*) In the eyes . . . a sharp tension.

THERAPIST   What was that thing in the body that compelled you to contact Danny – to "snatch that opportunity"?

CLIENT   My eyes – tension, on the sides of my eyes.

THERAPIST   Stay with that. (*speaks gently, conveying his concern*) Let's see . . .

CLIENT   In my neck area . . . shoulders . . . and throat. (*long pause*) I'm sort of drifting now (*seeming frustrated with himself*) . . . gotta get my mind back there.

THERAPIST   (*gently correcting*) Gotta get your *body* back there.

CLIENT   (*trying to recall*) Right. Well, I was checking my e-mail. First I was off-line, writing into my financial account program. Then I saw the phone line next to the laptop. I thought, *Oh, whatever. Let's just send an e-mail.*

THERAPIST   The feeling in the body, "Let's just send him an e-mail."

CLIENT   It's the same feeling as just before I look at porn. When I'm not getting along with Jill . . . I have this bored feeling, this irritability . . . and I go to the porn.

THERAPIST   Yeah . . . and the feeling?

CLIENT   And then there's the tingling, a surge in my genitals.

THERAPIST   Yes, stay with that.

CLIENT   An awareness of the first feeling of arousal. The beginning of something that feels good.

THERAPIST   "Arousal." "Something good." "Tingling." "Surge."

CLIENT   (*becoming more animated*) It was almost like "I don't care what's going on and what I'm about to do."

THERAPIST   Stay with that sensation in the body. What else do you feel about that now?

CLIENT   I was feeling a boredom. A "blah"... My shoulders are going down, there's a weight in the stomach... a deadness.

THERAPIST   *(nods)*

CLIENT   Then I'm suddenly feeling impatient... Yes, that's right. It was this underlying feeling of just being fed up with Jill and her never-ending criticism.

[Client then proceeded to productively explore, in detail, the anger and frustration toward his wife that had preceded his sudden impulse to act out, and the steps he needed to take to address that frustration.]

When homosexual enactment is most compelling. A client explains when he is most tempted to act out:

> Homosexual episodes are most likely when I sacrifice self-assertion. If I really don't want to do something, but I go along with it as if I do, I begin to feel minimized. Then I may notice attraction to other guys.
>
> It can be even subtler. For example, if I compare myself to another guy, I can be tempted to elevate him to a superior position and thereby shame myself. This is undoubtedly a distortion, because rather than humbly admit that talents vary from person to person, I am engaging in a mental "contest of personal worth," which makes me feel inferior to the other guy.
>
> Any time I shame myself this way, I am vulnerable to a homosexual episode.

Another man explained:

> It happens when I'm stuck in the gray zone – that foggy, confused, hard-to-think-clearly place where I lived a lot in my life. I get so shut down that I can't even identify what I'm feeling, which I know is really grief and pain and misery all wound up together in one big mess.
>
> During those times, I don't know what to do except stay there, then act out homosexually, then go back to that same shutdown place, and then act out homosexually again for just a little bit of relief. It's an endless, endless cycle.

A third young man described what leads him to seek out porn:

> I went to a gay porn site last night, but as soon as I got started, I remembered how depressed I had been. Not only had I been depressed but I had been avoiding doing anything about it.
>
> The power of these images is that it momentarily bolsters my sense of inadequacy, but then the sadness that comes from feeling that inadequacy.

The gap before enactment. Our clients tell us that there is an identifiable gap of time between the impulse toward homosexual enactment and their actual behavioral response. In that momentary gap resides *the will* – the last chance to choose. This is the final exit, the brief moment that lies between idea and reality. One man describes it:

> When the thought pops into my mind, at that moment in time, just before I cross over, I can choose to let it pass over me. But if I wait a couple of seconds too long, it'll be too late.

"Last week I didn't listen to my heart, and I had a fall," another client said. When asked about his feelings just beforehand, he said, "The attraction comes first as a tightness, a constriction in the chest – like fear – and then travels down into excitement in the groin."

Another man said that when he feels himself tempted, it helps to remind himself that "the gripping fear that I feel in my chest; it's not about him, it's about me – he is all that I feel myself *not* to be."

Another said, "I've come to identify that 'catch in the gut' before it's too late to avoid giving in to temptation."

Another man explains that brief gap of time as follows:

> The slightest response – just taking a second glance at him, looking left instead of straight ahead – can shift me into a different mode, and I'm gone. Before this point, it's only a possibility, a flash of consideration. I can still prevent the total sexual response.
>
> My freedom of choice is in that brief moment between thought and action. In that moment, I'm just a synapse away from the difference between a figment of my imagination and a disaster that will start that whole cycle over again.

Men report that once they behaviorally yield to the enactment impulse by looking for a partner online in a chat room, for example, then it's already too late to stop. One man explained this downward spiral in terms of the loss of self-confidence he feels as a result of sensing his willpower collapsing. "Watching myself give in," he said, "makes me give up on myself: 'See what you're doing again... you're weak, you're hopeless.'"

Overview of the Affective States

"Affective competence" refers to the way in which the person handles emotional experiences. Affective competence is possible only in the vitality states of assertion and grief – the only two self-states in which there is accurate self-awareness.

Recall Fosha's (2000) two negative alternatives to affective competence: "feeling but not dealing" (being flooded with affect, but distrustful of disclosure to the other) and "dealing but not feeling" (behavioral engagement, but without genuine emotional involvement, pp. 42–43). "Feeling" requires taking conscious ownership of one's internal emotions; "dealing" requires honestly expressing those emotions interpersonally. Feeling and dealing are preconditions for authenticity and for the integration of inner and outer selves.

Table 13.1 applies Fosha's criteria for the authentic self-state to the five self-states considered in the treatment of same-sex attraction.

Table 13.1 The Five Self-States and Fosha's Criteria

The Self-States	Feeling	Dealing
Assertion	Yes	Yes
Shame	Yes	No
Gray Zone	No	No
Homosexual Enactment	No	Yes
Grief	Yes	Yes

On the surface, homosexual enactment appears to contain the vitality affect of assertion, but it is actually an ersatz form of assertion due to its compulsiveness, which, by definition, involves minimal self-awareness and defies the person's willful intent. Without free agency, homosexual contact cannot be defined as a genuine assertive act. Further, there is a lack of authentic attachment to the other person.

When they are in the assertion stance, most clients say their homosexual temptation decreases or disappears. One client described it like this: "When I'm feeling assertive, I'm not just *able* to resist – the temptation disappears."

CHAPTER 14

Working Through the Scenario
Preceding Homosexual Enactment

The fruit of all my folly has been shame, regret – and knowledge
that whatever appears alluring in this world is but a dream.

– PETRARCH

Take on the true self, and live decisively out of it.

– A CLIENT

In this chapter we consider the self-states that typically lead to homosexual enactment, identifying how the client can choose to interrupt the
sequence of events.

Together, client and therapist retrace the preceding self-states, which
are (1) assertion, (2) shame, (3) gray zone and (4) homosexual enactment.

In the beginning of the session the client should first cognitively revisit
the scenario with the therapist, discussing what specific events led up to
the incident. With practice the client then moves by himself from cognitive
recall into kinesthetic memory, a phenomenon utilized in the performing
arts. The goal is, as one client said, "to understand it in a wordless way."
That is, he goes to his body and reexperiences the self-states as they actually
felt. Over time he develops the ability to recognize each self-state while
he is actually in it.

The therapeutic opportunity to work through the scenario preceding homosexual enactment will arise on two occasions: (1) when the client reports past homosexual enactment, and (2) when the client begins the therapy session mired down in the gray zone. Both occasions offer the client the opportunity to recall and identify the critical events that led back to his abdication of the assertion stance.

Examining the Preceding Scenario to Move the Client Out of the Gray Zone

It is particularly challenging to have a productive session with a client who enters the therapeutic hour mired down in the gray zone. For the client who is depressed and apathetic, shifting to an affective exchange with the therapist feels like an insurmountable task, something utterly beyond his ability. One man described the challenge to shift out of the gray zone as follows:

> Ugh, this is hard work! You mean I've actually got to feel my emotions? I really don't want to move out of this place, even though I hate it. This is going to require more effort, more energy, more focus, more commitment than I want to give. There's this thick, binding layer across my chest that dulls every emotion. It feels like being asked to force my way out of an encasement of bubble wrap.

As long as he remains in this passive-defiant state, the client cannot be reached on an affective level. In fact, it is this helpless, hopeless and inaccessible state that poses the single most formidable obstacle to treatment intervention and the working alliance itself. Any direct attempt by the therapist to shift the client's mood is met with intense resistance, leaving both of them frustrated and discouraged. So we apply a two-step procedure that gives the most favorable results:

1. Assist the client's recall of the preceding assertion-shame conflict – the one that created his present mood.

2. Utilize the assertion-shame conflict as the identified conflict for body work.

Success in these two steps results not only in the client's affective shift out of the gray zone (and renewed contact with the therapist) but also offers a lesson in identifying a past assertion-shame conflict, experienced as a shame moment, and by extension, he will learn how to avoid future homosexual temptation.

Most clients have no idea how long they've been in the gray zone. One middle-aged man admitted, "I've spent so much of my life in it, I don't even know I'm there." Another man said, "The gray zone – it's my zip code." Another explained, "At first, I can't recognize it when I'm in it. It's a soft, gentle, quiet thing; it seeps in like the twilight. You don't even notice that it's getting darker, till little by little, all the world is black."

Shame: The Obstacle to Grief

Even though the gray zone is a pre-grief or pseudo-grief state, in practical clinical work, it actually provides a poor gateway to access true grief. It is very rare that the client has the capacity to move from the "dead" state of the gray zone directly into an experience of his attachment loss. This is because the gray zone is a defense mechanism against feeling the pain of the shame that preceded it, which if fully felt will lead back to grief. Its dull, paralyzing mood traps the client and prevents him from recalling the preceding shame moment and thus from shifting into the vitality affect of true grief.

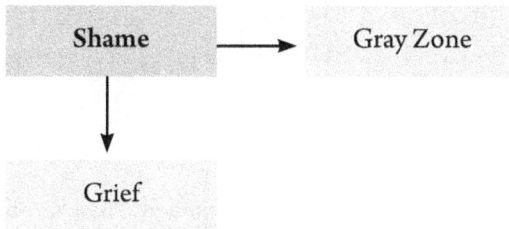

Figure 14.1 Shame leads to the gray zone or grief

Most often, rather than feel genuine grief, the client would rather dwell in the gray zone, eventually getting himself out of his paralysis through homosexual enactment.

Doing the Timeline Detective Work

The client usually has no idea why he is in the gray zone. Especially in the early phases of treatment, he resists the challenge to recall the assertion-shame conflict that preceded it, most commonly by simply "forgetting."

Once it has been agreed upon that the client is indeed in the gray zone, the task is to identify the event that preceded it. Recalling the events will require some focused inquiry. This literally means tracing back what occurred hours and often days prior to the session.

When the client does recall the shame moment, there is often an observable "Aha!" moment of recognition. Consider the following exchange between Bill and his therapist.

THERAPIST	OK. So how long did you feel this moodiness?
CLIENT	All day today.
THERAPIST	All day? You woke up feeling bad?
CLIENT	(*thinking back*) Yeah, I didn't want to get out of bed. I didn't feel like moving.
THERAPIST	OK. So what was yesterday like?
CLIENT	(*puzzled look, trying to recall*) Lousy...but yesterday was OK. Actually I was looking forward to meeting Ted for lunch.
THERAPIST	Fine. So, that you were looking forward to meeting Ted shows that you were in the assertive stance. But by nighttime, you were in the gray zone.
CLIENT	(*nodding*)
THERAPIST	How did you feel when you met Ted...where, did you say?

[Therapist asks where to help re-create the setting.]

CLIENT	It was in the cafeteria.
THERAPIST	OK...How did you feel when you first saw him at the cafeteria?
CLIENT	Happy. I was looking forward...excited, actually.
THERAPIST	How did you feel after lunch? Did you leave him or hang out some more, or...go anywhere else?
CLIENT	No. Um...that was it.
THERAPIST	How did you feel when you left?
CLIENT	Fine. (*hesitancy in voice*)
THERAPIST	Fine? (*waiting*)
CLIENT	I remember walking back to my car in the parking lot

and feeling... (*voice drops*) I don't know... (*suddenly voice becomes animated*) Now I remember. As I was walking back to my car, the thought suddenly popped into my mind of stopping at a porn shop.

Bill then proceeded to explain that he had felt in his body a "heavy" or "drooping" feeling at the time. Anticipating being trapped in a double bind, Bill did not mention to Ted or anyone else that he had been disappointed in Ted's lukewarm response to their meeting. Thus the detective work had narrowed the focus to Bill's unmet hope that his friend would show a special interest in him. Instead, he had been hurt (shame moment) by Ted's nonchalance.

Resistance to Recalling the Preceding Conflict

Childhood double-bind experiences make it difficult for a client to identify the shame moment. The most he may be able to recall is that "something happened" to him back then that made him "feel bad," but he doesn't know exactly what transpired.

Clients typically tell us, when asked to recall the embodied memory of a life event:

> For other people it comes so easily, but I have to stop and try to get in touch with how I really feel. I've got to ask myself consciously, *What's happening inside me right now? What do I really want from this situation?* or else I'll never be aware of how my body feels at all.

Resistance. Resistance to identifying the assertion-shame conflict can manifest in a number of forms. Most often the client will present vague storytelling mixed with indirect complaints. Rather than acknowledging authentic feelings of hurt or anger, he often simply reports, "That just annoyed [bothered, irritated] me." Or he will describe helpless confusion about identifying the preceding interpersonal events.

When he does identify the assertion-shame conflict, he may then minimize it, calling it "insignificant," "foolish" and "silly," or "no big deal," and instead proceed to avoid examining his feelings by simply blaming himself for the conflict.

Besides this avoidance and minimizing, we also see resistance in terms of illusions and distortions. The following are examples of illusions and distortions:

Illusions (narcissistically based false-positives):

- "It didn't bother me that he didn't care about me."

- "I don't care what other people think."

Distortions (shame-based false negatives)

- "I can't speak up – I'll just embarrass myself."

- "If I tell him how I really feel about what he did, it will break up our friendship."

- "Moving out will kill my mother."

- "This really bothered me, but I'm making a fuss over nothing."

- "Whatever I say to assert myself, it won't make a difference, and I'll still lose out."

- "Who am I to complain, anyway?"

One form of distortion is when the client serves as an advocate for his own shamer. Here he justifies the shamer's actions against him: "There's no need to tell him how I felt. I was overreacting, being petty; I shouldn't have been so devastated." Or "He stood me up for our appointment and then didn't call me, but I don't want to hold him accountable, because once in awhile, I can be late."

Two aspects of the shame moment: Somatic and cognitive. The shame moment has both bodily and cognitive aspects. The bodily experience is typically described as a tightness, gripping and clenching in the chest, followed by a dropping, sinking and collapsing in the mid-to-upper torso. These sensations alert the client to a shame moment that would otherwise go unnoticed by the cognitive functions.

The cognitive aspect is an unnoticed self-recrimination; a shaming self-statement prompted by the actions of others. Here, we need to remind our clients that while children can be shamed by adults, adults can only shame themselves. Therefore, it is critical to the success of treatment for the client to identify (which is to say, make conscious) the shame-based self-statement that he is telling himself during the shame moment.

Shame-Based Self-Statement

In order to work through the scenario preceding homosexual enactment, we must focus on the shame moment – that pivotal moment when the client shifts out of his assertive self-state. We can help the client identify and work through the shame moment by identifying the shame-based self-statement (SBSS) that likely precipitated it.

The therapist may help the client construct his SBSS by having him formulate it in a simple, present-tense sentence beginning with "I." For example, "I am a failure," "I am unacceptable," "I will never be masculine." This will facilitate the next step of evaluation.

Two criteria for the evaluation of the SBSS. Once the SBSS is constructed, it is evaluated against two criteria: objectivity and compassion. These two criteria offer the client an emotional distance from the overwhelming affect of shame. The evaluative process is done in a collaborative method with the therapist structuring, but not leading the client in assessing his SBSS against the two criteria of reality and self-care. The result of the assessment will be that the SBSS is either false or true.

If false. If objective evaluation determines the SBSS to be false, the therapist will notice the client's shift to the assertive state. For example, this twenty-eight-year-old medical student recalls a shame moment while at a barbecue:

CLIENT	I felt uncomfortable going into the group of mostly strangers. Tried to relax, had a beer, you know. So then I saw these guys laughing together in a corner...
THERAPIST	(*nods, listening*)
CLIENT	So, I felt uncomfortable and wanted to leave.
THERAPIST	What was the shame statement you were telling yourself at that moment?
CLIENT	That I don't fit in.
THERAPIST	Is that your statement?
CLIENT	(*changing his mind*) That I can't make friends.
THERAPIST	OK, (*repeating SBSS*) you're telling yourself, *I can't make friends.* How true is that?
CLIENT	Well, it's always been hard. (*after some consideration*) But

lately, things have been better; I have been making friends. In fact, it's a lot easier for me now. (*evident shift to assertive state*) It used to be true, but not anymore.

In this second example, a twenty-three-year-old man goes into a gym locker room. Afraid he will be aroused, he becomes overwhelmed with shame and then quickly leaves.

THERAPIST   What is the self-shaming statement you are telling yourself in that moment?

CLIENT   I'm telling myself that I am gay.

THERAPIST   Make it into an explicit self-statement, beginning with "I."

CLIENT   (*after a moment of consideration*) "I am gay."

THERAPIST   Good. So let's look at that statement objectively. Are you gay?

CLIENT   No. I get nervous, maybe aroused, but it's just fear. I really just want to connect, be one of them, but my body reacts in its old way.

THERAPIST   So, are you gay?

CLIENT   No! No way! (*demonstrates shift to assertive state*)

If true. If the SBSS is true by objective standards, the therapist then introduces (and in so doing, models) compassion. For example, a thirty-six-year-old client challenges himself to play softball with some men from work. In spite of his best effort, he performs poorly, making some serious errors. He recalls one shame moment during a critical play where he misses a fly ball.

THERAPIST   What is the shame statement you are telling yourself?

CLIENT   That I'm a lousy baseball player.

THERAPIST   Is it true?

CLIENT   Yeah, it is true; I am a lousy baseball player.

THERAPIST   (*attempting to prompt self-compassion*) Yes, but why is it true?

CLIENT   I don't know.

THERAPIST   (*knowing client's history*) When you were a little kid, did anyone take the time to teach you how to play?

CLIENT   (*sadly*) No. No one.

THERAPIST   OK, so you weren't a natural athlete. But did anyone take you under their wing and give you a boost to help you fit in with the other guys?

CLIENT   No. No one did.

THERAPIST   How do you feel in your body right now, when you say no?

CLIENT   Bad. Really bad.

THERAPIST   A better word than "bad"?

CLIENT   Sad. Yeah, it's true. I feel really sad, because it's true.

[Session continues into additional memories of childhood neglect by his detached father that lead into grief work.]

In the next example, a nineteen-year-old, post-gender type of client shamefully recalls as a little boy wanting to touch his father's penis.

CLIENT   It sounds really perverted, but I was maybe seven or eight, I would sneak up on my father when he was sleeping. He would get drunk and collapse on the couch. (*with great embarrassment and difficulty speaking the words*) I would touch his penis through his pants. Whenever I remember how I did that, I feel terrible.

THERAPIST   OK, so what is the statement you are making to yourself when you recall that?

CLIENT   (*long pause*) That it was sick.

THERAPIST   Make it an "I" sentence.

CLIENT   That *I* was sick. (*correcting himself*) That *I am* sick.

THERAPIST   All right, so "I am sick." How true is that statement?

CLIENT   Well, yeah! Of course it's true! What kind of kid would do that? Anyone would think it's sick.

THERAPIST   OK, by popular opinion, I guess you're right. But the question is, why did that boy (*it sometimes helps to foster self-compassion when the client evaluates his own behavior as if in the third person*) . . . why did that boy do that?

CLIENT   I don't know. (*pauses, then speaks with contempt for himself*) Weird!

THERAPIST   Let's think. What was that boy looking for? What was he trying to gain, to connect with? We've spoken about your father and how cruel he was to you, especially when he got drunk. Do you remember the humiliations? And the time he made fun of your little penis?

CLIENT   (*softening, silently nodding*)

THERAPIST   (*continuing*) So that was the only contact that kid could make! He wanted that male love and comfort.

CLIENT   It's true. When my father was drunk and passed out on the couch, that was the only time I could reach out to connect with him.

THERAPIST   That's right.

CLIENT   He made fun of my penis...

THERAPIST   So now, this way you could "settle the score." You could finally *take* – even aggressively *steal* – that male connection.

CLIENT   (*nodding sadly*)

[Client goes into sadness, then grief work about the father.]

Summary. A shame-based self-statement (SBSS), unevaluated, propels the client into the gray zone. But when it is evaluated, it either leads to assertion or to grief. And when followed through to completion, grief eventually shifts to assertion.

If the SBSS is objectively determined to be false, the client will experience a self-shift to assertion. If the SBSS is determined to be realistically correct,

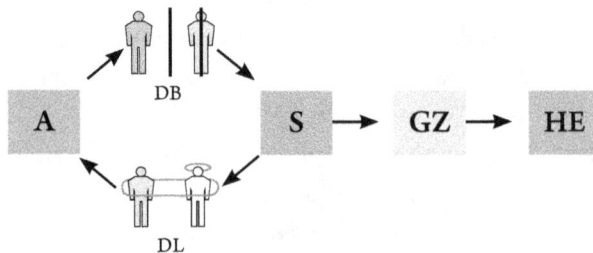

| A= Assertion | GZ= Gray Zone | DB= Double Bind |
| S= Shame | HE= Homosexual Enactment | DL= Double Loop |

Figure 14.2 Assertion-shame conflict model

when viewed by the client from a stance of self-compassion, there will be a self-shift to grief, which will eventually be worked through to assertion.

The more frequently the client practices this procedure in session, the more quickly he can carry it out on his own, during the shame moment.

Return to Assertion

I'm amazed at how much more involved I am now in my life.

        – twenty-seven-year-old client

In order to shift out of the gray zone the client must feel and express his emotion to the therapist, as he recalls it in the present moment, about the past assertion-shame conflict. By allowing himself to feel what he could not feel and express at the time (typically, anger at the shamer), he returns to his empowered self. This return to assertion is a return to the vitality affects.

The essential task of revisiting the preceding scenario is identifying the shame moment. This will take some "timeline detective work," but when the shame moment is identified, there will be a visible "Aha!" moment, shifting the client to the assertion state. The recall of the shame moment has the embodied quality of someone who has found his lost keys. The "surprise" effect is due not so much to "Oh, here are my keys!" but to "Oh, *here* is where I left them!" Likewise, to the client who has lost himself, "Oh, here is where I left me!"

The shift back to the assertion stance occurs immediately in a sudden and dramatic change. The attuned therapist can see exactly when that embodied shift happens. The client's posture becomes upright, with eyes focused; he has suddenly "come into the room."

Wow. I can see that I've been really "riding with my brakes on." I feel like my head just popped up above the surface of the water, and now, I see the bright world all around me.

If he is able to work through the preceding scenario from beginning to end, by the end of the session the client will have returned to the assertion state, with a corresponding vitality interaction in his relationship with the therapist.

Double looping the past assertion-shame conflict. After much practice the client gradually learns how to be self-aware in real time. He begins taking care of business, which means both "feeling and dealing" (Fosha, 2000, p. 42). Thinking back to his interaction with the shamer, he may also formulate a future plan of action – perhaps working on developing more genuine communication with the shamer.

With the shift back into the assertive state, there is an embodied transition into the true self. The man becomes more alive and present; he is focused, animated and more confident. This affective expansion is not to be confused with a wild euphoria or theatricality; instead, he is experiencing true emotional freedom, accompanied by a clearer head, a feeling of power and new insight.

In a quest similar to T.S. Eliot's stated life goal to "stay awake to myself," the struggler – by repeatedly working through the preceding scenario – gradually develops a sense of self-mastery, as described by a client in the following statements:

> Last night I started wanting to fantasize about men. I asked myself, *What's that feeling in my center chest, and what's it telling me? It's fear. Fear of what? I want protection, comfort. But from what?*
>
> One thing is clear to me after I've come this far; homosexual behavior is the consequence of feeling "less than" other men. It's what happens when I replay that negative voice about me. It's amazing how easily I can feel bad about myself. Then I remember, *Ah – here it is again, that voice telling me I'm weak.* But sex with men is only ersatz assertion; it's the seed germinated in the soil of shame.
>
> My homosexual impulse is a signal that I've just recently missed a lesson in assertion. I've got to keep my finger on the spot [touching the center of his chest] – like the little Dutch boy, keeping my finger in the dyke. If I don't, there will be devastation. I've got to be deliberate about this; I've been choosing not to deal with my issues, not thinking about what I'm bothered by – until it's too late, after I act out.

One obstacle in shifting the client from the gray zone to the assertion stance arises through his underlying belief that his failures of assertion are due to his special concern and deference for others. His seeming altruistic, self-sacrificing need to want the other person to not feel bad is actually an attempt to rid himself of his own internal distress. It is not so much that the other person must actually feel better but that he needs the other person "to feel better about me, so that I can then feel better about me too."

This unconscious game of "I'll make you feel good about yourself so that you won't make me feel bad about myself" finds its origins in the early mother-son relationship.

Guilt versus shame. Before he first felt shame, the child's experience was a state of pure innocence. He was at one with himself in his own Garden of Eden. Gradually, he became sensitized to shame.

Developmentally, shame ("you are bad") precedes guilt ("you did wrong"), since the child can feel shame before he is able to comprehend right and wrong behavior. Without having an awareness of his *behavior* as distinct from *himself*, the very small child feels like a "bad person" without realizing that it is what he *did* that was bad.

Since clients often confuse the two, it is important for us as therapists to convey the distinction between the guilt messages ("You did something bad") and the shame messages ("You *are* bad"). Guilt is the justifiable result of bad behavior; shame has no real justification. This distinction is facilitated by returning the client to his body. With practice he can learn to make a clear somatic distinction between guilt and shame. Utilizing body work, he begins to differentiate as follows:

Guilt. Guilt has decidedly different bodily sensations from shame. Guilt is characterized by a heavy-weighted sinking in the chest and is most commonly described as "sad and down," yet without marked anxiety or fear.

Shame. Shame is usually first felt as an overall bodily discomfort, then centralized in the abdomen as a queasy and jittery feeling, with butterflies (anxiety). With continued focus on the body, the client feels shame moving up to the chest and becoming a gripping tightness and constriction (genuine fear).

One client was especially articulate in grasping the implications of the distinction: "Listening to guilt, we better ourselves. Listening to shame, we just become what others want us to be. I'm working on diminishing the distractions of shame. When I do that, I can listen to the self-improving messages of guilt."

Three effective warning signals preceding homosexual enactment

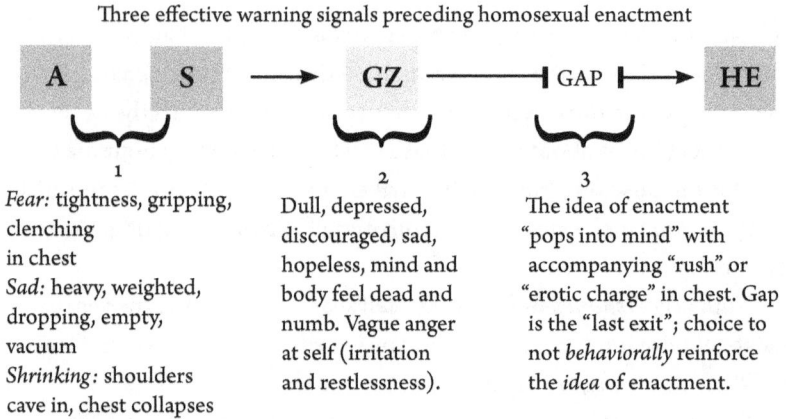

1	2	3
Fear: tightness, gripping, clenching in chest	Dull, depressed, discouraged, sad, hopeless, mind and body feel dead and numb. Vague anger at self (irritation and restlessness).	The idea of enactment "pops into mind" with accompanying "rush" or "erotic charge" in chest. Gap is the "last exit"; choice to not *behaviorally* reinforce the *idea* of enactment.
Sad: heavy, weighted, dropping, empty, vacuum		
Shrinking: shoulders cave in, chest collapses		

Figure 14.3 Avoiding the preceding scenario

Another client described his embodied distinction between guilt and shame like this:

> In guilt, I feel regret about my behavior (as distinct from feeling bad about me). But it's really about feeling bad for the other person; I caused him pain and I feel bad about that. I have real empathy; I feel affection or caring about him, so I feel bad about him feeling bad."

Another client put it this way:

> In shame, I feel s—tty about me. I feel sad, with a weighty emptiness in my stomach – it's a sensation of being weak, depleted, lifeless. I get upset about how that person feels about me, and I feel insecure around him. I want to undo my mistake to get rid of that bad feeling inside me.

A young lawyer explained:

> Guilt is sorrow for having hurt someone. "I really was unfair to him." Guilt feels rich, heavy, real.
>
> Shame is shallow and uncomfortable, but it has no other significance other than "I want to escape the discomfort."
>
> Guilt has a message, a lesson for me. It has a meaning about the way I relate to people. With guilt I feel conflict with myself; with shame I feel conflict with others.

The assertion-shame conflict. As part of the psycho-educational dimension of therapy, the therapist may point out the typical workings of the scenario preceding homosexual enactment, perhaps providing a diagram of the self-state sequence. As with all educational material, the diagram should be offered only if the client recognizes the scenario as relevant to his own life.

Regarding the shifting between assertion and shame, clients usually report three bodily responses:

1. Fear: tightness, gripping, clenching in chest
2. Sadness: heavy, weighted, drooping, empty, a vacuum
3. Shame: shoulders cave in, chest collapses, shrinking

With time and practice, and the development of somatic memory, many clients achieve the invaluable awareness that to avoid homosexual enactment, they must effectively confront the shame moments that precipitate them into the gray zone. As one man explains: "I know that staying out of the gray zone means staying in my integrity, staying honest with myself. I'm well aware of the triggers as they're happening, and if I ignore them, I know they'll get me to act out."

Only when the client is aware of the relationship of the gray zone to his homosexual temptation can he avoid enactment by taking advantage of "the gap" before he acts out and then utilize the vital opportunity the gap offers for self-reflection.

Clients generally report that the idea of homosexual enactment "pops into my mind" with an accompanying rush or energy surge in the chest. Meanwhile, the gap calls for the difficult task of inserting a wedge of self-control in that narrow time-space between the idea of enactment and the behavioral commencement of that idea.

The Client's Mastery of the Preceding Scenario

When I'm drawn toward gay stuff I think, "OK. What's the story I'm telling myself now about my situation?"

— a teenage client

My recovery from homosexuality requires a continual act of self-repossession.

— forty-two-year-old married man

My mantra has become *"Avoid* avoidance."

– a college student

When I went onto the gay website, as soon as I got started, I realized how depressed I had been all week.

– a client addicted to Internet porn

Stages of self-mastery. After repeatedly being made aware of his body's responses to the various self-states, the client is able to anticipate homosexual temptation by identifying his internal cues without the assistance of the therapist. With continued practice, the client is better able to avoid homosexual enactment by effectively dealing with shame moments as they arise. The shame moments will otherwise lead him into the gray zone.

Failure to assert leading to homosexual enactment. Clients report that when they are stuck in the gray zone, homosexual behavior is experienced as intense, exciting and compelling. Later, when they are living in the assertive state, homosexual behavior appears superficial and false.

In the following session transcript, we see the working through of the preceding scenario, beginning with the client reporting to the therapist his recent temptations.

This man, a forty-seven-year-old dentist, talks about signing on to gay chat lines while on a business trip. As a married man and a committed conservative Jew, he is dedicated to the well-being of his family and his role as the head of household, but to his considerable dismay, homosexual temptations sometimes overwhelm his will.

He begins by identifying "that compulsiveness in my gut," and through body work confronts his failure to assert himself in his work and at home.

THERAPIST   OK, can we go to that feeling just before you acted out?

CLIENT   OK...well, I'm alone – away from home – in this hotel room. No one to be accountable to. I'm trying to connect with guys, you know, to get a connection.

THERAPIST   A connection?

CLIENT   (*hesitant*) To get someone to come over.

THERAPIST   To have sex.

CLIENT   Yeah. To have sex.

THERAPIST   OK...

CLIENT   It's crazy and self-destructive. I often don't fall asleep till almost morning, even when I've gotta get up at 7 a.m. for the conference.

THERAPIST   Can you go to that feeling in the body? What is that feeling inside for the need to act out?

CLIENT   Well...boredom. But also that compulsiveness in my gut. There's a drive; my pulse is racing. It's like "the last hurrah before I get cured," like "Let me just get some excitement in."

THERAPIST   Let's stay with this.

CLIENT   There's a boredom, fatigue, but a sense of urgency, like "I gotta do this" kinda thing.

THERAPIST   In the body...

CLIENT   In my stomach, butterflies, like "get ready to go on stage – do something dangerous." Not necessarily a pleasant feeling.

THERAPIST   What's the "not pleasant"?

CLIENT   There's an aching, a kind of painful excitement.

THERAPIST   Where?

CLIENT   Hmm...At where the two ribs come together, lower part of the sternum. Right underneath that.

THERAPIST   And what's that feeling?

CLIENT   A tickle. I can't describe it beyond that. (*long pause*)

THERAPIST   Stay with that tickle. Let's see where that goes. (*waiting*)

CLIENT   A pressure at the sternum, like someone pressing in on my chest.

THERAPIST   Where exactly?

CLIENT   (*considers*) Right here. (*placing palm of hand on center chest*)

THERAPIST   Hmm...

CLIENT   (*after some moments*) It feels empty, uncomfortably empty.

THERAPIST   When have you felt this same empty discomfort in the past?

CLIENT   When I can't get my life together. What makes it worse is when I'm not getting along with Molly.

THERAPIST   How much would you say is about Molly?

CLIENT   (*looking sad and pensive*) Some of it is.

THERAPIST	In what way?
CLIENT	Her weight, her appearance. We're like roommates. I don't blame her. I've neglected her.
THERAPIST	Hmm... So what's the feeling?
CLIENT	(*nodding*) Inadequate. (*deep sigh*) My whole life is contrary to what I imagined it would be. Where I am in my life is not what I envisioned.
THERAPIST	What did you envision?
CLIENT	A large close family in the Jewish tradition. Going to Saturday services. A nice beautiful, comfortable home. And order... our home's not orderly.
THERAPIST	Stay with the feeling.
CLIENT	Powerless.
THERAPIST	Powerless.
CLIENT	Anger at myself for not living an orderly life. It's a chaotic life. The kids come and go.
THERAPIST	Do you have dinner together? Does Molly cook?
CLIENT	Sometimes. But mostly we order Chinese food. Sometimes we order Chinese food five times a week. Sometimes twice a day. Or somebody gets thirsty and drives down to the 7-Eleven store to buy a drink at 2 a.m.
THERAPIST	So what's the feeling?
CLIENT	Powerlessness. I feel powerless against my own disorganization. Acting out is my fantasy world to avoid feeling overwhelmed by my life.
THERAPIST	Yes...
CLIENT	You know, when I was in college I was totally disorganized. Could never get my papers in order. I'd sit down to study, and would spend an hour just getting *ready* to study. That's when I started acting out.
THERAPIST	So your homosexual behavior was an affect-regulator to adjust your emotional disequilibrium.
CLIENT	(*nods*) Yeah. (*considers*) And yet – you know what? I never acted out in grad school. Never acted out once. My life was structured from 9 a.m. to 4 p.m.

THERAPIST   So structure was the key...?

CLIENT   Yeah...being structured helps me a lot. I've always tried to tell Molly, I gotta be in bed by 10, but she can never get the house quiet, and it's chaos until the wee hours. That's when I want to go on the computer and do something to calm that agitation, that kind of painful urgency.

Another client told me:

> I can see that I will continue to suffer with same-sex attraction as long as I fail to deal with conflicts. The other day I noticed that old feeling of shrinking, caving in...that imploding, falling in on myself. Then I thought, *Oops! I know that feeling and I know what that will lead to.* Now I'm determined not to let that happen.

Aborted expression of anger as a catalyst to homosexual enactment. The client in this transcript describes his difficulty in expressing appropriate anger. (After the incident of aborted anger, he went to a gay bookstore for sex.)

THERAPIST   What happened when you tried to confront Tom about always forgetting the meeting?

CLIENT   Well, I tried to, but I couldn't. I knew I'd feel guilty later if I confronted him, and then I'd end up apologizing.

THERAPIST   OK. Stay with that. What do you mean you'd be guilty, apologetic?

CLIENT   Like, if I was direct with him, the pressure would be on me to smooth it all over afterward. Suddenly it would be quiet between us. There'd be an uncomfortable gap in the conversation.

THERAPIST   And how would that feel?

CLIENT   The anger I felt would just drop away from the core. I wouldn't be able to express it – not even be able to feel it any more.

THERAPIST   (*repeating meaningfully*) "The anger drops from the core"... Yeah. I visualize the collapse of the World Trade Center, when the center just implodes, collapsing inward.

CLIENT   Yeah, just exactly like that...yeah.

THERAPIST   (*at this moment, sensing a connection between them*) Then what? Stay with your feeling.

[Client seems to pull away, seems restless, shifting around.]

THERAPIST   You seem irritated now.

CLIENT   (*silent*) I feel restless.

THERAPIST   This is the hard part. (*pause, slowly and gently*) Go back to that "anger drops from the core." What's left? (*waiting*)

CLIENT   (*settling down, speaking slowly*) Nothing left but sadness. Emptiness inside. No energy left to express myself.

[At this point therapist feels interpretation is in order.]

THERAPIST   Does this fit what you're feeling? There's that familiar "antsy" anxiety in your body – the conflict where your anger hits up against the expectation of disapproval, which is shame, and then you just abandon yourself, collapse...

CLIENT   (*nods*) Yes. That's exactly what happens to me.

THERAPIST   You feel powerless.

CLIENT   Right. And that's when I go looking for sex.

Feeling slighted, entering the gray zone and moving toward homosexual enactment. Will and his therapist discuss his recent lunch with Tom, who seemed indifferent to him. As a result of Tom's indifference, Will found himself entering the gray zone.

CLIENT   (*facial expression reveals the affective shift into the "Aha!" experience*) Oh yeah, now I remember what happened beforehand. After I left Tom, walking back to my car, it occurred to me I could go act out. I didn't, but I thought about it.

THERAPIST   Why do you think it occurred to you just then, Will?

CLIENT   Don't know.

THERAPIST   Well, what did you feel about your meeting with Tom?

CLIENT   Well...a little disappointed, I guess.

THERAPIST   (*waiting*)

CLIENT   I didn't think his friend was gonna be there with him. The
              whole thing ended up being like ... just the two of them, like
              I wasn't even there. I felt left out.

At this point the therapist focuses the client on that conflict, "feeling left
out," by leading him through the two-triangle process – that is, to fully feel
and express in the present the embodied affect of "felt left out" (F/I – feelings and impulses) and associate it with the past (P). As is often the case
the conflict is between assertion and anticipatory shame. The therapist
supports the client in shifting into full assertion by challenging him to
role play.

THERAPIST   What could you have done differently? What could you
             have said to really represent how you felt?
CLIENT   (*some of his assertion dropping*) Um... (*hesitant*) That was
             hard, 'cause they were talking away.
THERAPIST   Go for it! Just tell him what you want to say...
CLIENT   (*more animated, sitting up, looking at the therapist*) I could
             have said, "Look, Tom, you said that we were gonna talk
             about our Baja road trip. That never happened 'cause your
             friend – not mine! – was with you and we never got around
             to it!"
THERAPIST   Great!

[Client continues to role play his assertive response.]

The Envy Moment

To help our clients better understand themselves, we explain how they
shift into homosexual enactment not only as a result of entrapment in the
gray zone but also as the result of an envy moment.

Consciously, the envy moment is experienced as a moment of sexual
attraction, no different from other moments of sexual attraction. But while
the experience is undoubtedly sexual, a closer analysis of what happens
in the body reveals something more complex.

Unlike the conscious choice to act out, in the envy moment the client unexpectedly encounters a compelling ideal masculine image which

seems to hit, jolt or shock him. By attending to the body, he discovers that beneath the surface of this seemingly instantaneous gay attraction lies a feeling of intimidation. Thus we see the envy as a particular kind of shame moment. When the therapist sensitizes the client to his embodied experience of such an envy moment, this deepens his understanding of the origins of his same-sex attraction.

The envy moment contains three distinct embodied shifts that follow in rapid-fire sequence. On coming to this awareness, one client described the experience as "a quick, one-two-three [quickly tapping his lap], well-oiled machine."

First, the unexpected encounter with the homoerotic image evokes a bodily sensation in the chest/sternum area that has been variously described as "tightness, gripping, clenching or sharp, stabbing pain." These sensations are associated with the emotion of fear.

Second, we see another set of sensations variously described as a feeling of "dropping, sinking, emptiness, sadness, feeling lost, slumping, hollow, caved-in at the lower chest beneath the sternum." These sensations are associated with the feeling of shame.

A third sensation quickly follows, generally described as a genital surge – an excitement, an erotic charge in the genital area which is described as "unquestionably sexual."

The first two feelings come so quickly, and without immediate awareness, that they may be described as unconscious. Our clinical experience has shown that very few men have previously been aware of these two emotions preceding sexual excitement. Only until the client is supported and taught to attend to his body memory in session (and with practice, outside the session during the actual envy moment) is he able to discern the significance of his sexual experience as a reparation for the shame posture.

Gay-activist psychologist Daryl Bem, in his attempt to explain the origins of sexual attraction, also links earliest sexual arousal to moments of fear (Bem, 1996). Many similar reports are found throughout the older psychoanalytic literature (i.e., clinical studies published before it was politically incorrect to address the subject).

The meaning of the "zap." As the client more deeply explores his bodily reaction during the envy moment, he discovers that beneath his "erotic

Unexpected encounter with homoerotic image
Distinct from homosexual enactment

Sensation	Location	Affect
Tightness, gripping, clenching, sharp pain in sternum	Chest	Fear
↓	↓	↓
Dropping, sinking, empty, sad, loss, slumping hollow, caving in	Chest	Shame
↓	↓	↓
REPARATIVE ATTEMPT		
↓	↓	↓
Genital surge, excitement, erotic charge	Genital	Sexual

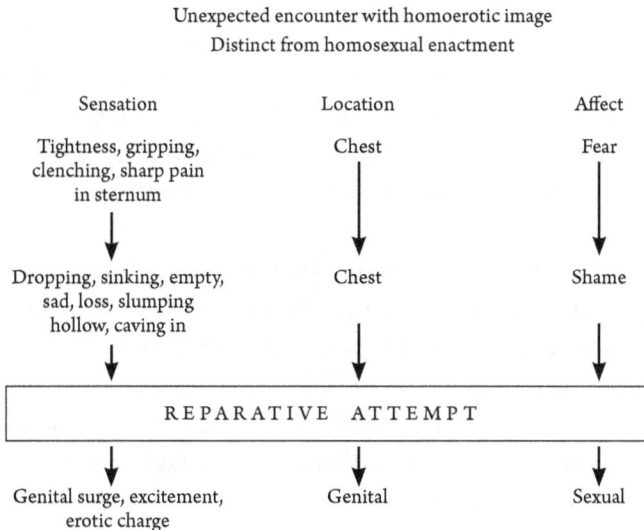

Figure 14.4 The envy moment, a particular kind of shame moment

zap" is actually a desire for deeper attachment. One man said, "When I see an attractive guy, my first gut reaction is a sexual urge. But if I really think about it, my deeper desire is, 'I'd like to get to know him; I bet he could teach me about masculinity.'"

An example of this underlying, authentic need is expressed by a thirty-six-year-old client:

> I was driving home last night. Ahead of me were these two guys, early twenties, on bikes. Seeing them started some sexual thoughts about them. I even went so far as to imagine three-way sex with both of them.
>
> Then I said, *Wait! What am I doing? What am I really attracted to?* I caught myself and realized what I wanted was to be with them – to ride along with them – to talk and laugh.
>
> What I really wanted was to be one of them. I never did that stuff when I was their age.

The envy moment: Bodily recall. The therapeutic goal is to turn the client's attention away from the eroticized other and back onto the self. This is the opposite of his focus during the envy moment, when he loses himself to the other man.

The application of body work returns the client to his own bodily sensations as he recalls this moment of attraction to another man. By staying with his body, he discovers subjective confirmation that these longings are a surface distraction from deeper, negative feelings about himself. What is first interpreted as "sexual" is subsequently understood to be an eroticized envy moment.

The client thus begins to understand that the envy moment is about his own sense of masculine inferiority. The person who is momentarily idealized offers a painful contrast to himself. Seeing the other guy, a representation of the masculine ideal, serves as a catalyst to jolt to consciousness his own background sense of inferiority. Feeling the embodied fear and shame, the man generates a reparative homoerotic fantasy. This neutralizes the humiliating contrast between himself and the other man, and provides relief from the affective destabilization generated by the comparison.

As one man explained:

> The power of the male image is its reflection of my own inadequacy. He is a shocking reminder of what I lack. The power lies not in what he is, but what I am not. And I can either go and pursue the distraction of what he is, or face the painful reality of what I am not.

Generating the reparative fantasy. Some comments from clients that capture this reparative fantasy:

> When I see a guy I'm attracted to, he becomes an object – another turn-on. He is no longer a person, but a catalyst for my imagination.

> When I see someone that turns me on, my heart constricts. There's a tension in my heart, an intense painful lump that just sits there. I'm the negative mirror-image of what he is. He's the positive reflection of my unhappy self.

> I think, *I could never be [masculine like] that. I could never feel that [masculine nature] in me.* It's this belief that determines the intensity of my attraction.

> The worse I feel about myself, the better those guys look. But the more I break down the attraction to its tangible elements and understand how

these elements fit into my past experiences, the less I'm controlled by attractions to other guys.

With self-knowledge and practice, clients can sense their vulnerability to the envy moment before it happens. Said one man:

> I'm doing well, but I know myself. When I get isolated and shut down and in the gray zone, I think, *Gee, let me see if I can find myself in that guy.*
>
> But then I'll realize, *Hey, this is not lust, this is actually envy and fear. OK – now it's reprogramming time.*

Some clients report that having an accountability partner is helpful in that moment between idea and enactment:

> It's got to be at the exact moment – I mean, I've got to literally interrupt what I'm doing, go pick up my phone, make a phone call and get out of that place ASAP.

> I have got to connect to somebody that knows me, understands me – someone I can be truthful with. They'll hear me out and allow me to double loop with them and get back to a place where I'm out of the gray zone.

The envy moment as an assertion-shame conflict. For every client there are specific masculine physical and personality traits lacking in himself that hold a compelling attraction. When asked to describe those specific qualities of masculinity he is sexually drawn to, the client will typically say, "I'm attracted to a guy who is self-assured, confident, has lots of friends and is popular, is self-sufficient, in control, and who knows who he is."

Then, when asked, "How would you like to improve yourself?" he usually says, "If only I were bolder, had greater self-esteem, more self-confidence..."

Harboring boyhood memories of masculine inferiority, clients feel immediate fascination for such traits. But when they identify and trace the childhood origins that trigger the attraction, the erotic change is lessened. Here's an example:

CLIENT   I distinctly remember when I was ten years old – the first time I knew I was gay.

THERAPIST   Tell me about it.

CLIENT   Well, I remember going to school, and we would save time by taking a short cut across the gym. We walked through the locker room and I saw a guy coming out of the shower. He was wet and naked and – wow! I felt sexual attraction.

THERAPIST   Wait a minute. Let's go over that again. Tell me exactly what happened.

[The client more deeply reflects on that defining moment, perhaps for the first time in his life. After a while, he speaks.]

CLIENT   I saw that guy and I thought, "Wow, I wish I was him!"

This man, as a boy, had been frail, sickly, suffered from asthma and had a hovering mother. What he had labeled "sexual" since the age of ten was actually an intense visceral response of envy to an idealized male image. But his experience was given a completely different meaning when he accepted the "gay" self-label.

In the following transcript, a twenty-seven-year-old college exchange student spoke of his own feelings.

CLIENT   I was sitting in the computer room at school and found myself noticing a guy. I found myself looking over at him a few times. So I tried to apply what you have been telling me. I went to my body and asked myself what I was feeling. I noticed I felt weak in my legs. (*slight laugh*) I always seem to feel things in my legs.

[This is an example of how the therapist must accept and appreciate how each client feels thing differently.]

THERAPIST   OK. Tell me about that.

CLIENT   Weak... a twitchy, shaky feeling in my legs, and with that, I noticed I was generally feeling insecure, uncertain – a feeling of nonconfidence.

THERAPIST   And how did that body awareness affect your attraction for the guy?

CLIENT   Well, it sort of placed it all in context. I mean, (*slight laugh*)

	I became more curious about myself and my body than about him.
THERAPIST	OK. Can you remember a time when you had those same sensations in your legs?
CLIENT	(*considers for a moment*) Um...well, I remember when I worked in a restaurant...
THERAPIST	How old were you?
CLIENT	About twenty-one or twenty-two. And I had trouble connecting with guys, customers, who were my age. I had trouble keeping eye contact.
THERAPIST	The feeling was the same?
CLIENT	The same weakness in my legs, I remember. I'd have this businesslike look about me, but I could not be genuine, sincere. (*thoughtful pause*) I've come a long way since that time.

[Therapist shifts into teacher-mentor role.]

THERAPIST	So let's look at what you've accomplished. In the moment you found yourself noticing a guy, which signaled you to shift your attention from him to yourself – from extroversion to introversion – and you noticed your legs felt weak and shaky, which you know means insecurity and uncertainty.
CLIENT	Yeah.
THERAPIST	So that shifted your perspective on that guy.
CLIENT	Well, it put it into a different context. Then it became less about him.
THERAPIST	Yes. And you were able to recall feeling that same weakness in your legs years ago, at a time of greater insecurity in yourself.
CLIENT	Yeah. So it became clear to me then that the homosexuality is a distraction from my weak feelings inside. It was really not so much about the other guy, but an escape into fantasy.

The envy moment resolution. Another man summed up his thoughts about resolving the envy moment as follows:

More and more, I'm aware that I'm making that leap directly from fear to sex – first feeling tight in the solar plexus, and then getting excitement in the groin. Very few times nowadays I feel the groin first. In fact, very rarely.

In the past, fear and sexual excitement would have happened so closely together, I never would have separated them. But now, I can see that divide – it's very apparent.

And frankly, when I feel the fear, I know that I'm gonna try to create the response in the groin. (*laughs*)

But knowing what I do now, takes the fun out of masturbation. I find I gotta work harder to get the image going.

Self-Awareness Brings Personal Power

Each client's growing self-awareness means greater sensitivity to his inner processes as they are happening in the moment.

The body work not only facilitates somatic recall of the critical events leading up to homosexual enactment, but it sensitizes the body to anticipate and respond to all future assertion-shame conflicts. In summary, the treatment modalities we use most often are the following:

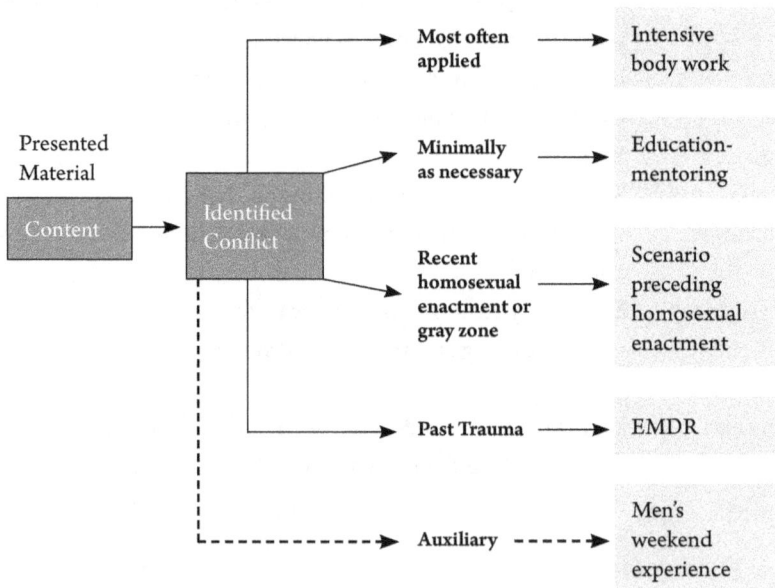

Figure 14.5 Basic intervention modalities

CHAPTER 15

Journaling

I might as well look at things. I've been running away from myself for too long.
— CLIENT IN HIS FIRST SESSION

Journaling is a powerful way for any man to challenge and examine the narcissistic illusions and shame-based distortions that lead to his self-defeating behaviors. The client will also gain an overall perspective on his ongoing trajectory of progress. This is particularly helpful during those inevitable times of disorientation and discouragement, as he rereads earlier entries and appreciates the progress he has achieved so far.

Since most men in reparative therapy tend to be overly concerned about what others think about them, there may be a temptation for them, while journaling, to write for some imaginary audience. One man admitted ruefully that "my journaling itself has become a performance." Such a client needs to be reminded, as he begins this process, that there is no one to impress and no one's approval to seek. He is writing only for his own self-understanding. Of course, the journal should be shown to no one.

Journaling helps clients attend to feelings, body sensations and thoughts, and fosters the cognitive integration of those subjective experiences. Above all, it teaches the client to take himself seriously.

It is often very difficult for men to slow down and take time to focus on their deep feelings. Further, the process is often agonizing, precisely because it requires a confrontation with oneself. One man described journaling as "a place of extreme discomfort. To sit down and write! When I first tried, my writing was tight, slow. I switched pens. It wasn't gliding, it wasn't flowing fast enough. I found every possible petty excuse not to settle down and relate to myself."

Clients often worry that a commitment to journaling will necessitate daily entries. But more important than a client's strict adherence to a schedule is the dialogue he has with himself, transforming his vaguely felt subjective impressions and half-formed insights into tangible form. But committing those subtle shifts in awareness onto paper will reinforce his commitment to personal growth. And most important, the journal will encourage his careful self-reflection on the critical scenario preceding homosexual enactment.

Unstructured Reflections

In time, the client may notice that when he does make a commitment to daily entries, he is making rapid progress. One man admitted, "I don't journal, though I know I should. In fact, I know I'm not doing well by the fact that I'm not journaling."

While journaling at any time is therapeutic, there are some occasions where writing out one's thoughts and feelings is particularly valuable: (1) directly after a therapy session, (2) during or immediately after an "upsetting" event or shame moment, particularly when it is part of the scenario preceding homosexual enactment, and (3) after homosexual enactment.

For many men journaling affords the rare occasion to dialogue with themselves without the influence of another person. It offers them the first opportunity they have ever experienced to evaluate their behavior, to "loop with the self" without external interference and judgment. This is particularly important for the man who has had intrusive, manipulative parental influence.

Besides the more or less daily entries, a monthly summary should be made as an additional therapeutic discipline. A review of those past entries often reveals overlooked themes and issues.

Structured Reflections

As a supplement to the unstructured format, the following journaling approach – based upon Albert Ellis's work in Rational Emotive Therapy – is also useful. It consists of five short questions to ask oneself after an upsetting occurrence: (1) event, (2) reaction, (3) assumptions, (4) assessment and (5) summary.

Using this format, the client can be given the following instructions:

1. *The event.* First, report the upsetting event. Describe in detail what actually occurred. Specify who did (or said) what to whom. Just the facts.

2. *Your reaction.* Describe in detail your internal reaction to the event. Include any emotions you felt, such as anger, hurt, depression, offense, shame, including your moods and bodily sensations. Also describe your opinions, ideas, urges and impulses. Include your behavior: What did you do? What did you say? How did you act out your reaction to the event? Consider the extent and intensity of your reaction. How exaggerated or extreme was your emotional reaction to the event? How overreactive was your behavior?

3. *Assumptions.* What assumptions did you make about the events? What did the event say to you? Why did the event create such reaction within you? How did you understand the event? What was the significance of the event that it so upset you? What interpretive judgments, presumptions and expectations did you make of the event which caused your reactions?

4. *Assessment.* Evaluate your assumptions in terms of reality, the way life really is. Then critique your assumptions in terms of any unrealistic (irrational) expectations you may have about life, about others and about yourself. Apply rational thinking to challenge these assumptions. Critique your irrational interpretations and look for emotional judgments. You should question any values, beliefs and attitudes that you may unrealistically assume to be true. Assess how your beliefs and attitudes caused your reactions.

Then apply your assumptions to these two criteria: *illusions* and *distortions.* As previously stated, *illusions* are narcissistically based assumptions that include unrealistic positive beliefs about what you can expect from life. Narcissism is the source of your illusions, telling you that the world, events and people will cater to your unique needs. Give special notice to words such as *should, ought to, must, need to* and *have to*. Consider grandiose expectations, assumed personal entitlements and any special consideration which you believe is "owed" to you.

Distortions are shame-based assumptions – unrealistic negative beliefs about what you can expect from life. Shame is the source of your distortions: *People will not respect, love, value me. Good things do not happen to me.* Consider ways in which you lower your expectations, deny your needs, avoid assertion and make excuses for others. Consider your evaluation of others' motivations based on your anticipation of their rejection, criticism, put-downs and humiliation.

5. **Summary statement.** Write a brief statement, including a summary of the above four points, and what you have learned about yourself.

Listening to the Body and Making Sense of Its Messages

Whether a client chooses to journal solely through free-structured reflections or to rely on the five-step format, the goal is the same: to apply reality principles to his unconscious assumptions. This provides the opportunity to realistically assess the narcissistically based illusions and shame-based distortions that control his emotional reactions to real-life situations. Through journaling, the client will begin to discern what is going within him and to keep a record of it while it is happening.

One man reported, "Journaling didn't make the pain go away, but it helped me tolerate the pain. The shift was not from 'pain' to 'no pain,' but from 'I want to run from the pain' to 'I can sit in the pain.' Feeling the pain feels *real*; when I feel the pain, *I* feel real."

Journaling thus helps clients attend to their body sensations, thoughts and feelings while integrating their meaning, and encourages them to take themselves and their feelings seriously.

CHAPTER 16

Counseling Teenagers

Every year, our clinic receives numerous calls from concerned parents of teenagers. The parents' calls typically result from some shocking discovery, often having to do with their son's visits to gay pornographic websites. This revelation usually prompts a long-overdue family discussion in which they face problems with the young man's developing sexual identity. The discussion often culminates in the parents bringing their son to therapy.

Directly clarifying our view of homosexuality to parents reduces their anxiety about the therapeutic process and encourages them to back off from pressuring their son to change. We do not simply support the child's notion about claiming any lifestyle option he chooses. The false claim of many therapists that they are operating with "therapeutic neutrality" on values-laden issues rightly frustrates parents. In practice this is not even a workable philosophy, much less an honest claim. In short, we believe that parents are owed some assurance of the direction the therapeutic agenda will take.

At the first session the teenage client is informed about our view of homosexuality and made aware that we differ from the mainstream psychological associations. With that in mind, we attempt to establish a working alliance.

As of this writing, several U.S. states have passed laws that put strong restrictions on therapists who work with minors with unwanted SSA. Gay activists succeeded in convincing legislators in those states that therapy involved techniques such as shaming the client, providing nausea-inducing drugs and electroshock treatment, and alienating him from friends and family. Of course, no therapist we know of, uses – or has ever used – such techniques. They have nothing to do with reparative therapy. The intent of the promoters of this law was to stop, not abusive therapeutic practices, but the promotion of a traditionalist worldview that gay activists dislike.

In California, the new law bans therapy for minors that involves "efforts to change behaviors or gender expressions – or to eliminate or reduce sexual or romantic attractions or feelings toward individuals of the same sex."

In light of this law, the approach we use at the Thomas Aquinas Psychological Clinic is now somewhat revised; in the therapeutic context of full acceptance – which was always the basis for reparative therapy – we encourage the client to investigate the motivations beneath his SSA, and we offer interpretation and provide scientifically based education. When he turns eighteen, we can broaden our approach.

Only a very small percentage of teenagers who are brought in unwillingly by their parents will actually continue in treatment. However, even when we fail to build a therapeutic alliance, these sessions offer an opportunity for teens to consider how their childhood experiences may have shaped their attractions, and to hear a perspective that they probably have not heard elsewhere.

The distinct needs of the young male between the ages of thirteen and twenty call for particular intervention strategies. (For preteenagers we take a different approach involving parental coaching, detailed in *A Parent's Guide to Preventing Homosexuality*.) Special challenges for the adolescent male include ambivalent commitment to therapy; intense sexual feelings; unstable personal identity; high susceptibility to the influence of media, peers and pop culture; suspicion of adult authority; teenage narcissism; rebellion; poor impulse control; the need to learn through experience; having an uncertain sense of morality; and high vulnerability to the influence of gay websites, especially gay porn. Added to this is the typical teenager's difficulty in maintaining a disciplined commitment to anything at all.

In spite of all these challenges, we continue to be impressed by the rare teenager who sustains a clarity and conviction toward overcoming his same-sex attractions.

Confidentiality

The issue of confidentiality is especially important when working with teenagers. It requires the therapist's ongoing sensitivity to preserve a working atmosphere of uncompromised privacy. Legal limits of confidentiality should be spelled out, including the therapist's obligation to inform parents about self-destructive behaviors, including dangerous sexual activities.

Often it is the parents who attempt to compromise the bounds of confidentiality, seeing the therapist as their paid agent to fix Junior. They may expect clandestine progress reports.

In the first session the client should be informed that although he has been asked by his parents to consider the possibility of a change in his sexuality, we agree from the start that therapy will not involve the therapist "changing" anything. Ultimately, his life choices must be his own, and if he feels manipulated or negatively judged, he is reminded that he needs to address this problem openly with the therapist. I reiterate, "Rule number one – never agree with anything I say unless it rings true for you."

Also during the first session it may be helpful for the therapist to explain that he will not convey specific details of the session to the parents, but instead will give them a general report of his overall progress. In practice, this is what most assures parents. Nevertheless, to avoid problems, the therapist should first clarify with the teen what he ethically can and cannot tell his parents about their sessions.

The Importance of Salient Men

To offset his susceptibility to popular cultural influences (television, movies and the Internet), the adolescent requires additional support beyond psychotherapy, most importantly from salient men. A "salient man" is defined as a male perceived by the client as both benevolent and strong. The therapeutic necessity for salient men cannot be overstated. Men who understand, accept and actively support the teen's efforts toward change are often the single most important factor in determining a positive therapeutic outcome.

Previously, we attempted to connect the client with other teens in treatment, but that strategy proved to us that youngsters are too susceptible to sexual temptation and are unable to offer support and wise guidance. Nowadays, we seek mature men as mentor-counselors and coaches, and for older teens, straight male friends such as an older brother. Most important of all, there is the father.

The Ongoing Role of the Father

Unlike the adult client, whose father may be aged, deceased or living elsewhere, the adolescent's father is likely to be living at home and able to participate in his son's treatment. To whatever extent possible, we attempt to include the father in the therapeutic process.

A critical evaluation must be made to determine the father's emotional availability. The father's psychological limitations will determine the extent to which he can actively participate in his son's change process, namely, through responding to his son's emotional needs. This evaluation will also determine to what extent the teen must accept (and grieve) his father's unavailability.

When appropriate, father–son dyadic sessions can be helpful to create a deeper level of communication. In such sessions the therapist is listening in terms of double binds and double loops. Father-son sessions help both client and therapist assess the father's realistic potential for responding to his son's needs.

Expose Versus Impose

If the teen disagrees with the therapist's views on homosexuality, then the foundation of the working alliance can simply be to "agree to disagree." In other words, the therapist *exposes* his *views* on homosexuality, but he doesn't *impose* the direction of treatment on the client. We explain that we see homosexual attractions as an adaptation to certain early emotional deprivations, and that the attempt to compensate for (repair) these early deprivations is, in our view, the reason for most same-sex attractions. Further, we explain that with corrective experiences in the present, those attractions can diminish.

It is important to remember that many homosexual clients, feeling betrayed by their earliest relationships, are hyper-distrustful and alert to manipulation. This is especially true for the adolescent client who is negotiating with an adult. By openly explaining his views on homosexuality, the therapist avoids covertly imposing his ideas and clarifies that the client is free to express and hold his own opinion.

The Gay Self-Label

For the teen who has come to therapy reluctantly, claiming a gay identity can serve as a means of distancing himself from the therapist. The gay self-label can serve a double bind function by engaging the therapist in intellectual sparring in order to keep an emotional distance.

The teenager may have already discovered the power of gay advocacy to neutralize his parents' influence. The therapist should avoid debate; rather than try to convince the client, he can return to discussing the young man's own experience, listening in terms of identifying an assertion-shame conflict.

Begin and End with His Experience: The Assertion–Shame Conflict

The high degree of narcissism common to all adolescents requires any therapeutic intervention to be closely linked to his immediate experience. Typically, the teenager's personal frame of reference must be the beginning and end of any intervention. This means that we do not focus primarily on the question of whether to be gay or not, but instead, we address the development of the confident, assertive, manly and strong person he himself wants to be – overcoming the false self that harbors feelings of intimidation, inhibition, unmanliness and hidden shame.

Fundamental to reparative therapy is the understanding that homosexuality is a symptom of this conflict. Without making changing his homosexuality the goal of therapy, but also without confirming the teenager in a gay self-label, the therapist may focus on assisting the teen in solving his day-to-day problems, which often involve interpersonal issues that manifest as assertion-shame conflicts. The client will soon discover that many of his assertion needs are direct or indirect expressions of his masculine drives. It is advisable that this understanding be clearly explained to him in the first session.

The therapist should know that supporting the client's assertion of self, even if he is gay-identified, may in fact diminish his same-sex attractions. More importantly an authentic therapeutic relationship with the therapist – a salient man who respects, values and understands him – will ultimately be of benefit to the client.

For the adolescent, sexual-identity issues are often confused with larger issues of personal identity and competence. "Who am I?" is the repeated theme in most early sessions. Developing a sense of himself as an autonomous person is the primary challenge for the adolescent.

The teen who is in conflict about his sexual feelings must now confront his problem directly. By mid-adolescence, he can no longer avoid the erotic conflicts that he has suppressed or denied. He may begin experimentation with Internet gay chat rooms, online pornography, phone sex and eventually homosexual behavior in a search for sexual identity.

Gay Identity as Fashionable

In today's culture teens are often actively encouraged to question and even test out their sexuality. A school psychologist told me that his caseload of teens reporting a sexual-identity crisis had doubled during one year. Many other school counselors report seeing an increasing number of students who believe they are bisexual or homosexual.

Our own clinical practice also reflects a greater proportion of younger teens questioning their sexual orientation. Thirteen-, fourteen- and fifteen-year-olds are increasingly announcing to their parents that they are gay. A transition that used to occur in the mid to late twenties or sometimes older now takes place in the early and mid-teens. More and more adolescents are "coming out" to their friends and parents. This is no doubt due to the increased presence of the gay identity as a fashionable and countercultur-ally in-your-face.

Although the Internet is a great education tool, it offers easy access to pornography and gay-activist misinformation. From the very start of treatment we recommend that parents consider adding protective blocks to their Internet server, and that they inform their teen in advance that as responsible parents they will make regular inspections of "usage history," their computer's record of websites visited.

Teens have always enjoyed provoking the older generation, particularly when they can link their rebellion to a struggle for freedom, self-determination and justice for a disadvantaged minority.

A number of studies show that youth who are dealing with homosexuality suffer from a higher level of behavioral and psychiatric problems than heterosexual youth, including suicide attempts and drug and alcohol abuse.[1] One recent study found "compelling evidence" that gay and bisexual youth present higher rates of generalized anxiety disorder, major depression, suicidal thoughts and even nicotine dependence (Fergusson et al., 1999). Effeminate boys in particular were shown to suffer from higher levels of psychiatric problems, including a deep sense of inferiority.

When the studies are taken as a whole, it is also clear that a teenager who self-identifies as gay is at high risk for infection with HIV or another STD, for psychiatric problems including suicidal ideation, and for self-destructive behaviors such as drug and alcohol abuse and prostitution. Although teasing and harassment by peers (which obviously does occur and can indeed be cruel) would be a contributing factor, no research has ever proven the alarming psychiatric problems of gay-identified teens to be due solely, or even primarily, to this peer marginalization.

We believe the higher rate of mental health problems in homosexually oriented youth reflects not only social disadvantage but problems that are intrinsic to the homosexual condition.

Activists bringing "safe-schools programs" to the public schools often win support by citing high rates of suicide attempts among sexually confused teens. The problem of suicide attempts will only be remedied, these programs claim, when society puts its stamp of approval on homosexuality. However, the fact that the elevated rate of psychiatric problems of gay-identified people *does not decrease* in gay-friendly cities such as San Francisco, or in gay-tolerant countries such as the Netherlands and Denmark, supports our view that there are problematic factors at work that are intrinsic to the homosexual condition itself.

Opening the Door for a Confused Teenager

The adolescent presenting for treatment has been exposed to a cultural message that says that homosexuality is perfectly OK and that it is just a complement to heterosexuality. But when we open the door to impressionable teenagers and urge them to go through it to try homosexual behavior, we expose them to terrible medical risks, as well as encourage them to habituate themselves to a behavior they may later, with greater maturity, come to regret.

The therapist needs to keep in mind that homosexual eroticism can be the result of many things: normal but temporary feelings of peer infatuation, need for belonging, the search for pleasure, or simple curiosity. It may be an expression of anxiety about growing into adulthood or a means of avoiding the challenges of heterosexual social relationships. A youngster who feels socially inadequate, overwhelmed by the pressures of dating or in conflict about his confusing sexual impulses may also resort to homosexual behavior by default.

In any event, a teenager's preoccupation with gay themes should cause parents serious concern, and properly addressing that concern requires appropriate professional intervention. Sometimes the youngster's preoccupations are also accompanied by overwhelming guilt, self-condemnation and even suicidal thoughts, particularly if his parents are critical, distant or abusive. Teenage depression and suicidal thoughts must be taken with utter seriousness. The therapeutic task is to affirm the teen's deep need for *same-sex emotional attachment* (the three A's: attention, affection and approval) as distinct from homosexual enactment.

When we consider how homosexual behavior serves to reinforce and deepen a gay identity, we see the absolute importance of early intervention. If childhood has passed, the teenage years yet remain a favorable time to address the emotional needs that lie at the root of homosexual behavior. Untreated, adolescent sexual confusion becomes increasingly unreceptive to treatment and is likely to result in the belief that "gay" is inevitably and ultimately the person's only possible self-identity.

How the Adolescent's Sexual Identity Forms

In helping the sexually conflicted teen, two issues need to be separated out: dealing with homosexual behavior, and whether or not the teen will choose to claim a gay identity. Let's first look at *homosexual behavior*.

The critical developmental phase leading to a homosexual identity is called the "erotic transitional phase" (Nicolosi, 1991). During the early teen years, if gender identification and emotional needs remain unmet in the prehomosexual child, once hormones stimulate adult erotic interests, sexual feelings will be directed toward satisfying those unmet love needs. It is precisely those emotional and identification needs that create the intense craving that characterizes homosexual desire. While never satisfying these childhood needs, homosexual behavior is easily confirmed into a habit pattern. The easy availability of gay pornography, now so readily accessible on the Internet, reinforces this addictive dimension.

Gay identity. Popular culture portrays the gay life very favorably, even glamorously. Many schools have gay and lesbian clubs and organizations, and pro-gay counseling programs encourage "sexually questioning" adolescents to try on a gay or bisexual identity.

The euphoric experience of "coming out" – of identifying oneself with an oppressed minority that is demanding social justice – appeals to the adolescent's romantic sensibility. Especially for youth, who typically feel misunderstood and unappreciated by parents and authority figures, the notion of a subculture with similarly oppressed youth, "where I can be accepted for who I really am," is indescribably appealing. Further, the gay subculture bestows great value on youthfulness. A young person who yearns to belong and who enters that world will quickly receive flattering attention, especially from older gay men.

Traditionally, mental-health professionals understood much of adolescent homosexual behavior as *experimentation* rather than as a means of discovering some sort of innate self-identity. They understood that for many adolescents, homosexual experiences represent nothing more than a "period of developmental curiosity" that will eventually be discarded as heterosexual interests predominate. And they recognized that with proper guidance, the young person would sort out the real meaning of his sexualized longings.

But today, the teenager's natural desire to "belong" to an embracing community, along with the extraordinarily easy availability of gay sex, can quickly lead any confused young person into a deepening gay self-identity. In fact, quite a few of my adult homosexual clients have told me they always assumed they were "straight" until their first homosexual experience; afterward, they believed that experience proved them to be gay.

A national survey, *Sex in America*, indicates that while only 2 to 3 percent of adult males are homosexual, 10 to 16 percent of all men go through a homosexual phase earlier in their lives (Laumann, Gagnon, Michael & Michaels, 1994). What if these young men had been confirmed as "gay" by a school counselor or gay program during that vulnerable phase? Another major study found that more than one-quarter of twelve-year-olds are *unsure whether they are heterosexual or homosexual* (Remafedi, Resnick, Blum & Harris, 1992). This 1992 study polled 34,707 Minnesota teenagers and was published in the prestigious journal *Pediatrics*.

This means that a gay school-counseling program, eager to identify and support every same-sex attracted teen, will find that about one-quarter of all early teens do in fact suffer from a *temporary* period of sexual-identity confusion. But most alarming of all, such teens might *erroneously be identified as homosexual* if they are affirmed as gay by a counselor at age twelve.

One reason for this high incidence of confusion, as mentioned earlier, is the media exposure our kids have to glamorized gay images. Internet websites, television, films, rock music, teen magazines and even public libraries offer very appealing pro-gay messages. For questioning youngsters, these messages are quite seductive.

A teenage boy called in to a radio talk show's host, a psychologist. The young man explained that he had attractions to men, but this created a conflict because he was a Southern Baptist. The psychologist advised him to accept himself as a "gay youth," and said that if he could not reconcile his "natural" gay identity with his religion, then he should think about jettisoning his religious beliefs and switching to the Metropolitan Community Church, which is gay friendly. This sort of advice – the uncritical assumption that a young person's experience means that he is "naturally" homosexual (and that sexual feelings take precedence over deeply held religious beliefs) – represents the pervasive misinformation that permeates our culture.

Adolescent Boys and Risky Behavior

Neuroscientists have recently gained better understanding of the high-risk habits of teenagers. The reckless experimentation characteristic of teenage boys in particular has traditionally been explained as a form of rebellion.

But studies have recently shown that risk-taking behavior is actually rooted in changes that are occurring in the brain.

During adolescence the brain undergoes a profound remodeling. The prefrontal neural cortex, which functions as the brain's command center, loses nearly half of its neural connections. Subsequently decision-making is shifted to brain regions that are governed by emotional reactivity. These massive changes predispose adolescents to take more risks. At the same time there is a drop in the brain's dopamine level during the adolescent years, which decreases the ability to experience pleasure. As a result, teens are drawn toward destructive behaviors such as drinking, taking drugs and experimenting with risky sex.

Valuing versus tolerating sexual diversity. The adolescent is often enthralled by the sociopolitical aspects of gay identity and the appealing thought of joining "the fight against oppression." Recognizing the role of adolescent sentimentality, pro-gay programs usually overlay encouragement to take part in a broad political agenda on top of the personal issues with which the teenager is dealing. What should remain a focus on the youth's own personal experience instead becomes a "call to join forces" with the gay political movement. The teenager is led to believe that *society's oppression is the thing that is standing between me and the possibility of happiness.*

Come out or seek change? Quite a few of the young men who come to us will decide to embrace a gay identity and will leave reparative therapy. However, others will succeed in deepening their sense of masculinity and developing friendships with straight males, whereby they experience a significant diminishing of their homosexual urges. For these young men, as time goes by, adopting a gay lifestyle seems to be less and less of an option for them.

One eighteen-year-old client had a good look at the gay community in San Francisco and was disgusted by the promiscuity, drug use, sadomasochistic sexual practices and unstable relationships. That visit taught him much more than I could. As he told me, "I used to envy those guys who are 'out.' I thought they were courageous, honest . . . they could be themselves. Now I'm not so sure that's what I want for myself."

Interventions intended to address adolescent homosexuality must be broad-based and individualized, because the teenager's same-sex attractions probably stem from many different sources. There may be conflicted feelings about females, and fear and envy of male peers. Years of teasing may have convinced the boy that "what they say about me must be true, so I might as well go ahead and just 'come out.'" All the while, the decision-making process is made more difficult by the easy availability of gay sex.

Building trust with adolescents. Anger, rebellion and hurt usually fester just under the surface as teenagers grapple with sexual identity. Although a young man may appear to be compliant, he is likely highly ambivalent about any adult who probes the deeper layers of his private life. Secrecy has always been his best defense against intrusion. Therefore we can expect suspicion and hostility directed at both parents and therapists.

Fortunately, even deeper than the adolescent desire to *hide* is the healthy desire to *be seen and understood*. What the adolescent male desires most is also what he fears most – to be truly "seen" by another man. Therefore, the first step in any kind of healing is to offer unconditional acceptance so that the teenager need not hide his conflicted feelings.

The young man also needs to hear this message from his parents:

> We love you, and nothing you do in your life will ever change that fact. We will do our best to respect your feelings and understand your perspective no matter what choices you make.
>
> But because we desire the best for you, we want you to seriously consider all your options. We do not think a gay lifestyle is a wise choice.

Separating Emotional Needs from Sexual Feelings

One sixteen-year-old boy was brought to me by his parents shortly after he had announced to them that he was gay. He came with them to the counseling session, but only very reluctantly. Even though the young man was resistant to being in therapy, a turning point in treatment occurred in our third session when I asked him, "Tell me, when do you *not* feel homosexual attractions?" His answer was immediate: "When I'm playing soccer."

From that moment on, he was able to realize that when he was feeling accepted and connected with other guys – especially on a physical level – his homosexual preoccupations disappeared. It was during times of social isolation and rejection that his same-sex fantasies resurfaced to preoccupy him.

By reflecting on this repeated pattern, the young man was able to realize that what he thought was an intrinsic, inborn part of "who he really was" was actually a situational reaction to feelings of gender inadequacy.

Very often the gender-confused adolescent has a physical handicap or limitation (such as asthma or a frail build) that, in his mind, blocks him from gaining full acceptance from males. It is up to both the therapist and the parents to help the adolescent make a realistic assessment of that limitation and to show him that very often this is an *excuse* to stay stuck in a posture of inferiority. His own obsessive focus on these limitations causes him to disqualify himself as equal.

As the therapeutic process continues, the teen often begins to understand that his same-sex attractions are, in fact, attempts to "repair" an emotional deficit – his own *perfectly normal and authentic* (but unfulfilled) needs for male attention, affection and approval. Homoerotic fantasies and romantic attachments may come to be understood by the adolescent as a reparative drive (however misdirected when eroticized) toward gender wholeness.

Correcting Popular Misinformation

Recently, a nineteen-year-old, gay-identified young man proudly informed me that Abraham Lincoln was gay. He had read this in a gay magazine. Fortunately, having heard the rumor myself, I was able to educate the boy on the historical reality. During Lincoln's times, travelers were often expected by an innkeeper to share beds, but the fact that Lincoln also shared a bed with other travelers did not mean that he was homosexual. I was able to use this distortion about Lincoln to provide an object lesson in the politicization of history.

The education of adolescents involves compassionately but clearly correcting popular misinformation, including the following myths:

- "Sexual orientation is biologically determined – once gay, always gay."

- "Gay men have steady, monogamous relationships." In reality, the expectation of sexual faithfulness, gay researchers now admit, is actually more likely to destroy gay men's relationships rather than keep them together (McWhirter & Mattison, 1984).

• "Every other culture and society throughout history has accepted homosexuality. Ours is the only homophobic society." Actually, no culture has ever elevated homosexuality to the same status as heterosexuality.

• "Animals, too, are homosexual." Same-sex behaviors are usually attributed by biologists to the stresses of captivity, biological pollutants, domestication, unavailability of the opposite sex, hormonal manipulation, misinterpretation of sex calls or odors, expressions of dominance, and immature sex play. But this does not mean the behavior should be considered normal.[2]

• "Attempts to change sexual orientation are dangerous; they only create greater unhappiness, depression and sometimes suicide." Serious depression due to failure to change is indeed a possibility, as it is whenever treatment fails for other problems such as obesity, anorexia, alcoholism or drug abuse. But to put this risk in better context, remember that suicide attempts are also precipitated by being told one *cannot* change.

• "Homosexually oriented people are identical to heterosexuals in every way psychologically and emotionally, except for the incidental detail of their sexual preference. As a group, they are as healthy as heterosexuals." In reality, homosexual men and women have been shown to suffer from a higher level of suicide attempts, substance abuse and psychiatric disorders (Sandfort, Graaf, Bijl & Schnabel, 2001).[3]

These and many other myths call for education and correct information. Any youth confronted with a fundamental choice in lifestyle deserves accurate information in order to make an informed decision about his future.

The Difference Between "Gay" and "Homosexual"

Essential to the healing of homosexuality is clarifying distinctions about labels. Just because a male experiences homosexual feelings does not mean he is obliged to assume the label of "gay." Unlike the word *homosexual*, which describes a sexual orientation, *gay* is a social-political identity, which says in essence, This is who I am, this is the "real me," and I can live out my same-sex attractions without any internal conflict.

Not all people who have these feelings choose a gay identity. The confusion between *homosexual* and *gay* is the result of a popular ideology promoted within our culture and increasingly in our public schools. The sexually confused boy is encouraged to *identify* with his sense of masculine inferiority and gender confusion, and to join forces with the other people who suffer from the same deficit. In so doing, he separates himself from the majority of conventional society and identifies with approximately 2 to 4 percent of the population, while excluding himself from the remaining 96 to 98 percent.

Will the Adolescent Stay in Therapy?

Young men who stay in reparative therapy come to see that their homosexual desires represent a far deeper need from males – it bears repeating that they are in search of the three A's: attention, affirmation and affection. With continuing counsel and inner work, many will take a path that leads beyond their same-sex attractions. But realistically, many other teenagers will drop out of therapy and make the decision to identify themselves as gay.

The road toward transformation is a long and winding one, and there will be continual temptations to give up the effort when that "one special guy" seems to come across his path. Still, even if there is a setback – sometimes a setback that may last months or perhaps years – there is still hope. Parents or therapists can offer options to the adolescent, although the final choice has to be up to him: guilt, manipulation, force or coercion will not free him from his attractions but will only cause greater alienation.

It's important to remember that change is a matter of *diminishing* homosexual feelings and *increasing* heterosexual attractions. Change moves slowly, on a gradual continuum, and there will inevitably be regressions. It is not a matter of "once homosexual, now heterosexual." And like *all* psychological change, the transformation will probably never be total. Realistically for most, there will be lingering attractions and temptations over the course of a lifetime.

Working with parents. Parental education and management can often become a significant part of the therapist's concerns. Usually it is the parents who have brought the adolescent into treatment. Either the adolescent has "come out," or the parents have discovered his homosexual interests. Finding gay pornography in the adolescent's room or discovering letters or e-mails indicating a same-sex infatuation has often alerted parents to the problem. For some time mothers may have had the uneasy suspicion there was another side to this obedient, compliant teenager.

Detective work by suspicious parents presents them with a potential ethical conflict. They want to respect their child's privacy, yet they are afraid to neglect a serious problem. "I'm a sneak," confessed one mother, "and I admit it. But I'll do whatever it takes to save my kid." Most parents easily understand her sentiments. However, a commitment to doing "whatever it takes" may ultimately provoke angry rejection by the teenager.

Parents need to understand that if their son doesn't want therapy, all that can be done is to provide information. The therapist can only offer him the opportunity to make an educated choice – that is, to make a life decision based on accurate information.

A number of teenagers have come to our clinic for counsel, have given themselves the opportunity to hear the option of reparative therapy and have declined the invitation. The reasons for their refusal are varied. One young man was very much involved in a relationship with an older gay man and feared losing the security of that mentoring relationship. Others have become enchanted by the gay self-label or the gay subculture. Many young people have so deeply identified with their homosexual orientation that the possibility of giving up that identity is too frightening. ("If I'm no longer gay, then who *am* I?") In all these cases, if therapy continues at all, the therapeutic relationship must proceed very, very slowly, with much support and little direct confrontation.

Even if the teenager decides to pursue a gay identity, he can gain much from the process of demystifying men and learning how to better connect with them as people. Regarding his habit of masturbation with gay pornography, one teenager describes how he was learning to develop more genuine human connections:

> The most liberating thing I've learned is that I don't have to live in the fantasy world of porn; there are no such people, no such places. Porn is not the real world.

It has become a hollow ritual, less real. I thought I was missing all of that, but those porn guys – they aren't really out there.

I'm feeling more and more free to find something real as a substitute for that old fantasy excitement.

For those who seek even more, Alan Medinger (2000), an ex-gay ministry leader, talks about the change in his life that "set him free to love," desexualized his unmet emotional needs, broke the power of his sexual addiction and met the deepest needs of his heart. Real and enduring change can happen, he affirms, "because I have seen it happen hundreds of times" (p. 240).

Considering the difficult realities of a gay life, many parents remain adamant in hoping their son will eventually pursue change. As Robert Spitzer, the psychiatrist who led the 1973 decision to remove homosexuality from the manual of disorders, said (2000), "in homosexuality, something's not working." As another father told me emphatically, "Living life as a *heterosexual* man is hard enough!"

The Power of the Media

One forty-six-year-old client recalled his experience as a seventeen-year-old trying to understand his same-sex attachments. Recalling an early 1980s pro-gay TV special, "An Early Frost with Marlo Thomas," he said:

I loved Marlo Thomas, and she did this story about a gay teenage boy who didn't really want to take this girl to a prom. The boy said something like, "When I see that special guy, I come alive." I thought to myself, "That's how it is for me: when I see that special guy, I come alive."

That confirmed for me that I must be gay.

Early gender-based trauma resulting in denial of gender, and later compensated for (repaired) by homoerotic attraction is, in today's culture, explained as an "innate gay identity."

But this is an all-too-easy explanation. In fact, it is an all-too-easy *untruth*. And it is an *untruth about human design* that will have a growing negative effect on family, religion, community and culture.

CHAPTER 17

Male Friendships

In childhood, I was never chosen for teams, so I learned to go where I would be chosen. That's why I go cruising today – so I will be chosen.

I've been helped a lot by the authentic brotherhood that I have received in men's groups, where I'm able to bond with straight men. That's powerful – when you get the stamp of approval that says you're OK.

Most homosexual men report feeling uneasy in the company of other males – a discomfort tracing back to early childhood. Beginning with alienation from the father, this unease is typical of the history of the homosexual man and is rooted in the etiology of the condition.

Our clients typically report a painful absence of close male friendships. The man dealing with same-sex attraction feels not only alienated from – that is, "different from" – but also "less than" other men.

Our clients' relationships are painfully distorted, because the assertive drive to relate as a man among men conflicts with their anticipation of shame for being exposed as not masculine enough. One client explained: "Even when I'm with another man, I still feel alone. I'm not letting them in, so I'm walled off – protected, guarded. Behind it all is the worry that they'll eventually lose interest in me."

The SSA male yearns to heal the father wound by finding closeness with other men; he continually seeks, yet is afraid of, masculine intimacy. This quandary, which leaves him chronically unhappy, is what Moberly (1983) calls "same-sex ambivalence."

A large part of the problem is that men struggling with homosexuality hold an idealized and unrealistic view of men and a naive understanding of the nature of male friendships. Their intense unmet emotional needs distort their expectation of what a healthy male friendship can be. Said one client, "I always think that finding that special friend means we're going to lock eyes, and it's [singing] 'Some enchanted evening.'"

Faced with the mystery and hard work of forming normal male friendships, some men discover rather odd tactics to avoid the unwanted intrusion of eroticism. "When I have to relate to another guy, I get so confused," said a client. "Just how is this done? A useful trick for me, is to ask myself, *So what would I do now if he were a female friend?*"

Yet the challenge of establishing and deepening healthy male friendships is an essential one for the man who desires to overcome his homosexual problem. Non-erotic intimacy is a basic requirement for the resolution of same-sex attractions – so much so that the client's progress can usually be evaluated by the level of intimacy of his male friendships.

In fact, for the first half of treatment, the quality of male friendships is a more important standard for assessing client progress than a reduction in homosexual enactments.

At the start of therapy many clients report that they already do have close male friendships. But closer inquiry typically reveals superficial relationships lacking in honesty, disclosure and full mutuality. These initial claims of close male friendships suggest a dimension of self-deception, based in part on wishful thinking. But more importantly, the client's belief that these friendships are actually "close" is based on his inability to realistically assess male emotional closeness due to his deep-seated, basic misunderstanding of males and maleness.

Men as Mysteries

Same-sex attracted men tend to categorize other men in extremes, deifying or demonizing them. They will psychologically split other men into "good object versus bad object," which diminishes opportunities to tolerate the normal disagreements that arise in all relationships. This childlike tendency to perceive other people's behaviors as either "all good" or "all bad" can, in some cases, be traced back to the triadic-narcissistic family's inability to foster the lesson of object constancy.

Remaining emotionally connected to another man while in conflict with him is of critical importance and an ongoing challenge in treatment. To receive or express anger within a male friendship is deeply threatening to the SSA man and will often evoke expectations of profound rejection. Men are perceived by him as mysterious, inscrutable, powerful forces that remain beyond the his reach or understanding. One man mused:

> All through my school years, the question I asked myself was, what do I need to do? To have? To show? What status markers do I need to display so that I can "get in"? How could I get to that warm, comfortable place of acceptance that I feel shut out of, and so painfully denied?
>
> I wanted to be wanted by that guy. But what was it about that guy? Actually it wasn't one guy, but a collective-type of guy that I wanted to be "in" with.

Therapist as Mentor

The challenge to establish and deepen male friendships can be daunting and is often discouraging. There seem to be no road maps; the world of men is a foreign culture. One client said about his attempt to initiate a male friendship, "How do I start? I don't even know what to say to him. Should I ask, 'How many sit ups can you do?'" Our clients lack the basic understanding of how males actually make friends. When other boys, during the latency period, were learning how to get along with the guys, our client was typically lost in a world of boyhood isolation, absorbed in fantasy and often stuck at home listening to Mom's complaints about Dad.

Consequently, therapy should include a crash course on how men establish and deepen friendships. Such desperately needed practical advice is provided by the therapist in his teacher-mentor modality. He offers a basic education about what men are like, how they relate, their ways of communicating and what to expect in a male friendship.

This need for basic education is exemplified by a seventeen-year-old student who describes how he stumbled into a shame moment because of his unrealistic expectations of male friends:

CLIENT
I was feeling good walking into church. In the back rows, I saw the girls sitting on the left and the guys on the right. My thought was, *Oh, here's a "reparative moment" – I should go over to the guys.* But I couldn't find a place to sit with them, no open seat, so I quickly swerved over to the girls. As soon as I did that, I knew I had made a mistake.

THERAPIST
There was no place for you to sit with the boys?

CLIENT
(*hesitant*) Well, I guess it was more their attitude. They... they didn't seem happy to see me.

THERAPIST
What exactly did you see?

CLIENT
(*hesitating*) They saw me walk in; they looked at me but they kept on talking to each other.

THERAPIST
What did you expect (*reveals his impatience*) – a standing ovation?

CLIENT
(*self-conscious laughter*) No! (*pondering*) I know it sounds stupid, they didn't seem happy to see me, and (*deep breath, as if summoning his courage*) I mean, the girls were like, (*high-pitched voice*) "Oh, David! Come here! Sit here!"

THERAPIST
So you expect guys to greet you like that?

CLIENT
Well...

THERAPIST
This is not how guys relate to each other. You just show up and then join in. There's no over-the-top greeting like girls do, or gay guys do with each other. You just join in and create a place for yourself.

CLIENT
(*nodding slowly*) I know you're right...but my insecurity takes over, and then I'm convinced it's all about me.

Gay Communication Versus Straight Communication

The negative implication of the word *straight* is of something rigid, narrow-minded and stiff. As one man said, "I have lived with gay roommates and straight roommates, and I can feel the difference. Gay men use a lot of innuendo and convoluted meanings. They say a lot just by what they *don't* say. But guys who are straight are direct, blunt, with no hidden meanings. I guess that's why gays call straights 'straight.'"

As they come to know straight men, clients notice other ways they are different than gays. One thirty-two-year-old said, "I notice that while straight guys are talking to each other, they'll often toss objects to each other. I never noticed this before, perhaps because I was intimidated. I didn't think I could catch, so I tried to ignore it – just make believe I didn't see it coming at me." Said another client, "I discovered straight men do (there's actually a word for it) – 'onomatopoeia' – you know, those whistles or sound effects when telling a story."

Psychiatrist Richard Friedman (1988) says that the prehomosexual boy can't accurately assess the intent of other boys' aggression and has difficulty distinguishing if the other boys are just playing rough or if they actually intend to hurt him.[1] Even in adulthood he becomes easily slighted by joking criticisms and is often put off by the rough way men typically engage each other. Straight men enjoy verbal sparring, teasing and good-natured put-downs. When straight men talk to each other there are more interruptions, disagreements, blunt contradictions and challenges. This benevolent but "edgy" hostility of friendly insults is likely to intimidate our client, giving him reason to feel unaccepted.

Intimacy must by definition include vulnerability and exposing his feelings to other men – something the client desires but at the same time deeply fears. Behind the homoerotic drive is often the simple desire to relate to another male on terms that may seem ordinary but, for the client, are deeply satisfying. Said one man, "Guys like me crave the simplicity and stupidity of straight guys."

An Experience of Silent Understanding

Disillusioned with gay sex, another client told me of a time when he was a teenager that captured the simple essence of what he actually sought from other men:

> Jim and I had been skiing all day. We had been out on the slopes together, speeding down the hills with fast turns, exploring different routes and trying out new jumps. But at the end of the day we were hungry and we

sat down at a wooden table across from each other. Over his shoulder I could see the snow swirling in the cold night through the window of the warm, lively ski lodge.

As we ate our pizza and drank our hot cocoa together, there was a silent understanding and acceptance between us. I didn't have to say something funny or clever or worry about saying the right thing. In fact, I wasn't even expected to say anything – I could feel that I was appreciated for just being there and being me.

During that simple meal, we shared much more than pizza. We felt as close as brothers, genuinely connecting. The most we probably said the whole time was "mmm" or "good food." But our simple silence somehow spoke much more deeply as we were relating heart-to-heart and man-to-man.

As I reflect upon that evening, I realize how much I value and long for times of emotional connection like that one; it's a kind of silent understanding and companionship between men that's so hard to explain, and yet so vital.

The Candy Machine

Another client, a sixteen-year-old boy, came to face the reality of his family situation. He had spent his childhood trying to "make things better" in a home in which his father was uninvolved with the family and his mother was needy for his attention but emotionally empty. He finally reached the conclusion that he could no longer hope things would get better at home, and that he needed to push himself to find some affirming peer relationships. Speaking longingly of what he wished he could have, he described this imagery:

> I'm just a little kid sitting next to a broken candy machine [his dad]. I'm hoping that if I keep putting more money in, I'll get some candy. But the machine isn't moving; nothing comes out. I can see all the pieces of chocolate and sweets through the glass, and the machine sometimes stirs a bit, making a little rattling sound, but nothing ever drops down the slot.
>
> I suddenly remember there's a candy shop two blocks down the street [male friendships]. That seems so very far away though. I don't

think I'm gonna go; I've never walked two blocks before. Besides, I could get lost or kidnapped. It's just so much easier to just sit here and kind of wait.

Four Categories of Male Friendship

Let's consider four categories of male friendships, in order of their increasing reparative value: (1) gay friend, (2) the non-gay homosexual friend, (3) the straight friend, (4) the straight friend to whom he is sexually attracted.

1. Friendships with gay men create the possibility of erotic attraction and a mutual sexual agenda. Honest friendship is diminished by flirtation and vague innuendoes, with each looking for cues of sexual receptivity from the other. Mutual game-playing and manipulation undermine the possibility of healthy equality, therefore diminishing the value of this sort of male relationship.

2. Celibate homosexual friendships with other non-gay homosexuals offer empathy and special understanding. Supportive groups of other SSA men can greatly facilitate the healing progress. However, such men are limited in their potential to break down the male mystique, which is usually reserved for the straight man. Challenges to these relationships include the likelihood of mutual anticipatory shame in the psychic makeup of both men, with slights and hurtful misunderstandings posing a continual threat. These friendships are preparation for the more challenging relationship with the less emotionally attuned and "ever-clueless" straight guy.

3. Heterosexual, nonsexually attractive friendships have more value to men in reparative therapy. Life circumstances often put the client into contact with such men, but he feels no motivation to establish a friendship because these men don't have "the look." When the man seems ordinary, and the old familiar sexual attraction is missing, he is uninteresting or boring. The client's dismissive contempt blocks a learning opportunity, since every man can teach him something about being a man.

4. Heterosexual male friendships with men for whom the client feels an erotic attraction offer the greatest opportunity for healing. Only through such associations can there be transformation from erotic attraction to true friendship – that is, the demystifying of the distant male. While the

SSA man will always have an aesthetic appreciation for another man's good looks and masculine qualities, as therapy progresses it will become increasingly evident that sexual fantasies simply don't fit into any mutually respectful friendship.

Over time, with increasing acceptance from the other man and growing familiarity, the original sexual feelings the client may have felt will naturally diminish: "It's like thinking of having sex with my brother." But when this familiarity fades (during times when the friend is absent), same-sex fantasies may begin to resurface. As a client said of his "gorgeous looking" straight friend, "When I'm with him I'm not thinking sexually about him. It's when I'm away from him, especially for a long time, that I think about him that way."

Shift from Eros to Philia

The transformational shift from sexual to fraternal (i.e., eros to philia) is the essential healing experience of male homosexuality. At every opportunity, this lesson needs to be identified and repeated. As one client told me, "When I was in college, I was in a fraternity. I played touch football and drank beer afterward. During that time in my life, I felt less homosexual, both in terms of my perception of myself and in my homosexual feelings."

Disclosing to a Straight Friend

A valuable therapeutic opportunity occurs when the client discloses his homosexual struggle to a straight friend. This decision deserves prudent consideration and can be very devastating if the straight friend fails to respond favorably. On the other hand, if the straight friend is able to listen, understand and affirm his friend's struggle, this leads to a deepening of their friendship. Disclosure to a straight friend can be powerfully healing.

The SSA male has difficulty accepting and internalizing the affirmation that his straight friend offers, because he holds the unconscious suspicion (a shame-based distortion) that "if my straight friend really knew about my homosexuality, he would not accept me." Disclosure, however, will remove one more layer of defensive separation that lies between him and straight men. "Before I told him I was dealing with SSA, when we would hug, I felt I was stealing something from him," a client explained. "But now that I've told him about my struggle, when we hug, I feel he is giving me something."

Healing occurs when a shame-based aspect of the self is revealed and responded to positively by a significant other. Whenever a person can reveal and disclose something negative, embarrassing or shameful, and present it to another person whom he regards as good and benevolent, and that second person hears that disclosure and still accepts the one who has confessed it, transformation occurs. Personal growth takes place through dynamic interaction.

How to tell a straight friend. How should the client disclose his homosexual struggle to a straight friend, particularly a straight friend he looks up to? From my many years of experience, there seems to be a basic outline that works best for this procedure.

First, when telling a straight friend, it is advisable to avoid such words as *homosexual* or *gay.* It is best, instead, to speak from personal experience. Unfortunately, many heterosexual men have been subliminally influenced by popular misinformation and tend to see their homosexually oriented friend as "gay," that is, someone fundamentally distinct from "straight."

That's why it is wise to speak in terms of childhood deficits and the need for acceptance by men. Reference to homoeroticism is best presented not as an identity but as a *consequence* and a *symptom* of these earlier unmet male needs.

Disclosure to the straight friend should be done in four steps – either during one meeting or over a period of time:

1. *Family background.* Offering information such as, "This is the kind of father I had . . . This is the kind of relationship I had with my mother, older brother, younger sister . . . These are my childhood experiences [sexual abuse, intimidation by peers, etc.]." The client can then describe the deficit that causes him not to feel confident about his masculine identification.

2. *Results of family background.* "I was left with feelings of insecurity, inferiority or inadequacy regarding my masculinity and my connection with other men. I didn't feel like one of the guys. I didn't know how to fulfill that deficit inside myself."

3. *Same-sex exploration.* "As a result of those feelings about myself, I found myself searching for masculine connectedness, and that search led

me to sexual behaviors and actions. These things left me dissatisfied, did not represent my values or who I really am."

4. *Healing through authentic friendships.* "Therefore, as a result of my sexual experimentation, I realize that it's not really sex that I'm after. What I really want is a healthy emotional connection with other men. Our friendship is important to me as an opportunity to fulfill my natural male emotional needs and to help me complete my heterosexual identity."

5. *Accountability (an optional fifth step).* The client may ask the friend to hold him accountable to report any form of homosexual enactment to him. This agreement works best if it goes both ways, with the straight friend disclosing "falls" regarding his own particular struggles.

When the struggler's story is presented to his friend according to this outline, most heterosexual men seem to understand. When the struggler reveals himself honestly to the mature and caring straight friend, the response is almost always positive.

What the Client Needs From a Straight Friend

There are certain responses our clients need from their straight friends. First, the client needs to be *understood*, not patronized, not categorized as "gay," but understood as to the nature of his struggle. The straight friend must truly appreciate and empathize with the challenges of his friend. To accomplish this the client will need to educate his friend on the developmental pathway, deficits, needs and desires which are the basis of his same-sex attractions.

Second, the client needs to be *accepted,* to see that his disclosure does not modify, qualify or diminish in any way the fundamental acceptance of the other guy. And he needs his friend's unconditional acceptance to be manifest and clearly demonstrated.

Third, he needs to be *supported* by his friend in his continuing struggle. The straight man should be actively encouraging about what his friend is trying to accomplish.

Fourth, the client needs a show of continuing interest so that he is able to tell the other guy the truth about his behavior. What he is saying is, "Please ask me about it." Sometimes disappointment arises when the friend shows initial support and understanding but never discusses the situation again. Typically, our clients fear mentioning their condition more than once for fear of "bothering or burdening" the other guy. Therefore, an important step in the process of telling the straight friend is to explicitly say, "I need you to ask me how things are going." This explicit statement has the advantage of freeing up the communication between the two men. It also gives the straight friend a responsive repertoire. .....

Each step builds on the preceding one. The heterosexual friend cannot show continuing interest unless he first *supports* the SSA man; he cannot support unless he first *accepts* his friend; and he cannot accept him until he *understands* him. I have always been amazed at the encouraging and supportive response of straight men to the SSA struggler.

Example of Confronting Resistance to Disclosure

Intense resistance to disclosing to a friend is exemplified in the following transcript. In this session both therapist and client have acknowledged that there would be a healing opportunity if Aaron disclosed his struggle to his best friend, Dave. Yet Aaron seems paralyzed in taking the first step.

CLIENT   I wanted to tell Dave, but it was the hardest thing to do!

THERAPIST   Let's focus on what exactly is so hard. What's it feel like?

CLIENT   (*becomes centered and focused after some time*) Discomfort... pain.

THERAPIST   Go to that pain.

CLIENT   The pain comes from the shame.

THERAPIST   (*ignores interpretation and moves back to the felt memory*) But where do you feel it?

CLIENT   In my stomach.

THERAPIST   The feeling?

CLIENT   It's... queasy... nervous. Anxious.

THERAPIST   Stay with those feelings. (*softly*) Just sit with them. (*after a while*) Where are they?

CLIENT   My chest. A pressure in my chest.

THERAPIST   Focus on that. What's the pressure feel like?

CLIENT   A tightness. Like a grip around my heart.

THERAPIST   (*gently, with encouragement*) Let's stay with that tight gripping around the heart.

[Moving to the second triangle.]

THERAPIST   Can you recall a time of feeling that same gripping tightness?

CLIENT   (*immediately*) Sure – when I was afraid of getting laughed at, doing something stupid or looking dumb in school.

THERAPIST   OK. What's the feeling?

CLIENT   Sinking, dropping...like I'm a zero, a nothing.

THERAPIST   Uh-huh.... How does that fit now, with the idea of telling Dave?

CLIENT   He'll withdraw, pull back from me.

THERAPIST   And that will make you feel...?

CLIENT   Horrible! Like, "Oh, my God. I've really turned him off!"

Aaron understood that his inability to "do the hardest thing" was grounded in the paralyzing fear of anticipated shame – the idea that he would be humiliated for exposing his weakness, shamed for sharing his shame. That is, he would be caught in a double bind. The therapist advised Aaron to disclose slowly, using the steps previously outlined.

As it turned out, each layer of exposure was met with Dave's understanding and support. After one month, Aaron and Dave committed themselves – with the support of their men's Bible study group – to be accountability partners, with Dave working on his own (heterosexual) Internet porn addiction.

Negative Projections onto Straight Men

One form of resistance in this process involves gay stereotypes about straight men. "Straight men are crude, coarse, insensitive, dumb s—ts, 'Neanderthals.'" The client is usually surprised when, in the course of time, the straight friend reveals his own doubts and insecurities. These revelations are invaluable in facilitating commonality and fostering a level playing field in the development of mutuality between two men of different sexual-orientation backgrounds.

The greatest barrier to healing is the shame the SSA man feels about his deep need for same-sex emotional nurturance. The sense that "I should have outgrown this by now" is an idea rooted in the shame felt from the rejecting father. One client confided:

These are old feelings that go way back to when I was a kid with other boys. The more competitive the group, the more ill-at-ease I felt. I did better with one guy, but with two, I would always feel like the odd man out. Then I'd start to turn inward and detach. I'd feel like the third wheel. I'm trying to be with them, but the other two guys are together with each other.

I'm afraid they'll get along better with each other than with me.

The Problem of Anticipatory Shame

Ambivalence – fear, but desire for authentic contact with loving men – is illustrated in the story of this thirty-five-year-old man. Faced with the choice of friendship with straight men or else a homosexual enactment, this client tearfully confessed: "I go around longing for friends, but then I'm hoping no one's around so I can indulge in my [gay] fantasies."

In the following transcript, he reports visiting a city where his two best friends live. Both straight men know about his homosexual struggle and have been affirming and supportive of him over the years. Yet while having dinner with them, he had already decided to homosexually act out after he left them. After a year of therapy he knew exactly what he was doing, making the conscious decision to pursue anonymous homosexual contact versus connecting with his two close but straight friends.

He begins by stating that it seems that straight men are simply not enough for him; he needs more, namely, sex.

> I just don't connect with them. Something's missing. I don't connect with them on some fun, intimate, belonging level. I just don't feel that intense connection that I get with a gay guy I'm having sex with. My friends can say all the right things, do all the right things, but my detachment is so engrained in me that I can't let them in. They love me, they see me, I believe they love what they see – because I show all of myself to them – but still, it's not enough.

Then he asked plaintively, "Why can't I take it in?"

In his heart he realizes that what is lacking is not about his straight friends but about his own ability to openly receive their friendship.

At this realization he becomes angry at himself (which can lead to further self-punishing homosexual enactment) and says, "This gay stuff is all I deserve since there's something wrong with me. I'm so screwed up ... what's my problem? Why can't I just be like them?"

THERAPIST   Now you're condemning yourself for not receiving their care for you. You're using that to punish yourself. Rather, the question is, "Why can't I take in their acceptance of me?"

CLIENT   (*staring blankly*)

[At this point, encouraging self-compassion rather than self-criticism, the therapist makes a direct interpretation, based on the client's previous description of the narcissistic parenting style he endured in his early family life.]

THERAPIST   As a kid, you felt your trust was betrayed. You believed you were loved, you assumed you were loveable, until one day you had the shocking revelation: "These people [his parents] don't see me! They've never seen me!" That shocking reality was intolerable. You shut down into the good little boy role, but secretly resolved not to trust what appeared to be love – *ever, ever again.*

CLIENT   (*nodding slowly*)

THERAPIST   Today, your friends are showing you love, but you distrust it and can't take it in – can't allow it to seep in, to sink in – to transform you.

CLIENT   (*suddenly overwhelmed with sadness, speaks through tears*) I'm sad that I hate myself so much ... (*sobbing*) I'm sad that I'm so scared, that I always choose to be alone!

THERAPIST   (*gently*) Yes ...

CLIENT   To be loved is to be controlled! (*with anger*) *To give my heart away is to be manipulated and controlled!*

THERAPIST   (*nods empathically*)

CLIENT   F—k them, I'd rather be lonely! And that's the choice I make repeatedly. (*long pause*)

THERAPIST   (*nods, waiting and listening*)

CLIENT   I *want* to connect with others ... but it's their connecting with *me* that I just can't trust ... *I just can't deal with!*

Regrets About Detachment

One client observed:

> I remember going to my older cousins' house. They were about twelve
> and I was nine. They could see I was shy, and in their own way, they
> tried to draw me out – each tried to get me to play. But I would have
> none of it. (*spoken wistfully*) I wish I could go back now and have it be
> different. I rejected them. If only I had opened myself up to them!

Another man said, "I think back at all the men who were there for me!
But I didn't notice, pay attention or take advantage of what they were
offering. I turned them away. I ignored them. I was too distrustful and
self-preoccupied."

Most of our clients' regrets are about missed opportunities and choices
made to self-protect. They speak about lost chances to connect with other
males – through activities rejected, feelings hidden, support turned away
and friendships offered but turned down.

Their greatest regret is usually about having chosen safety over challenges and self-protection over emotional vulnerability.

CHAPTER 18

Relationships with Women

While much of our treatment focus is on male relationships, success in reparative therapy necessitates the client's resolving any overidentification or enmeshment with the mother.

The therapeutic goal is for the client to relate as an adult male does with a woman. Unsupported by the father in childhood, many boys were unable to form a separate and masculine sense of self that makes them distinct from their mothers. One man explained it like this: "My father was in outer space, so I absorbed the world through my mother. I was so in sync with her ideas and feelings that I completely accepted her view of life." Regarding his present relationship with his mother, another gay-identified client proudly reported in his first session, "Everyone says we are identical. She's my best friend. We are two bookends."

But when mother and son maintain such an intimate relationship, a closer look reveals that the son holds not just an identification with his mother but an equally intense grievance toward her. Thus he remains in a hostile-dependent relationship.

While clients report that "no one understands me like my mother," at the same time they will complain that she has the unique power to annoy, bother or upset them like no other person. Men often report this paradox: they feel in some ways "most understood" but in other ways "least understood" by their mothers.

In adulthood, our highly sensitized clients continue to experience embodied shame reactions to subliminal signs of disapproval from maternal figures.

Mother's Power to Evoke a Shame Response

As a child, Brad found himself in the position of being his mother's surrogate husband. Burdened with the responsibilities of his mother's emotional life, he became sensitized to that look of disapproval, the unspoken message from her that "I've done something wrong, I've displeased her" or "She's upset, and it's my fault."

> The cold looks from Mom made me feel guilty. Going up to her and getting no response made me feel I had somehow disappointed her. Other times I just couldn't tell if she maybe was just tired. Or maybe I wasn't doing something to make her happy.

A fifteen-year-old described his exaggerated response to his mother's disapproval:

CLIENT   I can see her standing there with her arms crossed and her squinting eyes.

THERAPIST   What do you feel inside?

CLIENT   A tightening in my throat and neck. Everything goes dark around me.

In another example of a mother's power to evoke shame, the same thirty-nine-year-old man reported with cautious enthusiasm and hope a dating relationship with a woman – his first such relationship. We hear the inhibitory shift resulting from communication with his mother:

CLIENT   I called my mother and told her I was dating this girl. "Oh, I'm so happy for you," she said. "I'm so glad you told me!" But I heard something in her voice. I knew that when she hung up, she cried.

THERAPIST   Why would she cry?

CLIENT   Because she thinks she's losing me. (*wistfully*)...And it makes me sad that she's sad.

This excessive sensitivity to the mother's expectations and extreme anxiety about her disapproval sensitizes the client to feel he has to please all other women who come into his life. His fear of disapproval and dread of the woman's power to evoke shame, as well as her power to drain him, is the essential obstacle to such a man's future intimacy with another female. His essential challenge is to maintain his personal autonomy while in relationship with a woman. To do this, he must resolve the anticipatory shame about failing to fulfill the woman's expectations. In short, he must stop reenacting the mother-son relationship with other women.

One of our clients explained his initial problems with beginning to date women:

> Personally, I had great difficulty with feelings of engulfment and incest. Any time I would get close to a woman, I felt like I was getting close to my mother. My therapist helped me with this by allowing me to actually feel the very unpleasant feelings and to realize that I would not die because of them.
>
> He also helped me to connect with my anger and grief about my mother's emotionally abusive relationship with me. He helped me to set appropriate boundaries with women, and to feel good about myself for doing so.
>
> Fortunately, my wife is in many ways different from my mother. She is supportive of my masculinity and very respectful of my need for boundaries.

Another man explained:

> For me the biggest roadblock is about trusting women: that is number one. I can see that this stems from my mother, because her emotions fluctuate constantly, and she has the power to pull me into her down states. She doesn't confide in my other siblings. I'm always the first one to know whatever mood she's in.
>
> I need to work on my independence from her and to avoid being the surrogate husband that she considers me to be. In fact, I have started lately to remind her that she does have a husband.

Growing in Identification with Males: Relating to Women as a Man Does

As the client begins to deepen his heterosexual identification, no longer does he envy the gay man who has a partner, the way he once did. Increasingly, his ideal male is the man who can relate to a woman as a straight man does. One client reported, "I notice a change in the type of guys that I look at. Now I envy guys who are with girls – men who are in relationships with women." Another said:

> When I used to watch movies or television, if there was a love scene I identified with the woman. I felt like her and wanted to be loved like she was – by a man. Increasingly, I'm feeling more like the guy. In fact I've started to wonder, *What's it like for him to make love to her?*

In the course of treatment some men begin to express a readiness to enter into a relationship with women. This should not be initiated by the therapist but must arise spontaneously from the client himself. (This is in contrast to our explicit encouragement of non-erotic male friendships.) From our clinical experience, pressuring a client into dating is distinctly counterproductive. Only his own sense of readiness should dictate when the client seeks out heterosexual relations.

While many clients worry about their capacity for heterosexual performance, it is actually emotional intimacy with a woman that will pose the greater challenge. The insecurities and fears about their erotic abilities are often a displacement of his deeper fear of emotional vulnerability. At its base, the essential fear for the client is, If I trust a woman, she will take my power away.

The challenge to our client is to maintain emotional intimacy with a woman while still possessing his personal autonomy. This is a challenge for all men, but it is particularly formidable for the man with a homosexual past. The focus of therapy should be on his recurrent tendency to project onto the woman the fear that she is going to disapprove of and shame him.

The client may not identify the shame experience directly, but his parasympathetic hypo-arousal state is likely to be reported as feeling turned off, indifferent or just bored with the woman. He will often find himself feeling trapped into the old, familiar "good little boy" role when with her. When his feelings are explored more deeply, they are typically found to be a cover for unexpressed anger. This is typically expressed indirectly in passive-aggressive behavior toward her in the relationship, or by impulsive blowups of frustration and resentment. Both are unproductive and self-defeating.

Not all mothers of homosexual men were powerful personalities in the stereotypical "strong, controlling, domineering" style. Instead some men report quite the opposite experience: passive, helpless-dependent mothers. Yet a closer look at these two very different personality types reveals that they trigger the same inhibitory effect on their sons' assertive development. For example, one twenty-eight-year-old dance instructor recalls:

> When I was supposed to go to school in the morning I saw my mother become sad. She always cried the first day of school. It made me feel bad to have to leave her. She didn't want me to go; I didn't want to go, either. We both felt torn apart. I wanted to protect her by not going to school.
>
> When I did go to school, I was afraid something would happen to her. I think she never got enough love from her parents, so she needed to keep me very close.

The Importance of Friendships with Married Men

Typically, the client's parents did not provide him with an adequate model for married life. Consequently, it is important for him to have friendships with married men who can offer opportunities to view thriving marriages through the husband's eyes. Discussing adjustment problems with his married male friends, he will discover that women are not as threatening as he fears.

The source of the client's negative feminine introjections is commonly his earliest experience with the mother. In some cases the source is likely an older sister, a grandmother who has been closely involved in his life, or another family member. A helpful start in addressing negative feminine projections is to encourage the client to verbalize his opinion of women. He will typically include such descriptions as manipulative, disingenuous, controlling, smothering, devious and dominating. When we hear, "*All* women are [fill in the blank]" this is a good indication of a maternal projection.

A therapeutic technique that is sometimes helpful is to ask the client to imagine and then verbalize his ideal woman, one with whom he might picture himself to be in a relationship. Visualizing and articulating a positive feminine introject gives the idea validity. Asked to imagine the kind of woman he might someday marry, one client described her this way:

"She's not glamorous, but has a natural beauty. Low-key, but solid. She is very receptive, quiet. There is an integrity, but she is not wimpy. There is a modesty, an empathy and a loyalty – and I feel respected by her."

Same-sex attracted clients will often report that they want a woman to be independent, to be her own person, with a self-sufficient character. This is quite the opposite of what straight men tend to prefer – a woman who looks to them for emotional support.

The ex-gay man's need for an emotionally self-sufficient woman is typically traceable back to his fear of being "emotionally entangled and drained," as he felt with his mother. Men who felt responsible for their mother's feelings and for keeping her happy have a particular dread of finding themselves in another such relationship.

Learning to Trust a Woman

With this in mind, as he guides the client through a dating relationship, the therapist is watching for the client's abandonment of his authentic needs and his becoming oversensitive to the woman's expectations of him. The client must be mindful not to abandon the expression of his true gendered self. If he does, he will inevitably be angry at her, and this will be manifested in a variety of self- or relationally destructive reactions, including emotional withdrawal from her, hyper-criticalness, gay fantasies and finally homosexual enactment.

The client's successful shift to emotional and sexual intimacy with a woman will hinge on his ability to develop trust rather than to anticipate betrayal. Can he trust the woman with his feelings? Will she allow him to stay in his manhood? Yet ultimately, it is not the woman but he himself who abandons his own true gendered self. The essential challenge for the client is to enter into a relationship with a woman while maintaining contact with himself – being attentive to her while maintaining self-possession.

As he begins a relationship, the client should be monitored by the therapist, who keeps him honest with himself and helps him avoid going into the false self of the good-little-boy persona. Inevitably some relational conflict will emerge, obliging the client to hold firm in his assertive stance.

Many relational difficulties traceable back to the client's anticipatory shame are caused by projections of what he *thinks* the woman's expectations are of him, and these expectations are often distortions. The therapist may then suggest that the client go back to her and check out what he understood or "heard" her expectations to be. As a good father-figure (teacher-mentor), the therapist provides the masculine frame of reference from which his client learns to be man with a woman.

The client's tendency to self-compromise is often so unconscious that he is unaware of it until a relational crisis strikes. Early signs of self-compromise begin with feelings of boredom, irritability, annoyance or just feeling distracted. In a classic example of projective identification, he inevitably finds the woman to be demanding, critical and controlling – in short, he makes her his mother. These defenses are indirect expressions of anger that harbor his secret grievances: "She's controlling, bossy, inflexible [and so on]." Failing to maintain his self-possession and emotional connectedness, he lapses into ambivalence about his feelings for her and uncertainty about the relationship.

The "Void of Initiative"
We often see, in men struggling with homosexuality, a void of initiative in their relationships with women as they lapse into the old familiar role of the good little boy, very much like the placating relationship with the mother.

Many women in such a relationship will complain: "But he puts me in this leadership and decision-making position by refusing to take responsibility." Because he avoids initiative and assertion, the woman then must – out of necessity – assume the stronger role. He reacts to her initiative with disguised anger, while she remains unaware that he resents her now active, directive role.

Of the married men I have worked with, approximately 80 percent of the wives knew of their husband's same-sex attractions before the marriage. It is definitely an advantage to the man when his wife is so informed. In fact, he will often find her surprisingly accepting and tolerant of his difficulties. The qualifier is whether he will continue to be honest and include her in his growth process. She will usually be a very strong and loyal ally if he makes her a partner in his overcoming.

If, on the other hand, she senses that she is being excluded from the process – if he is withholding, secretive and does not include her – then she may radically withdraw her support and shift into a critical and rejecting posture.

The wife's involvement, I must clarify, should not include knowing details of his past. Neither should she be expected to serve as his accountability partner. That role should be reserved for a salient male. What she does need to know is that he has a sincere commitment to growth and change.

It is sometimes helpful to schedule a joint session with both the client and his girlfriend or wife. But the therapist must be aware that the client may want her to enter therapy in order to deflect focus from his own issues, preferring to believe that their relational difficulty – particularly his emotional detachment – is just "a communication problem." Inadvertently supporting him in this avoidance, the woman may hope that the relationship will improve if she joins him in therapy. But once they are in couples therapy, her openness about articulating her own needs may upstage his own unarticulated needs for masculine affirmation, which will prompt him to sink into a passive-avoidant posture in the session.

While these conjoint sessions may improve communication skills, the focus of treatment must remain on the client himself, and his goal should be to take responsibility for developing an honest engagement with her.

Ongoing Need for Male Friendships

No matter how successful his relationships with women may be, the man from a homosexual background will always need to maintain healthy male friendships. He requires steady contact with male friends so that he can succeed as a husband. We have found that most wives, including those who did not previously know of their husband's homosexual background, say that when their husbands spend time with their male friends they are happier, more attentive and more emotionally available to them and the children. But when their husbands fail to maintain these friendships, they become withdrawn, moody, irritable and emotionally detached from them and the children.

Intensity of Heterosexual Desire

Reparative therapy has been criticized by gay-affirmative therapists as being "nothing more than behavior modification." According to this view, treatment only succeeds in suppressing homosexual feelings. Indeed, most married ex-gay men report that their sexual experiences with their wives are not as intense and exciting as their earlier homosexual experiences.

Homosexually oriented men feel more comfortable relating to women than to men. They "split" women and think about them only from the waist up, with female friends viewed as sexless, genderless beings. But as shame is slowly diminished in therapy and the SSA man grows in self-awareness and self-assertion, he should gradually begin to find within himself a natural heterosexual response. However, because gay sex was driven by a profound deficit – an attempt to satisfy deep unmet needs of belonging and attachment – as a temporary stabilizer of affective disequilibrium, it offered a powerful erotic "zap" that temporarily lifted the depression and bridged the masculine disconnection. This zap, or electric charge, bridging emotional disconnection with (momentary) connection, will never be as powerful with a woman, partly because women are not "exotic"; they are in some ways too well known.

Another powerful charge in gay sex was its forbidden quality and its frequently impersonal nature, with strangers, and a sense of danger often added into the mix. This added further erotic intensity, which can feel much more exciting in the moment than sex with one's married partner.

However, the one-dimensional consideration of erotic intensity is an incomplete assessment of the ex-gay married man's sexual satisfaction. While ex-gay men report a qualitatively less intense experience, they do report a richer, fuller and more emotionally satisfying experience, accompanied by a deep sense of well-being. They describe a feeling of natural compatibility, rightness and oneness. One now-married man said, "When I look back on my homosexual experiences, it seems like we were two little boys playing in the sandbox."

Not the Straight Man's Path

The client who attempts to emulate the heterosexual man's way of relating to women, trying to fit in to the dating scene with its romantic-sexual intrigue, may be setting himself up for failure. The ever-straight man's pathway is different from the ex-gay man's. Ever-straight men are typically sexually attracted to the woman first, and only later get to know her as a friend.

For ex-gay men, the sequence moves in the opposite direction: friendship, affection and then sexuality. Here is how it works:

1. The man first comes to know the woman as a friend, someone with whom he enjoys common interests and activities.

2. He allows that friendship to develop into a growing and natural affection. Physical touch and holding will feel pleasant and good.

3. After establishing and maintaining a trustful friendship, that growing affection will naturally begin to express itself sexually.

This three-step sequence is reassuring to the client who has made the mistake of pressuring himself to feel sexual excitement in order to prove to himself he has successfully changed.

Some men may sustain a friendship with a woman for years before they become serious about her, not marrying until then. Many of these men then report very satisfactory emotional and sexual relationships. As they slowly grow in their heterosexual response, they usually describe their arousal toward their wives as less visually based, however, and lower-key and more tactile than sex with men.

Interestingly, married ex-gay men often report little sexual attraction to other women. This strange contradiction may be difficult for a heterosexual man to understand but is good news for the wife!

The Risk of Intimacy with Women

As we've seen, emotional closeness with a woman may feel dangerous because it evokes an abandonment-engulfment polarity. This either-or option may be traceable back to childhood experiences of insecure maternal attachment, with the mother's intermittent, on-and-off attunement in which the boy felt either swallowed up or abandoned/rejected by her.

Consequently, his adult stance with a woman may tend toward defensive disengagement, self-preoccupation or hyper-sensitivity to criticism. "I let Mom's critical and disappointed looks control me," one client, John, confided. "I end up trying to fix her problems or else running away from her. I always take responsibility for her feelings; I feel like it's my fault if she's not happy."

Maternal affective unpredictability leaves the boy feeling anxious, insecure and emotionally fragmented. For example, clients often report that at times of physical or emotional hurt, their mother's response to them provided strangely little comfort. A shrill emotional reaction by the mother to the boy's injury, for example (with her reaction upstaging and increasing his own distress), made the boy feel like the traumatic incident was more "about her" than it was about him.

Or perhaps he felt discomfited by the emotional incongruity between his mother's attempted words of comfort and her hyper-aroused emotional state. We often hear it reported that the mother's reassurance did not feel authentic; clients say her advice was simply not practical or did not match what they were feeling inside. To his deep feelings of peer rejection, one man recalls his mother advising, "Oh, forget them. Just don't play with those mean boys." Related to this, she made well-meaning but unrealistic attempts to bolster her son's self-confidence. Her excessive praise as to how great, special, good, smart or handsome he was did not match how others saw him, including how he saw himself. "I didn't believe that she believed it, and even if she did believe it, I knew it wasn't true anyway."

The following words of a thirty-four-year-old architect exemplify how acutely sensitive our clients are to the slightest sign of a woman's disapproval. Having grown up in a triadic-narcissistic family system, the man exhibited a conditioned, embodied response of shame to any suggestion of female disapproval.

CLIENT At our office party, Sandra gave me this look. She really bothered me. I think she had heard some rumors about me. I'm not sure.

THERAPIST (*Not concerning himself with what rumors she might have heard, but goes directly to his feelings*) How did she make you feel? You said, "bothered."

CLIENT Yeah. It was a look of worthlessness. She looked at me as if to say, "You jerk, I don't want to have anything to do with you."

THERAPIST	And the feeling...
CLIENT	The feeling...
THERAPIST	In your body.
CLIENT	"I've done something wrong."
THERAPIST	That's an idea. The feeling?
CLIENT	The feeling is anger.
THERAPIST	Stay with that anger.
CLIENT	I've disappointed her.
THERAPIST	That's an idea too.
CLIENT	A panic.
THERAPIST	Stay with "panic." (*the innate affect of anger is immediately inhibited by the client's panic response*) Where do you feel it?
CLIENT	In my head.
THERAPIST	(*moving the client back to the anger*) What's that feel like?
CLIENT	Tightness.
THERAPIST	Stay with tightness in your head.
CLIENT	A fear. Something like, "Oh God, I did something wrong." A fear...cold chills.
THERAPIST	Where?
CLIENT	All over my body..."I've got to make it right!"
THERAPIST	That's an idea; stay with the feelings.
CLIENT	It's depressing. A dread....I'm thinking, *I'm a disappointment.*
THERAPIST	That's an idea. Go to the body.
CLIENT	(*apparently stuck*)
THERAPIST	(*repeating client's words*) Depressing...dread. Disappointment. Where?
CLIENT	In my whole chest. A weight, a heavy weight.

[Therapist decides to move to second triangle.]

THERAPIST	Did you have these same feelings in the past, this same depressing, dreading, down, "I'm a disappointment" feeling?
CLIENT	For sure. When my mom gave me that look, like I'd disappointed her. Those same feelings kick in.
THERAPIST	Can you recall a specific event?

CLIENT   Yeah. I remember as a kid feeling sick. I guess I was feeling miserable and sorry for myself. I cried to my mom, "Why me?" And this is what she said: "Well, would you rather it be *me?*" I thought, *Huh?* It's that same feeling. I wasn't sure exactly what I had done, but I had somehow disappointed her, because I had said something that I guess was bad.

In the following session a twenty-five-year-old man is considering asking a girl to go out with him on a casual date. His nervousness leads to feelings of loss/abandonment that suggest associations to early maternal attachment loss:

CLIENT   I'm thinking about asking Katy out. Just for coffee or something, just to get to know her. I'm not so sure. I'm a bit nervous.

THERAPIST   Ok. Let's do some body work. What do you think?

CLIENT   Yes. OK.

THERAPIST   Let's go to that "nervous." Where do you feel it?

CLIENT   It's like an anxiety.

THERAPIST   (*nods*) Where?

CLIENT   In my chest.

[The client calls it "anxiety," but that is usually in the abdomen. He is probably feeling fear in his chest, but the therapist goes with it.]

THERAPIST   Good. Stay with that: "In your chest." Try to put descriptive words to it.

CLIENT   Tightness, nervousness, a void.

THERAPIST   Void. Where do you feel that void?

CLIENT   Same place, chest.

THERAPIST   (*speaking gently*) Ok. "Void." Stay with "void" in your chest. How does "void" feel in your chest?

CLIENT   A loneliness.

THERAPIST   Loneliness. Still in the chest?

CLIENT   (*slowly nods*)

THERAPIST   How does loneliness feel in your chest?

CLIENT   Like a hole. An empty area. Like an empty space... some-
             thing's missing inside.

[Therapist moves to the second triangle.]

THERAPIST   OK... any memory of that same emptiness? The "something
             missing" in your chest?
CLIENT   Being left alone as a child, in my bed. It's more an image, a
             picture. Not a specific incident.
THERAPIST   What's that little kid in bed feeling?
CLIENT   (*long pause*)
THERAPIST   (*nods, speaking gently*) How does that kid feel?
CLIENT   (*with a far-off expression*) Disconnected, lonely and empty
             inside.
THERAPIST   I wonder if there might be another memory with that same
             lost, empty feeling?
CLIENT   (*pause*) Getting yelled at by my mother over my room.
THERAPIST   How old?
CLIENT   Maybe... four. She would throw things out of my toy box.
             I'm outside my room, standing near the living room, watch-
             ing her throw my toys, and I'm feeling lost and disconnected.
             *What did I do wrong? What is this woman doing? How can I
             make it OK?*
THERAPIST   (*nods thoughtfully*)
CLIENT   I was feeling confused and afraid.
THERAPIST   Any connection between this memory and what's going on
             now?
CLIENT   Yes... (*slowly, thoughtfully*) Katy brings up this same kind
             of feeling in me of "void."

Besides memories of early attachment loss, we often see a conflict
between the boy's attempts at assertion and his mother's disempowering
intrusion. This is represented by the dream of a twenty-two-year-old man.
In the dream, he said:

I'm having sex with a girl in my room at college. I'm feeling connected
to her. But while I'm having sex, the scene suddenly shifts to my room

at home and my mother is trying to come in. The door is locked, but she's pushing hard and she's managing to get it open anyway.

This client described emotional domination well: "Women have to be appeased, humored and skillfully contained because of their power to dominate."

A thirty-year-old graduate student, Mike, describes a similar difficulty. He said he could not be spontaneous and free while also feeling connected to his girlfriend:

THERAPIST   Mike, what makes it difficult for you to sustain emotional connection with Annie and stay with yourself at the same time?

CLIENT   I guess I experience her as a drain, a drag and a burden. And it's kind of been why I've been basically ready to break up with her.

THERAPIST   Sure. And what's that like for you?

CLIENT   I shut down, I back off, I go in reverse, I pull away from her. I become cardboard.

THERAPIST   So let's go to the feeling of cardboard; what's that feel like in your body? Let's just spend a few minutes on this now.

CLIENT   You mean, what's behind it?

THERAPIST   Yeah. (*pauses, waits*) Let's just start with the feeling of cardboard.

CLIENT   Frozen. I feel frozen because I'm being watched. I feel like I'm being scrutinized. I don't feel free. I feel constricted and restrained. I shut down.

THERAPIST   You shut down. (*nods slowly*) You become cardboard, you become detached. What's the feeling on the inside? See if there's a feeling beyond, more deeply inside that...

CLIENT   There's some anger.

THERAPIST   (*waits*) Are you aware of the anger at those moments with her?

CLIENT   No.

THERAPIST   But you can feel the anger now, huh?

CLIENT   Yeah.

THERAPIST   (*speaking gently*) Mike, what's the anger feel like in the body? Can you identify it?

[Client shifts quickly from anger to sadness.]

CLIENT   Actually, it's just sad now.

[Therapist stays with the client's sudden shift.]

THERAPIST   It's sad now, isn't it? And you're feeling the sadness right now, as you're talking about this?

CLIENT   Yeah.

THERAPIST   Can you allow yourself to stay in the sadness for a few moments?

CLIENT   Yeah.

[Client appears to have some difficulty.]

THERAPIST   This is hard now, isn't it?

CLIENT   Yes.

THERAPIST   I want you to stay with this, Mike. This is hard.

CLIENT   Yeah.

THERAPIST   (*softly*) You're feeling that sadness right now?

CLIENT   Yeah.

THERAPIST   Mike, how are you feeling the sadness in your body right now?

CLIENT   (*slumped over; shoulders slowly drop*) I feel drained, collapsed, empty.

THERAPIST   Yes. Stay with that. Can you stay with that emptiness in your chest right now? Can you feel that?

CLIENT   Yeah.

THERAPIST   I think that emptiness has been there for many, many years – long before you met your girlfriend.

CLIENT   Yeah. It has.

[Therapist decides to move to second triangle of persons.]

THERAPIST   Do you remember a time as a kid when you felt that same sadness and emptiness in your chest?

CLIENT (*sadly*) Always.

THERAPIST Always. Long before you met Annie you had that empty feeling. Do you remember a particular time as a kid when you were very much aware of that lonely painful emptiness?...Maybe an incident or a particular moment that you recall?

CLIENT Well, let's see...I'm trying to think. (*sighs deeply*)

THERAPIST You can remember better if you stay with the body sensation of that emptiness.

CLIENT (*nods*) OK.

THERAPIST Staying with that sensation is going to help you remember.

CLIENT (*thoughtfully*) I remember being in my room at home a lot.

THERAPIST (*quietly*) Yes. Tell me about that...

CLIENT (*suddenly*) I'm just feeling some anger right now.

THERAPIST Do you feel anger?

CLIENT A little bit.

THERAPIST Tell me how you're feeling the anger in your body right now.

CLIENT In my chest.

THERAPIST OK. So that empty feeling in your chest has changed to another feeling in your chest, and that's anger.

CLIENT Yeah.

THERAPIST And how do you feel the anger in your chest? What's the sensation in your chest right now?

CLIENT A burning.

THERAPIST Exactly.

CLIENT Uh-huh.

THERAPIST Who are you angry at? Whose face comes to mind when you feel the anger burning in your chest?

CLIENT My parents...

THERAPIST OK. (*pause*) Stay with that burning in your chest, and see if a parent's face comes to mind.

CLIENT My mother. (*slumps down in his chair*) But the feeling just started to go away.

THERAPIST Can you visualize your mother's face and feel that burning in your chest right now?

CLIENT   No, as soon as I do it, the anger goes away, and then I just start to feel sad.

THERAPIST   Who are you feeling sad for?

CLIENT   Her.

THERAPIST   So instead of feeling anger toward her, you're feeling sadness for her.

CLIENT   (*sighs*) Yes.

THERAPIST   And anger toward yourself?

CLIENT   Yeah. That's true.

THERAPIST   And that leaves you feeling...

CLIENT   Well...dead. In fact, it's that same feeling I have when I'm with my girlfriend...that same feeling that I'm being "looked at and scrutinized."

Over time, it became apparent that Mike's shutdown response to Annie was a dissociative defense he had developed in relationship with his mother, which inhibited his natural impulse to assert himself and show anger. Instead, he felt guilty about his anger, and then would become overwhelmed and simply withdraw. In such cases, there is typically sadness for the other rather than a sadness for oneself, which reenacts the childhood no-win predicament of the double bind.

The False Self as a Defense Against Shaming

Fear of a woman's capacity to shame him evokes in the client the contrary feelings of fear and anger, which blocks his heterosexual response. Until he can resolve his fear of being shamed by a woman (and his anger at a woman's power to shame him), the man cannot access his biologically based sexual response to her. Consequently, resolution of his "shameability" is a prerequisite to developing his natural heterosexual response.

About his relationship with women, one man said, "I thought that to be the perfect man I had to always be with the woman where she was, at her emotional place. That's what I learned from my mother. To *not* attend to my mother was to let her down."

In anticipation of shame, the client creates an either-or predicament. One man described this predicament as "When I'm with a woman, I'm not 'with myself,' and to really be 'with myself,' I have to be alone."

A "Script to Be Played" Within the Narcissistic Family

This sense of powerlessness when confronted with a woman's feelings is exemplified by another twenty-one-year-old client, who speaks about a female friend at school who has formed a dependency on him. This brings back associations of the client's relationship with his mother and the caretaking, "placating" role he was expected to play within the triadic-narcissistic family:

CLIENT She's talking to me and I'm trying to be polite, but she takes up so much of my time. I can't get away. Yet I feel for her, you know; she's kinda plain-looking. (*hesitates*) I don't want to sound shallow, but... OK, she's fat. But she's also annoying.

THERAPIST Go to your feelings when you recall her.

CLIENT Anxious. (*pausing*) I've got to be "on," artificial. I have to hold up my energy.

THERAPIST What happens if you give up being "on," and you're not holding up your energy?

CLIENT (*immediately, as if he knows this all too well*) There's that defeated feeling... deflated, kind of. There's no energy there. Then I feel it in my throat... crying.

THERAPIST Stay with your body right now. Let's see what you might be feeling as you consider this.

CLIENT (*slowly*) In my throat, a frog in my throat, uncomfortable... flat, blah. (*pause*) I feel tired, and like crying.

[Therapist moves to second triangle.]

THERAPIST Did anyone else make you feel this same "crying/tired"?

CLIENT (*considers for a while*) Yes, my mother, whenever she would start crying.

THERAPIST Like when? Do you remember a particular time?

CLIENT There was always some invisible thing superimposed over me, a script for me, an idea about me, a role I was supposed to play, an agenda she had for me. It was everything else but just "me."

THERAPIST Uh-huh.

CLIENT My mother manipulated me to take from me. But if I tried

to be myself, then she said I was selfish and unloving. If I
pulled away from her she'd become ice cold, and then I'd
feel out on a limb – suspended, alone.

THERAPIST (*nods*)

CLIENT But I always needed to get back into her good graces, so I'd
immediately placate her, and then everything would be OK.
Then she'd switch back and resume our conversation.

Fixing the "Upset"

The therapeutic task is to interrupt the client's conditioned deflation
regarding an "upset" from a female, followed by his reflexive impulse to
fix things for her. Closer investigation reveals that it is not really about his
wanting to make her happy, but rather he must make her happy *about him*
so that he can feel happy (actually, secure) about himself.

Fear of the Mother Collapsing

One thirty-six-year-old man recalls a recent conversation with his mother,
in which he described how she drained him and "made him weak."

THERAPIST Go to your body right now. How does it feel as you think
of that conversation with her?

CLIENT It's stifling and frustrating. (*brief pause*) And…there's anger.

THERAPIST Where?

CLIENT In my chest and shoulders. I told her I needed a break from
her. Maybe that wasn't nice, but that's what came out of my
mouth. She seemed surprised, then hurt. Yeah, she got hurt.

THERAPIST And how did that feel?

CLIENT (*looking blank*)

THERAPIST Go to your body right now. What's the feeling?

CLIENT (*after some time*) A churning, an anxiety.

THERAPIST Let's stay with it.

CLIENT (*some moments later*) A ball of pain in the center of my
stomach. Tight. My mind, my brain hurts. I'm confused, sad.

THERAPIST Sad…

CLIENT (*suddenly blurts out*) She can't handle my being honest with

her. I've got this fear of her... of her completely collapsing.
I've got to bolster her.

THERAPIST   Prop her up.

CLIENT   All my life I was deprived of my friends and felt stuck with
my mother. Around a woman, I just feel dead; I don't feel
that freedom. Women make me weak. That's why I like the
[gay] bars – there I can feel alive and free.

I Lost Who I Was

Another young man tries to describe the feeling he has when he thinks
about dating a girl he's been attracted to. Memories of "feeling tied to
emptiness and sadness" are soon evoked.

CLIENT   But I'm hesitant to call her.

THERAPIST   Stay with "hesitant." What's underneath that?

CLIENT   Discomfort.

THERAPIST   How does discomfort feel?

CLIENT   A tightness, restrained...

THERAPIST   Where?

CLIENT   In the chest. (*touching center-chest area*)

THERAPIST   Stay with that; a restrained, tight feeling in your chest.

CLIENT   It's an emptiness...lost...

THERAPIST   Same chest area?

CLIENT   Yeah. Like I'm lost in a vastness.

THERAPIST   OK...stay with that. Keep attending and putting words to
that.

CLIENT   A blackness. Outer space. Vast openness.

THERAPIST   A black, vast openness...

CLIENT   There's a hole inside. I'm lost in it.

THERAPIST   (*nodding slowly*)

CLIENT   An emptiness. (*reflects for several moments*) Like, the blackness that's beyond the stars. (*begins to cry softly*) Somewhere,
I lost who I was.

THERAPIST   Yes...

CLIENT   I feel abandoned, disconnected. (*slowly, softly*) I just feel
tied to that emptiness and that sadness. *I can't get away.*

Relating to Women from the Assertive Stance

One man who finally succeeded in relating to a woman from the assertive
stance explained it like this:

> My job is to stay with myself when I'm with her. The secret is, it's
> not actually about her; she is not taking my power. I'm giving her my
> power.
>
>   In fact, she doesn't want the power – she actually wants a man who
> is masculine, confident and self-assured.

In summary, when a conflict arises with a woman, the client's task,
simply stated, is to

- consciously identify, then tolerate, the discomfort caused by her
disapproval
- identify his own valid needs beneath that bodily discomfort
- effectively express his needs to her
- negotiate his needs in an adult manner of communication
- continue to stay focused in his negotiations (i.e., to successfully double
loop) until he feels himself making the embodied shift back into the
assertive stance

The Good Little Boy Versus the True Gendered Self

A thirty-seven-year-old banker from the Midwest expresses his intense,
conflicting feelings for his mother. He has been visiting her regularly
because she is near the end of her life. Being with his mother again has
provoked a battle between his good little boy and true self, which leads
him into grief work.

CLIENT   Well, I went on a masturbating campaign; I think it was eight
times over three days. That was last weekend at her house. I
knew that it was Good Little Boy acting like Bad Little Boy.

THERAPIST   What's going on?

CLIENT   Mom's not taking in much food at all, and very little liquid, so it can't be too much longer, but she's just hanging on. I haven't been journaling, except either just before or just after our sessions. Being with her just drowns me. It's like I took a break from the conflict, the struggle. I just gave up and let Good Little Boy drag me around all day. Then I picked myself up and said, *This is stupid,* and since then, I've been conscious of working to stay in my true self, but it hasn't been easy.

THERAPIST   Uh-huh.

CLIENT   I feel pressure driving back and forth to be with Mom. It's something I want to do so I have no regrets, and it's also something I don't want to do because it interrupts my life so much. I have still been vacillating back and forth this week between Good Little Boy and True Self. She got sick so fast, and all those feelings of wanting to take care of her and please her came up again. I need to cut her loose emotionally and commend her to God's hands. I think I'm doing it and then I realize I'm missing her – I'm even missing my old role in her life, although I know I don't want it anymore. It's the feeling of loneliness, feeling unlovable and inadequate. It's the anger at her and at Dad and myself and God for my whole uncompleted masculinity.

THERAPIST   (*nods*)

CLIENT   It's the sadness I feel for myself, even though over these months, chunks of these feelings have broken loose and I've felt them and expressed them, but I know there's more. Without journaling they remain stuck deep inside me. The defenses I've built over my lifetime stay there, even when I don't want them to. So that's where I am.

[Therapist encourages client to identify his conflicts.]

THERAPIST   How would you encapsulate the problem you're facing at present?

CLIENT   I don't feel strong and confident like I did for so many weeks before her illness got so bad. I feel confident sometimes, but the conflict between those two selves is in the forefront now. It's like a tug-of-war.

THERAPIST   Yes...

CLIENT   Now it's like the true self keeps getting pulled right up to the line, and sometimes over it, in the tug-of-war. Good Little Boy wins, then True Self takes over again and pulls Good Little Boy the other way, and it's back and forth.

THERAPIST   (*refocusing client on the conflict*) Yes. So the conflict...how can we put this in words? Would you say the conflict is trying to stay in the true self, yet still, on some level, wanting to be Mom's good little boy?

CLIENT   Yes, that's as good way to put it as I can think of.

THERAPIST   You get pulled right up to the line?

CLIENT   Yeah, and sometimes I get pulled over it. I'm impatient for her to go, yet at the same time, I never want her to go, but I know she will go; it's going to happen. It's a conflict.

THERAPIST   It certainly is. Impatient for her to go, wanting her to stay.

CLIENT   Yeah. It's just not a pleasant place to be. It's like my progress is on hold. I just have to do the best I can to keep True Self in the driver's seat. I'm not sure what the resistance is at this moment, except those old behavior patterns.

THERAPIST   Do you want to try to work on those together today while you have a chance?

CLIENT   I do, but I don't know where to start.

THERAPIST   Let's just start with take a reading of what you feel right now. What are you feeling right now as you're sharing with me the conflict and what's going on?

CLIENT   I feel something positive – being able to articulate it and hearing myself saying it and having it make sense. It's like I'm exposing myself to it.

THERAPIST   You feel something positive inside of you.

CLIENT   Yeah. Encouraged. But I know that's not the feeling that I need to get in touch with. It's got to be the lonely, the angry or the sad feelings.

THERAPIST	But let's not anticipate what you expect to feel. Just go back to that "positive, encouraged."
CLIENT	(*closing his eyes*) I'm trying to get in touch with my body.
THERAPIST	OK.
CLIENT	(*pause*) I've got that rumbling in my stomach.
THERAPIST	Let's try to go beyond that rumbling in the stomach.
CLIENT	Anxiety...
THERAPIST	So what if we try to push against that, push beyond it.
CLIENT	It's anger.
THERAPIST	It's anger.
CLIENT	As soon as you said to push beyond it, I took a deep breath and my facial muscles relaxed and then became set – like strong, taking-a-stand angry.
THERAPIST	Yeah.
CLIENT	Does that make sense?
THERAPIST	You can feel it in your face?
CLIENT	Yes.
THERAPIST	Sure. Your muscles set. Sure. So there's anger. You're beginning to feel the anger, feel it in your face. Do you feel it anywhere else?
CLIENT	My fist.
THERAPIST	Uh-huh.
CLIENT	In my arms, all my muscles are like, poised for attack or defense. Like even the rumbling in my stomach has gotten quiet, like it's saying, "No time for this now, more important stuff to do."
THERAPIST	And that you're poised for attack or defense?
CLIENT	Uh-huh.
THERAPIST	Stay for a minute with your anger. It's right there now. You can feel it throughout your body. You have anger.
CLIENT	(*silent*)
THERAPIST	What's happening with that anger you're feeling in your body as we focus on it?
CLIENT	There's a feeling of strength along with it. I can feel my anger and be with the anger... I feel strong.

THERAPIST   Uh-huh. You feel the strength now. What do you feel in your body that is a feeling of strength?

CLIENT   Well, I don't feel weighted down. I feel like I have the energy to spring. I'm not aware of pain anywhere. I'm aware of a controlled flexing in my muscles.

THERAPIST   Uh-huh. You have this feeling of strength as you get in touch with your anger. And you feel that strength right now?

CLIENT   Yes.

THERAPIST   Feel it, the strength and the anger.

CLIENT   But I'm asking myself what the anger's about. Who it's aimed at, and it seems logical that it should be Mom, but that's not what's coming up for me; it's more like I'm angry at myself right now for not being stronger in that tug-of-war between Good Little Boy and True Self, and for letting my emotions drag me around this last week.

THERAPIST   So the anger, right now at least, is turned toward you.

CLIENT   Yeah.

THERAPIST   That's what you're experiencing: anger turned toward you.

CLIENT   Yeah.

THERAPIST   You're real good at turning the anger at yourself, but I think we'd be more productive if we can look around and see if that anger is toward anybody else. You said it's not toward Mom. You said that would be logical, but that it's not toward her.

CLIENT   Well...no. I am angry at Mom, I'm angry at her for pulling out of the game, for dropping the role. I'm angry at her for abandoning me.

THERAPIST   Abandoning you?

CLIENT   I have to keep reminding myself that this is about her; it's *her* life. It's not about me; it's not about her leaving me now.

THERAPIST   Yes. You're feeling angry at her because she's leaving you, she's abandoning you.

CLIENT   Yes.

THERAPIST   By dying.

CLIENT   Yes.

THERAPIST   Yes.

CLIENT   But even more, by the way she's dying. That she's "present" so little now, and I can't communicate with her.

THERAPIST   Uh-huh. Yes. She's alive but you can't talk to her.

CLIENT   Well, I can talk, but she can't talk back.

THERAPIST   But maybe there is something you want to say and you can't say it. Is there something you want to hear from her?

CLIENT   (*interrupting*) I know what I want to hear from her. I want her to say that she's sorry. I want her to say that she understands and that she takes responsibility for creating this good-little-boy role for me and for shoving it on me – for rubbing my face in it – for chaining me to it all my life. (*smiles slightly*) Those are angry words, aren't they?

THERAPIST   Yes.

CLIENT   Yeah.

THERAPIST   Yeah. I hear you saying you want to get this finally worked out where she takes responsibility, where you can hear her say that.

CLIENT   I want to hear her say it now while she's alive, and I know it's not possible.

THERAPIST   So what do you feel now as you're saying this?

CLIENT   Angry.

THERAPIST   You can feel the anger.

CLIENT   She's in this state of mental stupidity, this drugged state, it's like a metaphor for how she's been her whole life with me – completely ignorant of what she's done to me.

THERAPIST   (*pause*) Ignorant of what she's done. And you can *feel* this anger, right?

CLIENT   Yes I can.

THERAPIST   You want one last chance at a conversation, one last opportunity to have Mom admit, "I screwed up."

CLIENT   Yes I do.

THERAPIST   Yeah. (*pause*) And that's not going to happen.

CLIENT   No.

THERAPIST   Not in her drug-induced state; it's too late. Let's stay with this. What's that like for you, that you know it's just not going to happen, and you want it? Tell me what that's like for you right now, knowing it's not going to happen?

CLIENT   How can I describe it? What is it like for me?

THERAPIST   Yeah.

CLIENT   Staying with it just hurts.

THERAPIST   Uh-huh. You want to get away from this pain of knowing that it's not going to happen.

CLIENT   Right.

THERAPIST   Yeah. Let's try to stay with it, though. Let's try to stay with that pain, not shut down, not run away from it...just, "This is the way it is," right?

CLIENT   Yeah.

THERAPIST   "This is the way it is."

CLIENT   Yes.

THERAPIST   It's not going to be different. Stay with your anger, tell me what you feel and experience.

CLIENT   My jaws are clenching, my teeth are pressing against each other. The word *bitterness* comes to mind. I feel bitter.

THERAPIST   Yeah.

CLIENT   I feel bitter because it is bitter. I want to spit it out, it tastes bad.

THERAPIST   Yes. It really does. It tastes bad, bitter. It leaves a bitter taste in your mouth. Just try to stay with this, the way it is. This is reality; you have anger and bitterness. You can taste the bitterness.

CLIENT   I'm imaging myself talking to her and at the same time I'm trying to talk myself out of it. It's the conflict between True Self and Good Little Boy. True Self is telling me "How dare she have done this to you!" and Good Little Boy is saying, "Cool it, she's dying! What do you want from her?"

THERAPIST   Yes. But what *is* it that you want from her?

CLIENT   I want her to say, "I'm sorry." *I want her apology.*

THERAPIST   Yes.

CLIENT   *I want her to acknowledge her role...* I just feel those tears

come up in my eyes. I want her to feel the pain that I'm
feeling.

THERAPIST   Ah…

CLIENT   I want her to be with me in this pain – that will mean that
she loves me.

THERAPIST   Ah.

CLIENT   It's like what she's had for me all her life, it's not a full love…
it's been love at my expense. The love met her needs – it's
been for her. *It's been love on her terms.* Good Little Boy is
saying, "This is Mom you're talking about, what are you
saying?" And True Self is saying, "I've got to face the facts.
You better not back down, buddy, because this is the truth."

THERAPIST   This is the truth.

CLIENT   The feelings are not coming up from outer space; they're
coming from the inside.

THERAPIST   They're real. Yes.

CLIENT   It's hard to think that she hasn't genuinely known me. It's
hard to have that thought. It's hard to… that's why I keep
wanting to mitigate it. She loved me the best way she could –
the only way she could – but it still hurts because it wasn't
in the way that I really needed. If only she could see how I
needed to be loved!

THERAPIST   It does hurt, doesn't it?

CLIENT   A lot.

THERAPIST   Tell me where that pain is that you're feeling where it hurts
you.

CLIENT   It's in my heart. It's right at the core of me.

THERAPIST   There's a pain right there in your heart.

CLIENT   It's not me that's inept, it's Mom. It's not me that's inadequate,
it's Mom. (*deep sobbing*)

THERAPIST   Yes.

[The client continues with deep, long sobbing, but after some moments
he regains his composure.]

THERAPIST   "It's not me, it's Mom."

CLIENT	(*cries softly*)
THERAPIST	What's happening?
CLIENT	It hurts.
THERAPIST	Where?
CLIENT	It's in my throat, that lump.
THERAPIST	Yeah. (*pause*) Yes, it's right there in your throat now you feel something.
CLIENT	It shatters my whole image of how I grew up and the love that I thought I had. It shatters that whole image.
THERAPIST	Yes.
CLIENT	I don't want to believe it. The truth is hard.
THERAPIST	It's hard, it's painful right there in your heart, right in the core of who you are. Yes. (*pause*) Let's just sit here with this painful reality for a minute, OK?
CLIENT	Yeah.
THERAPIST	(*very gently, with compassion*) I'm here with you and I'm with you in the pain that you're feeling. I just want to stay here with you and be with you at this minute.
CLIENT	Thank you…
THERAPIST	I can't imagine how hard it is for you right now. (*pause*)
CLIENT	I still love her.
THERAPIST	You do love her, uh-huh. Of course you do.
CLIENT	I want so much to connect with her on an adult level.
THERAPIST	Yes.
CLIENT	I want so much to forgive her but I can't forgive her until she asks for it.
THERAPIST	Yes.
CLIENT	Otherwise it's just being that good little boy again.
THERAPIST	Yes, that's exactly right. That's exactly right. You don't want to play the game anymore; you want to stay in the strength of your masculinity as you relate to her. *You want to be who you really are.*
CLIENT	Yeah.
THERAPIST	And offer her real, genuine forgiveness, when the time is right. (*pause*) How are you right now?

CLIENT   I'm still hurting, but that's OK. I don't feel like I need to stop it or run from it. I feel OK to be with it.

THERAPIST   You feel OK to be with this pain that you still feel.

CLIENT   I'm feeling some peace with it.

THERAPIST   Yes, there's some peace, even with the pain....

CLIENT   I'm still feeling the anger of the whole situation.

THERAPIST   Yeah, but that's OK, because to be in touch with your anger is what's really needed because the feeling is true, it's genuine, isn't it?

CLIENT   Yeah.

[Therapist moves to meaning transformation.]

THERAPIST   Let's try and pull some things together, OK, in that couple of minutes that we have left. We started the session with you saying that you had that masturbation marathon, or whatever you called it there. How do you understand that now?

CLIENT   It was really the anger I have about what's happening and not being able to communicate with her about this.

THERAPIST   You were able to do some grieving there, you felt that pain in your heart, that pain and that disappointment and that sadness that it's not going to be any different, but then you were able to come to a peace along with the pain and the anger.

CLIENT   Yeah.

THERAPIST   Yeah.

CLIENT   That feels real masculine to me.

THERAPIST   It feels real masculine. It *is* real masculine.

CLIENT   Yeah, it feels real strong. "Strong even in my weakness"... strong in my emotional upset.

THERAPIST   Exactly.

CLIENT   I'm letting myself just "be" with my emotions, and they're real and honest.

THERAPIST   Uh-huh, and there's a strength in that. You were able to go into your weakness, you have gained the strength of your masculinity by facing it.

CLIENT   Yes. That's exactly right.

THERAPIST   Our time is about up. How do you feel about our time today?

CLIENT   Grateful. I've needed this for a whole week, and I've known it on some level but didn't know how to access it.

THERAPIST   Yeah. You've really fought to stay with the truth in this session.

CLIENT   Yeah.

THERAPIST   And you felt that bitterness and that bad taste in your mouth.

CLIENT   I was determined today to take the time to do it. I feel like I'm back in the saddle again.

THERAPIST   Good. I felt so privileged to be with you and work through this with you. You work so hard.

CLIENT   Thank you.

THERAPIST   Stay with it.

PART THREE
Grief Work

CHAPTER 19

The Role of Grief Work in Reparative Therapy

Sorrow is better than laughter,
because a sad face is good for the heart.
The heart of the wise is in the house of mourning,
but the heart of fools is in the house of pleasure.

— ECCLESIASTES 7:3–4

Over the years I have come to see that many of my homosexual clients are harboring hidden emptiness and despair. One married man, in a moment of emotional agony, confessed to me many years ago that his compulsive homosexual contacts were motivated by something "empty, dark and insatiable – a painful, lonely and despairing place inside."

The Core Injury: That "Hollow, Empty Place Inside of Me"
His experience has proven to be surprisingly common. Many other men have admitted to me that they are driven to seek out strangers to fill up that same dark, internal void.

Another man said something similar that caught my attention, although it took me a long time to fully grasp what he meant. After learning about his homosexual encounters, his wife had confronted him. This man told me that he hated his gay affairs; he loved his wife and would remain loyal to his family. But he spoke movingly of a black hole – a profound emptiness – that he suspected was not about sex and not about finding a lover, but about trying to fill "a vacant place" that could never be filled. This man had experienced profound parental malattunement.

Since that time, I have probed further into homosexuality's "deep grief" dimension.

My earlier understanding of homosexuality was of a symbolic attempt to repair a gender identity deficit (Nicolosi, 1991), but I now see it as something more: at its deepest level, *it is a defense against the profound pain of attachment loss.* Scores of men I have counseled offer additional supportive testimony.

These words capture the experience of many men: *"There's a hollow, empty place inside of me. It gets filled up with demons."*

In the following transcript one man describes this same empty place:

CLIENT   There is a hollowness inside me, in my very core. The color is black. It is about sadness and hopelessness, and it's something to be despised. *The black core is me*... I've always known it was there, and I've glanced at it from time to time, but now I'm looking right at it.

THERAPIST   (*softly*) And I'm with you in looking at it. We're looking at it together.

CLIENT   (*catching his breath*) It's something that I don't want other people to see... I've been working so hard to cover up. I want people to like me, and to see me as good.

THERAPIST   As if the black core makes you bad?

CLIENT   (*sadly nodding*)

THERAPIST   The black core is something you have inside, but it's not *who you are.*

CLIENT   (*staring blankly*)

THERAPIST   It's not only *not* who you are but something that got inside of you... that does not define you.

CLIENT   (*nods*)

THERAPIST   Yes. There it is.

[A long silence follows between them.]

THERAPIST   We're looking at it together now.

CLIENT   (*softly crying*)

THERAPIST   We are seeing it together.

CLIENT   (*long pause, then straightens up in chair*) I feel better; I can show somebody my blackness.

THERAPIST   (*nods*)

CLIENT   (*speaking slowly*) I feel calmer. I'm not as scrambled.

THERAPIST   Yes...

CLIENT   (*pondering for a moment, then speaks softly*) Do you think other people have this black core also? And they're covering it up too?

THERAPIST   (*nodding*) To different degrees, yes.

CLIENT   (*as if suddenly waking up*) I feel clear in my head now. I'm not as confused.

THERAPIST   (*nods*)

[Another long silence between them.]

CLIENT   (*another pause, then speaks decisively*) The shame of the black core has been separating me from people.

THERAPIST   Has kept you in hiding.

CLIENT   (*in a tone of surprise*) I feel more loving right now; I feel more love for everybody.

THERAPIST   Yes. When the shame disappears, suddenly there's a connection.

Shame Leads into Grief Work

Grief work reaches that painful, despairing place where we therapists must, from time to time, return our clients. Whenever a person has experienced an injury to the core self, reexperiencing the attachment loss that caused this injury is so deeply unsettling that it feels like *death*. It is emotionally agonizing and physically searing.

In the earliest phase of this work, a client is surprised by the extent and depth of his feelings. It is not unusual to hear him say something like, "I can't believe there is so much sadness in me!" The sadness may spill over into his daily life. It is very common for the client to report spontaneous crying during the week, "for no reason." Yet the benefits are powerful. One man explained:

Grief work is allowing me to generate my true deep sadness – feeling hurt and abandoned – all the loneliness that I wasn't able to explore as a child. I was often very sad; I felt alone in the midst of a large family and believed that I had no right to express my true feelings of being sad when I was hurt.

The message seemed to be that I did not have a voice, and not to even try to speak because my feelings would be discredited.

In the grief work I'm able to relive that pain and experience it in a safe environment rather than bury it and deny it and fear it. I'm gradually working this through now in a healthy way. I know now that we're meant to feel the pain, not to bury it.

And when I feel the pain, then my need to use the homosexuality to cover it up is so much less.

Working Through the Abandonment-Annihilation Trauma

Essential to reparative therapy's goal of resolving gender deficit is working through the perception of parental abandonment: the annihilation-abandonment trauma that has created the core injury.

The injury may have begun with an insecure attachment to the mother. It is also profoundly felt when the boy's gestures toward gaining his paternal love and fulfilling his masculine ambition have not been supported by the father. Any time there is a failure to develop the parental attachment bond, the person must address the shame of not having felt genuinely known and fully loved by one or both parents.

When he becomes a man, the child who experienced that loss must acknowledge and grieve it. Grief resolution requires releasing these body-held memories and then mourning the loss.

Learning to live in authenticity. The literature on the psychology of bereavement reveals the pathological legacy of unfinished grieving: an ongoing fear of emotional closeness and a limited capacity for genuine intimacy. This defensive avoidance of authentic emotions, which serves to protect against the core narcissistic hurt, is seen in the shame posture (formerly called "defensive detachment"), which we so characteristically observe in the men who come to us with SSA.

Attachment loss threatens survival. Attachment researchers, most notably John Bowlby, explain the infantile attachment process as rooted in a primal drive which, when thwarted, leaves as its legacy a sense of loss that is almost equivalent to death.

Human attachment needs are rooted in the elemental drive for basic survival. Therefore the man who has suffered an attachment loss will reexperience it as something like falling into a bottomless abyss – actually dying.

Understandably, the therapist will encounter significant resistance against approaching this unresolved loss. Seeing his client struggle through this death-like experience may bring up his own discomfort with grief, and perhaps require that he face his own unresolved losses. Further, he must be willing to return with the client again and again, as often as necessary, to this same place of profound discomfort. Consequently, grief work should never be attempted until there is sufficient positive transference to counter the entrenched defenses.

Yet when we pursue this painful work in reparative therapy, we see profound, durable treatment gains. The more the client is able to penetrate and resolve his attachment loss, the less he feels the need for homosexual behavior. The process proceeds as follows:

Task 1. To accept the reality of the loss – to come face-to-face with it.

Task 2. To acknowledge its meaning, to confront its significance, to *feel the emotional impact* of the loss while in contact with the therapist.

Task 3. To admit to oneself its irreversibility, and to accept the reality that there is no going back and "undoing" it.

Pathological Grief Defined

The term *grief work* was first coined by Freud (1917/1953). From his earliest writings, Freud understood this process to involve helping the client abandon his defenses in order to face a deep loss. He said it must involve "de-cathecting the libido" from the mental representation of the lost attachment, and when this was successfully accomplished, libido would then be reclaimed through recathexis into new healthy attachments.

Freud noted that success can be blocked, however, by the continuance of conflicting feelings toward the loved one – that is, when unresolved anger remains, which is then turned back against the self.

Freud's earliest formulations regarding grief remain central to reparative therapy in that homosexuality and its associated symptoms are understood to be a defense against attachment losses incurred in childhood, often within the triadic-narcissistic family.

Grief is a natural human state which should have not only have a beginning but also an end. Yet there is much personal variability in this emotional process; no two people grieve in the same way. Some people remain trapped in an intense and prolonged reaction against the loss of an emotionally important figure. Others, however, feel little need to repeatedly reenter the loss. But until the grief is resolved, all emotional roads will lead the man back to the original annihilation-abandonment trauma.[1]

Healthy grieving is a fully felt and conscious experience that does not involve prolonged suffering. Pathological grief, however, is marked by self-defeating, self-destructive, maladaptive behaviors.

Not surprisingly, the person with a homosexual problem shares traits characteristic of persons stuck in pathological grief: excessive dependency on others for self-esteem, subclinical depression, maladaptive behaviors, suicidal ideation, emotional instability, as well as difficulty with long-term intimate relationships. Unfinished grieving also results in a lifestyle of narcissistic self-protection (Deutsch, 1937).

We have observed all of those symptoms to exist at a high rate of frequency among our homosexually oriented clients. In fact, a *much higher-than-average* rate of psychiatric disorders has been shown, in recent studies, to exist among *all homosexual men*, as a group (Ferguson, Horwood & Beautrais, 1999; Bailey, 1999).

With unresolved grief as a ground source of same-sex desires, self-defeating, maladaptive behaviors are understandable. Homoeroticism masks the anguish of this profound loss and serves as a temporary – if ultimately unsatisfying – distraction from the tragedy of a core attachment injury.

In fact, the range and extent of the maladaptive behaviors of gay men is so large that it argues quite persuasively for the existence of an early, profound injury.

The Triadic-Narcissistic Family and Traumatic Loss

Gender is intrinsic to the structure of self in the same way that support beams are intrinsic to a building. As we have seen, within the triadic-narcissistic family structure, the boy's attempts at individualization and gender actualization are not adequately supported. The results can be disastrous for the temperamentally sensitive boy, whose peers will be quick to reinforce the implicit message that he is somehow unmasculine and defective.

The prehomosexual boy experiences this attachment rupture differently with each parent. He commonly feels that he has been ignored or belittled by his father and manipulated/emotionally used by his mother. Both parents may love the child within the limitations of their own personalities, but their interactions communicate to the child, on some level, that his true self is somehow unacceptable.

When this attachment loss is experienced, the child who has grown up within the triadic-narcissistic family system can neither share his distress nor even accurately conceptualize the nature of his loss. Yet his unmet needs persist, and the loss stays stored within the body's memory.

So we have seen that the developmental sequence is (1) primary attachment loss, (2) resulting gender deficit and (3) compensation through homoerotic activity.

Homosexual Enactment: A Symptom of Pathological Grief

I'm looking at my life, and it's really sad how I've lived it.

I didn't get here by myself – other people gave me a push along the way. But I'm absolutely determined to get out on my own.

Homosexual acting out is a narcissistic defense against truly mourning the loss of an authentic attachment to one or both parents. (It is ironic that *gay* is the word used to describe a condition that is a defense against profound sadness.) The homosexual condition can, for many men, be understood as a symptom of chronic and pathological grief.

The therapist serves as the "good parent" when he actively values a conscious reexperiencing of the pain. Whenever we return the client to his unfinished bereavement, he will be increasingly freed from the grief and shame that have been paralyzing his assertion and constraining him into a life lived through the persona of the false self.

CHAPTER 20

Approaching the Core Injury

Grief work is an encounter with profound anger
and sadness over unfair deprivation.

— MARTHA STARK, M.D.

For longer than he could remember, Brian had longed to establish a relationship with his father. He recently told me about his attempt to share his same-sex struggles with his dad.

> I finally spoke to him. It took a lot of nerve but I shared a lot of things with him. I sat down with him, and I said, "Dad, there's some things I want to tell you about – what I've been going through."
>
> I told him everything. Told him the whole condition. About my whole life, the hurts, the struggle – the therapy – everything. He listened for a long time and absorbed it all. Then he finally said, "Well, Brian, let's just look on the bright side. There are a lot of people worse off than you are." That was it – that was all he had to say.
>
> I walked away stunned. I didn't know what to think. I wasn't even sure what to feel about it.

Brian's experience is not unusual. It is rare that we see a father of a homosexual son who is able to respond with consistent emotional support to his son's desire for a closer relationship. The hurts that led to the son's same-sex attraction began with exactly this sort of parental malattunement.

But hurtful as these experiences have been – and continue to be in the present – I always encourage each of my clients to revisit painful childhood experiences where long-repressed memories can be retrieved and fully felt in the present, within the therapeutic setting.

In so doing, the client allows himself to fully experience those core psychic hurts from which he has tried to distract himself with repeated self-defeating behaviors. Gently and with empathic support, he is encouraged to revisit the original trauma of the attachment loss.

In the process of reexperiencing the loss, he may lapse into deep sobbing, followed by moments of reorganization, followed by new and even deeper waves of grief. The goal is for the client to fully grieve the reality of his loss while in emotional contact with the therapist. The essence of the client's grief is in the conviction that *"I am unloved because I am unlovable."*

Shame as the Gateway into Grief

The best time to move into grief work is when material is offered by the client that directly or indirectly suggests shame. To understand how shame opens the gateway to grief, we need to consider shame's developmental origins. In childhood the boy felt shame for his attachment loss, which made him feel unlovable. He also felt shame for his grief about the loss. Shame, therefore, caused the grief to be cut off, repressed and buried beneath a massive barrier of defenses.

The best openings into grief work are presented whenever the client reports complaints associated with shame. Discussions of the shame experience allow the therapist to lead the client into deeper emotions. Most often when shame is discussed, sad and angry feelings will also surface. These are the two innate affects that form the parallel paths to grief.

Grief work, the movement from shame to grief, is anger at other and sadness for self. At the same time, the therapist is attentive to the client's defenses against grief by returning to his shame. He does so by reversing that pathway and turning his anger at self into feeling sadness for the other (see fig. 20.1).

Many clients also learned to suppress their feelings to avoid upsetting

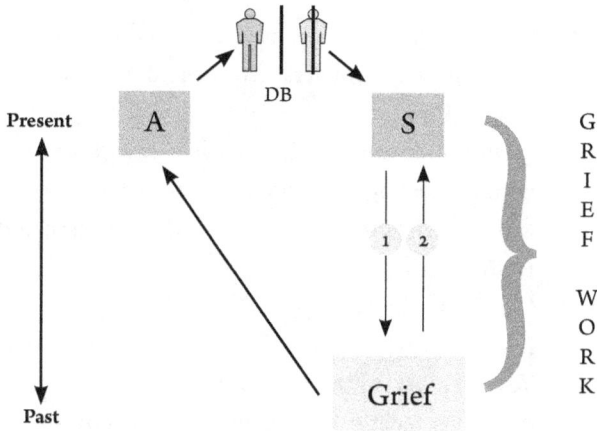

DB=Double Bind

1 = Shame to Grief: Anger at other, sadness for self

2 = Grief to Shame: Anger at self, sadness for other

Figure 20.1 Two pathways into grief

their mothers. "Fear of upsetting Mother" is a commonly heard theme in therapy.

This twenty-six-year-old man describes a shameful experience, from which he then moves to grief:

> I arrived early at a local club, so I stood at the bar waiting for my friends. I noticed this guy and thought, *Gosh, he's good looking.* He seemed confident, dressed casually stylish – as if unaware of how good he looked – and relaxed and at ease with himself while he stood at the bar with his girlfriend. They were with another couple who were like themselves. They would laugh and talk to their friends. I'm watching them, but especially him, while I'm standing there alone.
>
> What was really humiliating is that he noticed I was looking at him, and gave me a look like, "You pathetic pervert, what are you looking at?" (*slight laugh*) Maybe that wasn't what he was thinking, but that was what I was thinking. That's how I felt.

The therapist decides to do body work to help move the client from shame to grief.

THERAPIST   Go to the feelings now as you recall this situation.

CLIENT   (*slight giggle*) Embarrassed, ridiculous. The whole thing seems silly.

THERAPIST   (*gently dismissing his defensive humor with seriousness*) Stay with the feelings as you recall that incident.

CLIENT   (*deep breath*) OK. Out of place, awkward, just standing there, waiting for my friends.

THERAPIST   Go to your body...

CLIENT   Insecure, exposed, naked, shy, meek, tender, weak.

THERAPIST   Yes, OK...go to the body where you feel those feelings...

CLIENT   An empty feeling...a shame. I'd look at him and he'd notice, and I'd feel "caught"...a heaviness in my chest.

THERAPIST   Yes. Stay with that heaviness.

CLIENT   (*thoughtfully*) Sad...yeah...sad, deep inside my chest. My upper chest feels cold, blue. There's an empty space deep in the center of my chest. It's just sitting there, not moving. It wants to travel up (*gesturing, moving his hand from chest to throat*) to come out.

THERAPIST   What is it that feels like coming out?

CLIENT   Crying...A tightening in my throat, constriction; eyes watering.

[Therapist moves to the second triangle.]

THERAPIST   What is this about? What past memories?

CLIENT   Wanting to connect with men. Not ever having that connection. Not in childhood...*not ever in my whole life.*

THERAPIST   OK. (*pause*) Do you have a specific memory?

CLIENT   Sure. Plenty.

THERAPIST   OK...Can you give me one?...One with the strongest emotional charge.

CLIENT   Oh, yeah...at school, at the playground, never getting picked to play. Sitting on the sidelines with the girls, just looking at the boys play.

THERAPIST   What's the feeling now as you recall it?

CLIENT   That same awkward, "not belonging" feeling...

THERAPIST So the feeling is...

CLIENT Empty, sinking...

[After some moments the client's grief approaches the larger aspect of his life.]

CLIENT I'm feeling little bursts, little painful shots of... fear. Fear of the cold, hard facts. I'm so pathetic – I'm thirty-five and I've never had a girlfriend, never even gotten started in life. No home, no children. I go back and forth between the shots of fear and the dull, dead heaviness. The fear is that each year it gets harder.

[Here, the client has moved beyond same-sex attraction and gender inferiority to profound loss of self-identity.]

CLIENT I don't know what intimacy is, what connects everyone. I don't even know how to feel deeply. How do people connect? What does it feel like? I'm on the outer edge of human relations. I'm on the outer edge of humanity.

Deeply entrenched resistance surfaces any time the client comes in contact with the affects which are associated with grief, because they evoke feelings of even deeper abandonment-annihilation (the double bind).

Rejecting the Rejected Self

The following transcript illustrates a client's process of self-shaming for his deep loss. He minimizes himself, as well as the efforts of the therapist to double loop.

CLIENT It comes to me, like a voice: *I'm not all that I think I am.* It's like, if I go to my sadness, then I'm gonna lose control, I'll be weak... worthless. I'm gonna be the very thing I pushed away from, so long ago.

THERAPIST What was it you pushed away from, Bill?

CLIENT I pushed away that "thing"... (*with contempt*) that was *me*, is what I pushed so far away... That person who was weak, who felt rejected. I didn't want to be him anymore. Nobody liked him. My parents didn't like him – and I didn't, either. So I become stoic and acted it: *I'm not feeling any pain.*

THERAPIST   (*nodding thoughtfully*) So you rejected, denied to yourself, your weak side.

CLIENT   I don't know how to forgive him … forgive *me* … for his weakness. That person is so much *not* what I want to be; in fact, he's the opposite. It's so much easier for me to forgive someone else's failings than my own.

THERAPIST   Maybe sometime, somewhere, someone went inside you and caused you to split off from your "sad" self … to deny it … and so you need someone to help reconnect you back to that part of you.

CLIENT   Right now I'm feeling silly, stupid – like I've been making a big deal out of nothing.

THERAPIST   OK. Tell me about this, Bill.

CLIENT   It's humiliating. I feel weak complaining about this.

[Therapist tries to keep the client feeling his feelings of "humiliation" and "weakness" (i.e., shame), thinking that it may lead him into grief work.]

THERAPIST   Let's look at what you've just said, how you feel silly and stupid for complaining. Did anyone do that with you … make you feel silly for complaining?

CLIENT   (*becomes more serious*) Yeah, my dad, he'd make me feel stupid or dumb for crying. I had to hide it … even my telling you these things right now, you must be thinking – what a weak little wimp this guy is.

[Reassurance would rob the client of the chance to work through his shame. Resisting the temptation, the therapist uses this as an opportunity to work through a shame-based distortion. He will offer reassurance, but not until the end of the session.]

THERAPIST   So tell me more about what you think I must be thinking about you right now.

CLIENT   (*deep breath*) Like, *This guy's never gonna make it* … Like you're being nice and kind to me, but underneath you're laughing. You've gotta be thinking, *This guy's such a faggot.*

THERAPIST   Stay with that. How is that?

CLIENT   (*long silence*)

THERAPIST   (*softly*) Please try to just sit with that feeling right now. Tell me, what's the feeling?

CLIENT   (*eyes shift downward*) A real pain, like it really hurts.

THERAPIST   Where? Where's the pain?

CLIENT   My whole chest. (*very long silence*)

[Therapist waits with him a long time, then, speaks.]

THERAPIST   What's that feeling?

CLIENT   (*looking down*) Really sad … like I'm just nothing, a nobody.

[For the remaining time, therapist and client sit in the grief with few words exchanged. Finally, the client then goes into a description of some of his deeply felt childhood shame experiences, with their body memories. As the therapist brings the session to a close, the delayed reassurance is offered.]

THERAPIST   Bill, I want you to know I recognize how difficult this work is for you, how hard it is to go into those feelings, and to sit with them and really feel them – how you feel them in your body.

CLIENT   (*thoughtfully*) I never realized that I had feelings like that – memories with feelings in my body attached. But they really *are* there.

THERAPIST   I admire your perseverance for pushing past that shame with no reassurance from me, and going into and staying with and truly feeling the full extent of that weakness, and the real depth of that sadness.

Grief work gradually disempowers shame. Clients who can successfully sit in their core sense of abandonment will later report much less inclination to feel shamed, which permits them to stay longer in the assertion stance.

Freud's "Melancholia" as Our "Gray Zone"

Freud's (1917/1953) distinction between "melancholia" and "mourning" corresponds to our distinction between the "gray zone" and "true grief." Freud's says the person undergoes "mourning" (healthy grieving) when there is a fully conscious loss of the love object.

Melancholia (pathological or aborted grieving), however, is where one part of the ego sets itself against the other in order to "keep alive" the lost object. The person remains unable to transition out of pathological melancholia into healthy mourning because of guilt and ambivalence about his anger toward the loved one for emotionally abandoning him. Melancholia involves "self-reproaches and self-revilings" with "a delusional expectation of punishment" (p. 154). It allows the person to feel "sadism and hate toward the object, but turned upon the self" (p. 162).

In our application of the same concept, the client blames himself – more accurately, his unlovability – for the attachment loss, which prevents his pathological melancholy (the mood of the gray zone) from being transformed into a conscious experience of the loss, followed by healthy and constructive grieving.

Revolt Against the Loved One Transforms into Depression

The key to the clinical picture of melancholia, Freud says, is that the self-reproaches are actually reproaches against the loved object, but they have been shifted around and put into the person's own ego. Ego identification with the object is thus maintained, neutralizing the guilt and self-blame the person feels for the fact that the love object disappointed him. As a result, the would-be revolt against the loved one transforms into the "crushed state" of melancholia. Freud's description of the "crushed state" is very suggestive of the flat affect of the gray zone.

Freud speculated that for melancholia to occur, the love object must have been one that was essential to ego development (i.e., a parent). The love object disappoints the child, and he experiences abandonment-annihilation trauma. Narcissistic identification with this disappointing love object serves the important function of "keeping the loved one alive" (after all, he felt essential to the child's survival) within the self as an introject.

It is this narcissistic identification with the disappointing love object that postpones healthy mourning.

In Freud's melancholia (the gray zone) the cause of the grief is the *unconscious memory of past loss*. The memory of the attachment loss is then reactivated in the present whenever the person feels slighted, rejected or disappointed.

Our therapeutic task is to take the pathological melancholia and make the loss conscious and complete – that is, to transform it from the ongoing depressive state of the gray zone and into healthy, productive mourning.

The therapist helps the client substitute self-compassion for self-criticism, so that he may face his losses realistically and grieve them constructively. The working alliance supports the client's ego whenever his narcissistic defenses (illusions and distortions) fail to protect him against the flood of shame.

Fear of Pain

> My whole personality is constructed to avoid that dead spot.
> – forty-five-year-old client

Grief work is met with deeply entrenched resistance precisely because of the intense pain it generates: the pain and shame of lost love. This pain is so acute that the client literally feels that if he reexperiences it, he will be annihilated. This primal sense of "dying" is biologically rooted in mammalian group-survival mechanisms. The desperate quality of the client's distress is understandable because this "expulsion from the pack" is, as we have noted, a virtual death sentence for the rejected pack member. But it is actually not the pain but *the fear of the pain* that is the greatest source of resistance.

One client explained how for many years, he lived in a state of buried grief and anger that he was unable to access until he entered therapy:

> You could say that I grew up the gray zone, which represented the unspoken and unconscious agreement I had with my parents, namely, that I would kill off the feeling parts of myself and in return, they would love me. Living in the gray zone fulfilled my parents' expectation that "Thou Shalt Not Be Aware."
>
> This was not only a flight from grief – it was also a flight from anger.

Entering the Pain

Most clients believe that they cannot enter the pain and survive. One man's words illustrate this poignantly: "My persona, my image to the world is like a balloon – I'm always blowing or puffing it up, keeping it afloat. Behind my pain is a sense of nonbeing. Behind it all, I feel pain and shame that I'm actually so empty."

Said another man of the emptiness within:

> My whole personality is constructed to avoid this dead spot, this place of isolation. There's deep ache, a knife turning in my gut. It's a black hole … it's weird, spooky, scary, unreal. I'll disappear if I go down into it.
>
> I want to run away from it; it's something bad and disgusting, some reality that I don't want to know. What's in there is – *me!* A "real me" that is unlovable. If I go down into that place, I will die.

Another client, recalling the same interior place, said:

> I'm screaming and screaming. No matter how much I scream, the pain won't go away. I'm terrified because my father can't figure out how to comfort me. He doesn't know what to do about me. I can feel his helplessness. He doesn't know how to love me. There is no one else to take away the pain.

Some men who are mired in deep despair will deny their childhood unhappiness in order to justify (on an unconscious level) their hatred of themselves for feeling so sad. Rather than looking at and tending to their wounds – which is the work of bereavement – they choose to escape into some sort of painkilling distraction or self-punishment.

One man confessed, "I want to run from the pain and just pretend that everything's OK, my parents are OK, I'm OK, and that what I did last night [homosexual enactment] is OK." I interpreted this to him as his internalization of the critical parent who says, "You're not supposed to cry, you're not allowed to feel sorry for yourself." But to deny the existence of the loss, I told him, is to continue to punish himself.

In a corrective grief work experience with the therapist, the client allows himself to free-fall into a full experience of the sorrow.

Entry into Grief Through Body Work

The grief feels heavy and drags you down, like when they make you
wear those x-ray vests.

Our session begins with the client's reporting of his life events since
our last meeting. The therapist should be listening for a conflict, usually
one that pits the client's authentic needs against the expectations of others. When he senses that the conflict may lead to grief work, the therapist,
in collaboration with the client, may agree to move into deeper feelings
of sadness.

Grief work should not be approached until there is sufficient positive
transference established to allow the client to release his lifelong defenses
against feeling the deepest level of pain. The client will always harbor an
unconscious need not to reexperience his feelings of loss. But when there
is a good working alliance, he will eventually choose to work with the
therapist to oppose his own defenses.

To proceed, the client must remain focused on his feelings in the
here and now. The therapist should keep him focused on his feelings
and impulses but avoid a discussion of anxiety. The client will feel various – even contradictory – feelings, but by carefully attending to them, he
will eventually identify a single core feeling. Each core feeling will lead
to a deeper core feeling, moving ever deeper, many times, down into an
essential sense of abandonment-annihilation.

During this process, defenses and manifest forms of anxiety are systematically separated out so that the client can concentrate on the emotions
and impulses that lead to grief. Other pathways into deep grief are envy,
jealousy and frustration, which then lead to the two even deeper affective
pathways of anger and sadness.

When an innate affect is fully felt and expressed, the client is led to
the second triangle, where memories and associations are linked with the
present. This phase then concludes with the double loop, where the client
has the experience of feeling unconditionally understood and accepted in
this loss by another human being.

The "triangle of understanding" concludes with the final phase of meaning transformation, where the client develops a "coherence of discourse"

(Main et al., 1985). This integrative opportunity was denied the child who grew up in the chaotic structure of the triadic-narcissistic family, where he was often made to feel bad for feeling sad: "You're upsetting everybody else. There's no reason to be unhappy. You have everything you need, and nothing to complain about." Now, as an adult in therapy, he can recreate a coherent narrative by making his past attachment losses meaningful and understandable in the present time.

In an overall view, then, we conceptualize grief work as requiring four tasks:

1. recalling any traumatic childhood events

2. going beyond recall to feel and express the associated affects (sadness and anger) in the present time with the therapist

3. facing the painful consequences of those past traumatic events as they affect his life today, that is, the chronic emptiness, the inability to feel and trust, and the inability to relate intimately to others and to love

4. resolution of past losses and developing realistic expectations for the future

While studies of grief had previously focused on the child's reaction to physical abandonment by a parent, John Bowlby (1988) extended this clinical study to include the often-hidden effects of emotional abandonment. The child's first reaction to abandonment is "protest," then "despair," marked by "apparent withdrawal of attention from ongoing life" (pp. 93–96).

Gender-disturbed boys (a large proportion of whom grow up to be homosexual) have often been observed to experience depression, emotional detachment and social isolation. Homosexual men very often recall their childhoods as characterized by isolation, dreaminess and fantasy, and in adulthood they repeatedly report a feeling of "emptiness" and "black void" inside.

Accessing the pain. One client, Rob, describes a home situation that suggests the narcissistic family, along with his sense that he was emotionally abandoned. In this session, after initial resistance, he worked hard toward reaching his core pain. Here are some excerpts from that process:

CLIENT   "Going there" scares the hell out of me.

THERAPIST   Can you go to that feeling in your body? Right now? Can you feel in your body that feeling "It scares the hell out of me"?

CLIENT   (*long pause*) In my whole body?... Like, *No, I don't want that!*

THERAPIST   Sure. But how would that feel?

CLIENT   Like a shock, a wound.

THERAPIST   Stay with that, Rob. See if you can find a centrality to that "wound," that "shock." Try to stay with it.

CLIENT   This is so F—kin' depressing. I hate this.

[He sounds angry, but the therapist is not sure, so he accepts his word.]

THERAPIST   OK, then... Let's try to look at that instead – that "depressing." Where is that located?

CLIENT   My stomach, my heart.

THERAPIST   Where is the feeling stronger, stomach or heart?

CLIENT   (*considers*) In my heart.

THERAPIST   What's the feeling?

CLIENT   (*sighing*) Just sad. Heavy.

THERAPIST   Where?

CLIENT   Here. (*points to center chest*) I'm tempted to run away...

THERAPIST   From?...

CLIENT   From the pain... and from all that sadness. I'll feel this sadness for no reason; sometimes I begin to ask myself, *Am I just making this sadness up?* Maybe I'm just feeling sorry for myself for no reason.

THERAPIST   (*nods, waits*)

CLIENT   Mainly, I just want to belong. I feel the terror of not belonging. But then, if I try to belong, I'm just as afraid they're going to find out the truth – that I'm not like them.

THERAPIST   And where does that leave you?

CLIENT   Stuck.

THERAPIST   How does "stuck" feel?

CLIENT   (*considers for a moment*) Numb.

THERAPIST   Stay with "numb," that numb feeling of being "stuck."

CLIENT   (*long pause*)

THERAPIST   What's happening?

[At this point, client rambles a bit but then moves to the second triangle. Therapist follows his lead.]

CLIENT   At the bottom of it all, there's self-hatred. I feel stupid, never good at anything.

THERAPIST   (*returning client to here and now*) How does that feel right now as you sit here with me and talk about it?

CLIENT   (*long pause*) Desperation. I hate myself.

THERAPIST   Let's stay with that desperation. (*softly*) Let's just stay with that.

CLIENT   (*heavy sigh*) I feel I'm on the edge of a black abyss. I'm afraid to go in, because I might not come out. No one took care of me, or understood what I was going through. Nobody loved me always alone. Always darkness. Never a purpose. I remember being a little kid, standing in the middle of the kitchen... I did not belong, and I did not feel loved. Standing there in a roomful of people, but feeling totally alone. I couldn't say anything about having those feelings.

THERAPIST   Why not?

CLIENT   (*heavy sigh*) It would anger my father.

THERAPIST   And your mom?

CLIENT   I couldn't tell her. My mother was always complaining that we didn't love her enough. But how could we love *her* when *we* didn't get enough ourselves? How could we tell her when *we* were feeling bad? When I would cry, she'd yell "Shut up! Shut up! I can't take this any more!"

THERAPIST   (*nods thoughtfully*)

CLIENT   (*crying now*) My parents tore my heart out and left me alone to bleed.

THERAPIST   (*waits*)

CLIENT   The real hurt is that I don't know who I am, so how can I expect someone to love me or care for me if I don't know who I am?

Sadness and Anger: Parallel Paths to Grief

My body was a battlefield throughout my childhood. The rage is gone, but the sadness is still there. It's a background feeling that always leaves my body feeling so tired.

When a man senses that he has suffered a core attachment loss and decides to fully face that tragic loss, he must access it on an emotional as well as intellectual level. This often means moving out of shame and into grief.

The parallel roads that will lead him away from shame and to grief are the two core emotions of sadness and anger. When reexperiencing the grief of that loss, he will feel sadness for himself and anger toward the people who could not fully understand and love him.

Some confusion arises along these parallel roads, however, when anger that would be appropriately directed toward others is turned against the

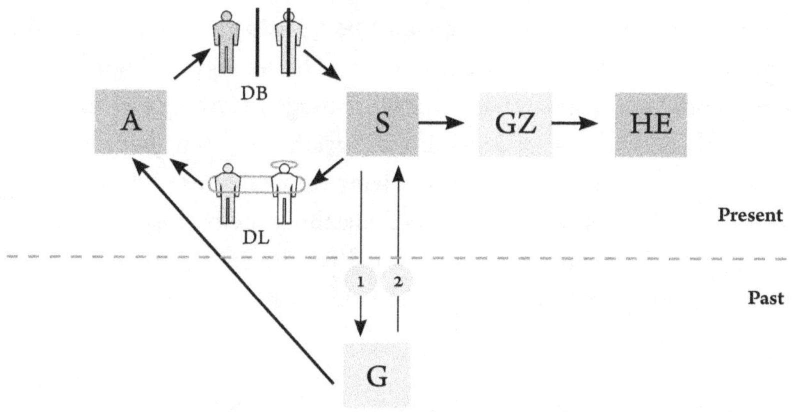

A= Assertion   GZ= Gray Zone   G= Grief
S= Shame   HE= Homosexual Enactment   DB= Double Bind
                     DL= Double Loop

1 = Shame to Grief: Anger at other, sadness for self
2 = Grief to Shame: Anger at self, sadness for other

Figure 20.2 Shame and grief

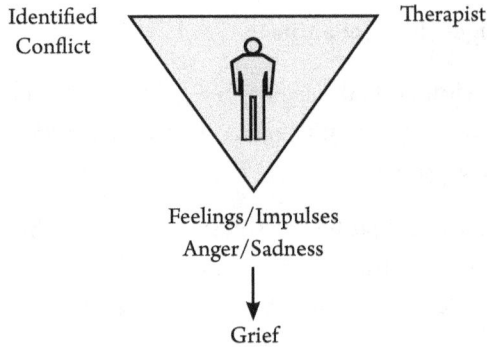

Figure 20.3 Triangle of containment

self in self-defeating, self-punishing ways. The child of the narcissistic family has been taught that to be sad is to be shameable. Therefore sadness becomes a signal to attack himself with self-punishing anger, leading back to shame.

The pain of the sadness is not so much in the feeling itself but in his critical self-appraisal that says he must be weak, pathetic – a sissy and a crybaby. In order to touch the deepest level of his feelings and impulses, the body work he will undertake is utilized through the triangle of knowing.

In his early phase of accessing his grief, one client became overwhelmed with sorrow and then suddenly stopped himself short, saying something that many of our clients think about themselves: "I'm sounding just like a sniveling, little baby wimp." The therapist's task is to remain vigilant to the ways in which the client blocks the grief and turns against himself for feeling sadness.

Hating Oneself for Being Unhappy

Anger is often directed against the self as a defense against the intolerable pain of internal emptiness. As children, many clients conspired with their parents against themselves for feeling sad. They still do so today, as evidenced by such statements as "I hate myself for being so pathetically unhappy." Anger turned against the self is not only a self-punishment for "being weak," but it also preserves the good image they may hope to harbor of loved ones who have hurt them.

Clients will often say something like, "I get angry at my weakness because my father laughed at me when I cried." Or they report "frustration," but this is typically the collision of two forces: anger pushing up against guilt.

When this occurs it may be appropriate to shift into Neborsky's (2001) confrontational style, where an immediate and direct intervention is made. While conveying respect and appreciation, the therapist addresses the client's internalized parental condemnation of his anger:

THERAPIST   Do you see what you are doing now? You are being critical of yourself for feeling sad. Calling yourself a "wimp" is disrespectful to your experience of hurt and pain. (*pause*) Who called you wimp?

CLIENT   My dad. (*touching upon his genuine sadness*) Sometimes I think about hurting myself. Punishing myself for feeling weak. To feel sad is to be weak.

THERAPIST   So you say your dad cut you off from your sadness...

CLIENT   (*nods*) When I showed my unhappiness, my dad's basic message to me was, "It's all your fault." As a kid, my sadness set me apart from the family.

THERAPIST   This is the same message you tell yourself today. "It's all my fault."

In the following session, the client is able, for the first time, to resist turning the anger against himself. Rather, he allows himself to fully feel his overwhelming loss and then revels in the vitality of the experience:

CLIENT   (*allowing himself to feel the loss*) I feel my chest closed down – closed in, numb, boxed in... emotionally flat. (*some moments later*) I feel a great sadness. My eyes are teary.

[Therapist and client sit together in a long silence.]

CLIENT   (*suddenly speaks again*) I feel a heat radiating out from the center of my chest, spreading up and out. It's an energy within me. The anger wants to kill off the part of me that is sad.

THERAPIST   (*nods*)

CLIENT   As the anger comes up, it's getting absorbed by the sadness. (*long pause*) Waves of energy shooting up from my chest center. I'm almost ready to cry, feeling very vulnerable, weak.

THERAPIST   (*waits*)

CLIENT   But now the anger is dominant, very strong. It's like the big bully here, (*passing his palm across his chest*) and the stronger "anger" is bullying the weaker "sadness." My sadness wants to be spared but is being pummeled by the anger which wells up – beating down and towering over the pathetic sadness. Whenever that sadness comes up, the anger says "no!" (*some moments later*) Now the anger is gone. I feel lifeless...

THERAPIST   (*nods*) Lifeless and wiped out.

CLIENT   (*sits up*) It's scary to realize I have these huge emotions, but at the same time it's cool to have such passions and emotions that are actually from me. I can see them and know that there's *life* there! I'd much rather *feel* the feeling inside instead of spilling it out in some "gay way." I *felt it* this time – I didn't have to jump in the car, do harm to myself or act out sexually in some way.

Sitting Together in the Abyss

I look inside and I'm staring at blackness. It's empty, and it has always been empty inside.

As the client approaches these deeply painful levels of grief, the therapist must move ever more slowly and gently. His task is to remain present to him in his sadness, containing and supporting him while he "sits in the ashes" of the loss.

When the client's defenses are dropped and he enters the despairing depths, the therapist replaces his focused pressure with a more passive "attendance," dwelling on the nuances of the client's experience. He steps back to provide a supportive containment while the client occupies his very personal grief space.

When the client reaches the true depths of his despair, he no longer resists feeling the painful feelings, but chooses to inhabit them on his own – settling in and allowing long, silent moments to pass by together as he becomes acquainted with, explores and then simply dwells in the abyss.

This experience of grief is often so deep that it is a death-like experience, as described by this twenty-eight-year-old man:

> Feeling like this takes me back so far. I feel all alone, like I don't really exist. The basic feeling is "dead, numb." I feel no love; no one around for me. I'm in my house, but nobody's home. I'm alone, and everything is still.
>
> If I go deeper into that pain, I'm gonna die. It's like a shadow that envelops me – a soul death. I want to run from it and just pretend that everything is OK... that what I did last week is OK... that my parents were completely OK... that life really was OK.
>
> But as I sit still now, I can hear the silence of the house. I don't know where my mom and dad are. All is dark... quiet... abandoned. Nobody's home; they left me there. I must have done something terribly wrong.

Another client describes the same feelings of attachment loss in these words:

> I feel the fear of disconnectedness, and in my chest, an emptiness which reaches down to my abdomen. There's a dull pain down into the base of my intestine. Something inside my head is spinning around, dizzy, doesn't know where it belongs.
>
> I don't know what to do about what I'm feeling. That's when I break down... because there's no hope of stopping the feelings now.
>
> This is the truth... I am broken-hearted.

What If?

At the lowest point of the grief process, the client thinks about how his life might have been. What if he had chosen to *confront* the many challenges that he pulled back from? What if Dad had not left home and had been there to break up his unhealthy closeness of just "Mom and me"? if Dad had been there to protect him from the teasing of his friends? What if he had had a mentor when he was being picked on, on the sports field?

if someone had noticed he was into porn, had figured out he was being molested by those older boys? Might he, then, have been "one of the guys" – those mysterious males in possession of that elusive masculinity that now seems, for him, always just out of reach?

He deeply feels his lack of self-confidence, his loss of a life as a "a normal guy" who is attracted to women, a man like other men who is so *easily* and *naturally* inclined toward marriage and family. There is a hole in the center of his heart, and he knows it can never be filled by another man. One client observed:

> I'm sad about my childhood. If only I could go back and relive it now. All those wasted years! I believed that they were right about me – that I was weak. Maybe I could have hit a home run in Little League, taken a girl to the prom? . . . I wasted so many years living out my parents' script, playing the good boy, the pleaser.

Who Am I?

Grief work addresses this "defective self," the inauthenticity that is the root cause of their same-sex desire that our clients sense to exist within them. And yet, they will also grieve the impending loss of his old, familiar identity, "The false self I've fabricated, in place of who I was meant to be," as one man put it.

During the weeks of ongoing grief work, the client may feel a persistent sadness between sessions. This man begins his session with these words:

CLIENT   I've been crying all weekend. I'll cry in bed, especially in the morning. I started crying in the shower, just holding myself, feeling scared and just sad. This is so different from the past.

THERAPIST   How's that?

CLIENT   Now I'm being heard.

THERAPIST   By whom?

CLIENT   By myself. I'm telling myself that this time I'm "there for me."

THERAPIST   (*nods*)

CLIENT   I'm telling myself just to go ahead and cry, that it's OK. It's

> really and truly OK to just cry and grieve what I've lost...
> to admit it now, and this time, to feel it.

Describing his own grief experience, another twenty-two-year-old man says the therapy session felt like entering a "timeless state" where sensations are mixed with colors and feelings, pain is blurred with thoughts, and memory fragments surface and resurface in a continual ebb and flow. During such an experience he fully feels the trauma of his loss – his perception of having been cut off from authentic parental and gender attachment, and his continuing longing for deep human closeness. In an almost trancelike state, he remains immersed in an intense self-absorption with only intermittent contact with the therapist.

His feeling of loss comes in waves, often with deep sobbing, then followed by moments of reorganization, followed by deeper waves of grief, in which he again confronts his despair. He is now doing what he could not do as a child – grieving (and repairing) the attachment loss. This subjective, nonverbal, preconscious and deeply personal experience is all part of the psychic reorganizing process.

Robert describes the progress of his grief work:

> I would see continual images during the session and sometimes they would be connected to an emotion, which would grow stronger as I would keep at the near-impossible task I had been instructed to do – "Go to your feelings."
>
> While I was doing that, there would be no images or ideas – only myself in the room with my shrink, and my body feeling its pain. The pain would be this deep throbbing... a foreign feeling that lingers there like a painful, silent, spreading death.
>
> It would start with a dragging feeling in my lower chest, and then grow heavier, and then become a cold, heavy stone, and then a dagger relentlessly carving into one place within me, and then sticking into a single point on the bottom of my chest – a feeling that was at first cold and then heavy; and finally, it just hurt. All that time, I'd be fully aware of my vacant, quiet environment.
>
> This is the grief experience. Those who sit Shiva [a traditional Jewish

mourning process] undergo this same kind of process, which brings them solace and comfort and, finally, the strength to go on.

How long do I have to sit at the bottom of the abyss? I'd wonder. *I don't know what I have to do to come out on the other side. Won't it always be the same – just like this? At least it's hopeful to realize I can't ever feel any more hurt than this…*

After the session finished, I cannot say I'd feel exactly elated, but something better – I would feel whole. By plunging into my deepest fear, confronting my most daunting insecurity, I slowly became to feel much more whole and secure.

In the months that followed the session, the [homosexual] symptom diminished in importance and my larger life narrative grew more prominent in my mind.

The Boy in the Black Room

> That deep, scary, dark place! I'm a boy in a black room. That's a metaphor for my whole life… for who I am.

In the course of grief work, it is not uncommon for clients to spontaneously recall the same archetypical scene from their early lives that we call "The Boy in the Black Room." Some men called it "that big, sad place" or "that place that's all dark, where I'm all alone." Variations of this same primal, terrifying image emerge as the client reexperiences feelings of profound abandonment: "I am this scared, helpless little kid, just sitting there in a dark void… a black room with no wall, no door… a little boy who is totally by himself, naked, all curled up, his knees to his chin."

A twenty-eight-year-old teacher described how he perceived himself: "a boy in a black cell, crying out – but nobody hears him." After some hesitation he broke into deep sobs, and then, gathering himself together, he continued in a child-like voice:

> I'm in a dark room; I can't see anything. I want to get out, but there's no door. The walls are smooth – no edges or markers, no window, no doorknob. It's lonely, completely empty inside… There's no connection to anybody or any thing.
>
> This is my whole life. I can never connect to any human being.

Another client, a thirty-five-year-old executive, having begun his grief work in previous sessions, starts out the session by facing a life of emotional neglect.

THERAPIST   So what do you want to work on today?

CLIENT   I want to talk about what I was dealing with this week. I've been feeling kind of like a "little boy in the basement" needing comfort...It's a physical weight on me just thinking about that.

THERAPIST   Sure.

CLIENT   Mostly I just kind of feel hurting and wanting comfort.

THERAPIST   Let's take a moment to focus on that hurting feeling.

CLIENT   (*pauses to collect his thoughts*) OK. Well, I feel sad, betrayed and lonely...First I start to feel anxious, but then when I sit with that, then I feel that deep sadness and a "stinky, gut sense" that I am just sad and alone.

THERAPIST   (*gently*) Are you feeling those feelings right now?

CLIENT   Yeah, I am.

THERAPIST   "Feeling sad" is located where in your body?

CLIENT   In the back of my throat. There's tears under there somewhere and a lump and tightness in my throat...My stomach feels like it's in a knot. It's that kind of frightening feeling when you first start to go on the roller coaster, that kind of "Oooh!" thing like when you're ready to go down a hill – "Whoa, here we go!" and then you just tense up and think, *I'm going to be sick here*, that kind of thing.

[Therapist tries to move client back to feelings of sadness.]

THERAPIST   Could it be that you are afraid of the sad feeling beginning to well up inside you? That you get tense and anxious about that "roller coaster ride"?

CLIENT   (*nods*)

THERAPIST   So let's try to just push that anxiety aside for a minute and focus on the sadness that's there. I think that's the feeling that we need to focus on – the sad, lonely feeling.

CLIENT   It's that lonely and betrayed feeling...I feel just so miserable and just terrible. It almost gives me a headache to feel it. Right now I have a pain in the head on the front part of my forehead, that kind of headache.

THERAPIST   (*nodding, with understanding*) Like a tension headache.

CLIENT   Yeah – right in the front, behind my eyes and my nose. That's what happens when I think about the sadness I've got here, and my head starts hurting... such a long chain of pure anguish.

THERAPIST   Yes, there's real anguish to it, from what you're saying.

CLIENT   It's a lot of pain... even my whole head is hurting. That tension goes into my head and it just kind of feels lonely, sad and dark. I see myself just sitting in a corner in a dark basement.

THERAPIST   You can see yourself there? You're a little boy.

CLIENT   Uh-huh, I'm a little boy in the basement, about two, and... I don't know... right now, I'm afraid.

THERAPIST   (*softly, attentively*) You feel very *little* right now, and scared.

CLIENT   Uh-huh. Real little and afraid. Kind of sitting on the floor in the dark, all alone. It's the same when I'm in my bedroom... I'm alone and it's dark. Very sad. A terrible feeling.

THERAPIST   (*in a quiet and steady tone*) Yes. Where's that sadness, that terrible sadness that you're feeling? Let's just focus on that together. Where is that in your body?

CLIENT   Now it's right in the middle of my forehead, like someone just punched me in the nose, and my brow is real crumpled.

THERAPIST   Yes.

CLIENT   Like tears, but they are dry tears because you can't cry anymore and you just have dry tears. You can't even make tears anymore because it just hurts so bad.

THERAPIST   Yes.

CLIENT   It's dreadful.

THERAPIST   (*with understanding*) Yes, it is. And part of it is that you feel lonely in your sadness, you're all alone.

CLIENT   Uh-huh.

THERAPIST	In the dark.
CLIENT	The dark, yeah. In a dark hole. Just so bad…
THERAPIST	(*slowly, expressing his deep feelings for the client's genuine, traumatic loss*) You're in the dark hole and you feel so bad.
CLIENT	Right.
THERAPIST	You feel terrible.
CLIENT	(*unexpectedly*) "I don't want you. I just don't want you"…I don't know if Mommy or Daddy said that to me, but I knew that: they don't want me.
THERAPIST	(*somewhat surprised*) You hear a voice saying that to you now? You heard someone say to you, "I don't want you"?
CLIENT	"I never wanted you." Yes.
THERAPIST	Whose voice is this, "I never wanted you"?
CLIENT	Daddy's.
THERAPIST	It's Daddy's voice saying, "I never wanted you."
CLIENT	Yeah. (*begins to cry deeply*) I don't know what I'm going to do. I don't know what I'm going to do. (*in anguish*) Because they don't want me anymore. They don't want me.
THERAPIST	What are you feeling inside as you're telling me this? "I never wanted you."
CLIENT	(*continues to cry*) Very sad. (*crying*) It's hard. (*desperately*) Why don't they want me?
THERAPIST	So sad.
CLIENT	I'm all alone. Nobody wants me.
THERAPIST	Not wanted…
CLIENT	Nobody wants me.
THERAPIST	(*with deep feeling*) Yes. I can see the sadness you're feeling and the tears.
CLIENT	Moaning and groaning…
THERAPIST	Moaning and groaning deep within you, huh?
CLIENT	Yeah.
THERAPIST	Something that's moaning and groaning deep inside of you.
CLIENT	(*exhausted, depleted*) I just moan and cry.
THERAPIST	(*softly*) Yes. There's a pain way down deep inside, isn't there?
CLIENT	Uh-huh.

THERAPIST	(*gently, attentively*) Can we go there together? I'm going to go there with you.
CLIENT	(*in little-boy voice*) OK. (*taking a breath, gathering himself*) All right.
THERAPIST	Yes. It's a pain way down deep.
CLIENT	Uh-huh.
THERAPIST	Yeah. Let's go there together. You have somebody with you.
CLIENT	(*crying deeply*)
THERAPIST	You're not alone, though. We're together. Let's look at this pain. Let's go there together.
CLIENT	(*muttering, crying*)
THERAPIST	It's really painful. So painful. Yes. But you're not alone. I'm with you. Yes. Let it out. Just let it out.
CLIENT	(*crying*)
THERAPIST	Yes. Very deep, very painful.
CLIENT	Yeah.
THERAPIST	You're not alone this time. Go ahead. I'm right there with you. All right. Tell me what you're feeling now.
CLIENT	I've just been abandoned.
THERAPIST	Abandoned?
CLIENT	Yeah.
THERAPIST	You felt that abandonment, didn't you?

[Therapist makes the mistake of speaking in the past rather than keeping the immediacy of the present response – perhaps a defense against some momentary empathetic discomfort.]

CLIENT	Uh-huh.
THERAPIST	It must have been terrible.
CLIENT	It was bad. (*gasping*) It took my breath away.
THERAPIST	(*softly*) It just took your breath away, didn't it?
CLIENT	Uh-huh. It took my breath away.
THERAPIST	Go ahead, catch your breath. That was deep. That was really deep.
CLIENT	I don't know if I've ever moaned and wailed so hard.
THERAPIST	I don't think I've ever heard you moan and cry so hard.

[As is commonly seen in grief work, the client needs to "catch his breath," that is, recoup, take a break. Rather than plunge directly into deep grief, most clients need to "level off" to catch their bearings before they move to a deeper level.]

CLIENT	I'm a little dizzy. (*laughs*)
THERAPIST	Feel a little light-headed from the experience, huh?
CLIENT	Uh-huh. Yeah, I got all numb, you know when you over-breathe. Got all tingly and everything.
THERAPIST	(*with concern*) Almost faintlike, huh?
CLIENT	Uh-huh.
THERAPIST	The emotion coming out of the whole experience. Yes. Do you think you can talk about it now?
CLIENT	I think so. I'm tired. I've caught my breath.
THERAPIST	You were feeling abandonment, you said. What are you feeling now?
CLIENT	Now I'm numb.
THERAPIST	You're feeling numb?
CLIENT	Uh-huh, mainly just numb and tired. But starting to feel anxious though.
THERAPIST	You're starting to feel some anxiety now...
CLIENT	Uh-huh. Because it makes me nervous to feel that sad.

[Therapist now shifts to making meaning of the grief experience.]

THERAPIST	Yeah. Besides, the feeling is so powerful, so deep and so strong.
CLIENT	Very, very strong. It kind of took over. Like it was one big wail.

[Therapist moves to double loop.]

THERAPIST	Did it help to have someone with you?
CLIENT	Yeah. I don't think I could have gone there without you. When you said, "I'm right here," I was able to moan and wail.
THERAPIST	It felt like I was right there with you.
CLIENT	It felt like you were there and you were comforting me.

THERAPIST   (*gently*) That's what you always wanted, isn't it? Someone to be there in that deep, abandoned kind of hell?

CLIENT   Yeah. That dark hole. It's cold and all alone. And just felt so…I don't know…coming from the bottom of my gut. It's low and felt so sad. Overwhelmingly sad. Overwhelmingly abandoned. That it was just so strong, so intense. (*reflective pause*) Yeah, very, very intense.

THERAPIST   It's the place that you've tried to stay away from and tried to gloss over, isn't it?

CLIENT   Uh-huh. Tried to avoid the pain and look for the comfort. Never go to the pain – it was *never* a place where I could go or wanted to go.

THERAPIST   Right.

CLIENT   I've avoided it.

THERAPIST   When this feeling starts to come up, you have to do anything you can to just make it go away.

CLIENT   Right.

THERAPIST   Yeah.

CLIENT   I'd change the subject…

THERAPIST   Fantasy.

CLIENT   Fantasy, yeah.

THERAPIST   Something to anesthetize yourself, distract yourself, make it go away.

CLIENT   Make that awful pain just go away. I don't want to go there.

THERAPIST   So, in many respects this pain has controlled you.

CLIENT   Yeah. I'd say so, pretty strong. You have to do everything to avoid it. You have to organize everything just not to face it.

THERAPIST   Absolutely. It's all about that abandonment. *Nobody wants me. I'm all alone. What am I going to do? What's wrong with me?*

CLIENT   *What's wrong with me?*…Yes, and *How come I'm unwanted?*

THERAPIST   Yeah. It's being back there in that crib in the middle of the night.

CLIENT   Uh-huh. *What's the matter with me? How come nobody wants*

me? Yeah. I'm screaming. All the horrible moaning, screaming at the top of my lungs. Everything in my little body
moaning. *What's wrong with me?*

THERAPIST   And nobody came?...

CLIENT   Nobody came.

THERAPIST   Nobody came to comfort you.

CLIENT   No. I hurt too much. I'm in a lot of pain. There's just so much
"black." I felt that black... everything was black. There wasn't
any light. It was all black.

THERAPIST   Yes. It was a black world for that little boy.

CLIENT   It was just terrible. It was just awful. I couldn't even catch
my breath. As a little one, I couldn't catch my breath, just
moaning so hard.

THERAPIST   Yeah.

CLIENT   Not so sure if you're going to pass out. Too much.

THERAPIST   Yeah. All you want is... what?

CLIENT   To be loved.

THERAPIST   Yeah.

CLIENT   I'd like to be covered by love – wanted and loved. I want to
be wanted and loved when I'm feeling all alone.

THERAPIST   You wanted to be able to sit in a room and feel not all alone
and sad...

CLIENT   Exactly.

THERAPIST   But all secure.

CLIENT   Secure and warm and comfortable and tight. When you're
squeezed, you feel tight. I don't know. It gives you comfort...
when you feel all comfy and all that stuff, you know?

THERAPIST   Snug as a bug in a rug.

CLIENT   Yep.

THERAPIST   Yeah, that's exactly it. That's what you want to feel. When
you sit in your hurt now, today, that's what you want to feel.
Not the anxiety and the dread that something's coming over
you and you don't know what it is, not the sadness – but
this time, to feel loved and secure and snug.

CLIENT   Right. Yeah. That's what I want.

THERAPIST   (*gently*) Right. Are you still feeling some of it now as we talk?

CLIENT   Uh-huh. Still that kind of need for comfort, but I'm starting to relax, not so anxious now.

THERAPIST   Right. You're not alone. Did you feel it with anybody else? Did you ever get the feeling of being snug and secure and loved?

CLIENT   Yeah, once in a rare while with my dad... that is, when I could talk to my dad. And I sometimes feel it when I talk to Steve and Jack, and with Jim [his straight friends]... the people that I love.

THERAPIST   How are you feeling now?

CLIENT   I feel pretty good actually. A lot better. I feel tired.

THERAPIST   Well, I'm not surprised you feel tired. You had an emotional workout. Emotional calisthenics. (*smiling*)

CLIENT   It feels like I just ran a mile. I feel a lot better.

THERAPIST   Good.

CLIENT   (*nodding*) I feel a lot more confident. When I feel those feelings, I can face them and it's not so horrible. I've gone and just *faced it* – I've been there and come back – *I've survived*.

Alone and Abandoned

Variations on the primordial image of the "Boy in the Black Room" have been described by various clients:

- "My heart is in a cage, there are spikes all around the cage, with big nails sticking into my bleeding heart."

- "I'm on this desert island – flat, barren and lifeless. No one's there and I'm alone and stuck with nowhere to go. It's been this way my whole life."

- "I'm on a lunar landscape, nothing all around. It's not Earth, but a different planet, a Never-Never Land."

- "I'm hit with smothering waves of oppression, and my insides are empty and hollow."

The images collectively reported by our clients capture the vast sense of emptiness they almost universally feel at a deep core level. One client reported a repetitive dream he had over many years in childhood: "I had this dream where I'm floating through space, through eternity. Alone, there's no God, no nothing." These dreams are metaphorical images of a deeply felt, childhood sense of abandonment.

Consider the following man's experience:

I want to tell you about this dream. I had just moved into a new house and it was getting dark. I was the only one; it was only me – no furniture, no pictures, nothing but me in the house. I started getting scared.

I wanted to talk to somebody, so I tried calling my parents on the phone. When I dialed, Dad picked up at the other end, but all he said was, "Here, talk to your mom," as he always does. So she got on the phone, but she said the same thing, "I can't talk now."

I said, "No, you've got to – I'm really scared. I need somebody." She got pissed off and said, "I can't, I haven't got time," and hung up.

I was frantic and scared and lonely with nowhere to go and no one to go to. And it was a big, dark house and I was standing in the middle of this big empty room with no furniture. That was the end of the dream.

When I think back on that dream, I recall what little self-worth I had as a kid, how hard I worked for acceptance. I can picture a little boy, all alone in a crib with his arms held high and stretched upward, but empty, crying out, "Aaah!" Nobody there to hear him...never a hand reached down.

This man's "Big Black Room" is his boyhood closet:

As a kid, I had a recurrent nightmare: I used to pray I wouldn't have it again. The dream was that I was standing at the door of the closet in my room, and I'd be pulled in and grabbed by the hanging clothes and shoes and everything.... They were sucking me into some all-consuming, black unknown.

In another dream, I can see myself sitting alone in the dark corner of my basement. Little, afraid and on the floor.

That was a very sad little boy inside there [pointing a finger to his chest].

Grieving the Father

I keep hoping that someday, Dad will love me the way I've always needed him to.

The lost father-son relationship is inevitably a source of excruciating pain to men who struggle with same-sex attraction. An articulate young man shared a powerful childhood memory as he worked through the process of grieving his father.

It must have been late afternoon, about the time Mom would call me and my brothers for dinner. It was hot, which explains why I was wearing just my T-shirt and shorts. Playing in a neighbor's yard, I did not respond as promptly as I should have. Perhaps her anxiety over my lack of immediate response fueled Dad's fire.

A few minutes after our failed appearance for dinner, this man – it was Dad – appeared at the far end of the block, in a white T-shirt and holding a long stick. His eyeballs were bulging and ugly purple veins were popping out of his temples. His face was red with anger, and his desire to inflict punishment was all I saw. I was frozen with fear. I can remember not moving – only to begin to run when that big stick hit me on the back. I was running as fast as my little legs could, but with each step feeling the whack of that stick on my back and butt. I am sure that I cried loud and hard as I was chased all the way back home.

I hurriedly entered the house. I remember just being in a panic. I was frightened and confused and panic-stricken. My dad's screaming seemed to be nonstop. I tried to find refuge in my mom, who was not prepared for what was about to take place.

Throwing me down into my seat at the kitchen table, he took a large mouthful of food and then began to scream. He screamed and screamed and screamed. I remember not crying, not even moving. It hurt too much anyway from all of the beatings with the stick. With his mouth full of food, he garbled on about how bad I was, and then finally he picked up his plate of food and threw it back on the table top and screamed at my mom; "You can just dump that food in the trash!" Then he left. I do not know where he went or what he did. Neither did I care.

I remember the dead silence after he left the room. My mom sat there apparently as stunned as I was. After a while she got up and washed off my cuts and bruises and tried to comfort me. I do not remember crying. But I do remember at that moment, turning myself completely off.

In fact, as I think of it, that day was the beginning of my feelings of worthlessness. That day taught me that I could be hated by someone, and that I was a burden.

My father hated to be bothered by anything he had to do for us or with us. Nothing was done with genuine caring, but with a visible burden of obligation. I just wondered why I even existed. Every interaction with him reminded me of how I was an imposition on his time and his composure. He'd spend all evening drinking and sitting in front of the television.

I think that day was the day that I decided not to give him any kind of satisfaction, especially around his precious TV. F—k his lousy television!

I felt unwanted, frightened and that I shouldn't even exist. *I am a burden, I am worthless, and I am unlovable.*

I felt that somehow, since I evoked all of this anger in this man, maybe I wasn't supposed to exist... maybe I *was* really a great problem, since my needs caused such a negative reaction. Maybe I *was* damaged to begin with. Looking back, I can see clearly why I detached from him.

How much I wished that I was wanted – *that I was a joy to somebody*, that I was safe, that I was worthwhile, that I was welcomed into life.

As I reflect on that, I remember feeling like it was never safe to tell anyone about those feelings. It also occurred to me that Mom and my brothers were no more safe with Dad than I was. And we could not even talk about it among ourselves.

I believe the source of my problems today can be traced back to how I felt like a burden – an unwanted, useless, time-consuming burden.

Here, another forty-year-old man begins with his fantasy of being held by a strong man. With little direction from the therapist, his free associations lead him back to earlier rejection from his father and brothers. He talks about the deep need that still remains to be held and protected by another man.

CLIENT	I'm being held by a strong, good-looking guy.
THERAPIST	Stay with that image.
CLIENT	Feels real good, that feeling wanted; there's a warmth that comes from being touched. There's a peace inside.
THERAPIST	OK. Stay with those warm feelings.
CLIENT	I feel satisfied, calm, secure … "captured" … there's a transfusion of love.
THERAPIST	(*nods*) Yes. You're feeling "captured," held …
CLIENT	When this guy holds me, I'm secure as a person … worthy … (*frowns thoughtfully*) But then, those other feelings come. Feeling not appreciated by Dad … rejection … not part of the team with my brothers and Dad … "at odds" … always the loner.
THERAPIST	What are you feeling as you say this?
CLIENT	(*considers*) Heaviness in my heart, deep disappointment, disconnection … a trauma, a pressure in my chest … and shame – I can't measure up.
THERAPIST	Disappointed, shamed …
CLIENT	I'm a failure in the eyes of Dad and my brothers. There's the hurt of rejection, of the loss. And there's betrayal. This is not the way it's supposed to be, and it's ripping my guts apart.
THERAPIST	Yes. It's not supposed to be like that.
CLIENT	(*nods, long pause*) And all the time this is happening to me, I'm losing my soul – just losing my innocence.

"Recoiling" from Masculinity

A middle-aged man described how he had just returned disappointed from a trip with his father. He had hopes of connecting with him on deeper level, but now he faces the sad reality of his father's apparently insurmountable emotional limitations:

> It just makes me very sad. I tried to put things out to him, but nothing seemed to resonate. He doesn't respond. He wants me to do well, wants the best for me – but he doesn't take the next step to really care, to actually enter my life. I think he always had the ability, but just didn't choose to be involved. He simply chose not to be there.

Clearly my life could have been easier . . . because his not being there for me kept me away from a big part of myself.

Because of that I have moved away; I've "recoiled" from the part of me that would have come to me from my father, and I fall back into the fantasyland which prevents me from being an adult man.

I still haven't made peace with his choice to not be a part of my life . . . It torments me, keeps me unsettled. A man forty years old and I shouldn't be spending so much time in that fantasyland – wasting time, going into avoidance, just chasing my tail.

I know I was ripped off and deprived of something critical to me. My attitude used to be, *Why do I want to grieve? I'm OK; it's no big deal!* But there's anger and sorrow. It's made my life very hard. If he hadn't pulled away from me, I know my life would have been a very different one.

Will, a twenty-year-old college student, expressed his resentment about his father's not having corrected his effeminate ways, such as his childhood preference for playing with the girls. "Dad," he told his father in a recent phone call, "you had your friends – your own father and brothers and activities. I had none of that. You had no interest in my being masculine. If I had a son, I know I'd push him toward the boy toys. I'd encourage him to have a typical boy's life. But you just dropped me on Mom."

Will told his father he hoped for a closer relationship. As they parted, his father promised to try to understand Will's struggle with same-sex attraction. Will also began to hope that his father would now finally become engaged in his life.

Six long weeks passed before he finally called Will back.

"I'm sorry I took so long to get back to you about what you told me about your problems," he said. "As for your childhood, I had to consult with your mother. She saw some signs when you were a child, but I never noticed your effeminacy. We just don't remember your being so different. None of this really quite added up."

After that phone call, Will told me, "I started second-guessing myself. Maybe I was just blaming him for my problems. But in reality, the hope I had, just a few weeks ago, once again turns to disappointment. I am ashamed of him. He's confusing; I can't relate to him or figure him out.

"The words that come to mind to describe my feelings for him are 'disdain, anger, repulsion, sadness.' Mostly, I see him as weak. Why doesn't my struggle matter to him?"

Grieving the Father Wound

In the following transcript, another client, Jim, also grieves the inadequate relationship with his father. He has decided to surrender his lifelong illusion that someday, somehow, he will at last receive his father's affirmation.

Jim begins our session by expressing feelings of intense ambivalence after receiving a lunch invitation from his father. His feelings for his dad lead to fear, then sadness and finally to grief.

CLIENT	My father called and wants to get together for lunch. I hate to keep saying no. I feel guilty about this, but I really don't want to go.
THERAPIST	So, what's the feeling?
CLIENT	It's like ambivalence in a way.
THERAPIST	Under ambivalence there is a feeling. Stay with that.
CLIENT	Fear. There's a total fear under that.
THERAPIST	Can you feel the fear?
CLIENT	Yes.
THERAPIST	How does the fear feel?
CLIENT	Well it's a nervous thing.
THERAPIST	Where do you feel it?
CLIENT	I can feel it right now talking about it.
THERAPIST	Yeah, but where?
CLIENT	My whole body. It's making me upset to talk about it ... Like in my chest; just kind of a shakiness inside my body.
THERAPIST	Can you stay with that feeling in your chest? Where in your chest do you feel the fear? Can you show me where?
CLIENT	(*touches center of chest*) Yeah. It's here – right in my heart.
THERAPIST	Yes, go to that feeling, focus on that. Tell me what that feeling in the center of your heart feels like.
CLIENT	(*long pause*) It's incredibly sad.
THERAPIST	Can you stay with that "incredibly sad"?
CLIENT	(*long pause*) It's an overwhelming feeling. Every time I think about him ...

THERAPIST   (*interrupting*) Right now, just try to dwell in the overwhelming feeling of sadness. Can you allow yourself to feel the overwhelming feeling of sadness?

CLIENT   (*silent*)

THERAPIST   Stay there, Jim. (*softly, patiently*) Speak to me from that place if you can.

CLIENT   (*silent*)

THERAPIST   (*gently*) You feel it in your body, don't you? Where do you feel it?

CLIENT   Yeah, I kind of feel it in my eyes, my heart.

THERAPIST   What is it that you feel in your eyes?

CLIENT   It just tenses up in my eyes. But the sadness, it's mainly in my heart. The heart and soul of me. Because even though he's nice to me now, I just don't trust him, because all it takes is one big blowup at me, and then I'm devastated again.

THERAPIST   What does that hurt – that devastation – feel like?

CLIENT   A horrible, burning feeling.

THERAPIST   (*returns the client to the experience in his body*) Is that the feeling you're feeling now?

CLIENT   Yeah. Kind of feeling of worthlessness, nowhere to go. Nowhere to run. Not being good enough... inferiority.

THERAPIST   (*gently, reassuringly*) That hurts, doesn't it?

CLIENT   It does. My whole being is just destroyed... That feeling of worthlessness has been my whole world.

THERAPIST   You're feeling it pretty fully now, aren't you? It doesn't take much for you to go right there, does it?

CLIENT   No.

THERAPIST   Jim, stay with the feeling. "Nowhere to run," that "inferiority, my whole being is destroyed"... What do you feel in your body when you hear your own words?

CLIENT   It's kind of like entering the core of my being, and it's all black there.

THERAPIST   And what's the feeling at the core of your being? What do you feel right now?

CLIENT   Worthless...

THERAPIST	Worthless.
CLIENT	As a man...the masculinity thing. That's what was so destroyed...my feeling about myself as a man.
THERAPIST	Do you feel like you're feeling it fully, or is there a little deeper you can go? Deeper into the sadness, deeper into the grief?
CLIENT	I just want to run away from it.
THERAPIST	I know you want to run away from it. Just stay there for a while.
CLIENT	OK.
THERAPIST	Can you go back to that "feeling worthless" you spoke about? (*gently*) Go to that feeling. Can you tell me what "worthless" feels like to you in your body, right now?
CLIENT	Humiliation. Total humiliation. Lack of love.
THERAPIST	You're feeling lack of love right now?
CLIENT	Yes...from my father.
THERAPIST	A lack of love from your father. OK. Do you feel the lack of love right now from your father?
CLIENT	(*heavy sigh*) Yeah. I do.
THERAPIST	What does it feel like, his not loving you?
CLIENT	It feels like everything has been taken away from me...It's the feeling that I'm absolutely nothing.
THERAPIST	How does your body feel?
CLIENT	Really tired. Very sad.

[Client seems on the brink of tears.]

THERAPIST	(*quietly*) Is there a desire to cry? To release those feelings?
CLIENT	There is.
THERAPIST	Can you allow yourself to go into that?
CLIENT	If I think about what he's said to me and what he has called me, I can get sadder and sadder. He used to call me sissy, faggot. He used to say these things to me in front of my brothers. How can you do that to a kid, your own son? But I was taught *not* to be sad (*describes the double bind*) so now, it's hard for me to take those feelings seriously.

[Therapist identifies the double bind and then quickly returns the client to sadness.]

THERAPIST   You were told not to be sad. But we don't need to do that now. What if you were to go ahead and release that stress, what would happen?

CLIENT   I just don't know how to get there. I always prefer to cry alone.

THERAPIST   Try not to back away. Trust in the sadness and try, however you can, to express it to me. Let me in on whatever you're feeling inside right now.

CLIENT   I'm feeling like a loser... pathetic.

THERAPIST   You're labeling yourself. That's a self-putdown. That's how you move away from the sadness; you tell yourself, *I'm such a loser. I'm so pathetic.* You step out of your sadness and go into critically evaluating yourself for having those feelings. You don't need to keep doing that now.

CLIENT   (*sighs*) This feeling just overwhelms me.

THERAPIST   Shall we sit together in the silence of what that feels like – that feeling of "being overwhelmed"?

CLIENT   It's like a dam inside me that wants so much to break.

THERAPIST   Exactly... like a dam inside of you.

CLIENT   Like a dam in my heart.

THERAPIST   Your heart... that's right. You need to respect that. To respect the grief.

CLIENT   (*long pause, begins to sob*)

THERAPIST   Yes, it's OK. It's OK.

CLIENT   (*fully sobbing*)

THERAPIST   I'm with you, it's all right. Just honor that heart feeling. We're going through this together.

CLIENT   God, it's so huge. It hurts. It really hurts.

THERAPIST   It's huge. It's painful. You feel your grief now.

CLIENT   God... It's like drowning.

THERAPIST   Drowning in grief. Absolutely. OK... OK.

In later sessions, Jim began to find resolution of his grief through a realistic acceptance of his father's emotional limitations.

Exploring Sadness, Anger and Longing

A married man, Bob, vacillates back and forth between sadness, longing and anger as he works through his father issues. This session is an example of the exploration of ambivalent feelings.

CLIENT	When I think about my relationship with my father, it just hurts.
THERAPIST	Where in your body do you feel the hurt?
CLIENT	(*considers*) In my heart.
THERAPIST	Can you allow yourself to feel the hurt in your heart – right in the center of your chest?
CLIENT	Yes. It's like arrows into my heart from what he did to me.
THERAPIST	Stay with that and let's see where that feeling takes you. Focus on that feeling and see where that goes.
CLIENT	OK. (*takes a deep breath*) He made me feel like I was an embarrassment to him. That was the pervasive feeling: "My son is an embarrassment." He was always ashamed of me. As a kid, I was so paranoid that I was going to make the wrong move or say the wrong thing. I'd think, *But what have I done to embarrass him? I just don't understand.*
THERAPIST	(*nods*) OK. Let's stay with that. What's the feeling you feel for your father right now?
CLIENT	It's still a hurt feeling...
THERAPIST	Is it just in your heart, or does it feel like it's in other parts of your body?
CLIENT	When I talk about it, my face tenses up, my eyes tense up, I get kind of uptight.
THERAPIST	"Uptight" is a fear of the feeling.
CLIENT	Yeah, there's a fear of the feeling. It's scary for me to start thinking about it.
THERAPIST	It's scary for you to start *feeling* it.
CLIENT	To feel it, yes. Even more so.

THERAPIST	What do you want to do with your father? Do you just want to just "kiss him off" forever? Or do you hope to have some relationship? Do you want to communicate with him?
CLIENT	(*with some feeling*) I want a relationship with him.
THERAPIST	You want to tell him about yourself, about your feelings, about your pain, and what you've gone through.
CLIENT	Yes. But when I start thinking in that direction, I get all bent out of shape. I would be too scared to do that with him at this point.
THERAPIST	You don't think he would understand you?
CLIENT	I don't know how he'd react. I'm scared that he would shame me, even now, today. There's still that element of fear there. If he shamed me again, it's like a reservoir would break, and I would cry and never stop.
THERAPIST	Do you love your father? Is there a love for him?
CLIENT	Yes, I do.
THERAPIST	Can you feel it?
CLIENT	(*thoughtfully*) Yes. I can.
THERAPIST	What's it feel like? Tell me about your feeling of love for your father.
CLIENT	It's a mixed emotion. I see him struggle with his own issues, and I know he maybe *wants* to do right, but doesn't know how. I don't know. (*shrugs shoulders helplessly*)
THERAPIST	Can you go inside yourself right now and find that feeling for your father now? What does it feel like?
CLIENT	I don't enjoy doing it.
THERAPIST	But you can feel it, right?
CLIENT	I can feel it.
THERAPIST	What does it feel like in your body?
CLIENT	It's real distant. It's like I want to approach that love for him, yet on another level, I don't – I really want to stay away. I guess I want to love him, but it's a struggle.
THERAPIST	Do you think that you'll ever get what you want from your father?
CLIENT	The closest I've ever been to him was when Mom died, a

few years back. I think that's the only time I've hugged him for two whole seconds. Because he was just a mess. I think that's the best connection I've had with him ever. Two seconds! He finally was vulnerable because he was crying. He had his defenses down. He's usually such an *a—hole* – I'm sorry. But seeing him like that was refreshing; he was finally being real.

THERAPIST Can you come to terms with the fact that you may never get what you want from your father?

CLIENT That's where the sadness is.

THERAPIST That's where the grief is. You tolerated his neglect with the hope that he might someday turn around.

CLIENT As a kid I guess I hoped that one day he'd see the truth; he'd realize what he'd done to me.

THERAPIST Every child has to hold on to that hope. Now the hard part is to be willing, if necessary, to let go of that dream. It's a very hard thing to do. That's where the real sadness comes from.

CLIENT Yeah. That is hard. There's something in my heart that just springs out to have that relationship, even though it was so incredibly painful. It seems like my hopes can't ever be filled, yet there's still this screaming, aching heart that says, *How I want my father's love!* But I can't figure out what I have to do to get it. It's hard to imagine living without it forever. Doing without it gives me a real, physical pain.

THERAPIST You feel it right now...

CLIENT I do.

THERAPIST Where do you feel it?

CLIENT In my eyes...

THERAPIST Sure you do.

CLIENT ...and in my heart.

THERAPIST Yes, that's the hard reality. You say that you never did feel his love. What you did have, though, was your hope. Now, you think you may have to give it up, and that's very hard...It's despair. But there's life on the other side. It's not going to kill you. Letting go of that hope, if you must, will free you to recognize that there are men in your life who can give it to you – who can still affirm you, be in relationship with you.

CLIENT   I think I've let go of that hope about my dad, very slowly, over the years, without actually realizing it.

THERAPIST   Now you're really taking in the actual loss of your father, and it makes you feel very alone. You may get this connection from other men; you may develop your own resources within yourself – but from him, your dad, you're pretty convinced it's not going to happen.

CLIENT   (*sadly*) Yes.

THERAPIST   What do you feel in your body right now?

CLIENT   I'm still thinking, *But what am I doing wrong? What can I do to get my dad to like me? I gotta try something else. There's something wrong with me.*

[Client goes to a discussion of ideas, and therapist permits him, perhaps hoping it will lead back to his feelings.]

CLIENT   I got the same thing from the other boys at school. I have memories of crying so hard, I would go out in the backyard, look at the stars and hold my dog and cry and cry, cause I couldn't share this with anybody. There wasn't anybody who would understand me.

THERAPIST   What are the feelings now?

CLIENT   Anxious, pins and needles – all over.

THERAPIST   Stay with that.

CLIENT   Tightness in my chest...

THERAPIST   (*encouragingly*) Stay with that.

CLIENT   A sinking tension in the back and shoulders, there's like a shield...freezing up. I'm thinking, *Here it is, his love... right in front of me, and I could take in – if I just knew how!* OK; there's also some anger.

THERAPIST   Where?

CLIENT   Shoulder – I have the energy to push him away. (*pause*)

I'm tense and ready for that. There's anger because I was
humiliated by him, squashed and put down. I was a vehicle
for his entertainment.

During subsequent sessions that continued to explore his ambivalent
feelings, the client came to fully accept the sad reality that he must look
elsewhere for masculine connection and affirmation.

Reconnecting with the Self While Entering the Pain

Facing the loss of the loving father, and the fully felt realization that same-
sex longings have developed as a defense, is perhaps the most difficult
aspect of grief work.

Over time the client fully grieves the reality of his loss while staying in
emotional contact with his therapist. He faces that reality in the presence
of a supportive man who accompanies him as he immerses himself in
the pain. Gradually, he reconnects to those parts of himself that he once
defensively renounced.

Discarding their illusions and distortions, many clients must face the
fact that a profound attachment loss has set into motion a life of unfulfilled
longings and frustrated dreams.

CHAPTER 21

Defenses Against Grief

This "morphine of the soul" [sex with men] can kill a person if taken in too
large a dose. Oh, it suppresses it for a while, but then it rises up again and
deceives the mind with even more illusions…
I lived with these illusions for twenty years – that time
of shame when I began this "voluntary death."

Grief work will inevitably encounter two powerful defenses – illusions
and distortions. We will now take a closer look at those defenses and the
ways in which the therapist can assist the client in overcoming them.

False Positives and False Negatives

Illusions are narcissistically based false-positive ideas. An example of a
typical illusion is "I'm looking for a woman who is very beautiful, sensitive
to my needs and will completely understand me. Only when I find such a
woman will I consider myself ready to get married."

Distortions, on the other hand, are false-negative shame-based ideas.
They emerge from the damaged self, and they lead to self-defeating, self-
destructive and maladaptive behaviors. An example of a distortion is, "No
girl would ever want me if she *really* knew me."

These illusions and distortions are perpetuated by the client in the present in order to protect himself from facing the painful losses of the past.

They distract him from accepting the reality that his life is not working, and they deflect his attention from the challenge to change.

Grief work inevitably evokes in the client the primal dread of discovering he actually is a nothing. *"I am unloved because I am unlovable"* is the most common, core negative belief that we uncover. Stripped of his illusions and distortions, the client feels as if he were left suspended without any sense at all of who he is: "But if I give up my false self, then who will I be?" "If I give up these illusions, I'm afraid I won't be good enough."

These are, of course, modes of self-protection that serve to deflect attention from psychic pain. In the context of same-sex attractions, they represent manifestations of unwillingness to do what the client himself recognizes would be in his own best interest.

Even when the man is sincerely and deeply committed to change, and determined never to go back to homosexual activity, usually *he still chooses*, consciously or unconsciously, to cling to his old narcissistic illusions and shame-based distortions.

Ways of Avoiding Grief

One culturally supported defense against grief, of course, is to resort to the solution of calling oneself gay. This usually results in a total denial of underlying losses and reparative motivations. As long as a man continues to cling to the fantasy that same-sex attractions and behavior will solve the ongoing crisis of his loneliness, his self-alienation and his deep feelings of emptiness, he perpetuates the painful losses of the past and is condemned to repeat them.

Defenses against engaging in grief work include denial, a sense of entitlement and overwhelming anxiety. For some clients the anxiety generated by their ongoing, present-day losses may already seem too much to bear. Such men prefer to smother themselves in shame-evoking distortions rather than confront their true, core-self losses, and thus move on with their lives. It seems easier to anesthetize themselves in the illusion that somehow "everything will eventually be OK," than apply a disciplined commitment to examine their attachment loss.

Should these illusions and distortions tracing to childhood trauma remain unexamined, a nagging emptiness will remain. As one man explained, "I'm very outgoing; I project a good image. But when I go home at night, I feel this eerie aloneness and apprehension."

The following sections of this chapter discuss some of the most frequently encountered illusions (false positive) used as defenses against grief work.

The Illusion of the "Good Enough" Family

Adult children of the narcissistic family system often enter therapy in denial of the depth of their familial dysfunction, and may only later admit that much in their family life went wrong. "I had a great family. They had nothing to do with any of my problems today." They often hold the illusion of having had a good enough, if not in fact a superior, home life. In contrast, clients from other pathological family types will more readily recognize the underlying dysfunction they survived.

Whatever their awareness of their family dynamics at the start of therapy, by the conclusion of grief work, clients are brought face-to-face with the full impact of whatever damage was wrought in their childhood. Children of the narcissistic family will eventually confront their illusion of having had the "too-perfect, too-respectable family" – and come to see that "It really *was* that bad." Their families looked normal, maybe even ideal, in the image they projected, but somehow, in some confusing and intangible way, they usually admit that "something about it just felt strange."

The contradictory messages they received about being loved, yet somehow emotionally used for one or both parents' needs were so confusing to sort out that it was easier to retreat into "Everything really was OK."

Or if they recognized that it wasn't OK, then "It must have been my own fault. I was the child that caused the problems. There was something wrong with me. I was too [sensitive, selfish, ungrateful, needy, etc.]."

The narcissistic family is described by Donaldson-Pressman and Pressman (1994) as follows: "Dad may have been a nine-to-five type, Mom a homemaker who baked cookies for the PTA. There were simply no problems.... The parents were home when the kids were home, the family ate dinner together six nights a week, and nobody over drank, did drugs, smoked, swore, or hit anybody. They were apple-pie normal" (pp. 22–23).

The child who grew up in such a family, which looked good on the outside but was somehow "rotten at the core," was never allowed to accurately attune to his own feelings and develop his own perception. In adulthood, sharing memories with a brother or sister often gives him a more objective view of the underlying dysfunction. Recalling childhood experiences is especially helpful if that sibling is in therapy too, and therefore is able to offer additional memories and further insight.

Many clients eventually come to resign themselves to their father's and mother's human limitations, and give up the need for them to be better than they were. But for some men, there may never be a genuine closeness. As one of our clients explained:

> My parents' way of operating was to give me a bare minimum of affirmation to keep me emotionally dependent. Therapy has allowed me to feel better about who I am and to rid myself of the codependency that my parents fostered. It has allowed me to finally establish boundaries and to insist on respect.
>
> Sadly, I don't feel very close to my parents today, but I don't regret this, because the previous closeness was unhealthy. It required that I sacrifice my true needs for their benefit.

The Illusion About What Homosexual Enactment Can Provide

Our clients typically report a lifelong emotional numbness. They claim that only sexual conquests with a variety of men offer an intense-enough excitement (however brief) to "bring them alive."

When they finally confront their fear of annihilation-abandonment, clients are able to stop their compulsive search for another man. They have learned that feeling their pain in the present, in the presence of a supportive and attuned man, offers a profound encounter with the past that alters their perception of gay relationships. From that experience there comes a growing openness to receive the masculine acceptance and affirmation they have always craved.

Confronting the losses in his life and his growing desire for real intimacy, one man confessed to me:

I am sad that things turned out this way for me. Even now, whenever I see a father and his little son, I feel I want to be that little boy. It's the same stab – a deep longing, yearning...so deep.

I'm sad for all the time I lost in my life – sad for who I was. I was weak, scared, negative, very critical of myself, envious of other guys, and lonely when others were having fun. I missed a lot of opportunities. I didn't live as I could have. When I talk about it now, I think, "What a tragic waste of time!"

What an illusion that I could solve all this with another guy.

A forty-five-year-old client also spoke of his own regrets about his years in the gay community:

Homosexuality has robbed me of life, and leaves me empty. The very thing that I use to soothe and distract and relieve the pain, actually keeps me in the pain.

Looking back, I can see that I hitched my wagon to the wrong star.

Compensating for the Losses

By attending to his body, this twenty-eight-year-old was able to distinguish between the illusion of homoerotic fulfillment, and the reality of a deep male friendship.

THERAPIST	What do you feel inside when you feel a homosexual attraction?
CLIENT	A surge in my chest – a leap, a charge like an electric shock in my upper chest, shooting up into my shoulders and arms.
THERAPIST	Can you now contrast those feelings with those moments of real friendship with guys – when you really feel genuine and affectionate?
CLIENT	Oh, yeah, that feels totally different. During those moments, I feel clear. My whole body, not just my chest but my whole body, feels open, free and lighter. I actually feel taller. My vision clears. When I'm into that kind of friendship, I feel calm and very real.

Another client described how therapy was helping him give up his illusions about what another man could give him:

> I'm learning to identify the essence of this thing [homosexuality]; I used to believe it was just about sex. But it's really about so much more. When I was young, this thing got into the middle of me and stayed there, and I made it the "blank, white paper" upon which the whole story of my life was written. Now I see the pain that has been in the background all my life; homosexuality is just a symptom of all the damage that pain had been causing me.

One man told of his twenty years of gay encounters, where sex with men had been his way of fleeing from the internal emptiness:

> It is perhaps the most difficult thing for me to do – to willingly confront my own anguish – because my instincts turn me sharply away from the pain and back toward my old painkillers. But this morphine of the soul can kill the person if taken in too large a dose.
>
> In reality, it's powerless to kill the pain. Oh, it suppresses it for a while, but then the pain rises up again and deceives the mind with even more illusions.
>
> I lived with these illusions over the course of twenty years – that time of shame when I began this voluntary death.

Giving Up the Illusion of Finding "That One Special Guy"

Part of the grief process must involve the client's abandonment of the narcissistic illusion that there's one man "somewhere out there, if only I can find him" who will meet all his emotional needs; a special man who holds the key to finally making him feel connected to himself. He has to let go of the image of the fantasy man who will be his best friend, childhood pal, spiritual guide, 24/7 therapist and mentor, hotline consultant, cuddle-buddy, and coach and – while totally masculine and straight-acting – still be willing to engage in gay sex.

Gradually, he comes to realize that he must abandon this illusion in order to experience the affirmation of true male friendships characterized by mutuality, dignity and equality.

In the following transcript, Greg confronts his rage that his friend Brad is failing to fulfill his narcissistically based illusions about what a man can offer him. As he does so, he identifies the relationship as a reenactment of his unsatisfying relationship with his father, that is, as a repetition compulsion.

CLIENT   I'm enraged that Brad doesn't show interest in me. I'm so F—king angry at him! I try not to be. Part of me knows that it's not his fault; I can't expect him to understand how much I need him; I have too-high expectations. I want to be more important in his life and I'm not. I'm obsessed with him; if he doesn't notice me when I walk into the office, I'm depressed all day – and angry at him. I know I have no right to be, but it's just so unfair... he means so much to me! I'd do anything to get him to like me more.

THERAPIST   (*nods*) Brad is very important to you.

CLIENT   Yes. But I'm so tired of obsessing over him, so I try to act disinterested, you know, unavailable – and he doesn't even notice! When I hear him on the phone talking to his buddies, planning the weekend, he's so animated! It drives me nuts with jealousy. He's just an eighteen-year-old kid. But he's so F—king into himself!

THERAPIST   And not into you.

CLIENT   I'm angry that I'm weak and needy. That I let myself get to such a desperate point. Because what I want from him has no basis in reality. We can have these wonderful conversations and the next morning it's obvious that I don't matter to him. It pisses me off!

THERAPIST   Makes you so angry at your neediness.

CLIENT   I'm also angry that, as important as he is to me, I don't let him really get to know me. I know I'm not fully disclosing myself to him. In fact (*moving to a deeper truth about himself*) I know it's not really about him – it's really about me.

THERAPIST   (*nods*)

CLIENT   I'm so scared; I don't want to lose him. I'm so hurt; I love him so much. I just want to be loved back! I don't want to be needy! And I'm scared I'm gonna mess it up by seeming so needy.

THERAPIST Can you feel the pain of accepting Brad as he is – accepting the limits of what he's willing to offer?

CLIENT I still don't want to give up the hope. I'm scared of going back to where I was. Back to watching some DVD at home alone on Saturday night. (*taking a deep breath*) It's painful to accept that I'm not gonna get him the way I want him. The way I need him.

THERAPIST Stay with that. What's that feeling?

CLIENT I feel abandoned.

[Here the therapist cannot resist the temptation to move away from body work and suggest an interpretation.]

THERAPIST You're trying to change him into someone he isn't, or at least someone he doesn't want to be for you.

CLIENT I keep hoping that I can get it – better, deeper – I don't know, closer. (*sadly*) I've tried to change him, but it hasn't worked.

THERAPIST It's the death of the illusion.

CLIENT (*nods sadly*)

THERAPIST You say you love him, but you try to refashion him. But all you can do in reality is invite him, rather than manipulate him.

CLIENT I know.

[Therapist returns to body work.]

THERAPIST OK. Let's go to some of these feelings for Brad.

CLIENT (*nods*) OK…

THERAPIST When you think of him now, how do you feel?

CLIENT (*with eyes closed, concentrating*) Love.

THERAPIST Love. OK. Stay with that.

CLIENT Anxious…

THERAPIST How does "anxious" feel? Where?

CLIENT	(*considers for a moment*) My stomach. A pain.
THERAPIST	A pain in your stomach. OK. Stay with that.
CLIENT	A tightness in my upper stomach, a gnawing. Like I've been punched there. All clenched in a knot.
THERAPIST	Where?
CLIENT	My sort-of chest area, pressing down, closed down, bound, constricted.
THERAPIST	Constricted. How does constricted feel?
CLIENT	Like I'm a failure. That it's my fault that he doesn't care about me.
THERAPIST	Stay with the body.
CLIENT	Unpleasant. Hopeless. Discouraged. Depleted. I'm just inadequate. There's nothing I can do or say to Brad. Everything I try doesn't work. I feel like a nothing.

[Therapist tries to shift attention from Brad back to his body.]

THERAPIST	How does that feel in your body, that "rejected"?
CLIENT	Rejected? Well, there's a heavy weight. He really doesn't love me.
THERAPIST	In your body…
CLIENT	Tight, compressed, depressed, hopeless.

[Therapist decides client has gone as deep into his feelings as he can, and shifts to second triangle.]

THERAPIST	Greg, try to go back to your body memories. Have you felt this depressed, rejected, hopeless feeling at another time?
CLIENT	(*nods, considers*)
THERAPIST	With anyone else?
CLIENT	Dad. I see myself in my playroom in the basement. I got it all fixed up…
THERAPIST	How old?
CLIENT	Um…Maybe eleven. I got the place all fixed up just the way I liked it. My tapes, my movie posters on the wall. It was *my* place. I felt so proud of it. He came down the stairs

and just ranted on and on about how I was hiding in the basement, avoiding the family, avoiding doing things and avoiding him. How I was selfish, didn't care about anybody else and was just a loser and a loner. He just belittled me, depreciated everything I had set up in the room. He took away all my happiness.

THERAPIST   So there's a felt connection between Brad and your Dad. How's that?

CLIENT   That same hurt...that same rejected, disinterested feeling. Making me a nothing. A nobody. Worthless. The same fear, that desperation.

THERAPIST   So your father had that same effect on you...

At this point the client began to come face-to-face with his illusion. Greg began to see that he was attempting to resolve his past conflict (with Dad) in the present (through another unavailable man, Brad). But before the therapist could fully connect the past to the current, Greg started to become defensive.

CLIENT   (*abruptly interrupting*) Right now I feel like I want to defend my father. (*slight laugh*) I know it's crazy but I wanna say "You're wrong about my dad."

THERAPIST   (*nodding seriously*) Sure. OK. Stay with it. Tell me how I've got it wrong.

CLIENT   (*in an angry, pleading tone*) I want to say, "Leave my dad out of this!" There's a part of me that wants to shout, "You don't know my dad! How can you suggest that any part of this goes back to him? I'm F—ked up. I'm a fag. I'm defective. All this has nothing to do with him. My dad was right! It's the truth! I'm a loser."

THERAPIST   (*listening, waiting*)

CLIENT   (*sadly, desperately*) I want you to fix me so that my father will love me, and then I won't be alone anymore. (*now speaks less forcefully*) I do this with other guys too, making excuses for them for moving away from me. "It must be my fault. It must be about me."

THERAPIST	You feel like you must have done something wrong to lose them...
CLIENT	(*verging on angry tears*) I don't want that experience to control my life. I know my father was a tyrant! A bully!

Now that the client's defensiveness has begun to falter, his intensive work goes more quickly. Most importantly, as he speaks, he can better feel and then express the many changes in his body as he begins to identify what they mean.

CLIENT	I feel anger now.
THERAPIST	Where do you feel it, Greg?
CLIENT	My chest.
THERAPIST	Who is this anger about?
CLIENT	About all the Brads in my life. (*pause*) And also about my dad....
THERAPIST	What's the feeling?
CLIENT	There's a tightness, and a fear.
THERAPIST	(*nods*) Let's just sit with that awhile.

[The client spends several minutes assessing his body shifts between anger and fear, as he reexperiences the feelings of rejection and attachment loss, and describes the body memories associated with those experiences. Then, there is a shift.]

CLIENT	Now I'm starting to feel more expansive... (*breathes deeply*)...In fact, I can tell the difference now as I speak. (*settles back in his chair*)
THERAPIST	(*nods*) How does that feel?
CLIENT	I feel open...relieved...relaxed (*pausing to attend again to his body*)
THERAPIST	(*nods with encouragement*) There's a relief there.
CLIENT	I'm feeling so much more free – I can even breathe more easily now. When I get scared, I get tight. Yes...this is so much better. I want to stay this way – stay open and expansive!

[The session continues to its conclusion.]

The False Self in Interactions with Women

When a man grew up living in the role of the good little boy for his mother, he usually continues to portray this same stereotyped image (in adulthood, we call it the false self of the "nice guy") to the outside world. The nice guy is characterized by a veneer of compliance and passivity, but it overlays deeply repressed hurts, and especially anger, which trace back to a deep resentment toward his mother for putting him into this false role. His role as the good little boy fulfills his need to feel special, as well as his mother's own need to feel the same. Meanwhile, on the inside, the man who spends his life stuck in this stereotyped self remains intensely confused about his real needs and true identity.

Jordan, a thirty-six-year-old architect, has been addressing his grief issues for the past three months. He begins the session.

CLIENT   (*looking away*) I've been feeling angry lately. I don't know what or whom I'm angry at. I'm angry that I'm not perfect. That I have to take responsibility like every other person. (*looking up at the therapist*) Why can't you fix it so that I don't have to take responsibility like every other person? I'm angry that I have to give up my (*searching for a word*) my pseudo-solutions.

THERAPIST   Your what?

CLIENT   My pseudo-solutions – that is, my shortcuts. The world does not reward me for pseudo-solutions.

THERAPIST   Such as?

CLIENT   Such as continuing to choose to manipulate others and never really living with integrity. I try "integrity" for a while, but never really live it boldly, consistently.

THERAPIST   Yes…

CLIENT   I take all this pride in being so likeable, a nice guy. I always gotta be a "really great guy." (*grins sarcastically*) I can't just be Jordan, but I've got to be "Jordan to be adored." In reality, I just want to be another man among men, not this "great guy" among men. But I'll make the simplest little mistake, and then I feel this deep anger toward myself, and beat myself up. I beat myself up like my dad did to me. I realize my father punished me for just being myself. He called me selfish; he always accused me of hurting him and other people in my family. But in beating myself up, I am doing again what he did to me. I am identifying with the aggressor, and I do not need to do that.

THERAPIST   Your anger at yourself is part of the process of letting go of the false self.

CLIENT   Yeah, sure, it's easy for you to say. And I resent you for knowing it.

THERAPIST   So, it's anger at me?

CLIENT   I want to get angry at you rather than sit in the exposure of it.

THERAPIST   (*nods*)

CLIENT   I'm pleasant, nice, loving, friendly, charming … But the fact is, I'm really not so nice. I resent people when they burden me with their problems and I have to appease them. (*long pause*) I fear the power of a woman to shame me. I'm scared to death that they'll take advantage of my shame … There is Vicky at work, the receptionist. I walk in to the office and I get into this "charming, friendly guy mode." And she talks to me about her life, and I listen attentively, smile, even though it's not like I really do give a s—t. She drains me; I cannot walk through the office past those women at the front desk as my true self – as just a regular guy. It's a habit; I can't *not* get into that false role. She showed me pictures of her trip to Hawaii for, like, ten minutes. Like I give a s—t. It's tiring, exhausting, and I resent her. Why do I do this?

THERAPIST   Why *do* you play that game?

CLIENT   I fear her disapproval. If I disappoint her expectations that I care about the little details of her life, then she will shame me. I remember being three or four years old. My mom was as insecure with my dad as I was. She needed to feel special, and I needed to feel special. We consoled each other. When I think back, the truth was that I hated my mom for putting me in the position of her protector and confidante.

THERAPIST   It was an unspoken understanding between the two of you.

CLIENT   Yeah, a mutual adoring relationship kept us protected from our shame; the shame that my father made us both feel about ourselves. I'm angry at my mother for doing that to me – making me so special – and at my having to make her feel special in return. (*long pause*) I just wanted to be her son, not her girlfriend...

THERAPIST   Yes. But both of you needed to feel special about yourselves.

CLIENT   (*nods*) I'm feeling really sad right now that my mom and I never really, honestly knew each other – we never really saw each other for who we were.

As demonstrated by Jordan's frustration and anger, we see how difficult it is to abandon the nice-guy persona. After all, this persona offered him a special relationship with his mother and defended him against the shame of feeling not really known and loved for who he was.

Common Distortions (False Negatives)

Some of the more commonly encountered distortions that manifest in grief work follow. All distortions serve to protect the client from shame and grief.

The distortion of helplessness.

> I am shameable, and therefore I can only establish shame-based relationships.

*   *   *

> Nobody should have to see my anger.

*   *   *

> I'll never be man enough to satisfy a woman, and I have only myself to blame.

Because of repeated double bind experiences in childhood, many clients are stuck in the perception that they must accept a no-win situation. This leads them into the distortions of helplessness and hopelessness. Helplessness is about their perceived inability to have any impact in relationships, while hopelessness is about life itself. Many men stay mired in this "helpless and hopeless" mode.

The following is an example of helplessness.

CLIENT   My mother really annoyed me last night.

THERAPIST   What happened?

CLIENT   She does this... this thing...

THERAPIST   (*waiting*)

CLIENT   OK... What happened was (*sounds exasperated*) I flew into the city where my mom lives. I had only a few hours' layover and I rarely see her. So we met for dinner, just for a quick visit. In the middle of the dinner her cell phone rings, and she leaves the table with me just sitting there – gone for twenty minutes! I mean, how disrespectful! I was furious. When she returns, I say to her – very politely (*slowly and deliberately*) – "Mother, did you need to be gone for so long?" She shoots back, "Who are you tonight, my date?" (*client stares at therapist blankly*)

THERAPIST   And you said?

CLIENT   I was speechless! (*pausing, reflecting*) I couldn't make a fuss about what she said. I would have upset her and ruined our dinner.

The distortion of hopelessness.

I can't make straight male friends. They'll never accept me.

*   *   *

This "being an adult" thing is a pain in the a—.

Internalizing the message of helplessness leads the client into a lifelong, vague but pervasive sense of hopelessness: "Why bother trying?"

Efforts such as expressing appropriate anger, or seeking help and understanding from others, are considered to be useless. He has come to believe that there is no way out. "What's the use? I've felt sad like this before, and trying to do something about it was a waste of time."

Or we hear, "When people meet me, I just assume they won't like me." And "I'll never be man enough for other guys to respect me."

Hopelessness is a shame-based judgment of the self when the person is mired in gray-zone affect. As the client works through it, he eventually strikes the foundation of his suffering, and here he reaches the low point at which grief work begins. Genuine, deep grief is reflected in the words of one shattered young man: "My pain is so deep, so profound, that no one can understand it; nobody can relate to it. My life script is that there's nobody who really cares about me."

The distortion of anger turned inward. Anger directed against the self is often a recapitulation of the double bind predicament. This predicament is, "If I fully feel and express my grief, I will upset my parents and suffer parental attachment loss; I will be ignored, punished or will feel their disapproval. On the other hand, if I ignore my grief and assume all the blame (i.e., directing the anger at myself) for displeasing my parents, I will be rewarded with their attention, and something that feels like love." The child has thus abdicated his authentic emotional life for a semblance of love and attention, but on his parents' terms.

Ultimately, anger at parents who emotionally abandoned him will be turned to anger against himself (i.e., "There must be something wrong with me for displeasing my parents"; "I must be unlovable"), which results, in adulthood, in an ongoing pattern of self-deprecation.

As the client first begins expressing his anger at a malattuned or negligent parent, the therapist remains vigilant for a shift into self-directed anger. This can be tricky because, at times, the self-anger may appear justified. For example, this thirty-two-year-old man, Sam, is angry with himself for impulsively going to a gay bar, picking up a stranger and taking him home to have sex.

CLIENT   (*shouting, leaning forward, face flushed*) I'm angry for doing something so stupid. After six months of sobriety, after two years of therapy, and after all that I know!

THERAPIST   Yeah…You are wondering, *After all that I know, why did I act out?*

CLIENT   Because it feels like I'll never get better, like it will always be with me. (*noticeable shift to sadness*) I'm stuck.

THERAPIST   What are you feeling now?

CLIENT   (*desperately frustrated*) Sad! (*eyes tearing*) No matter how
            hard I try...I can still end up doing something like this.

Later, Sam began to face the full reality of how utterly unfair and
difficult the struggle to overcome his homosexuality really was. This
realization could have provided a gateway for grief work, but during this
session, his way into productive grief was blocked by self-anger: Sam had
become stuck in the rut of blaming himself over and over for his fall into
homosexual enactment.

As a childhood victim of the double bind, Sam had (understandably)
blamed himself for the loss of parental attachment. The internalized
parental message was that feeling hurt or sad is unacceptable. The shaming accusation sounds something like, "Stop making a fuss," "Get over it,"
"You're looking for sympathy," "Big boys don't cry," "Quit feeling sorry for
yourself!" and "You're upsetting Mom/Dad/the family."

Because he had internalized the critical parent, Sam interpreted his
hurt feelings as mere self-indulgence. He was, in essence, saying, "Being
critical of myself is a way of stopping the grief at feeling misunderstood
and unloved." His anger is turned away from the others who hurt him and
directed instead against himself in the form of self-defeating behavior followed by continual self-reproach.

Grief work is often aborted by the client himself when he hears the
voice of the critical parent: *What am I doing? I'm not supposed to cry. I
shouldn't feel sorry for myself! I'm just being silly.*

Or, if the client doesn't feel any grief, he may criticize himself for
not feeling it. For example, although he describes a painful, lifelong gulf
between himself and his father, he may be unable to feel the pain of that
attachment loss: "Why can't I care about not having gotten my father's
love? What's wrong with me? I'm not doing this right." At times, the
blame is projected onto the therapist: "I can't do what you expect. I'm
failing in therapy."

Anger deflected into guilt.

When I did get angry at my mom, it broke her heart.

                                    – thirty-five-year-old client

The simplistic belief that anger is invariably "bad" represents a childhood lesson that was taught and is not easily eradicated. The following two examples illustrate the client's confusion about his right to acknowledge anger.

Jeff, a twenty-one-year-old architect, shows us the double bind that kept him from feeling anger at his parents. His parents were divorced, and during his childhood his father had been scheduled to pick him up every other weekend. "I waited for him at the window, but a lot of times he'd be very late or not show up at all. I would get mad, but still, I kept forgiving him."

Pushing past his defense of "having forgiven Dad," Jeff finally allowed his anger to lead to genuine grief:

THERAPIST   Why would you keep forgiving him if you were mad at him?

CLIENT   I just didn't want to say anything.

THERAPIST   Yes, but you *felt* the anger – even if you didn't express it.

CLIENT   Sure. I was afraid if I got mad, then he wouldn't come by at all. If I would complain to my mother, she would yell at him, and then he'd stay away altogether.

THERAPIST   So you really didn't "forgive" him, then – you just didn't express the anger.

CLIENT   Yeah... I suppose that's true.

This admission opens Jeff up to feel his sadness, which he finds to be in direct conflict with his false self as the compliant, cooperative son, and he suddenly develops a fear of feeling the sadness. He knows his father conveyed the message that he was unlovable, but Jeff refuses to feel the anger at the hurt:

CLIENT   Basically my entire life I have always felt rejected by my dad. It's always in the back of my mind. Why would he leave my mom and me? He couldn't be man enough to take care of his family, to be there when a little kid needed him. But then when I let myself feel the anger, I get mad at myself that I get upset.

THERAPIST   So you're telling yourself you don't have a right to be upset. Where did that come from?

CLIENT   I guess I anticipate people not really caring about my anger. And anyway (*a sudden divergence*) I'm feeling guilty – I picked up a guy for sex last night, so it doesn't give me the right to get angry at my parents, because, after all, look what I'm doing with my life.

THERAPIST   (*a bit confused*) So you're saying that because of what you did last night, you don't have a right to your anger?

CLIENT   Every time I got upset, my dad got angry. Then he wouldn't come around any more. So I had to act happy for him. To keep him coming around.

THERAPIST   What do you mean, he got "upset"?

CLIENT   He got angry at me, and then I felt guilty.

THERAPIST   And now, your "payoff" for being such a compliant son is to become depressed and to pull away from your authentic feelings…

[Client seems shut down (dissociated) and remains silent. Therapist decides to keep the pressure on.]

THERAPIST   But you're here now – what are you going to do about it? Do you want to bring your father's voice into this room today?

CLIENT   (*in a flat voice*) I don't know. It doesn't matter. If I get mad or not, it doesn't make any difference. (*using the defense of helplessness*)

THERAPIST   What do you want to do about it? (*gently*) There's got to be some anger there.

CLIENT   Not really.

THERAPIST   You don't feel anger? What do you feel instead?

CLIENT   Tired.

THERAPIST   OK. Tired of what?

CLIENT   Nothing.

THERAPIST   I don't think you're tired of nothing. You're tired of not allowing yourself to live. It takes effort to shut yourself off from life. From relationships. From living.

CLIENT   What "living"?

THERAPIST   Yeah, what living? Do you want to continue to live your life like this?

CLIENT   (*defiantly*) Yeah, yeah I do!

THERAPIST   So now you're getting angry at me...

CLIENT   (*silence*)

THERAPIST   That's OK to feel angry at me. *Feel the anger.* Stay with it.

CLIENT   (*crying*) It's so hard. (*long pause, sobbing*) It's not like he just out-and-out abandoned me. It would have been easier for me to deal with him if that were true...

THERAPIST   So in some ways, you had the hope of a relationship.

CLIENT   Really, what I feel most of all is resentment. It feels unfair. Why should I have had all this happen? I'm angry that I have to deal with all this and that I'm in this situation.

Sadness for the Other

Besides anger at the self as a defense against appropriate – and grief-inducing – anger at the other, we also see sadness (pity) for the other as a defense against feeling sadness for the self.

When twenty-two-year-old Allan returned from a visit to his parents, whom he had gone to see with the goal "to connect with Dad," he reported that things did not go well. Here, we see how the father's nonresponse evoked Allan's anger toward himself as well as sadness for the father. When this was pursued further, Allan eventually saw that this sadness was really for himself.

CLIENT   I thought we'd have this chance to talk on the drive back to the airport. I tried to get him to open up, talk about real stuff. I didn't get far.

THERAPIST   How did that feel?

CLIENT   When I ask my father for something and he doesn't give it, I feel angry. But then I feel like I wanted something from him that he *couldn't* give, that he didn't *have* to give.

THERAPIST   What was that like?

CLIENT   Disappointing. I felt I was wrong – like I was asking too much of him. Like I was some self-righteous prick.

[The client is defending against the loss by blaming himself. The therapist confronts the defense directly.]

THERAPIST Let's go back to what you said, "When my father doesn't give me what I want, I feel angry." Go to your body; what's that feel like?

CLIENT It feels...nauseous...tight...actually, heavy.

THERAPIST Where?

CLIENT Stomach...and chest.

THERAPIST Where is it strongest, stomach or chest?

CLIENT (*considers, nodding slowly*) In the chest.

THERAPIST Let's stay with that awhile. (*long pause*) Any changes?

CLIENT (*remaining attentive to his body*) There's a sadness...

THERAPIST Where?

CLIENT In the chest and throat.

THERAPIST Which one is stronger?

CLIENT Throat.

THERAPIST (*slowly nods*) What's that feeling in the throat?

CLIENT I'm repulsed by him.

THERAPIST (*hearing the beginning of anger*) OK, stay with that.

CLIENT It's sadness.

[Therapist is surprised by this change of direction, but follows it.]

THERAPIST OK – what's that sadness about?

CLIENT I see him as being defective, inadequate.

THERAPIST Is that sadness for him, or sadness for you?

CLIENT (*immediately, with feeling*) Sadness for me. Sadness that he just can't give it. *That I will never get it.*

In grief work, many clients must continue for some time to face the reality of the unfairness of their life, their deep attachment deprivation and the difficulty of their struggle against homosexuality.

CHAPTER 22

Homosexual Enactment as an Opportunity for Grief Work

Grieve, mourn and wail. Change your laughter
to mourning and your joy to gloom.

– JAMES 4:9

From time to time, a client will begin the session by reporting that he has engaged in an unwanted homosexual enactment. This provides a good opportunity for continued grief work. The same opportunity arises when the client reports having only wrestled with serious temptation.

In such cases we proceed with the two-triangle sequence. Using the homosexual enactment as the identified conflict, the client reports sexual arousal – typically expressed as a genital surge, erotic charge and a feel-ing of adventurousness and restlessness. When encouraged to go deeper into those feelings to find the "feelings behind the feelings," he typically returns to the predicament of the gray zone; that is, feeling bored, restless, "blah," lonely, trapped and disconnected from significant relationships.

Allowing himself to go even deeper, the client then drops down to a more profound level of sadness, commonly expressed as feeling "empty" or "hollow," with a sense of "nothingness," "blackness" and "despair" inside. On a physical plane, these feelings include pain, ache, hurt and woundedness.

With his therapist's support in accessing his deepest feelings, his

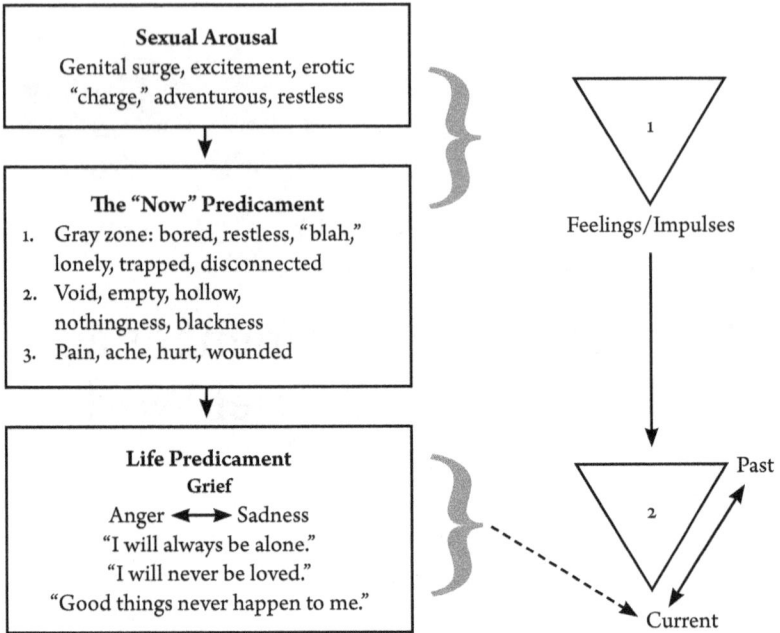

Figure 22.1 Homosexual enactment as an opportunity for grief work

sense of rootless despair often expands beyond his present predicament (unwanted SSA) and into the larger context of his very personhood. Linking his current life with his past, through the interweaving pathways of anger and sadness, he enters a profound level of despair: "I've been utterly abandoned in life." "I am broken, damaged and unlovable." "I am empty inside." "I am nothing, I am no one."

By repeatedly returning to these deeper feelings, most clients begin to see their same-sex attractions as a drive to compensate for attachment loss trauma.

The following are some illustrations of homosexual enactments that served as opportunities for grief work.

The Attempt to Heal Gender Inferiority
This client begins the session by reporting an incident of unwanted sexual acting out. Through body work, he moves beyond the memory of sexual arousal to consider his overall life predicament.

CLIENT	I've been thinking the last three days about going out. You know, to the bathhouse.
THERAPIST	OK... Do you want to do some body work on this?
CLIENT	(*indifferently*) Yeah. OK.
THERAPIST	Shall we go to your body now?... Let's attend to what's going on inside of you as you think of going to the bathhouse.
CLIENT	Well – not that I really wanted to go there. It's just that it's been in the back of my mind.
THERAPIST	OK.
CLIENT	I've been kind of toying with the idea.
THERAPIST	And that's a conflict for you?
CLIENT	Yes.
THERAPIST	OK. Shall we look at what's behind that conflict?
CLIENT	(*heavy sigh, nods*) OK. Well... I feel tense.
THERAPIST	(*nodding*) Uh-huh.
CLIENT	Yeah. In fact, tense and tight.
THERAPIST	Where?
CLIENT	Here. (*passing hand over abdomen*) And of course, there's some excitement too at the idea of going. There's one right here in the Valley.
THERAPIST	Where do you feel that excitement?
CLIENT	Chest. Like a nervous excitement... and a genital excitement, like in my crotch, my d—k.
THERAPIST	Yeah.
CLIENT	(*long pause*)
THERAPIST	Where does that excitement feel stronger, chest or genitals?
CLIENT	Arousal, I guess, at the possibility of going for it.
THERAPIST	OK. So the possibility of "going for it" increases your excitement.
CLIENT	(*encouraged*) Yeah.
THERAPIST	OK, so go with that... what do you feel?
CLIENT	Well... I feel arousal. Excitement in my penis. Like I'm kinda getting hard. (*pauses; seems lost in thought*)
THERAPIST	Yeah, but stay with me. What's happening?
CLIENT	(*long pause*) Less excitement now. (*pauses to consider*) I'm

running through the images about what would actually happen there, and I don't feel the excitement as much.

THERAPIST   Less of a charge…

CLIENT   The truth is, (*sighs*) I feel like a loser. I'm really looking to be held and reassured. I hate my body…It feels small and skinny and insufficient. I'm really unhappy about how my body feels and looks, and I'm lonely.

THERAPIST   (*nods, waits*) OK…Let's go to your feelings. What was that all about?

CLIENT   I know what it's all about. I get scared of growing up.

THERAPIST   OK. Let's go to your feelings now about that.

CLIENT   (*considers*) Tightness and compression. A feeling of dread.

THERAPIST   Yeah, stay with that…

CLIENT   (*considering*) I feel small…dark…black inside.

THERAPIST   Where?

CLIENT   In the center. Something is pulling all the corners of my chest together.

THERAPIST   Yes. Stay with that.

CLIENT   A cold hard lump. (*deep breath, then begins to speak rapidly*) It's really scary. There's no door to escape, I'm just stuck here with this cold hard presence inside. I just want to die from the inside out. It's so intense, so threatening that I'd rather die than feel it. (*sighs deeply*)

THERAPIST   (*nods, waits*)

CLIENT   I can't believe it can ever possibly go away. It's too big and too present inside me, and it's crowding out my world. (*pauses to consider before continuing*) In fact, it's just me and *it*, locked in a room, and the room is getting smaller and it's getting bigger and it's pushing me up against the wall.

THERAPIST   Yes. And where is that?

CLIENT   (*attends to his body, considers for a moment*) Here. (*hand over chest*)

THERAPIST   Yes…

CLIENT   (*long pause*) My chest cavity hurts like someone has punched me in the sternum. It feels like there's this black rock that sits right under the sternum. It's cold, black, hollow. (*almost whispers*) Feeling this, just hurts!

THERAPIST   (*gently*) I'm with you on this … Of course. It's very painful …

CLIENT   (*long pause*) The truth is, (*sighs*) I've reached my hell. This thing – this black thing inside – has completely taken over my life.

THERAPIST   I'm with you. This is the most difficult thing you could be doing.

CLIENT   (*tearfully*) It's so empty … There's nothing inside here. (*touches his chest*) Yes. (*speaks resolutely*) I've hit the truth of the matter. It's completely empty inside.

Hiding in the Darkness

The following client, who had fairly recently started therapy, began the session by reporting a failure – he went to a gay bookstore and was disgusted by the encounter he had in the restroom with a stranger.

Encouraged to recall his state of mind before he decided to act out, he said, "I was very depressed that morning. I couldn't stand being with myself – couldn't even get up and go to work. I came in late."

Invited to do body work in recalling the events of that morning, he began, "I feel an emptiness, a desperation. I just want to feel loved. I don't even love myself or want to be with myself."

Regarding the pain of emptiness in the center of his chest, the therapist asked if the client could recall a time in the past when he had felt such a sensation. He answered without hesitation, "Hiding in the darkness under my bed."

THERAPIST   How old were you?

CLIENT   Four, maybe five.

THERAPIST   What was that little boy feeling?

CLIENT   No connection with anyone. Just isolation, complete aloneness.

THERAPIST   Stay with that little boy …

CLIENT   He's unloved, unwanted.

[Client becomes stiff and expressionless.]

THERAPIST   You look like you're moving away. Can you go back to that little boy?

CLIENT   (*sighs, then speaks softly and sadly*) He feels weak and abandoned.

THERAPIST   Can you touch that little boy's pain?

[Client is silent.]

THERAPIST   What would you say to that little boy now, if you could?

[Client remains silent.]

THERAPIST   (*pointing out his defense*) I wonder if it is your fear and shame that blocks you from making contact with that little boy who's hiding in the corner of that dark closet?

CLIENT   (*pensively, nodding slowly*)

THERAPIST   Is there anything you would want to tell that little boy?

CLIENT   (*tearing up, then taking a deep breath*) I would tell him "Somebody loves you, you're a good kid – a *great* kid, you're handsome and lovable, and you have innate goodness!" (*desperately*) But nobody ever told him that, nobody did.

THERAPIST   You felt alone and abandoned.

CLIENT   I am still exactly like that kid – very much alone, then and now. There is no guy out there, never has been. All that's left is the constant, never-ending search. It's an addiction – I know it – but if I don't give in to it, I'm just left sitting alone in the pain and desperation.

THERAPIST   (*long pause*) What's in the body now?

CLIENT   A sinking, dropping feeling. I feel bitterness about my mom and dad. "What was wrong with you?" (*wailing now*) "Why did you even have me?" (*sobbing*) "All my life I tried to get it from you, but I never did. All my life I thought, *If I could only do things the right way – if I could do them at the right time... then, would you love me?*"

THERAPIST   (*nods, waits*)

CLIENT   Until Dad died, I kept trying to pull it out of him... just one little word from him that he loved me.

THERAPIST (*nodding, speaking softly*) Just a word...

CLIENT (*through tears*) My family said to leave him alone, I was upsetting him, but I kept trying. My brother said to stop bothering him because he was too old and sick to deal with me. But if I can't get it from my own father, (*shouting now*) who can I get it from? Who in this world is left? (*sobbing*)

The Boredom of Being with Myself

In our third example, a twenty-six-year-old man begins his session reporting his return to a gay bathhouse.

THERAPIST OK, so you said you went to the bathhouse last night. So what were you feeling that led up to that?

CLIENT Well...it was Thursday night. Bored, I guess. Just bored with myself.

THERAPIST Boredom means you haven't been giving yourself freedom to express yourself.

CLIENT (*nods*) That makes sense, I guess. I've been feeling stuck. Uptight...

THERAPIST Shall we do some body work with this?

CLIENT (*shrugs*) OK.

THERAPIST Let's go to that boredom. Right now, just try to go back to that feeling of boredom. What was that feeling like when you made the decision to go there?

CLIENT Often, going to the bathhouse is a way of saying, *OK, you've handled your day at the office, why not go ahead now and have a little bit of fun.*

THERAPIST That's a reason, not a feeling. Let's stay with the body. Talk to me about what it feels like inside of you when the get that feeling about wanting to go to the bathhouse. You're sitting in your apartment, and...

CLIENT (*considers for a moment*) Hmm...Well. (*nods*) Yes. First... there's an aloneness.

THERAPIST So you're aware of a sense of aloneness.

CLIENT Yeah. Just a loss of interaction with any other person and not very interested in myself, either.

THERAPIST   So stay with that – "I'm not interested in myself"...

CLIENT   There's a sense of separation there.

THERAPIST   What's the sensation in your body?

CLIENT   It's pretty passive.

THERAPIST   OK. What's it feel like in the body?

CLIENT   It's very flat...

THERAPIST   Tell me about the flat, how "flat" feels in your body. That's important.

CLIENT   Well... "flat" equals nothing. Nothing equals boring. Boring equals "Let's do something else now." (*seems apathetic*)

THERAPIST   (*softly*) You don't want to go there right now, do you?

CLIENT   I guess not. (*pause*) There's nothing there. The feeling is just "empty." Flat.

THERAPIST   I think it's important to bring your attention there, and to go to that flatness and emptiness. Because we've gone beyond boredom now; we've gone to "flat." But this is up to you; do you want to do this?

CLIENT   (*reluctantly*) Yeah, I guess. But there's nothing really there, nothing to talk about. It's very ordinary and predictable and... (*long pause*)

THERAPIST   (*waits*)

CLIENT   Actually, it's agonizing. It's agonizing to feel that.

THERAPIST   (*focusing on that strong word*) Right now, how do you experience "agonizing"? Can you, right now, feel this "agonizing" in your body?

CLIENT   Physically, it hits me right at the top of the sternum. When I say the word *agonizing*, I feel like this word is right here, sitting right here at the sternum.

THERAPIST   (*gently*) So that's it.

CLIENT   A huge explosion above it and below it.

THERAPIST   You're feeling that "explosion" feeling right now.

CLIENT   Yeah. Just pushes up and pushes down, and it's agonizing.

THERAPIST   "Agonizing"...

[Therapist reinforces the strong sensation and encourages the client by using his own words.]

THERAPIST   There's a body sensation of agony, and you're feeling that right now in the center of your chest, and it's pushing up and it's pushing down, and it's going both directions and it's cutting right in, yes?

CLIENT   (*nodding, grimacing*) Yes. It's an ugly feeling.

THERAPIST   The pain is so uncomfortable that you don't want to go there, you'd rather stay flat – stay bored – and distract yourself by going to the bathhouse. But right now, what really is important is for you to feel that I'm with you and present with you right now in this feeling of "agonizing," which is the "explosion in the sternum." That's where your pain is. I'm following you – you take the lead.

CLIENT   (*nods*) OK. I'm feeling that pain in the sternum.

THERAPIST   (*softly*) Stay with the body, because the body is where you need to be. Feel it fully and put it into words. Let me be with you so I know what it's like for you to be there.

CLIENT   But why do I have this pain?

THERAPIST   Right now you and I are going to move away from the question of why; we'll go there later, OK? First, you and I together need to go to that feeling and look at it.

CLIENT   Sometimes I feel like I'm stuck with this pain inside forever. I've been to that feeling inside before... It's negative and it always will be. I (*deep breath*)... This is not fun.

THERAPIST   That's right. But it sounds like you're there now. Inside that feeling.

CLIENT   But I'm making the choice not to look at it. I'm looking away.

THERAPIST   (*gently*) But we *are* looking at it. You and I are both looking at it right now.

CLIENT   It's just... (*long pause, and voice becomes tremulous*) It's eating me up in there. It fills me up, getting bigger the more I think about it.

THERAPIST   That's right; the more you get into the feeling, the bigger it gets. Can you tell me how you're feeling it... that "bigger" in your body?

CLIENT   It's very expanded in my stomach and my chest.

THERAPIST   Right. What does that feel like, that thing expanding inside of you?

CLIENT   Pressure.

THERAPIST   Could this be the feeling that you've been running away from, but now you're going inside of it?

CLIENT   (*eyes closed, pauses, then speaks softly*) It's just taking over my torso.

THERAPIST   Absolutely. That's right, it's taking over, it's expanding. The more you look at it, the bigger it gets with this expanding and taking over of your torso.

CLIENT   It's an expansive, painful presence just taking up mass. It seems like above my stomach, pushing down on my stomach. (*long pause*) Now it seems to be up to my throat.

THERAPIST   Yes. That's where you're feeling this heavy expansive pressure, a physical presence from the top of your stomach to the bottom of your throat. What's it like to be carrying that inside of you?

CLIENT   It's filling me, consuming me like a cancer, and not allowing me any room.

[After some minutes of sitting together in the presence of this deep feeling, the therapist senses that this is as far as the client is capable of going in this session, so he decides to move to the second triangle.]

THERAPIST   Jack, do you remember feeling this same heavy, agonizing presence in your body another time?

CLIENT   A lot of times. But nothing specific.

THERAPIST   (*gently*) Stay with it...

CLIENT   (*thoughtfully considers*) Well...Yes...when my mother would leave and I'd be home alone with my dad. Just the two of us.

THERAPIST   And?

CLIENT   There was this eerie, empty feeling in the house. He would drink and I'd stay out of his way. She wouldn't protect me. (*long pause*) I think she was just as scared of him as I was.

THERAPIST   (*nods*)

CLIENT   Sometimes, he'd just come after me. No reason, just start after me.

THERAPIST   Any particular memory?

CLIENT   Oh… (*hesitant*) he'd slap me around.

THERAPIST   Can you give me a picture of it?

CLIENT   An actual incident?

THERAPIST   (*nodding*)

CLIENT   Uh… well, one time, a library book was overdue. I must have been about eleven. He shoved me onto the kitchen floor. Left me there crying, and just drove off.

THERAPIST   Can you feel right now what that boy was feeling then, on the kitchen floor?

CLIENT   (*thoughtfully*) Sad. Yeah – that same sad feeling. Alone and abandoned…

[Client then spends several emotional minutes deeply dwelling in the feeling of aloneness and the sense of worthlessness. We now shift to near the end of the session, at the meaning transformation phase.]

THERAPIST   Jack, we started with you reporting a homosexual enactment. What did you make of this session? What did you take away from this?

CLIENT   (*speaking slowly, thoughtfully*) I can see that I'm sitting on a lot of sadness. A lot more than I ever realized.

THERAPIST   Do you think that ties in, in any way, with the trips to the bathhouse?

CLIENT   (*thoughtfully*) Yes. For me, I think it's escapism.

THERAPIST   From what?

CLIENT   (*considers*) It's my way to run and hide from the emptiness.

THERAPIST   (*nods*) To run away…

CLIENT   (*deep sigh*) Yeah. In fact, I think this has been what I've always done.

Breakthroughs Achieved Through Grief Work

I feel sad that the truth is the truth, but I make peace with the sadness that the truth is the truth.

                                              – thirty-year-old client

Asked what he had learned about himself through grief work, one man explained,

> Through grief work, I discovered that the pain was real. It hurt not in some sort of vague, ethereal or abstract way, but it hurt physically in my body, and I had never realized or experienced that before. I felt it in my gut, you know?
>
> I had many layers of fear and shame that had been covering up my sadness. I've been experiencing this most of my life, but I just denied it or repressed it or medicated it away. But now I realize that I actually felt pain – physical pain – and I just never knew that or wouldn't have known that, had I not gone through grief work and the experience of actually feeling the body memory of that pain.

Another man spoke of the power of feeling the sadness in the session, while in emotional contact with the therapist:

> For so long, I had sacrificed parts of myself to keep other people happy, and I learned that this was not only unnecessary, it was harmful.
>
> Here, I've been able to express my grief without shame. This has helped me feel more and more authentic. To feel these feelings and share them with another man has been a completely new experience.
>
> No one is mocking me or telling me "It's not healthy to cry" or "Just act like a man."
>
> Accessing this grief helped me to understand the story of my life, what really happened to me, and to make sense of my past. Gradually, I have learned to look at what's happening inside me – and to trust the body to tell me what's really going on.

When the client repeatedly works through this underlying grief, we see the fundamental foundation of his unwanted homosexual enactment slowly and gradually erode, and finally dissipate into the background.

> Now I can look a man in the eyes – even a good-looking man – and relate honestly and openly to him, not look away. Whenever I can do that, I don't think about gay porn or other guys.
>
> Grief work helped me get in touch with all of my feelings – especially

the negative ones that I didn't want to feel. When I am connected to my true feelings, I feel strong, masculine and alive. That's when I'm no longer drawn to looking at other men, and my life can go on.

CHAPTER 23

Resolution of Grief

A Life Without Illusions and Distortions

The road to being real is being sad.
— TWENTY-FOUR-YEAR-OLD CLIENT

∽

Today, I can truly say, "I walk before the LORD / in the land of the living."
— THIRTY-FIVE-YEAR-OLD MAN, AT THE COMPLETION OF THERAPY,
QUOTING PSALM 116:9

This book has been about the devastation of grief and shame. Indeed, almost all of our men harbor intense memories of feeling misunderstood, feeling alone, and having never been truly and deeply known. Some of them were especially and profoundly hurt – belittled and abused by family members and peers. For such people, Martha Stark (1994a) observes:

> Genuine grief means being able to sit with the horror of it all, the outrage, the pain, the despair, the hurt, the sense of betrayal, the woundedness; it means accepting one's ultimate powerlessness in the face of all this; and it means deciding to move on as best one can with what one has – sadder perhaps, but wiser too. (p. 25)

Seeing People Clearly

After having gone through the grief process, clients have a more accurate view of people who have been influential in their early lives. While the grief process reveals much about significant family members, it also brings a greater acceptance of them, with a certain mature resignation – "I wish it had been different, but that was Dad" – where the client needs the people in his life to be neither better nor worse than they really are.

Another, equally essential part of the grief process involves giving up the unacknowledged sense of entitlement that the people in his life today are obliged to compensate for his past hurts. No person in his present life deserves to be the recipient of his anger over past relationships, and no one deserves to be idealized as "the solution" to compensate for his early attachment losses.

Resolution of grief is complete when the person is able to surrender the illusions and distortions that he has used to cover over the pain of the loss. With completed grieving, he can live much more genuinely, transparently and realistically.

We cannot, of course, speak of "grief resolution" in the real sense of "undoing" any of those painful realities. Rather, the client must make a practical adaptation through incremental phases of acceptance, followed by gradual adjustment.

The loss must be slowly assimilated, with a gradual integration of its consequences.

Who Am I?

After assimilating the loss, the person must thoughtfully consider who he hopes to become.

Freed from the hidden power of grief and the defenses it evokes, its illusions and distortions, he spontaneously expresses curiosity about his emerging identity. *Who is this person I am becoming,* he wonders, *as I discard the false self?* As the illusions and distortions are unmasked, he begins to recognize this new man – a new man who needs neither to idealize and aggrandize other men, nor to deprecate them.

Growing in self-sufficiency, he is better able to give and receive male love in the only authentic way there is: through mutuality within a non-erotic friendship. He can now abandon the compulsive homosexual enactment that has driven him to try to fill his male emotional and identification needs in a sexual way.

Besides this, he begins to discover a qualitatively different sort of emotional fulfillment – healthy relationships with women where he need not fear engulfment and being required to surrender his separate, masculine selfhood.

Developing the Capacity for Authentic Relatedness

Grief work is a profoundly humanizing process in that it demands the abandonment of powerful, seemingly essential-for-life narcissistic defenses, and sets in motion a gradual movement into deeper humility and transparency.

Therapy has provided the holding environment that allowed the man to explore, reexperience and assimilate that past trauma. By experiencing the pain of his grief and letting go of the lost attachments, he is liberated from old, repetitive patterns of self-sabotage.

Throughout this time he has vacillated back and forth in a tension between the inhibitory affect of shame and the need to experience and express his vitality affects of sadness and anger.

It is through the resolution of sadness and anger that a door abruptly opens to personal growth, identity transformation and new ways of relating. The man now experiences a sense of inner cohesiveness and self-integrity. One twenty-three-year-old man described this transformation by saying, "I'm so much more real, so much more tangible to myself now."

Little by little, he grows beyond the emotional isolation and chronic loneliness that have so long limited him, and develops a deep emotional investment in authentic human relatedness.

The deep inner emptiness has begun to be filled. And along with this new, heightened capacity for genuine intimacy comes a diminishment of homosexuality's illusionary power.

Facing the Father Wound

For most men, grieving the lack of a salient father has been a strategic and indispensable part of the therapeutic journey.

In the following journal entry, a young man realistically admits what he missed, and explains how he has come to terms with the loss:

Dad failed to give me something essential. He didn't stamp me or mark me with something that other guys have; I'm missing that sign of validation. I'm different, and I know I'm lacking something.

He didn't give me that something that other men received, and there's a loss I feel about that.

I can accomplish in sports, achieve tasks, do a job, go to work, go to therapy, bond with guys – but I will never, ever really get this thing I've missed. I say this not in anger or despair. I can live with that something missing in me, and it's not going to destroy me or urge me to act out. It's uncomfortable, but it doesn't have to control me. But I will always know it's there, and I know how it got there.

Before, it was the nonacceptance of that "something missing" that was the source of the homosexual impulse. My nonacceptance of that lack is what created the false hope that some man, some day, would give me what I had missed.

Other men can give me something that makes the lacking OK to live with; I know that. Now, I seek a different type of embrace.

Resolving the father wound is one of the most important prerequisites before the client can claim his true gendered self. He has faced his painful inability to feel like a normal guy, one who is comfortable with other males, attracted to women, and able to fulfill the natural human inclination toward marriage and family. He has had to feel – fully feel – the painful awareness that his life might have been different. He has lingered for quite some time in that "hole in the center of my heart," that deep emotional void that he knows can never be filled by gay fantasies.

"For all those years," said one forty-five-year-old man, "I turned away from my destiny as a man, a father and a husband. I understand now why all these distractions couldn't satisfy. I sought them out because they supported my denial.... They distracted me from the pain."

Returning to the True Gendered Self

It doesn't help me to idealize other guys; I have to make do with what I have. Homosexuality now has far less power over me. When I see a good-looking guy I will maybe look at him, but not have his whole image just "suck me in" where I have to "drink him in" and try to get from him what he has.

At the close of therapy, there will be a time of mourning over the past – those lost years when, our men tell us, they were not fully living. A middle-aged client described this awareness in a therapy session:

> Now my life makes sense. Now I see clearly what I need to do. By my fear, I've denied myself a normal boyhood, manhood . . . denied myself being a husband and father. I've turned away from the life I was meant to live. I spent so many years of just waiting around, not growing up, just "killing time."
>
> So much of it goes back to fear. In the center of my chest I feel the heavy truth that I've spent forty years of my life not taking action; afraid of men – afraid of women – afraid of living.

Abandoning the Shame

> I've let my shame-wound separate me from people.

Rejecting the self-inflicted shame is a foundational step in the client's movement into wholeness. By now, he has fully felt the shame with the support and understanding of the therapist, and at last, he has set it aside. With the deepest part of this shame dismissed, a new life has opened up, characterized by more mature aspirations and realistic hopes:

> I have learned that the power of the male image is not in what he is, but what I am not. And I can go pursue the distraction of what he is, or I can face the painful reality of what I am not.
>
> For the first time in my life I'm not running away from myself. I'm feeling what it's like to not feel shame. It's amazing to walk around and not feel shame!

The man coming out of homosexuality will demonstrate a new willingness to express his doubts, confusion and insecurity whenever those feelings arise. He is now much more willing to accept the unknown, and he has a growing comfort with the same uncertainties that previously felt so paralyzing. Before, he spent his life "anchored in vulnerability," as one man aptly said, but it was that lifestyle of avoidance that made him weaker.

Another client, nearing the end of therapy, summed up as follows:

> My therapy has helped bring about in me more self-acceptance, peace and feeling accepted by men, more than was ever conceivably the case in the years since puberty started. If one thing angers me in life it is this: when gay apologists claim that to reject a "gay identity" is to be in denial of my true self. My personal experience tells me the opposite!
>
> When I feel masculine within, I have no emotional need to draw on the men "out there" who are external to me. This is because I feel at one with them. If, however, I don't deal with my shame, then my masculinity becomes "covered over" and my heart then gravitates to symbols of masculinity found outside myself. I then feel disconnected both from myself, others, particularly men, and from God. I also see more of the beauty of the opposite sex now than I ever did previously.
>
> Were these changes an accident unconnected to my therapy? I think not. Was my therapy "dangerous," as some critics with an ideological ax to grind try to claim? Well, if getting more self-acceptance and feeling now that I belong around men is "dangerous," then I want more of it!

And so we see that on the other side of the therapeutic process is the discovery of a new and authentic identity that emerges from a life lived in the assertive state. Along with this newly discovered assertion comes humility and transparency, supported by deeper clarity and conviction.

Grieving the Missed Opportunities for Male Friendships

> Homosexuality is the "friend" that's been there for too, too long.... But it's never really been a friend.

Our men often express their deep regret about having rejected many willing and capable father figures who reached out to them over the years – men they could have bonded with, but instead, dismissively ignored. They feel acute remorse about having avoided these affirming men who tried to make themselves available to them. They will spontaneously recall certain teachers, coaches, uncles or male peers who showed a clear indication of interest. But now, looking back, they see that they avoided the challenge of their invitations. One man told me: "I think back at all the men who were there for me.... But I didn't notice, pay attention or take advantage of what they were offering. I turned them away and ignored them. I was too preoccupied with myself."

Our clients' regrets center around a lifetime of choosing to self-protect versus choosing to reach out. They speak of challenges avoided, feelings not expressed and friendships not made. One man told me:

> I remember being invited by one of the popular kids to learn to play baseball. He was about thirteen, and I was a few years younger. He wanted to take me under his wing because he could see I was being picked on. But I acted like I didn't care about him, so after a while, he just gave up and left me alone.

He concluded wistfully, "I wish I could go back to relive those years right now – I would have it all be so different."

Growth in Compassion and Connectedness

As one man explained, "Last night I had a salient conversation with myself about giving to others. I can empathize with other people more because now I can feel more. I want my personal journey to end with deeper relationships."

As they work their way through grief resolution, many men express regrets not only about people with whom they've failed to make friendships, but about people they've failed to help, or even abused and exploited. A twenty-five-year-old man cried sorrowfully in recalling a long-forgotten incident involving sex play he had initiated with a vulnerable eight-year-old playmate when he himself was ten.

Another thirty-five-year-old had the startling realization that his father had ignored his younger brother, not just him. He came to see that his own loss had obliterated his awareness of his brother's similarly acute suffering, and now he felt compelled to go back and reach out to him.

There is deeper sensitivity to others' feelings. "Now I tend to think," one man explained, "*Gee, maybe I've hurt this person.* Even when what I did to the person seems to be justified, I still think about their feelings. Before, it was pretty much all about me."

A married man described the change that had occurred in his family life:

> I think of all the time wasted – just *wasted* – on dreaming and fantasy about mysterious and unknown guys. I think of all the years on the porn websites, looking at the bodies of men. Those were years that could have been given to my wife and kids. It was a time when I was not fully present at home, really *listening* to my kids.
>
> I remember coming home once from a stressful day at work and wanting to get relief by going to my porn sites. My daughter was there, doing her homework online. I told her to get off the computer, that I had some "important work" to do. How sick is that?
>
> I've become so much more attentive to my wife, rather than with my mind half distracted onto a porn image. Now, when she talks to me, I can put my full attention on what she is saying and feeling. I know she too feels more connected to me as a result.
>
> And guess what? Now my kids are opening up to me too, telling me about stuff I had no idea that they were interested in.

A young man described his new freedom from envy:

> How great it is not to live with that background feeling of shame…where I don't feel "less than" other guys. I can go to the gym and can actually focus on my workout. If I see a good-looking guy, it's like, *So what?*
>
> The other day I saw this young guy doing this exercise. Before, I would have focused on his body, but the thought that came to me this time was, *Oh, that exercise he's doing would be good for me – for my lower back problem.*

As the narcissistic defenses are relinquished, they are replaced not only by greater humility but also gratitude. There is a surrender of grievances and grudges, and of the self-absorbed preoccupations that caused them to ignore and abuse others.

Thus we see an overall shift from entitlement to gratitude, from self-abnegation to assertion, from narcissism to humility, and from emotional isolation to authentic attachment.

Our men develop a more clear-eyed view of life, and a sense of inner cohesion and integrity. And with these changes come much more mature aspirations and realistic hopes – particularly regarding what other men can and cannot offer in a relationship that is characterized by the brotherhood of equality and mutuality.

Leadership

Therapeutic resolution brings with it the understanding that *being a man* requires serving others, taking on a position of leadership. "And I thought I had nothing within me to give!" clients have often told me at the end of therapy. Passage through the grief process has awakened a surprising new desire to reach out to others.

Some men feel called to enter community services or a parachurch min-istry with the mission of helping other men come out of a gay lifestyle. A former client wrote me:

> As with other life-changing events, I feel the need to tell others, to share what I've learned with other strugglers. I just feel compelled to help.
>
> There is no way I could justify homosexual activity in terms of God's plan for my life. As part of his creation and as part of his Kingdom, I was created to live as a heterosexual, and I can't make any sense of it any other way. I was made by him in his image, designed to be one with a woman. Anatomically, men and women fit together, and we complement each other in terms of disposition, temperaments, and personalities.
>
> Even if you want to take God out of the equation and look at me as just a biological creature, then still you have to deal with the fact that anatomically, I "fit" only with a woman, because procreation occurs in that way. The behaviors that occur in homosexual sex are not natural – they clearly are harmful.
>
> If I don't share what I've learned, I feel unworthy of the gifts that I've received. I used to disclose my hurts for what attention I could get for myself. Now I want to share about my hurts for the sake of others;

share about my pain as a way to minister to another guy's pain. I just feel it's part of what God intended me to be.

I want more than anything to be of help to other guys.

The Final Phase of Meaning Transformation: Resolution

And so we see how grief work has fostered the full development of the observing, reflecting part of the mind, which provides resolution and conviction about who one is. The man who has completed this process is free to move forward as an active, creative agent in bettering his life.

Another benefit of grief work is the tendency to be much less critical of other people. With that attitude comes the ability to accept one's life as it is, and the people in it as they are, without the need to distort reality. Brief bursts of these constructive attitudes appear intermittently throughout the therapeutic journey but will not reach sustained expression until the final phase of therapy. Any hurt and anger at parents turns into a certain benevolent acceptance: "They were what they were." "I know they loved me in their own way." "I realize that they didn't 'get it' from their own parents, either." There is an acceptance of people as they are. Thus the client discovers a new, more mature sort of love and attachment to his significant others – even to those who have hurt him.

He will – it is true – still live with the background awareness of some lingering unproductive, self-defeating and maladaptive stances toward the world. There will still be some emotional blocks that inhibit him. There will still be some intermittent attractions to men, especially during times of stress. But he will have surrendered most of those obsolete patterns of thinking and behaving. He will have given up the illusions and distortions that other people must be as he expects them to be. He will have learned to make the most of what is good, true and possible.

He will have let go of rigid patterns and emotional responses that were life-limiting, and instead he will now be fully engaged in life. He will be fully involved in the process of "becoming what I want to be."

His self-criticism will be appropriate: no longer beating himself up with shame and self-blame, he will know the difference between constructive self-criticism and shame-based distortions. There is a newfound sense of self-determination and a belief in the possibilities of the future. As one man explained, "In the past, I made the worst self-appraisals and simply assumed the worst about myself. But now there is a clarity of wants and needs – strength in my voice – and a deeper way of communicating." Another man explained:

> While it is true that I often felt very much "alive" when I engaged in homosexual activities and pursuits, I also later felt empty and depleted. I must admit that I never really loved those that I had liaisons with. I was interested in what they could give me and how I could benefit.
>
> For me, the gay life was anything but gay. In my life, homosexual attraction represented my neediness, envy and feelings of inadequacy. I have finally found happiness in my marriage, and satisfaction in fulfilling the potential of the heterosexual man I was meant to be.

One sixteen-year-old told me how "getting connected" back to himself was in turn allowing him to connect to the rest of the world: "I'm beginning to feel in touch with something solid, deep and real. When I make contact with myself, my homosexuality is nowhere."

Into and Out of My Darkness

Another man, writing in his journal, reflects the experience of many other men who have found their way through the change process. The darkness that they were sure was "death" had proved to be something very different: an opening into life.

> The blackness that I thought was so painful and all-consuming is a sham. I am bigger than it is. I came about this discovery by allowing myself to go to the place of black emptiness that sits in the center of my chest. It's a cold, hard, elongated orb – like a rock. It stretches from one side to the other of my chest cavity.
>
> When I went to this cold, dark place, I didn't just look at it from afar; I allowed it to envelop me. I went inside. It hurt my stomach and made me feel very afraid because I didn't see anything beyond it. It had me believe that in the darkness there was no end, no place beyond it. "This is it – my hell, and I have played host to it for my whole life." This was the end of the line, with nothing more left to see. I wanted to die from the inside out, because only in dying could I escape.

But as I stood in this emptiness, I realized that there was nothing inside this space to be afraid of. I, "me," was the one bringing in life – not it; I was illuminating this dark place.

My headaches, which had been bothering me for many years, became less troublesome. I had a feeling of peace come over me.

The part of me that initiated the journey was bigger than that dark place! I felt confident; I began to see that I would survive this darkness.

There was something very affirming about going into – and then staying in – this darkness, and then coming out aware that it was much less cold, black and all-consuming than I had feared it to be.

I take away gold from this experience; I feel love for me. I feel that I matter, and I prove this by realizing that the darkness is inferior to me, less than me. I am the one who holds the opportunities and possibilities and strengths. The darkness deluded me into thinking that it held the power.

No, indeed – *I hold the power.*

Freed from the dominating power of grief and the defenses it evokes, a new identity emerges for the man who seeks it. It is the true gendered self that brings with it the capacity for healthy male intimacy. There is now a quiet but sure conviction: *I am man enough.* And along with this heightened capacity for genuine male intimacy comes a profound and ever-growing diminishment of homosexuality's illusionary power.

Eye Movement Desensitization and Reprocessing (EMDR) in Reparative Therapy

EMDR is a valuable treatment modality in the repertoire of the reparative therapist. It has been found to be effective in addressing past gender-shame traumas, diminishing unwanted homosexuality and enhancing heterosexual potential (Goldwasser, 2004).

This chapter provides a brief introduction to the practice of EMDR and a description of how it can be easily modified for use in reparative therapy. This chapter is not intended to prepare the therapist for its actual application. Formal training is necessary through the EMDR Institute. (Introductory educational material may be obtained through www.emdr.com.)

Brief History of EMDR Therapy

For generations individuals have observed that a good night's rest can help a person feel more resolved about the previous day's conflicts and stressors. The need to "sleep on it" is something people say is helpful before making a big decision or assessing the impact of an event. People notice that a good night's sleep often results in a greater feeling of mental clarity.

Studies of sleep physiology in the 1950s discovered that rapid eye movement (REM) – a continuous lateral back-and-forth movement of the eyes which occurs during deep sleep – appears related to a person's ability to feel resolved about previous life experiences.

The originator of EMDR therapy, Francine Shapiro, was the first to publish material on EMDR's effectiveness. The body of literature which has accumulated since Shapiro's earliest study has led the American Psychiatric Association to approve EMDR as a treatment, and to score it highest in effectiveness in the treatment of trauma-induced symptomatology (Shapiro, 2002).

Proponents of EMDR therapy claim rapid results for disorders such as PTSD, anxiety, depression, panic attacks and phobias. Indeed, the efficacy of EMDR therapy has been extensively substantiated by multiple peer-reviewed studies, particularly in regard to the treatment of trauma-related phenomena (Bisson & Andrew 2009, Denny 2005).

While instructing clients to recall their trauma memories while guiding them through certain patterns of eye movements, EMDR therapy transforms disturbing traumatic memories into memories which are no longer disturbing. For example, a client seeking treatment for childhood sexual abuse may recall an abuse memory as a "10" on a 10-point scale of disturbance, but after several EMDR sessions, he will no longer recall the memory as disturbing. In addition to this change, negative cognitions, such as "it was my fault," tend to vanish and be replaced with more realistic beliefs, such as "I'm not responsible for someone else's behavior." When conducted properly, EMDR therapy produces clients who consistently report a permanent adaptive resolution to the negative memories.

When Trauma Becomes Overwhelming

Addressing the underlying neurophysiology of the traumatic experience, EMDR is guided by the Adaptive Information Processing model. According to this model, maladaptive memory networks are the underlying basis of psychopathology. This is due to the traumatic experience's overwhelming nature, which interferes with the brain's natural ability to encode and store the information. This dysfunctionally stored memory and its associations (body sensations, emotions and negative cognitions) are reactivated during therapy as the client holds them in mind, and then reprocessed to an adaptive resolution through the EMDR process.

EMDR is typically conducted in a "three-prong approach:" past, present and future material, which is treated in that order, with the present symptoms being a starting point so that the past traumas (the first prong) can be uncovered.

For example, a client's presenting complaint is that he believes he is "weak" no matter what does. The EMDR therapist would begin by asking the client for present triggers of this symptom (going to the gym and feeling intimidated by stronger guys, difficulty standing up to his boss, quickly giving up on himself when trying out a sport). The therapist would ask the client for the body sensations and emotions he associates with this negative experience, as well as the negative belief about himself: "I'm weak."

Once this negative state has been identified, the therapist guides the client to think back to earlier times when he felt this way. As the client recalls these experiences, the therapist writes them down and creates a "target list" of his past memories related to the "weak" emotional state. Each memory is rated by the client on a 10-point "SUD" scale (Subjective Unit of Disturbance). The client is asked what he'd rather believe about himself: for example, "I'm strong." This alternative belief is called the Positive Cognition. The client and therapist then reprocess all the memories one by one, adding new Positive Cognitions to be associated with each memory, thereby completing the first prong (past traumas).

Client and therapist then move to the second prong, the client's present-day triggers (seeing other strong men at the gym, difficulty standing up to the boss, etc.), which are to be reprocessed, one at a time, until the disturbance level reaches 0 on the 10-point scale.

Once this is completed, therapist and client move on to the final prong: future template work. For each present-day trigger, a future adaptive response is installed: "Instead of believing I'm weak, I see those strong guys in the gym as social equals and I confidently ask them if they have any tips they can teach me."

This standard approach described here (called the Standard Protocol in EMDR therapy) can be easily adapted to decrease homosexual attractions. Many reparative-therapy clients worldwide have used this modified approach and report powerful and lasting effects. The following are several specific methods that reparative-therapy clients have found useful.

To do this, we begin with the client's homosexual attraction itself.

Using EMDR to Reduce Unwanted Attractions

The client is first asked to imagine his "ideal sexually attractive guy" who elicits a strong sexual charge. He is asked, "How do you feel about *yourself* in comparison with him?" thereby ascertaining the shame statement that underlies his erotic attraction. Clients almost universally report shame statements such as, "I'm not enough," "I'm weak," "I'm nothing," "I'm inferior." This is the core shame statement, or "negative cognition" (in EMDR terms) that is targeted for reprocessing. The rationale behind this first step is the reparative principle that the client's homosexuality is often driven by eroticized envy, a shame-based mindset that the other man is the idealized representation of what the client believes he cannot be – i.e., he is the missing part of his own masculinity.

When his underlying shame is successfully reprocessed, he will often notice a spontaneous decrease in his shame-based symptoms (envy, idealization of other men, disqualifying himself from non-sexually connecting with other men, etc.). He is left with non-shame based feelings toward the other man and a perceptual shift occurs: "I would like to walk up to him and get to know him," "I see he's stronger than me, but I no longer envy him, I just appreciate this about him in a way that doesn't leave me feeling lower than him."

Thus we identify and reprocess the shame-based trauma experiences in the client's history, his present shame triggers, and we work through how he would like to respond to these triggers in the future. Over time, he gradually overcomes his shame-based identity. *This corresponds with the real work of reparative therapy, which isn't sexual-orientation change. It is self-identity change* (from shamed to non-shamed) which results in a significant diminishment of unwanted same-sex attractions as a byproduct.

Tips for Correctly Identifying the Client's Negative Cognition

The negative cognition is not directly about the other man ("He's better than me"), but rather a negative evaluation that the client makes about himself that expresses a sense of defectiveness ("I'm a loser," "I'm inadequate").

There are always two elements to shame – the right hemisphere's somatic experience (sometimes described by clients as slouching shoulders, looking down and a sense of painful contraction in the chest), and the left hemisphere's experience, which is a cognition in the form of a verbal negative self-evaluation ("I'm just a loser").

When the client states that the shame statement "feels true," and he feels the corresponding sensation in his body, then both elements have been locked in the central nervous system and are being correctly accessed. A successful eye movement reprocessing of any memory associated with this state will result in a spontaneous dissipation of the validity of the (left hemisphere) negative cognition, as well as the (right hemisphere) negative somatic associations.

The treatment goal is to integrate the dysfunctionally-stored trauma memory and to bring it to an adaptive resolution. New insight and meaning transformation of the original memory are common spontaneous phenomena during this process. The same memory which initially led the client to believe "I'm a loser" then acquires a new association; the positive, adaptive belief, "I can speak my mind."

Neurobiology of Homosexual Attraction

Though a popular slogan today is "love is love," our neurobiology tells a different tale. Men with same-sex attractions have been found to show significant amygdala activity when they're exposed to a homosexually-arousing image, unlike heterosexual men when exposed to a heterosexual-arousing image (Safron, et. al, 2007). Although the amygdala is involved in numerous functions, it plays a major role in the processing of shame and fear.

The authors state that due to the speed of the neuro-imaging, the amygdala activation in homosexually oriented men did not seem to be the result of shame originating in social constructs (which requires social-referencing, and would take longer to be generated). These are the same, fear-based responses that clients report feeling beneath their homosexual attractions. A study published in The American Journal of Neuroradiology declared in its title, "Patterns of brain activation during visually evoked sexual arousal differ between homosexual and heterosexual men." The article concludes by stating that "different neural circuits are active during sexual arousal in homosexual and heterosexual men." (Hu et al, 2008, p. 1890).

The amygdala and other limbic structures play a major role, as we have said, in storing trauma memories. Brains of subjects who have been diagnosed with PTSD eventually resemble the brains of those who do not, after being treated with EMDR (Bossini et al, 2007). This change from a "PTSD brain" to a "non-PTSD brain" is evident in both brain structure and brain function. One example of this change is increased thalamic volume in individuals who have been treated with EMDR therapy (Bossini, 2011).

The observed reality of neuroplasticity (the brain's capacity to rewire itself) challenges the dogmatic view of many gay activists that "sexuality may be fluid for some people, but no form of psychotherapy can initiate this change." Neural imaging demonstrates that the brain can, in fact, achieve significant changes at deep, limbic levels relatively quickly when effective interventions such as EMDR are employed. Since EMDR has been shown to cause noticeable changes in limbic physiology and anatomy, it is well-suited for use with our treatment population of same-sex-attracted men.

Trait Change vs. State Change

A temporary shift in one's mindset is sometimes referred to as a "state change." While reprocessing a few individual memories is often helpful to the client and sometimes results in a brief change in mindset, this in itself is often not enough to elicit a "trait change" (a significant, enduring shift in the client's experience of himself). It is through the systematic and thorough reprocessing of an entire neural network that trait change can be achieved. For example, if the client's primary shame statement is "I don't fit in," then trait change would require thoroughly and systematically reprocessing (1) past memories associated with this negative belief; (2) present triggers which continue to elicit it and (3) installing adaptive future responses to these present triggers. If this three-prong approach is done correctly, it should result in the client no longer "defaulting" into this shame state in the future.

For clients with unwanted homosexuality, the second prong (present triggers) would include erotically attractive males who trigger the client's shame statement: for example, "I'm weak." This second prong is where direct reprocessing of homosexual stimuli takes place and where the client often notices his greatest symptom reduction in his same-sex attractions.

Early Sexual-Abuse Memories

Reprocessing memories of early sexual experiences usually provides powerful breakthroughs in the therapy. In our experience at our clinic, approximately 25% of clients report having had sexual-abuse experiences in their childhoods with older men. This roughly fits national self-reports by homosexual men (Doll et al, 1992, Holmes & Slap, 1998).

Below is a sample vignette of EMDR treatment with a 19-year-old man with unwanted homosexuality. Note the EMDR terminology: "SUD" = Subjective Unit of Disturbance, and "VOC" = Validity of Cognition (i.e., how true a cognition feels).

Clinical complaint: unwanted homosexual attraction. Trigger: seeing a man with broad shoulders who looks strong and confident in his body.

Negative cognition (the belief the client has about himself when he compares himself to the other man): "I'm defective."

Body sensation: "pain" in chest and "slouching" feeling in torso.

Trauma target list (past)

Seeing photos of "perfect looking guys" on the internet. Age: 14. SUD: 8

Positive cognition: "I'm equal." VOC: 3

"Feeling embarrassed to go out of the house because my younger brother makes fun of me because of my acne." Age: 13. SUD: 10.

Positive cognition: "I'm ok as I am." VOC: 5

"Looking at my confident, older brother and realizing how different I am from him." Age: 19. SUD: 7.

Positive cognition: "I can be confident with or without his approval." VOC: 3

"My only male friend left me on the last day of school without saying goodbye." Age: 8. SUD: 5

Positive cognition: "Others' actions don't determine my value." VOC: 6

"My father is in the back yard, sharing his sports interests with other young guys that I feel I can't join in with. "Age: 11. SUD: 5

Positive cognition: "I'm alright as I am." VOC: 3

Once all the SUD levels have reached 0 or 1, and VOC levels of the positive cognitions have reached 9 or 10, the client is ready to proceed to the second prong – present triggers.

Present triggers (present)

Seeing someone who is confident in his body. SUD: 6

Being called "gay" (especially by a masculine guy). SUD: 4

"My acne – seeing my own face in the mirror." SUD: 5

Seeing guys who have an ideal friendship – with trusting, masculine best friends. SUD: 10

Once all the SUD levels have reached 0 or 1, the client is ready to proceed to the third prong – installing future templates as responses to the present triggers.

Template (future)

Seeing someone who is confident in his body – "I walk up and talk to him with confidence."

Being called "gay" (especially by a masculine guy) – "I can walk away feeling assertive."

"My acne – seeing my own face in the mirror" – "I know it doesn't define my worth as a person. I can still go out and be confident with my friends."

Seeing guys who have an ideal friendship – trusting, masculine best friends – "I'm happy for them and I can continue my day without letting that bother me."

EMDR to Increase Heterosexuality

When both client and therapist believe the time is right, the client may use EMDR to explore his heterosexual potential. It is imperative that the client engages in this work only when he feels motivated to do so (never out of pressure from his therapist, family members, etc.).

The essential rationale is this: just as shame-invoking memories and triggers are reprocessed to decrease homosexuality, shame memories also constitute roadblocks against the client's heterosexual development. When the client is able to first identify and reprocess sources of his shame and fear regarding women, then he is able to explore and experience the positive feelings he may have toward women.

Educational Preparation Before EMDR

An analogy that often helps the client is to imagine a small plant that is sitting under two heavy rocks. The heavy rocks prevent the plant from growing and becoming the tree it is designed to be. We don't need to teach that plant how to grow. We don't need to force it to grow. It knows exactly what to do. The rocks simply need to be removed and with minimal assistance, the plant will grow by itself. The plant represents the client's potential heterosexuality, and the rocks sitting directly on top of it represent shame and fear.

In order to help the client explore and develop his heterosexuality, we must first identify and reprocess the sources of his negative affect that are activated when he begins to feel close to a woman with whom he would like to explore a heterosexual relationship. This is in complete contrast to historical psychological attempts to increase heterosexual attraction (which usually failed). In the past, psychologists would attempt to have the client view heterosexual pornography, or use other methods, to try directly to manufacture some positive heterosexual feeling. These efforts likely failed because trying to manufacture a positive feeling (especially a romantic or sexual feeling) very rarely works for anyone, regardless of sexual orientation.

It's important for the client to know that this is not a method of trying to "make" him feel an emotion. Some clients may feel an expectation (from themselves or their therapists) to experience a sexual feeling for a woman. This often unrealistic expectation should be put to rest immediately. Clients benefit from their therapist letting them know that the sequence of feelings he is likely to develop for women is often the reverse from men who have never had SSA.

Typical developmental sequence for feelings of attraction toward women:

HETEROSEXUALLY-ORIENTED MEN:

Sexual attraction → romance → affection → warmth → friendship

HOMOSEXUALLY-ORIENTED MEN:

Friendship → warmth → affection → romance → sexual attraction

Both groups of men ultimately can experience this full range of emotion toward the women they are attracted to, even if the development of those feelings occurs in reverse sequence.

Exploring and Increasing Heterosexuality

The client is first asked to think about a woman he would be open to having a dating relationship with. This could be a real-life woman he knows or an image. Clients can perform an internet search with the key words of characteristics they would like in a woman, such as "safe, warm, funny woman" and pick the image that they like best. Some clients can quickly identify women they are attracted to. Others need more time, and this is understandable, particularly if the experience of heterosexual attraction is novel to the client.

This first protocol is designed to identify and reprocess negative emotions that become activated through emotional closeness with a woman that the client is interested in pursuing. The second protocol is designed to help him develop positive emotions in this intimate context, such as safety, comfort, love and arousal. The second protocol is not recommended until the first protocol has been conducted. Clients who revert to negative emotions during the second protocol would likely be better served going back to the first protocol to continue reprocessing their negative emotions, and they may need to do this more than once.

The basic structure of the outline (below) is simply a modified "inverse protocol" which is well established in EMDR literature. EMDR practitioners have used this protocol with success, and reparative-therapy clients often report this method to be helpful in both exploring and then developing their heterosexual potential.

Decreasing Negative Affect in Heterosexual Interactions

This protocol closely follows the the vignette provided earlier in this chapter. However, here we begin with an ideal image that the client picks, representing the kind of woman he'd like to date. As he is asked to imagine interacting with her, the therapist conducts eye movements until the client reports a negative response after several sets. One client for example imagined having lunch with a woman he would like to date, but after several minutes of positive feelings, he began noticing a tightness in his chest. He reported feeling a fear that came over him, imagining her having an expectation that he would now be obliged to make her happy for the rest of the afternoon and onwards. Instead of using this as an opportunity to interpret the parallels between this imagined scenario and the client's narcissistic mother, the therapist instead created a target list for the client.

As he imagined the moment he was "stuck" with her, the client was asked what his negative cognition was that went with the tightness in his chest and feeling of being "stuck." "I'm powerless," he reported. From there, the 3-prong approach was employed.

The scenario is as follows:

1) The client identifies a woman with whom he's open to a dating relationship.

2) He imagines interacting with her in a way he wants, while paying attention to the sensations in his body, until he reports a negative feeling he believes he cannot overcome.

3) Using his negative cognition and the associated body sensation, the three-prong approach is employed.

Increasing Positive Affect in Heterosexual Interactions

The client revisits the image of a woman in whom he's interested. It's not uncommon for him to change this "ideal" image from time to time, and this occasional change usually reflects a refinement in the kind of woman he's interested in.

While engaging in eye movements, the client imagines relating to her in the way he'd like.

Once he feels comfortable with this, he is asked to imagine her reciprocating his actions in a way he'd like (for example being open, caring and appreciative of him when he is assertive toward her).

These first two steps are repeated while the client continues to perform eye movements. He is encouraged to explore different ways he would like to act toward her and different ways he would like her to respond, while noticing the sensations in his body and going with the actions and responses that feel comfortable and positive.

Clients who have little to no history of having a romantic relationship with a woman will likely proceed more slowly during this process. One way of helping clients explore how they would like to give and receive affection is to mention "The Five Love Languages" (Chapman, 1992). According to this model, people give and receive love through (1) words of affirmation, (2) physical touch, (3) quality time, (4) gifts, and (5) acts of service.

The therapist may suggest the client "try on" different methods of expressing his affection like he might "try on" clothes in a dressing room. Explore, be open, and if you don't like what you see, change it to something you like better. Free of his previously held negative affect, the client at this point may be learning his "love language" for the very first time. He is encouraged to have fun with this process and explore these different ways of heterosexual relating while the eye movements are occurring.

It may also be helpful to remind the client, if he becomes "stuck," that this woman represents the qualities he wanted. For example, if the client wanted a "safe, encouraging" woman, and he begins imaging her to be scolding and punitive, he is gently reminded by the therapist that this is not how a safe, encouraging woman would likely act. The therapist should redirect the client back to scene of the woman relating to him from her core positive attributes.

If the client reports feeling positive affect in his body during this process, the therapist may find it helpful for the client to simply sit with those positive body sensations and "freeze frame" the enjoyable scene while performing the eye movements. This can be a helpful opportunity to facilitate the positive-affect tolerance that is needed to simply "be" with the good feelings he can have with this woman, with no perceived agenda or expectation that he must do anything with these feelings. Experiencing positive emotions while in the context of an emotionally close and vulnerable moment with a woman may be a very new and unfamiliar experience for our clients, so if he feels a good feeling while only imagining holding a woman's hand and nothing more, this is often time well spent.

EMDR for Body-Image Shame

Many clients report feeling shame about some aspect of their body, and often report feeling attracted to men who are confident and comfortable in their own bodies. One powerful method of decreasing the eroticized envy and idealization of men who are "comfortable in their own skin" is to help the client decrease his sense of shame about his own body, and EMDR can provide powerful assistance to accelerate this work.

For the client who wants to work on decreasing his body shame, it is useful to first begin with discussing the specific part of his body he feels shame about with his therapist. For example, lack of muscle, "love handles," moles, etc. The client may bring a picture of this part of his body to show his therapist (without nudity of course) or if he wants, he may even take his shirt off during the session to show his therapist directly the part of himself he feels shame about. Obviously, there should be common-sense caveats to this process – (1) no nudity, (2) the therapist never removes any of his clothing, and (3) the therapist and client do not touch during any of this process.

Once the client has revealed the area of shame to the therapist, he is asked to take in a deep breath and feel the therapist's acceptance and nonchalant response. If he can accept this, it will powerfully decrease whatever shame, anxiety and fear the client may have.

The next step is for client and therapist to use EMDR to target the residual shame. This can be done in two ways. If the shame is very substantial, the standard protocol (mentioned above in this chapter) that uses the 3-prong approach can be used.

The other option is to simply target the part of the body directly, having the client either look at this part of his body or visualize it, and reprocess the part of the body directly as a "present trigger." Note that past trauma memories may spontaneously be reported by the client during this process, indicating the need for the standard protocol approach of past, present and future traumas to be reprocessed.

It's important to note that the specific physical elements that the client finds sexually attractive in other men are usually the same physical elements that he himself feels most ashamed of. This recognition can further help the client recognize that his same-sex attraction is a form of reparative attempt to compensate for his deeper shame issue.

Body Dysmorphic Disorder (BDD) has recently been categorized by the American Psychiatric Association as an anxiety-based disorder, which is a manifestation of OCD (Obsessive Compulsive Disorder). For clients with actual body dysmorphia (which is rare), EMDR treatment can be counter-productive. BDD clients present with an obsessive disordered view of the parts of their body they are not happy with, and reasoning with these clients is notoriously difficult. Absolute statements, such as "I'm completely unlovable as long as my nose is this big," may indicate Body Dysmorphic Disorder and since EMDR is a trauma treatment and BDD is ultimately an anxiety disorder, BDD clients are likely better served with another treatment intervention such as exposure with response-prevention and cognitive-behavioral therapy. Most reparative therapy clients do not have body dysmorphia disorder and EMDR is an excellent treatment approach.

Eye Movements to Facilitate Free Association

EMDR has numerous clinical applications which therapists are continuing to refine. One application worth mentioning is to incorporate eye movements to accelerate free association, which leads to further insights. For example, a client might report, "I'm feeling strange about that last interaction I had with my mother. I don't know what it was that's still bothering me;" or "That insight we came to a moment ago was really powerful – I wonder how I might apply it to the other areas of my life." The simple incorporation of eye movements during moments in which the client reflects on these matters seems to accelerate the process of linking neural pathways, bringing spontaneous insight, with no interpretation needed from the therapist. Adaptive solutions can sometimes emerge directly from the client's unconscious.

EMDR vs. Body Work

Like EMDR, Reparative Body Work – the "Triangle of Containment" –

also attempts to neutralize bodily gender-shame trauma so that the client will be less receptive to same-sex attraction. The rationale of both treatments is the same, but the applications are different. Metaphorically, we might say that EMDR and Body Work both speak the same language, but EMDR is a form of shorthand, representing more direct neuro-transformative treatment. Body Work requires more conscious awareness and therefore, the client's greater ability to tolerate uncomfortable affect.

In Body Work, the therapist is the conduit between the client's left brain and right brain. In EMDR, the client's two brain hemispheres are integrated directly, with the therapist "getting out of the way."

As a metaphorical comparison, Body Work would be equivalent to the daytime integrative process (verbalizing a distressing event to a concerned friend), while EMDR is equivalent to the nighttime sleep-integrative process of REM.

Regardless of which method is used, many clients will move on to work through their conflicts from a higher, religious/spiritual perspective, with an expansion of self that goes beyond the mere release of trauma. This can grow into a broader understanding of their past experiences and a deeper appreciation of their identity as whole and healthy men.

Bibliography

Bisson, J., & Andrew, M. (2009). Psychological treatment of post-traumatic stress disorder (PTSD). *Cochrane Database of Systematic Reviews* 2009, Issue 3. Art. No.: CD003388. DOI: 10.1002/14651858.CD003388.pub3.

Bossini, L., Fagiolini, A., & Castrogiovanni, P. (2007). Neuroanatomical changes after EMDR in posttraumatic stress disorder. *Journal of Neuropsychiatry and Clinical Neuroscience, 19,* 457–458.

Bossini, L., Tavanti, M., Calossi, S., Polizzotto, N. R., Vatti, G., Marino, D., & Castrogiovanni, P. (2011). EMDR treatment for posttraumatic stress disorder, with focus on hippocampal volumes: A pilot study. *Journal of Neuropsychiatry and Clinical Neurosciences, 23,* E1–2. doi:10.1176/appi. neuropsych.23.2.E1.

Chapman, G. (1992). *The five love languages: How to express heartfelt commitment to your mate.* Chicago: Northfield Publishing.

Denny, N. (1995, March). An orienting reflex/external inhibition model of EMDR and thought field therapy. *Traumatology,* 1(1), 1–6 Article 1.

Doll, L.S., Joy, D., Bartholow, B.N., Harrison, J.S., Bolan, G., Douglas, J.M.,

Salzman, L.E., Moss, P.M., Delgado, W. (1992). Self-reported childhood and adolescent sexual abuse among adult homosexual bisexual men. *Child Abuse and Neglect,* 16(6), 855–64.

Goldwasser, Norman. A Multi-Modal Trauma-Based Treatment Paradigm for the Treatment of Ego Dystonic Homosexuality. *NARTH Annual Conference Report* November 12–14, 2004, p. 31–38 (www.narth.com).

Holmes, W., & Slap, G. (1998). Sexual abuse of boys: Definition, prevalence, correlates, sequelae and management. *Journal of the American Medical Association,* 280(21), 1855–62.

Hu, S.H., Wei, N., Wang, Q.D., Yan, L.Q., Wei, E.Q., Zhang, M.M., Hu, J.B., Huang, M.L., Zhou, W.H., & Xu, Y. Patterns of Brain Activation during Visually Evoked Sexual Arousal Differ between Homosexual and Heterosexual Men. *AJNR Am J Neuroradiol.* 2008 Nov;29(10):1890-6.

Safron, A., Barch, B., Bailey, J.M., Gitelman, D.R., Parrish, T.B., & Reber, P.J. (April 2007). Neural correlates of sexual arousal in homosexual and heterosexual men. *Behav. Neurosci.* 121 (2): 237–48.

Shapiro, F. (2001). *Eye movement desensitization and reprocessing: Basic principles, protocols, and procedures* (2nd edition). New York: Guilford Press.

Notes

Introduction

1 Writers who argue for the ethics of some form of reorientation therapy include the following:

Rosik, C.H. (2003). Rosik's paper outlines common motivations for pursuing change, updates the current state of knowledge regarding the effectiveness of change efforts, and provides ethical guidelines for therapists. He also offers an examination of moral epistemology to assist marriage and family therapists in understanding divergent perspectives about reorientation treatments.

Throckmorton, W. (2002). Throckmorton describes the role of religious variables in the change process, and he notes that "some change," which is described by the client as helpful, does indeed appear to occur for many clients who seek reorientation.

Yarhouse, M.A., & Throckmorton, W. (2002). The three primary arguments cited in the literature in favor of a ban on sexual reorientation therapies are that homosexuality is no longer considered a mental illness, that clients who request change are motivated by internalized homophobia, and that sexual orientation cannot be changed. The authors present three arguments in favor of providing reorientation therapy: respect for the autonomy and self-determination of persons, respect for different value systems regarding the moral status of same-sex behavior, and the existing scientific evidence that some efforts to change sexual orientation can be successful.

Yarhouse, M.A., & Burkett, L.A. (2002). Yarhouse advises psychologists to demonstrate respect for religion as an aspect of diversity, noting that conservative religion is a legitimate, though often overlooked, expression of diversity. He discusses ethical questions that arise when a client's religious views clash with his same-sex attraction. Further, he identifies ways in which gay-affirming theorists and religious traditionalists could better appreciate each other's perspective.

Yarhouse, M.A. (1998). Yarhouse refers to the American Psychological Association's 1992 Ethical Principle D, "Respect for Rights and Dignity," as an important ethical principle for psychologists who work with same-sex attracted clients who seek change. He advocates for their ethical right to receive treatment – emphasizing the therapist's professional responsibility to affirm the clients' rights to dignity, autonomy and agency.

And finally, Rekers, G. (1995).

2   There is much evidence in the older literature (before homosexuality was removed from the Diagnostic Manual) that sexual reorientation occurs for some clients. For the most recently published evidence for change in sexual orientation, see the following:

Spitzer, R.L. (2003, October). Spitzer's study tested the hypothesis that some individuals whose sexual orientation is predominantly homosexual can, with some form of reparative therapy, become predominantly heterosexual. The participants were two hundred self-selected individuals (143 males, 57 females) who reported at least some minimal change from homosexual to heterosexual orientation that lasted at least five years. The majority of participants gave reports of change from a predominantly or exclusively homosexual orientation before therapy to a predominantly or exclusively heterosexual orientation. Reports of complete change were uncommon. Female participants reported significantly more change than did male participants. Spitzer concluded that the participants' self-reports were by and large credible, and therefore that change in sexual orientation following some form of reparative therapy does occur in some gay men and lesbians.

Nicolosi, J., Byrd, A.D., & Potts, R.W. (2000b). This study presents the results of a survey of over eight hundred dissatisfied homosexually oriented people who were questioned about their beliefs regarding conversion therapy and the possibility of change in sexual orientation. There were seventy closed-ended questions on the survey and five open-ended ones. Of the participants, 726 reported that they had received conversion therapy from a professional therapist or a pastoral counselor. Of the participants 779 (89.7%) viewed themselves as "more homosexual than heterosexual," "almost exclusively homosexual" or "exclusively homosexual" in their orientation before receiving conversion therapy or making self-help efforts to change. As a group the participants reported large and statistically significant reductions in the frequency of their homosexual thoughts and fantasies that they attributed to conversion therapy or self-help. They also reported significant improvements in their psychological, interpersonal and spiritual well-being.

See also Byrd, A.D., & Nicolosi, J. (2002). This paper synthesized studies of treatment of individuals identified as homosexual using the meta-analytic technique. A large number of studies (146) evaluating treatment efficacy were identified, most published prior to 1975, fourteen of which met inclusion criteria and provided statistics that could be used in a meta-analysis. Analysis indicated that the average client receiving treatment was better off than 79 percent of those in alternative treatments, or as compared to pretreatment scores on several outcome measures. This analysis of fourteen studies suggests that treatment for homosexuality can be effective.

See also Jones, S., & Yarhouse, M. (2007). A review of this study of change can be found at <http://narth.com/docs/rekersrev.html>; Byrd, A.D., Nicolosi, J., & Potts, R.W. (2008).

Chapter 1: Overview

1   There are a number of recent studies, including Nicolosi, J., & Byrd, A.D. (2002). Limitations of Bem's 1996 theory are outlined. We propose an alternative model to explain male homosexuality, that is, reparation of early boyhood trauma.

It should also be noted that Bem fails to identify the narcissism that would characterize a relationship in which the man seeks a gender-mirror image of himself in a partner. We propose that it could only be from a false self of detached admiration and longing that the boy would become susceptible to an erotic (reparative) response toward masculinity.

2   Childhood environmental factors are further detailed in Nicolosi, J., & Nicolosi, L.A. (2000).

3   Regarding the guarded stance toward relationships, the gay-identified man is rarely able to invest all his feelings, including his sexual desires, into a relationship with one person, with fidelity, for a lifetime. A prominent cultural observer, Andrew Sullivan, who is himself a gay activist, says that he discovered to his surprise, after many years in gay life, that he would need to cultivate two distinct sets of relationships: his lovers, and his loyal and caring friends, but the two groups would not overlap. Why should this be true? Cut off from an aspect of his authentic feelings, the gay-identified man relies on eroticism for pseudo-attachment to masculinity and as a temporary regulator of affect – particularly as a regulator of his depression and shame. This results in a lifestyle of sexual relationships that are split off from authentic and lasting emotional attachment.

Chapter 2: Family Dynamics

1   The life of actor Montgomery Clift is a fascinating study of the narcissistic family (an extreme version). Clift was a broodingly handsome classical actor who is considered to be one of the greatest screen stars of the Golden Age of film. He led a tormented life, dying prematurely after many years of drinking, drugs and a long string of affairs with men (as well as a few women). He portrayed a haunting vulnerability and sensitivity that was as much who he was off screen as on screen.

In *Montgomery Clift: A Biography*, author Patricia Bosworth (1978) describes Monty's father, Bill, as passive, good-natured and very dependent on his charismatic wife, Sunny. A successful man in the business world, Bill nevertheless deferred to this strong-willed, opinionated woman at home. "My father would do anything in the world to please Mother," Monty's sister, Ethel, said (p. 23). "She made everyone – including her husband – feel that no one with any brains could possibly disagree with her and still be a person of consequence" (p. 31).

Indeed, Sunny was known as a vibrantly attractive and intelligent woman. She was "energetic, sometimes venomous, always triumphant in any situation" (p. 284).

Sunny herself had been adopted as an infant into a family that apparently abused her, and she was never able to locate her birth parents. She had been told, however, that her bloodlines made her a "thoroughbred." Her primary goal in life, biographer

Boswell says, was to raise her children as "the thoroughbreds they were" so they would never know the uncertain identity and insecurity she had suffered in her life. There were two boys (Monty and Brooks) and one girl (Ethel). Sunny did not seem to respect their gender differences: "Monty and the others were being raised as triplets, given identical haircuts…clothes, lessons, and responsibilities, regardless of age or sex."

Brooks, the tougher son, rebelled – fighting and talking back to his mother when he was told he must dress like his younger brother and sister. "I wanted to be myself," he explained later. Brooks (who grew up to be heterosexual) was married and divorced several times. However, "Monty appeared the most docile, the most obedient of the three children. He did precisely what he was told." Biographer Bosworth notes that his "independent impulses, his drives, were curbed again and again" (p. 31) by his mother.

In spite of the intense pain the relationship brought him, Monty, his brother Brooks later recalled, "had a secretive relationship" of mutual specialness with their mother, which Brooks and his sister "never intruded upon." (p. 50). In contrast, Monty and his father "rarely communicated about anything," and in the morning, they would both read the paper while sitting at the breakfast table, "rarely exchanging a word" (p. 55).

Isolated from his male peers, the sensitive and gentle Monty also developed an intense closeness to his sister Ethel. "Throughout his life Monty relied on Sister for comfort and advice…. Their insecurities made them inseparable. By the time they were seven they were sharing every secret, every fantasy" (p. 26).

In the Clift family there was apparently no room for anyone but Sunny to vent anger or express opinions. The father deferred to his wife in family disagreements and did not defend the children. " 'Ma was always right.' She would tell them that her entire life was dedicated to, and sacrificed for, her children, so 'the least they could do' was to behave and keep her happy." "All three children felt profound anxieties they could not comprehend" as Sunny tried harder and harder to "cast everyone in their assigned roles, and deny their individual needs" (p. 38).

By the age of twelve, Monty (who was being tormented by his male peers) had found the one love of his life – acting. His brother, Brooks, said acting was the perfect release for Monty because when he played someone else, he was at last freed from his old role – the one created for him by his mother: "Now he [Monty] no longer had to live up to the image Sunny imagined for him," Brooks said (p. 44).

Monty's closest lifelong friends (most notably, Elizabeth Taylor) were, like his mother, magnetic, strong-willed women with whom he became enmeshed in intense (platonic) relationships. "As time passed, Monty slept with both men and women indiscriminately in an effort to discover his sexual preference, but his conflict remained obvious," says his biographer (p. 67).

The rest of Montgomery Clift's life was marred by alcoholism and depression. The hostile-dependent relationships he developed with women caused him recurrent distress (p. 369). He had a near-fatal car accident when he was driving home drunk from a party, which left him with permanent facial disfigurement. The death of this brilliant and magnetic actor – in a tragic end, alone at age forty-five in a hotel room – was said to be brought on by complications from his longtime depression, drug use and alcoholism.

2   In a March 12, 2006, episode of CBS TV's *60 Minutes*, interviewer Leslie Stahl introduces two nine-year-old fraternal twins – one typically masculine in his interests, and the other, feminine. She asks the boys if they are "proud" of who they "are," and to Stahl's evident approval, both boys nod enthusiastically. Then she asks the more feminine boy if he wishes he were a girl or a boy. He answers, "A girl." How a boy could be "proud" of being discontented in his own body and wishing he were a girl is not explained.

Chapter 3: Homosexuality as a Shame-Based Symptom

1   It is important to note that our developmental sequence is the opposite of the gay-affirmative sequence put forth by Isay, who posits that the boy is somehow born homosexual, and the poor father-son relationship so often observed among SSA men is not a cause of that SSA, according to Isay, but a result of the father's disgust with the boy's biologically based gender-nonconformity (i.e., nonmasculinity relative to other boys).

Our own developmental model does acknowledge that there may be a biological predisposition to nonmasculinity in some boys, but this predisposition is not seen as central to the boy's failure in secure gender identification. In our model the challenge of male bonding involves a nonsalient father who does not reach out to his son with the salience and consistency that are necessary to attract the temperamentally vulnerable boy into his own masculine sphere. (We also propose that an attachment difficulty with the mother may have first handicapped the boy before he could meet the challenge of bonding with the father.)

Chapter 5: Homosexuality as a Reparative Drive

1   The "gay identity" is a recent social construct. About one hundred years ago, in England, upperclass, effeminate men who were sexually attracted to others of their own sex began to label themselves as a separate group of people. In the United States the concept of a "gay identity" was popularized in the late 1940s or early 1950s. Until then there was no idea of a separate class of "gay people"; all people were understood to be designed for heterosexuality, even though some of them engaged in homosexual behavior. For example, in ancient Greece, men who engaged in homosexual behavior did not consider themselves to be a different kind of man from other men.

Chapter 9: Reparative Body Work

1   Many of our clients report feeling touch-deprived by their fathers and will describe their homosexual desires as largely motivated by the need to be held, touched and physically comforted by a stronger male. Ironically, I have found the admission of this need to be more difficult for the client than their admission of unwanted homosexual

behavior. This appears to be the result of their overwhelming childhood shame for the desire to receive affection through touch from the father.

Recently, there has been some advocacy for the therapeutic benefits of "holding." (Counselor Richard Cohen, for example, has been an advocate for this approach.) This approach involves passive hugging of the client by the therapist or a male friend or family member. It usually is carried out in a formalized manner to avoid eroticization or, in the very least, misunderstandings.

In contrast, we understand the need to be held as regressive and as reinforcing the sense of dependency and weakness. Holding may reinforce the illusion that the client can return to being a little boy. What appears more transforming is for the client to feel and express the need to be held, and to have this need respectfully understood by another salient man (i.e., through the double loop), where the client admits his deep longing to be held; it is understood and accepted by the therapist, and he experiences the therapist's acceptance of that need.

We believe that while therapeutic "holding" may gratify for a while, there is no lasting transformation. Instead, when we "double loop" the lost opportunity for the father's touch, the client finds the interior strength necessary to withstand his past deprivation.

Chapter 16: Counseling Teenagers

1 Kourany (1987); Erwin (1993); and Prenzlauer, Drescher & Winchel (1992). See also Remafedi (1987); Remafedi, Resnick, Blum & Harris (1992); Schneider, Farberow & Kruks (1989); Rich, Fowler, Young & Blankush (1986).

2 For a critique of the book *Biological Exuberance: A Study of Diversity*, which uses animal same-sex behavior as a model for the normality of human homosexuality, see James Phelan (1999, August). Is homosexuality normal for some animals? *NARTH Bulletin*, 19.

3 See also Bailey, J.M. (1999), which found substantially higher levels of mental health problems among homosexually oriented people.

Chapter 17: Male Friendships

1 Friedman (1988) found a significant correlation between difficulty with male peer relationships during boyhood and later homosexual orientation. He reports male-male bonding relationships to be "frequently painfully distorted during the juvenile phase of childhood in homosexual males" and hypothesized that this phenomenon was "of central etiological significance" in the development of homosexuality (p. 240).

Chapter 19: The Role of Grief Work in Reparative Therapy

1 In this conceptualization I am adopting Johnson's (1987) synthesis of Kohut's "annihilation" and Masterson's understanding of abandonment.

References

Adler, A. (1969). *The science of living*, New York: Doubleday.

Alpert, M.C. (1992). Accelerated empathic therapy: A new short-term dynamic psychotherapy. *International Journal of Short-Term Psychotherapy, 7*(3), 133–56.

Alpert, M. (2001). Accelerated empathic therapy. In *Short-term therapy for long-term change*. New York: W.W. Norton.

Amato, P.R. (1993). Children's adjustment to divorce: Theories, hypotheses, and empirical support. *Journal of Marriage and the Family, 55*, 23–38.

Amsterdam, B., & Levitt, M. (1980). Consciousness of self and painful self-consciousness. *Psychoanalytic Study of the Child, 35*, 67–83.

Bailey, J.M. (1999). Homosexuality and mental illness. *Archives of General Psychiatry, 56*, 883–84.

Basch, M.F. (1976). The concept of affect: A reexamination. *Journal of the American Psychoanalytic Association, 24*, 759–77.

Bates, J., Bentler, P., & Thompson, S. (1973). Measurement of deviant gender development in boys. *Child Development, 44*, 591–98.

Bates, J., Bentler, P., & Thompson, S. (1979). Gender-deviant boys compared with normal and clinical control boys. *Journal of Abnormal Child Psychology, 7*, 243–59.

Bates, J., Skilbeck, W., Smith, K., & Bentler, P. (1974). Gender-role abnormalities in boys: An analysis of the clinical ratings. *Journal of Abnormal Child Psychology, 2*, 1–16.

Bateson, G., Jackson, D.D., Haley, J., & Weakland, J. (1956). Toward a theory of schizophrenia. *Behavioral Science, 1*, 251–64.

Bem, D.J. (1996). Exotic becomes erotic: A developmental theory of sexual orientation. *Psychological Review, 103*, 320–35.

Bieber, I., et al. (1962). *Homosexuality: A psychoanalytic study of male homosexuals.* New York: Basic Books.

Bieber, I., & Bieber, T.B. (1979). Male homosexuality. *Canadian Journal of Psychiatry, 24,* 409–21.

Blackwell, J. (2004). *The noonday demon: Recognizing and conquering the deadly sin of sloth.* New York: Crossroads.

Bloch, D. (1984). *So the witch won't eat me: Fantasy and the fear of infanticide.* New York: Grove Press.

Bly, R. (1990). *Iron John: A book about men.* Reading, MA: Addison-Wesley.

Bosworth, P. (1978). *Montgomery Clift: A biography.* New York: Harcourt Brace Jovanovich.

Bowlby, J. (1977). The making and breaking of affectional bonds: Aetiology and psychopathology in light of attachment theory. *British Journal of Psychiatry, 130,* 201–10.

Bowlby, J. (1988). *A secure base: Parent-child attachment and healthy human development.* New York: Basic Books.

Bradley, S. (1980). Female transsexualism: A child and adolescent perspective. *Child Psychiatry and Human Development, 11,* 12–18.

Bradley, S.J. (2003). *Affect regulation and the development of psychopathology.* New York: Guilford Press.

Browning, F. (1993). *The culture of desire.* New York: Vantage Press.

Buber, M. (1958). *I and Thou* (2nd ed.). (Ronald Smith, Trans.). New York: Charles Scribner.

Bühler, K. (1990). *Theory of language: The representational function of language* . Philadelphia: John Benjamins.

Butler, A.C. (2000). Trends in same-gender sexual partnering, 1988–1989. *Journal of Sex Research, 37,* 333–43.

Buxton, M.S. (2004). Ethical treatment for people who present with unwanted homoerotic attraction. In *NARTH Annual Conference Reports 2004.* Encino, CA: NARTH <www.narth.com/docs/confreports04.html>.

Byrd, A.D., & Nicolosi, J. (2002, June). A meta-analytic review of treatment of homosexuality. *Psychological Reports, 90,* 1139–52.

Byrd, A.D., Nicolosi, J., & Potts, R.W. (2008). Clients' perceptions of how reorientation therapy and self-help can promote changes in sexual orientation. *Psychological Reports, 102,* 3–28.

Chance, P. (2003). *Learning and behavior* (5th ed.). Belmont, CA: Wadsworth Thomson Learning.

Chasseguet-Smirgel, J. (1984). *Creativity and perversion*. New York: W.W. Norton.

Coates, S. (1990). Ontogenesis of boyhood gender identity disorder. *Journal of the American Academy of Psychoanalysis, 18*, 414–18.

Coates, S., & Person, E. (1985). Extreme boyhood femininity: Isolated behavior or pervasive disorder? *Journal of the American Academy of Child Psychiatry, 24*, 702–9.

Coates, S., & Wolfe, S.M. (1995). Gender identity disorder in boys: The interface of constitution and early experience. *Psychoanalytic Inquiry, 15*, 6–38.

Coates, S., & Zucker, K. (1988). Gender identity disorder in childhood. In *Clinical assessment of children: A biopsychosocial approach*. (C.J. Kestenbaum & D.T. Williams, Eds.). New York: New York University Press.

Cohen, R. (2000). *Coming out straight: Understanding and healing homosexuality*. Winchester, VA: Oakhill Press.

Coughlin Della Selva, P. (1996). *Intensive short-term dynamic psychotherapy: Theory and technique*. New York: Wiley.

Damasio, A.R. (1999). *The feeling of what happens: Body and emotion in the making of consciousness*. New York: Harcourt Brace.

Davanloo, H. (1978). *Basic principles and techniques in short-term dynamic psychotherapy*. New York: Spectrum.

Davanloo, H. (1980). *Short-term dynamic psychotherapy*. New York: Aronson.

Davanloo, H. (1995). Intensive short-term dynamic psychotherapy: Spectrum of psycho-neurotic disorders. *International Journal of Short-Term Psychotherapy, 10*(3, 4), 121–55.

De la Huerta, C. (1999). *Coming out spiritually: The next step*. New York: Jeremy P. Tarcher/Putnam.

Deutsch, H. (1937). Absence of grief. *Psychoanalytic Quarterly, 6*, 12–22.

Dickinson, E. (1960). To learn the transport by the pain: Poem 167. In *Complete poems of Emily Dickinson*. New York: Little, Brown.

Donaldson-Pressman, S., & Pressman, R.M. (1994). *The narcissistic family: Diagnosis and treatment*. San Francisco: Jossey-Bass.

Drescher, J. (1988). *Psychoanalytic therapy for the gay man*. Hillsdale, NJ: Analytic Press.

Erwin, K. (1993). Interpreting the evidence: Competing paradigms and the emergence of lesbian and gay suicide as a "social fact." *International Journal of Health Services, 23*, 437–53.

Fast, I. (1984). *Gender identity, a differentiation model: Advances in psychoanalysis theory, research, and practice* (Vol. 2). Hillsdale, NJ: Analytic Press.

Fenichel, O. (1945). Acting. *Psychoanalytic Quarterly, 15,* 144–60.

Fergusson, D.M., Horwood, L.J., & Beautrais, A.L. (1999). Is sexual orientation related to mental health problems and suicidality in young people? *Archives of General Psychiatry, 56*(10), 875–80.

Fisher, S., & Greenberg, R. (1995). *Freud scientifically reappraised: Testing the theories and therapy.* New York: Wiley.

Fitzgibbons, R. (2001). Gender identity disorder in children. *Lay Witness* (Steubenvill, OH). Available online at <www.narth.com/docs/fitz.html>.

Fitzgibbons, R. (2005, December 5–6). The psychology behind homosexual tendencies <zenit.org>.

Fleming, S., & Robinson, P. (2001). Grief and cognitive-behavioral therapy: The reconstruction of meaning. In *Handbook of bereavement research.* (M. Stroebe et al., Eds.). Washington, DC: American Psychological Association.

Fosha, D. (2000). *The transforming power of affect: A model for accelerated change.* New York: Basic Books.

Fosha, D. (2005). Emotion, true self, true other, core state: Toward a clinical theory of affective change process. *Psychoanalytic Review, 92*(4), 513–51.

Fraiberg, S.H. (1959). *The magic years: Understanding and handling the problems of early childhood.* New York: Scribner.

Freud, S. (1895). Project for a scientific psychology. *Standard Edition, 1,* 281–397.

Freud, S. (1911). Formulations on the two principles of mental functioning. *Standard Edition, 12,* 213–26.

Freud, S. (1914). Remembering, repeating and working through. *Standard Edition, 12,* 145–56.

Freud, S. (1917, 1953). Mourning and melancholia. In *Collected papers of Sigmund Freud* (Vol. 4) (Joan Riviere, Trans.). London: Hogarth Press.

Freud, S. (1918). Lines of advance psycho-analytic therapy. *Standard Edition, 17* (1917–1919). London: Hogarth Press.

Freud, S. (1920). Beyond the pleasure principle. *Standard Edition, 18.*

Freud, S. (1933). New introductory lectures on psycho-analysis. *Standard Edition, 22,* 80.

Friedman, R.C. (1988). *Male homosexuality: A contemporary psychoanalytic perspective.* New Haven, CT: Yale University Press.

Goldwasser, N. (2004, November 12–14). A multi-modal trauma-based treatment paradigm for the treatment of ego-dystonic homosexuality. *NARTH Annual Conference Reports.* Encinco, CA: NARTH <www.narth.com/docs/confreports04.html>.

Goldwasser, N. (2005a, November 12). Using EMDR to actualize heterosexual potential. Paper presented at NARTH Annual Conference, Washington, DC.

Goldwasser, N. (2005b). Utilizing EMDR to heal undesired sexual attractions and to help actualize sexual potential. Paper presented at EMDR International Association Annual Conference, Seattle, WA.

Green, R. (1976). 110 feminine and masculine boys: Behavioral contrasts and demographic similarities. *Archives of Sexual Behavior*, 5(5), 43.

Green, R. (1985). Gender identity in childhood and later sexual orientation: Follow-up of 78 males. *American Journal of Psychiatry*, 142, 339–41.

Green, R. (1993). *The sissy boy syndrome*. New York: HarperCollins.

Green, R., & Money, J. (1966). Stage-acting, role-taking, and effeminate impersonation during boyhood. *Archives of General Psychiatry*, 15, 535–38.

Greenson, R. (1968). Disidentifying from mother: Its special importance for the boy. *Journal of the American Psychoanalytical Association*, 56, 293–302.

Hadley, J. (1992). The instincts revisited. *Psychoanalytic Inquiry*, 12, 398–418.

Hatterer, L. (1970). *Changing homosexuality in the male: Treatment for men troubled by homosexuality*. New York: McGraw-Hill.

Herrell, R., Goldberg, J., True, W.R., Ramakrishnan, V., Lyons, M., Eisen, S., & Tsuang, M.T. (1999): Sexual orientation and suicidality: A co-twin control study in adult men. *Archive of General Psychiatry*, 56, 867–74.

Horner, A. (1984). *Object relations and the developing ego in therapy*. New York: Jason Aronson.

Horner, A. (1991). *Psychoanalytic object relations therapy*. Northvale, NJ: Jason Aronson.

Horney, K. (1945). *Our inner conflicts*. New York: W.W. Norton.

Horney, K. (1950). *Neurosis and human growth*. New York: W.W. Norton.

Isay, R. (1987). Fathers and their homosexually inclined sons in adulthood. *Psychoanalytic Study of the Child*, 42, 275–94. New Haven, CT: Yale University Press.

Izard, C.E., Porges, S.W., Simons, R.F., Haynes, O.M., Hyde, C., Parisi, M., & Cohen, B. (1991). Infant cardiac activity: Developmental changes and relations with attachment. *Developmental Psychology*, 27(3), 432–39.

Jay, K., & Young, A. (1979). *The gay report: Lesbians and gay men speak out about sexual experiences and lifestyles*. New York: Summit Books.

Johnson, S. (1987). *Humanizing the narcissistic style*. New York: Norton.

Jones, P. (2000, January). Androgyny: The pagan sexual ideal. *Journal of Evangelical Theological Society*, pp. 443–69.

Jones, S., & Yarhouse, M. (2007). *Ex-gays? A longitudinal study of religiously mediated change in sexual orientation*. Downers Grove, IL: InterVarsity Press.

Kagan, J. (1994). *Galen's prophecy: Temperament in human nature*. Boulder, CO: Westview Press.

Kleeman, J.A. (1966). Genital self-discovery during a boy's second year. *Psychoanalytic Study of the Child*, 21, 358–92.

Kohut, H. (1971). *The analysis of the self*. New York: International University Press.

Kourany, R.F.C. (1987). Suicide among homosexual adolescents. *Journal of Homosexuality*, 13, 111–17.

Lamb, M.E. (1987). Predictive implications of individual differences in attachment. *Journal of Consulting and Clinical Psychology*, 55, 817–24.

Lamb, M.E. (1997). *The role of the father in child development* (3rd ed.). New York: John Wiley.

Lasch, C. (1991). *The culture of narcissism: American life in an age of diminishing expectations*. New York: W.W. Norton.

Laumann, E.O., Gagnon, J.H., Michael, R.T., & Michaels, S. (1994). *The social organization of sexuality: Sexual practices in the U.S.* Chicago: University of Chicago Press.

LeDoux, J.E. (1996). *The emotional brain*. New York: Simon & Schuster.

Lewis, C.S. (1960). *The four loves*. New York: Harcourt, Brace & World.

Lewis, H.B. (1980). "Narcissistic personality" or "shame-prone superego mode." *Comprehensive Psychotherapy*, 1, 59–80.

Lowry, C., & Zucker, K. (1991, June). Is there an association between separation anxiety disorder and gender identity disorder in boys? Poster presented at the meeting of the Society for Research in Child and Adolescent Psychopathology, Zandvoort, The Netherlands.

Main, M., Kaplan, N., & Cassidy, J. (1985) Security in infancy, childhood and adulthood: A move to the level of representation. In *Growing points of attachment theory and research* (I. Bretherton and E. Waters, Eds.) (pp. 66–104). Monographs for the Society for Research in Child Development No. 50. Chicago: University of Chicago Press.

Malan, D.H. (1963). *A study of brief psychotherapy*. Philadelphia: Lippincott.

Malan, D.H. (1979). *Individual psychotherapy and the science of psychodynamics*. London: Butterworth.

May, J. (n.d.). EMDR: A power tool in the treatment of attachment disorders. The Family Attachment and Counseling Center <www.familyattachment.com/pages/emdr.html>.

McCullough, L. (1994). The next step in short-term dynamic psychotherapy: A clarification of objectives and techniques in an anxiety-regulating model. *Psychotherapy, 31*(4), 642–54.

McCullough, L. (2001). Desensitization of affect phobias in short dynamic psychotherapy. In *Short-term therapy for long-term change* (M. Solomon et al., Eds.). New York: Norton.

McCullough, L., Kuhn, N., Andrews, S., Kaplan, A., Wolf, J., & Hurley, C.L. (2003). *Treating affect phobia: A manual for short-term dynamic psychotherapy.* New York: Guilford Press.

McWhirter, D., & Mattison, A. (1984) *The male couple: How relationships develop.* Englewood Cliffs, NJ: Prentice-Hall.

Medinger, A. (2000). *Growth into manhood: Resuming the journey.* Colorado Springs: Waterbrook.

Menninger, K. (1958). *Theory of psychoanalytic technique.* New York: Basic Books.

Moberly, E. (1983). *Homosexuality: A new Christian ethic.* Greenwood, SC: Attic Press.

Morrison, Andrew P. (1989). *Shame: The underside of narcissism.* Hillsdale, NJ: Analytic Press.

Nathanson, D.L. (1987). A timetable for shame. In *The many faces of shame* (D.L. Nathanson, Ed.). New York: Guilford Press.

Nathanson, D.L. (1992). *Shame and pride: Affect, sex, and the birth of the self.* New York: Norton.

Nava, M. (1992). Abuelo – My grandfather, Raymond Acuna. *A member of the family: Gay men write about their families* (John Preston, Ed.). New York: Dutton.

Neborsky, R. (2001). Perinatal trauma and resistance to emotional closeness. Presentation at a conference, "Core Factors for Effective Short-Term Dynamic Psychotherapy," Milan, Italy.

Neborsky, R. (2004). Recognizing and working with an Oedipal focus in I.S.T.D.P., Part II, Working through sexual feelings. *ADHOC Bulletin of Short Term Dynamic Psychotherapy – Practice and Theory, 8*(2), 48–59.

Nicolosi, J. (1991). *Reparative therapy of male homosexuality.* Northvale, NJ: Jason Aronson.

Nicolosi, J. (1993). *Healing homosexuality: Case stories of reparative therapy.* Northvale, NJ: Jason Aronson.

Nicolosi, J. (1993). Treatment of the non-gay homosexual man. *The Journal of Pastoral Counseling, 28,* 76–82.

Nicolosi, J. (1999). The gay deception. In *Homosexuality and American public life* (C. Wolfe, Ed.). Dallas: Spence.

Nicolosi, J. (2001). The removal of homosexuality from the psychiatric manual. *The Catholic Social Science Review, 6,* 71, 77.

Nicolosi, J. (2003). Finally, recognition of a long-neglected population. *Archives of Sexual Behavior, 32*(5), 445–47.

Nicolosi, J., & Byrd, A.D. (2002). A critique of Bem's "Exotic Becomes Erotic" theory of sexual orientation development. *Psychological Reports, 90,* 931–46.

Nicolosi, J., Byrd, A.D., & Potts, R.W. (2000a). Beliefs and practices of therapists who practice sexual reorientation psychotherapy. *Psychological Reports, 86,* 689–702.

Nicolosi, J., Byrd, A.D., & Potts, R.W. (2000b). Retrospective self-reports of changes in homosexual orientation: A consumer survey of conversion therapy clients. *Psychological Reports, 86,* 1071–88.

Nicolosi, J., & Nicolosi, L.A. (2002). *A parent's guide to preventing homosexuality.* Downers Grove, IL: InterVarsity Press.

O'Donohue, W.T., & Caselles, C. (2005). Homophobia's conceptual, definitional and values issues. In *Destructive trends in mental health* (R. Wright & N.A. Cummings, Eds.). New York: Routledge.

Orlinsky, D.E., & Ronnestad, M.H. (2005). How psychotherapists develop: A study of therapeutic work and professional growth. Washington, DC: American Psychological Association.

Paulk, J., & Paulk, A. (1999). *Love won out.* Wheaton, Ill.: Tyndale House.

Peiser, K., & Sandry, M. (2000). *The universal 12-step program: How to overcome an addiction and win!* Avon, MA: Adams Media Corp.

Perloff, R. (2004). Free to choose. In *NARTH Annual Conference Reports.* Encino, CA: NARTH <www.narth.com/docs/confreports04.html>.

Perls, F.S. (1969). *Gestalt therapy verbatim.* Lafayette, CA: Real People Press.

Petrarch. *The canzoniere, or rerum vulgarium fragmenta* (M. Musa, Trans.). Indianapolis: Indiana University Press, 1999.

Phelan, J. (1999, August). Is homosexuality normal for some animals? *NARTH Bulletin,* p. 19.

Prenzlauer, S., Drescher, J., & Winchel, R. (1992). Suicide among homosexual youth (letter to the editor). *American Journal of Psychiatry, 149,* 1416.

Preston, J. (Ed.). (1992). *A Member of the family: Gay men write about their families.* New York: Dutton.

NARTH. (1997, December). Psychiatrist "reassures" parents about lesbian experimentation. *NARTH Bulletin*, p. 12. [Cited in Elite Schools Face the Gay Issue. *New York Times*, June 13, 1997, B7-B8].

Radin, N. (1994). Primary-caregiving fathers in intact families. In *Redefining families: Implications for children's development* (A.E. Gottfried & A.W. Gottfried, Eds.). New York: Plenum.

Rekers, G. (1995). Homosexuality: Development risks, parental values and controversies. In *Handbook of child and adolescent sexual problems* (G. Rekers, Ed.). New York: Lexington Books.

Remafedi, G. (1987). Adolescent homosexuality: Psychosocial and medical implications. *Pediatrics, 79*, 331–37.

Remafedi, G., Resnick, M., Blum, R., & Harris, L. (1992). Demography of sexual orientation in adolescents. *Pediatrics, 89*, 714–21.

Rich, C.L., Fowler, R.C., Young, D., & Blankush, M. (1986). San Diego suicide study: Comparison of gay to straight males. *Suicide and Life-Threatening Behavior, 16*, 448–57.

Richards, P.S., & Bergin, A.E. (1997). A spiritual strategy of counseling and psychotherapy. Washington DC: American Psychological Association.

Richards, P.S., & Bergin, A.E. (2000). *Handbook of psychotherapy and religious diversity*. Washington, DC: American Psychological Association.

Rosik, C.H. (2003). Motivational, ethical, and epistemological foundations in the treatment of unwanted homoerotic attraction. *Journal of Marital and Family Therapy, 29*(1), 13–28.

Rothschild, B. (2000). *The body remembers: The psychophysiology of trauma and trauma treatment*. New York: W.W. Norton.

Rubin, T. (1975). *Compassion and self-hate*. New York: David McKay.

Saghir, M., & Robins, E. (1973). *Male and female homosexuality: A comprehensive investigation*. Baltimore, MD: Williams and Wilkins.

Sandfort, T., Graaf, R., Bijl, R., & Schnabel, P. (2001). Same-sex sexual behavior and psychiatric disorders: Findings from the Netherlands mental health survey and incidence study (NEMESIS). *Archives of General Psychiatry, 58*, 85–91.

Satinover, J. (1995, April). Reflections from Jeffrey Satinover. *NARTH Bulletin*, p. 3 <www.narth.com/docs/satinovr.html>.

Schiffer, F. (1998). *Of two minds: The revolutionary science of dual-brain psychology*. New York: Free Press.

Schneider, S.G., Farberow, N.L., & Kruks, G. (1989). Suicidal behavior in adolescent and adult gay men. *Suicide and Life-Threatening Behavior, 19*, 381–94.

Shapiro, F. (2001). *Eye Movement Desensitization and Reprocessing (EMDR)* (2nd ed.). New York: Guilford.

Schore, A. (1991). Early superego development: The emergence of shame and narcissistic affect regulation in the practicing period. *Psychoanalysis and Contemporary Thought, 14,* 187–205.

Schore, A. (1994). *Affect regulation and the origin of the self: The neurobiology of emotional development.* Hillsdale, NJ: Lawrence Erlbaum.

Schore, A. (1996). The experience-dependent maturation of a regulatory system in the orbital prefrontal cortex and the origin of developmental psychopathology. *Development and Psychopathology, 8,* 59–86.

Schore, A. (2002, March 9). Regulation of the right brain. Continuing Education Seminars presentation. Los Angeles: University of California at Los Angeles.

Schore, A. (2003). *Affect regulation and the repair of the self.* New York: W.W. Norton.

Schore, A. (2007, February 2–3). The science and art of psychotherapy. Presentation at Skirball Center, Los Angeles.

Segal, L. (2007, August 19). Nureyev: Dancing around the lies. *Los Angeles Times,* 12.

Seligman, M.E.P. (1992). *Helplessness: On depression, development, and death.* New York: Freeman.

Shapiro, F. (2002). *EMDR as an integrative psychotherapy approach: Experts of diverse orientations explore the paradigm prism.* Washington, DC: American Psychological Association.

Shapiro, F. (2005). *Eye Movement Desensitization Reprocessing: Basic principles, protocols and procedures* (2nd ed.). New York: Guilford.

Shapiro, F., & Forrest, M. (1997). *EMDR: The breakthrough therapy for overcoming anxiety, stress and trauma.* New York: Basic Books.

Siegel, D. (2002, March 9). Interpersonal neurobiology of the developing mind. Continuing Education Seminar presentation. Los Angeles: University of California at Los Angeles.

Siegel, D. (2007). *The mindful brain.* New York: W.W. Norton.

Siegel, E. (1971). *The h persuasion.* New York: Definition Press.

Smith, D., & Orlinsky, D. (2004). Religious and spiritual experience among psychotherapists. *Psychotherapy: Theory, Research, Practice, Training, 41*(2), 144–61.

Socarides, C., & Freedman, A. (2002). *Objects of desire: The sexual deviations.* New York: International University Press.

Solomon, M., Neborsky, R., McCullough, L., Alpert, M., Shapiro, F., & Malan, D. (2001). *Short-term therapy for long-term change.* New York: W.W. Norton.

Spitzer, R.L. (2000, February 29). Videotaped interview by The Reichenberg Fellowship. New York City.

Spitzer, R.L. (2003, October). Can some gay men and lesbians change their sexual orientation? 200 participants reporting a change from homosexual to heterosexual orientation. *Archives of Sexual Behavior, 32*(5), 403–17.

Stark, M. (1994a). *Working with resistance.* Northvale, NJ: Jason Aronson.

Stark, M. (1994b). *A primer on working with resistance.* Northvale, NJ: Jason Aronson.

Stern, D. (2002, March 9). Why do people change in psychotherapy? Continuing Education Seminar presentation. Los Angeles: University of California at Los Angeles.

Stoller, R. (1985). *Presentations of gender.* New Have, CT: Yale University Press.

Stringham, E. (2004). Advocating for reparative therapy and traditional moral perspectives on homosexuality (pp. 102–11). In *NARTH Annual Conference Reports.* Los Angeles: NARTH <www.narth.com/docs/confreports04.html>.

Tabin, C.J., & Tabin, J. (1988). Bulimia and anorexia: Understanding their gender specificity and their complexity of symptoms. In *Bulimia: Psychoanalytic theory and treatment.* (H. Schwartz, Ed.). New York: International University Press.

Tabin, J. (1985). *On the way to the self: Ego and early oedipal development.* New York: Columbia University Press.

Thompson, M. (1995). *Gay soul: Interviews and photographs.* New York: Harper.

Throckmorton, W. (2002). Initial empirical and clinical findings concerning the change process for ex-gays. *Professional Psychology, Research and Practice, 33*(3), 242–48.

Tomkins, S. (1981). The quest for primary motives: Biography and autobiography of an idea. *Personality and Social Psychology, 44,* 306–29.

Tomkins, S. (1982). Affect theory. In *Emotion in the human face* (2nd ed.) (pp. 353–95). New York: Cambridge University Press.

Tomkins, S. (1991). *Affect/imagery/consciousness,* Vol. 3. *The negative affects: Anger and fear.* New York: Springer.

Tuber, S., & Coates, S. (1989). Indices of psychopathology in the Rorschachs of boys with severe gender identity disorder: A comparison with normal control subjects. *Journal of Personality Assessment, 53,* 100–112.

van den Aardweg, G. (1985) *Homosexuality and hope: A psychologist talks about treatment and change.* Ann Arbor, MI: Servant Books.

van den Aardweg, G. (1986). *On the origins and treatment of homosexuality: A psychoanalytic interpretation*. Westport, CT: Praeger.

van den Aardweg, G. (1997). *The battle for normality*. San Francisco, CA: Ignatius Press.

Watzlawick, P. (1967). *Pragmatics of human communication* New York: Norton.

Whitebook, J. (1995). *Perversion and utopia: A study in psychoanalysis and cultural theory*. Cambridge, MA: MIT Press.

Winnicott, D.W. (1965). *The maturational process and the facilitating environment*. New York: International University Press.

Wolfe, G. (2003). *Malcolm Muggeridge: A biography*. Wilmington, DE: ISI Books.

Wolverton Mountain Enterprises. (2005). The lesson of the pike <www.wolverton mountain.com/articles/pike.htm>.

Worden, W.J. (1991). *Grief counseling and grief therapy: A handbook for the mental health practitioner*. (2nd ed.). New York: Springer.

Wright, R.H., & Cummings, N.A. (2005). *Destructive trends in mental health: The well-intentioned path to harm*. New York: Routledge.

Yarhouse, M.A. (1998). When clients seek treatment for same-sex attraction: Ethical issues in the "right to choose debate." *Psychotherapy, 35*(2), 248–59.

Yarhouse, M.A., & Burkett, L.A. (2002). An inclusive response to LGB and conservative religious persons: The case for same-sex attraction and behavior. *Professional Psychology: Research and Practice, 33*(3), 235–41.

Yarhouse, M.A., & Throckmorton, W. (2002). Ethical issues in attempts to ban reorientation therapies. *Psychotherapy: Theory/Research/Practice/Training, 39*(1), 66–75.

Zucker, K., & Bradley, S. (1995). *Gender identity disorder and psychosexual problems in children and adolescents*. New York: Guilford.

Zucker, K., & Green, R. (1992). Psychosexual disorders in childhood and adolescents. *Journal of Child Psychiatry, 33*, 107–51.

Index

www.ingramcontent.com/pod-product-compliance
Lightning Source LLC
Chambersburg PA
CBHW021842020426
42334CB00013B/150